TESI GREGORIANA

Serie Spiritualità

—— 2 ——

SELVISTER PONNUMUTHAN

The Spirituality
of Basic Ecclesial Communities
in the Socio-Religious Context
of Trivandrum/Kerala, India

EDITRICE PONTIFICIA UNIVERSITÀ GREGORIANA
Roma 1996

Vidimus et approbamus ad normam Statutorum Universitatis

Romae, ex Pontificia Universitate Gregoriana
die 20 mensis aprilis anni 1996

R.P. Prof. Bruno Secondin, O. Carm,
R.P. Prof. Robert Faricy, S.J.

ISBN 88-7652-721-4

© Iura editionis et versionis reservantur

PRINTED IN ITALY

GREGORIAN UNIVERSITY PRESS
Piazza della Pilotta, 35 – 00187 Rome, Italy

ACKNOWLEDGEMENTS

This dissertation is the result of a research to discover the spirituality of Basic Ecclesial Communities in the socio-religious context of Trivandrum/Kerala, India. Throughout the research, I have been experiencing God's unending love and guidance in manifold ways through my professors, benefactors and friends: by prayers, guidance and financial assistance. I am not able to mention all of them. Nevertheless, with a sense of gratitude I place on record all the professors of the Institute of Spirituality at the Pontifical Gregorian University, Rome, who helped me to study spirituality *from the people's point of view*. I am privileged to have Prof. Bruno Secondin, O.Carm., as my moderator. He helped me with his continuous encouragement, critical comments and guidance throughout my research work. My sincere gratitude to Prof. Robert Faricy S.J., the second reader of this dissertation, for his suggestions. I am grateful to Prof. Herbert Alphonso S.J., the President of the Institute of Spirituality, at the Gregorian University, for his timely interventions and suggestions throughout my doctoral studies.

I thank Prof. E.J. Thomas, Principal of Loyola College, Trivandrum and Shaj Kumar, who helped me to conduct the questionnaire survey in 1994, in Trivandrum. I place on record the valuable remarks and suggestions given by Professors: M. Amaladoss S.J., S. Raimon, A. Thottakara CMI, R. Wehinger, R. White S.J., and friends: F. Athikalam, J. Culas, R.B. Gregory, H.M. Nayakam, J. Jolly, J. Ponnore, J. Prasad, P.L. Rufus, A.R. Serrao and J. Vadakkedom. I am indebted to Sr. M.A. Clarahan RSM, Fr. E. Klump FM Conv., and Fr. T. Kearns I.C., who helped in the draft of this work.

My special thanks also goes to those whom I interviewed: M.S. Pakiam, the Bishop of Trivandrum; B. Penha, the Auxiliary bishop of Bombay; S. Amirtham, the Bishop of CSI, Trivandrum; I. Pinto, the Bishop of Shimoga; J. Fernandez, the Bishop of Quilon; Fr. J. Edwin, a pioneer of BEC experiment in India; M.M. Thomas, a theologian of India; M. De C. Azevedo, a theologian of Brazil; D'Silva, Profssor of St. Pius College,

Bombay; Mr. T. Achari, former Joint-Director of the State Planning Board, Kerala; Sr. Philomin Mary, who took an active part in the fishermen's struggle in Trivandrum. My sincere thanks also go to all those who responded to the questionnaire, and the lay people, seminarians, priests and sisters of the Diocese of Trivandrum. I extend my sincere thanks to the Archivists of *Archivium Generale Ordinis Carmelitarum Discalceatorum*, Rome and the Council for World Mission Archives, School of Oriental and African Studies, London, and the Librarians of different universities and institutes in Rome.

I am grateful also to the Congregation for Evangelization of Peoples for providing me with the necessary scholarship for my stay in Rome. With gratitude I remember the former and the present members of the staff of St. Peter's College, Rome: Fr. A.J. Verschur, and Fr. M. Müller, the former and the present Rectors of St. Peter's College respectively; Fr. B. Pallan, the Vice Rector, Fr. G. Lupsek, Fr. M. Lapasansky, Bro. Francesco and Rev. Sisters of the Ancelle Missionarie. I would like to thank the La Salette Generalate Community of Rome where I was accommodated in the first year of my stay in Rome. My sincere thanks also go to Mother Benedetta Ferroni and the Oblate Sisters of the Sacred Heart of Jesus, in Rome, for their timely help and hospitality for the completion of this dissertation. I cannot forget those priests and parishes — in Italy, Germany, England and Spain — who helped me in one way or other during my holidays. A special thanks goes to Herr W. Schmitt and the parishioners of Böfingen, Ulm; Msgr. D. Maltinti and the parishioners of Montopoli; Herr H. Riedle and the parishioners of St. Josef, Biberach; Herr. D. Scholtz; Padre M. Bru, Don C. Calzolari, and Fr. A. Charleton. I thank C. Valentino for his fraternal co-operation in preparing the text for publication.

I remember with gratitude my parents, brothers, sisters and their families whose prayers constantly accompany me. I recall with gratitude the late Bishop A.B. Jacob of Trivandrum, who participated in the joy and sufferings of the people of God of Trivandrum till his death. I thank my Bishop M.S. Pakiam, who sent me to Rome for higher studies and supported me with his prayers.

Last but not the least I remember the people of God of Trivandrum to whom I dedicate my work.

GENERAL INTRODUCTION

Standing at the threshold of the third millennium, one of the great concerns of the Church, regarding the continent of Asia is «to illustrate and explain more fully the truth that Christ is the one Mediator between God and man and the sole Redeemer of the world»[1]. In this mission one has to take into account two important realities which are inherent in the Asian culture: the first is the community consciousness; the second is the spiritual or religious experience. As Christianity is basically an Asiatic religion we see that the early Christian community had combined both these aspects (Acts 2,42; 4,32). The word «Christians» was attributed to those who followed Jesus Christ because of the fellowship which the disciples cherished (Acts 11,26).

However, those who presented Christianity to the various parts of Asia could not combine these two — spiritual and communitarian — aspects of Asian culture and kept themselves aloof from the mainstream of the life of the people, of their struggles and of their dreams. They failed to identify themselves with the people, even though in terms of charity many praiseworthy services have been rendered.[2]

In this context, the self understanding of the Church by Vatican II as «People of God»[3] gives everyone a new impetus to combine the community and spiritual aspects of the human person. In a prophetic voice, the Council Fathers also remind the «People of God» that the plan of God «at all times was to make men holy and save them, not as individuals without any bond or link between them but as a community, making them into a people who might acknowledge him and serve him in holiness» (LG 9). The emergence of the Basic Ecclesial Communities (hereafter abbreviated as BECs), as the new way of being the Church is the outcome of

---

[1] JOHN PAUL II, Tertio Millennio Adveniente, n. 38.

[2] See FAPA, xxiii-xxx.

[3] See LG 9. See also Y. CONGAR, «The Church: The People of God», 7-19.

the new understanding of the Church[4]. The BECs are known by various names and function in different contexts. The theological exploration of BECs is developing[5].

1. Significance of the Study

The emergence of BECs is one of the significant developments that has taken place in the local Church of Trivandrum since the Second Vatican Council. This dissertation studies the spirituality of BECs in the socio-religious context of the Latin Rite Diocese of Trivandrum in the State of Kerala, India. Trivandrum is the capital city of Kerala. The Diocese has a Catholic population of about 4.00.000. The people come from different castes, social backgrounds and ecclesiastical traditions such as *Padroado* and *Propaganda*. It is in these different ecclesiastical traditions and in the socio-religious plurality of the region that BECs have emerged as a pastoral option in the Diocese. Though many like J.P. Pinto[6], and G.De Lima[7], have undertaken studies on various aspects of BECs in the general context of India, to our knowledge, no research has been done to discover the spirituality of the BECs in the context of Trivandrum where more than 2.600 BECs exist today; hence the relevance and originality of the study.

BEC is *a new way of being the Church* within a local Church. Since BECs exist in the concrete situations of the people they will be a means of «evangelization»[8], as well as Christian formation. BEC is one of the best means to witness Christ and to preach His Gospel in the pluralistic cultural and religious situations of India[9]. Cardinal S. Pimenta, the Archbishop of Bombay in his address to Pope John Paul II on 13 December 1995 remarked:

---

[4] The terms like Basic Christian Communities, Small Christian Communities and Basic Ecclesial Communities are generally used to designate the same meaning in the catholic circle. For a smooth reading of our work we use the term Basic Ecclesial Communities [BECs].

[5] The recent studies on BECs other than those on Latin American countries show contemporary relevance of the theme. See A.L. PICARDAL, *An Ecclesiological Perspective;* G. GAZO, *Pour une Sainteté Ecclesiale Aujourd'hui;* G.U. DA SILVA, *Ecclesial Basic Communities;* J.V. KODA, *Small Christian Communities.*

[6] J.P. PINTO, *Inculturation.*

[7] G. DE LIMA, *Local Church.*

[8] PAUL VI, *Evangelii Nuntiandi*, n. 58.

[9] See *CBCI Evaluation Report*, ns. 632. 204.

Your Holiness will be glad to hear that the Church in India has taken the programme of forming Basic Christian Communities very much in its pastoral planning and work. In the 1992 General Assembly of the Catholic Bishops' Conference of India, the Bishops studied this pastoral strategy and adopted it as an effective way to make the Church aware that it is a communion, with a mission in and to the world. Since then several Dioceses have been working to make this a concrete pastoral programme. We are happy to be able to tell Your Holiness that the three Regions — Western, Andhra and Kerala - (Latin Rite) — have not been lagging behind in implementing this programme. Formation programmes for Bishops, priests and people are held; pastoral teams have been formed, and other such means employed so that our parishes adopt and implement this programme. We have taken more than the first steps. *Sed longa adhuc restat nobis via.* Obviously, not all can or do move with the same speed, but we understand that our objective cannot be achieved in a few years. We will continue our efforts[10].

As BECs have an authentic ecclesial spirituality, they could work as a leaven in the society which has the Indian spiritual background. Since pluriformity is the characteristic feature of the Church in India, the study of the spirituality of BECs in Trivandrum in the context of its plurality may give vitality to the BECs in Trivandrum. It may also inspire other local Churches in Kerala and India to promote BECs in their own particular contexts and vitalize the Christian life. This study may shed further light on the field of inculturation in the Indian context which would enable one to be fully Indian and authentically Christian.

2. Method and Limits of the Study

The methodology employed in this study is theological and analytical. The BECs in Trivandrum are formed on the basis of the teachings of the Church. It is from the theological foundation that the ecclesial spirituality is derived. It is analytical for we contextualise the ecclesial life in a particular socio-religious context. In the analysis, we also compare the ecclesial life in the past and in the present which helps one to see at a glance the immediate pastoral relevance of BECs.

We limit our study to the spirituality of the BECs in the socio-religious context of Trivandrum/Kerala. After an analysis of BECs in general, as well as the socio-religious context of Trivandrum in particular, we try to understand the specific roles of BECs in Trivandrum, highlighting their spirituality.

---

[10] S. PIMENTA, «La nostra Chiesa», 7.

3. Structure

This dissertation is divided into five chapters with a general conclusion. The first chapter is a comprehensive presentation of the phenomenon and the spirituality of BECs. The second chapter introduces the socio-religious background of the local Church. The third chapter describes the emergence of BECs in Trivandrum. The fourth chapter analyses the functioning of BECs in a theological perspective. The fifth chapter explores the Spirituality of BECs in the socio-religious context of Trivandrum. In the general conclusion we sum up our findings of the study.

4. Content

The *first chapter* examines the Phenomenon and the Spirituality of BECs in general. Since BECs are a *new way of being the Church* within the local Church we begin our study with a discussion on the different dimensions of the local Church. In order to have a comprehensive vision of the local Church and its dimensions, we try to understand the meaning of Church in the biblical context. In the light of the Bible and the teachings of the Second Vatican Council, we explain the relation between the universal Church and the local Church. The presentation of the historical development of the BECs in the Church and the papal teachings will help the reader to have a general understanding of how BECs are becoming a source of «great hope for the life of the Church»[11].

The *second chapter* gives a holistic view of the socio-religious context of Trivandrum. The existence of different caste groups within the same diocese is a peculiarity of Trivandrum and most dioceses in India. In our study we deal with different castes. The Brahmins and the Nairs play an important role due to their influence on the socio-religious context of Trivandrum. The castes such as the Mukkuvar, the Nadars, the Izhavas and the Dalits represent the majority of the Christian population in the Diocese.

Despite the caste differences, we see a *harmonious* co-existence of Hindus, Christians and Muslims representing three of the major world religions in the capital city of Trivandrum[12]. There are also cases in

---

[11] JOHN PAUL II, *Redemptoris Missio*, n. 51.

[12] Within a radius of 200 meters one can see that St. Joseph's Cathedral, Palayam of the Diocese Trivandrum, Palayam Muslim Mosque and a Temple dedicated to the Hindu God.

which in one family there are people professing different faiths. A short description of various Churches of oriental rites and other important Christian denominations as well as their impact on the Diocese is discussed in order to understand the socio-religious context of the Latin Catholics of Trivandrum. The division caused by the *Padroado* and *Propaganda* administration is reflected clearly in the Diocese. A basic understanding of these differences is important for understanding the genesis, nature, function and spirituality of BECs in Trivandrum.

The *third chapter* introduces the emergence of BECs in Trivandrum. Since the life and work of St. Francis Xavier and later the Carmelite Missionaries have made a lasting impact on the people and the ecclesial structure of the parishes, we analyze the early forms of ecclesial communities. We also take note of the influence of Vatican II on the local Church of Trivandrum and elucidate various factors which have contributed to the emergence of BECs in Trivandrum. This chapter also sheds light on the various problems which existed in the Diocese and how the Diocese was able to overcome them.

The *fourth chapter* is the result of the field study, in view of this dissertation, carried out in the Diocese of Trivandrum in 1994. Through a process of decentralization and people's participation there are more than 2.600 BECs and nearly 10.000 lay animators working at the service of the development of the people at the grassroots level. In its functioning, the approach of BECs towards the Word of God, the liturgy, the consecrated and non-consecrated ministers and the mission of the Church have formed part of our investigation.

The *fifth chapter* discusses the spirituality of BECs and its challenges in Trivandrum. Since the BECs in Trivandrum are the natural outcome of the renewal process initiated in the Diocese with the Second Vatican Council and the Golden Jubilee celebration of the Diocese they have contributed to the revival of Christian life. We try to present the spirituality of BECs of the Diocese in accordance with their functioning today. However, as the functioning of BECs is in the process of maturing their spirituality also has the same feature.

In explaining the spirituality of BECs in Trivandrum we present also the possible challenges which the BECs will have to face in their journey. The chapter also presents a general tendency of the various local Churches in India towards BECs. Showing the relation between the BECs in Trivandrum and in other local Churches the reader is led to know how BECs can become a source of *great hope for the life of the Church* in India. As BECs function in a pluralistic cultural and religious situation, we discuss how BECs could have a meaningful dialogue with other religions. In other words, basing itself on the ecclesial norms, the study explores the possibility of forming basic human communities which is the urgent need of the Church in India.

The dissertation concludes with the summing up of the findings of the study and indicates the scope for further theological and missiological research on BECs.

CHAPTER I

The Phenomenon and the Spirituality
of Basic Ecclesial Communities

The plan of God, at all times, was to make men and women holy and to save them, not as isolated individuals without any bond or link between them but as a community, making them into a people who might acknowledge him and serve him in holiness[1]. This plan of God is realized in and through the Church. BECs are a *new way of being the Church* within a local Church.

The scope of our study in the first chapter is to understand the phenomenon of BECs in the Church and to discover the spirituality of the BECs in general. Since BECs are *a new way of being the Church* within the local Church, we discuss briefly the different dimensions of the local Church. The presentation on the phenomenon of the BECs in the Church and the papal teachings on BECs provide us with a general picture of the BECs at present. Then we have a theological reflection on the BECs. In the last part of the first chapter we will see how a new ecclesial spirituality.is evolving through BECs.

1. New Dimensions of the Local Church

In the twentieth century we notice a new ecclesiological interest in the Catholic Church. This interest is articulated in the life of the people especially after the Second Vatican Council. Ecclesiology is no more the monopoly of the theologians or the elite few. Every Christian, realizing his or her vocation through baptism, begins to feel the Church (*consentire ecclesiae*) and to live the Church (*vivere ecclesiae*). The emergence of

---

[1] See *LG* 9.

BECs could be seen as one of the fruits of this new ecclesiological awareness in the Church.

1.1 Self Awareness of the Church

The Church, from the very beginning of its existence, has an extraordinarily deep awareness of her own being. It is this self-awareness that helped her to begin the process of reflection on herself at the very early stage[2]. The first Jewish Christians, who followed the monaic traditions, apart from its *ideal* life of being «faithful to the teaching of the apostles, to the brotherhood, to the breaking of bread and to the prayers» (Acts 2,42)[3], expected that the new converts could come to their fellowship only if they first became Jews[4]. The divine intervention in the life of Paul on his way to Damascus (Acts 9,3-12), the divine command given to Peter to baptize the Roman Centurion Cornelius (Acts 10,9-48) and the first Apostolic Council at Jerusalem (Acts 15) were real manifestations of the openness to the Spirit of the early Church. It is this openness and awareness[5], that helped the Church to convoke different Councils[6] and to make a «prophetic consciousness»[7] at the time of great heresies and to proclaim the «message of the brotherhood and of salvation»[8] to the world. And it is this sense of self-reflection and its

---

[2] H. DE LUBAC, *The Splendour of the Church*, 3.

[3] Acts 2,42 speaks of the life pattern of the early Christian community and it has a strong heritage from Israel. See *NJBC*, 1340-1341. The Bible quotations, unless specially mentioned, are taken from *The New Jerusalem Bible*.

[4] See K. RAHNER, «Towards a Fundamental Theological Interpretation», 716-727. In this article Rahner refers to the three epochs in Church History. The first is «the short period of Jewish Christianity», the second is «the period of the Church in a distinct cultural region, namely that of Hellenism and of European culture and civilization" and the third is «the period in which the sphere of the Church's life is in fact the entire world» (ID., 721). When discussing the second period K. Rahner ignores the presence of Christianity in India. According to the historical evidences Christianity was in existence at least in the 3rd century along with the most of the European countries.

[5] Paul VI deals with the term «awareness» extensively in his first encyclical. See PAUL VI, *Ecclesiam Suam*, ns. 18-40. «We think that it is a duty today for the Church to deepen the awareness that she must have of herself, of the treasure of truth of which she is heir and custodian and of her mission in the world» (n. 18).

[6] See M. SCHMAUS, *Dogma 4: The Church*, 76-79.

[7] PAUL VI, *Ecclesiam Suam*, n. 22.

[8] «The Church needs to reflect on herself. She needs to feel the throb of her own life. She must learn to know herself better, if she wishes to live her own proper vocation and to offer to the world her message of brotherhood and of salvation» (PAUL VI, *Ecclesiam Suam*, n. 25).

earnest desire for «renewal»[9] or *aggiornamento* that prompted Pope John XXIII to convoke the Second Vatican Council.

As on the day of Pentecost, when each one heard the Apostles in each one's language (Acts 2,8), so the Second Vatican Council, «the most significant ecclesial event»[10] of this century, made it possible to understand the nature of the Church to its members who live in the changing world of the present and in the years to come[11].

1.1.1 *Lumen Gentium*: Point of Reference for the Local Church

All the Council documents show the spirit of *aggiornamento* aimed at by Pope John XXIII. However, the document on the *Church* has a unique position as it is the point of reference for all the other documents[12], and for *discovering* and developing[13] future theologies. And there is no doubt that the document on the Church reflects the mind of the Fathers of the *World Church*[14] who, inspired by the appeal of *aggiornamento*, changed

---

[9] Pope John XXIII convoked the Second Vatican Council as a part of the renewal of the Church. How the idea also influenced Pope Paul VI is seen from his first encyclical. See PAUL VI, *Ecclesiam Suam*, ns. 41-57.

[10] JOHN PAUL II, «Homily for Closing Mass of the Ninth Synod», 1.

[11] It does not mean that the whole Catholic community came to know about the theological openness by way of Vatican II. Neverthless, this became the point of reference for all the further theological developments of this century.

[12] «With something like unanimity it has been hailed as the most momentous achievement of the Council, both because of its important contents and because of its central place among the Council documents. The other constitutions, decrees, and declarations, for the most part, deal either with particular sections or elements in the Church (Eastern Churches, bishops, religious, seminarians, laity), or with particular activities of the Church (such as liturgy, communications, education and missions), with the relations of the Church to outside groups (ecumenism, the non-Christian religions, the modern world). The Constitution on Divine Revelation deals with the sources of the Church's doctrine, and the Declaration on Religious Freedom with the relations between the Church and civil society. Thus in one way or another the entire work of the Council is centered about the theme of the Church» (A. DULLES, «The Church: Introduction», 10).

[13] A theological development on local Church takes place with Vatican II. See G. VODOPIVEC, «La Chiesa Locale e la Missione», 97-139. See also G. GHIRLANDA, «Universal Church», 233-271. See also F.A. SULLIVAN, «The Significance of the Vatican II», 272-287.

[14] According to K. Rahner Vatican II is the Church's first official self-actualization as the world Church. By the term «world Church» what he means is that the Council was the representative body of all nations. Until Vatican II, the bishops who represented other nations were either from Europe or from North America. See K. RAHNER, «Towards a fundamental Theological Interpretation», 716-727. Hereafter we use the word «world Church» as it appears in the understanding of K. Rahner.

the *original schema*[15] of the document on *the Church* prepared by the Theological Commission. And, what we have at present in the *Dogmatic Constitution on the Church* is the result of much discussion and self-reflection by the world Church on the *mystery of the Church*.[16]. The theological significance of the self-understanding of the Church in the document, which is expressed through various images[17], is a great shift from the traditional way of understanding the Church as an unchangeable reality[18]. It was a shift from the «monolithic ecclesiology»[19] of the past to the communitarian ecclesiology. It is in this context of the ecclesiological shift that we understand the local Church, which the Council preferred to name «particular Church», with its new dimensions.

1.2 *The Term «Church»*

The Church, which Jesus Christ founded, is one, holy, catholic, and Apostolic. The same Church is understood by various images such as «People of God», «Body of Christ», «Temple of the Holy Spirit» in the Bible. Vatican II says, «This Church, constituted and organized as a society in the present world, subsists in the Catholic Church, which is

---

[15] «The original schema, prepared by the Theological Commission before the first session in 1962, resembled the standard treatise on the Church as found, for example, in most of the theological manuals published between the two world wars. Influenced by centuries of anti-Protestant polemics, the writers of this period placed heavy emphasis on the hierarchical and juridical aspects of the Church, including the supremacy of the Pope» (A. DULLES, «The Church: Introduction», 10).

[16] See A. DULLES, «The Church: Introduction», 10-11.

[17] Some of the images used in the *LG* are «people of God», «Temple of the Holy Spirit», «Body of Christ», «a sheepfold», «the sole and necessary gateway to which is Christ (Jn 10,1-10)», «a flock, of which God foretold that he would himself be the shepherd (Is 40,11; Ex 34,11f.)», «a cultivated field, the tillage of God», « building of God (1 Cor 3,9)».

[18] See K. RAHNER, «Structural Change», 115-132. According to A. Dulles even today, many middle-aged Catholics are actually uncomfortable with any other paradigm of the Church than that of *societas perfecta*. See A. DULLES, *Models of the Church*, 29. The nature of un-changeability existed up to the Second Vatican Council apart from the ecclesiological concern of the theologians from the beginning of the 19th century. See A. GRÉA, *L'Eglise et sa divine constitution*.

[19] «Prior to Vatican II it had become quite common to look on the Church as a gigantic corporation in which all true authority is located at the top, and flows downwards through the bishops to the laity at the bottom. This monolithic ecclesiology did not do justice to the idea of catholicity as identity in diversity — the idea that has been the leitmotiv of the present study» (A. DULLES, *The Catholicity of the Church*, 133). See also E.R. HAMBYE, «Image of the Church», 293-310; M. VELLANICKAL, «Image of the Church in the NT», 333-346.

governed by the successor of Peter and by the bishops in communion with him» (*LG* 8). Nevertheless the word «Church» is practically absent in the Gospel. So an understanding of the concept of the Church is needed.

The word «Church» comes from the Greek word *ekklēsia,* which means gathering of people. It has also a secular significance[20]. In LXX the Greek word *ekklēsia* occurs about 100 times. In LXX it has a religious significance and represents exclusively the Hebrew word *qāhāl*[21]. However, the Hebrew word *qāhāl* has different meanings. For example, in Genesis, Leviticus and Numbers, 21 times the word is translated by the word *synagōgē*[22]. But wherever the word *ekklēsia* is used in the LXX for *qāhāl*, it indicates God's assembly, characterized by having answered Yahweh's call[23].

Coming to the NT, Jesus Christ's followers did not use the term *synagōgē* for their gatherings. The only exception is in the letter of James 2,2. It seems that the followers of Jesus Christ consciously avoided the term *synagōgē* as the term could not contain the full significance of the Christian fellowship[24]. They preferred the term *ekklēsia* to signify their

---

[20] It also means a political force. «Celles-ci juridiquement, assemblées du "peuple" intervenant dans le gouvernement des villes, étaient une institution marquant l'unité institutionnelle de toutes les cités du monde grec» (L. CERFAUX, «L' Église», 899). Usually the gathering, *ekklēsia,* opened with prayers and sacrifices to the gods of the city. So it has a religious connotation too. See L. COENEN, «Church», 291. See also M. SCHMAUS, *Dogma: The Church,* 3.

[21] The word *qāhāl* probably related to *qōl* means both a summons to an assembly; and the very act of assembling. In Deuteronomy (9,10; 10,4) *qāhāl* means the congregation gathered to conclude the covenant at Sinai. See L. COENEN, «Church», 292-293. See also L. CERFAUX, *La Théologie de l'Église,* 81-100.

[22] The word *synagōgē* is also used to mean assembly, place of assembly, harvest (Gen 1,9; Ex 34,22; Lev 11,36). This word has a religious connotation reminding the great events of salvation history and of the promises to Israel (Num 14,7ff). This word also acquired an eschatological significance in Is 56,8; Ezek 37,10. In the NT the word *synagōgē* occurs nine times in Mt, eight times in Mk, fifteen times in Lk, twice in Jn and some nineteen times in the passages of Jas, Rev and in Acts. The word is used to describe either the meeting place of the local Jewish community or the congregation itself, representing the total number of Jews. See W. SCHRAGE, «"Ekklesia" und Synagoge», 178-202. See also L. COENEN, «Church», 292-293.

[23] The preference of the word *ekklēsia* by the LXX is also to be seen in the etymological context. *Ekklēsia* comes from *ekkaleō* (I call from, I convoke) of itself which indicates that Israel, the people of God, was the assembling of men convoked by divine initiative. See *DBT,* 72. See also L. COENEN, «Church», 295-296.

[24] «Once the Law of Moses had effectively taken central place in its life, liturgy and institution (cfr. Moses' seat in Mt 23, 2), the idea of the synagogue must have seemed so rigid to the Christian that he separated from it in favour of a reformed Christian assembly. It was, no doubt, also felt that a word with such connotations could not be used to

gathering. It is striking to note that the word *ekklēsia,* with the exception of Mt 16,18 and 18,17, is absent in the Gospels[25] whereas it is frequently found in the Pauline corpus[26]. From the frequent use of the term in the letters of Paul we assume that it was Paul who developed the concept of *ekklēsia* in the NT.

Paul uses the word *ekklēsia* intending *ekklēsia tou theou* as in Acts 20,28 (Church of God)[27]. He uses the word in the singular (Rom 16,23; 1 Cor 14,23) and in the plural (2 Cor 11,8; 12,13; Phil 4,14). A Church does not depend on the number of persons. His main concern was the building up of the Church[28]. Even a small fellowship as a house Church could be called *ekklēsia.* Paul writes: «The churches of Asia send their greetings. Aquila and Prisca send their best wishes in the Lord, together with the church that meets in their house» (1 Cor 16,19).

According to Paul, each community is Church in its fullness[29]. In 1 Thess 2,14 Paul speaks of local Churches: «For you, my brothers, have modelled yourselves on the churches of God in Christ Jesus which are in Judea». Sometimes he uses the word Church pertaining to the whole geographical area. For example, in 1 Cor 1,2 he speaks of the Church of God in Corinth. In his letter to Galatians 1,13, he says, «[...] I persecuted the Church of God in my attempts to destroy it». Paul's use of the words

---

describe fellowship and an event, at the centre of which was the proclamation of the Gospel of freedom from law and salvation available only through Jesus Christ» (L. COENEN, «Church», 297). It is also to be noted that the verb form of the word is used in an eschatological sense (Mk 4,1; 5, 21; 6,30; 7,1).

[25] According to O. Cullman all the early Christian writers use *ekklēsia* only for those fellowships which come into being after the crucifixion and resurrection of Jesus. See O. CULLMANN, *The Early Church,* 118. See also R. SCHNACKENBURG, «The Pauline Theology of the Church», 223.

[26] In Paul's un-contested letters it is found 44 times (in Deutero-Paulines, 15 times; in the Pastorals, three times). See J.A. FITZMYER, *Paul and His Theology,* 95.

[27] When Paul gives an attributive or predicative definition of *ekklēsia,* he uses primarily the genitive *tou theou,* which is added to the singular (1Cor 1,2; 10,32; 11,22; 15,9; Gal 1,13; 1 Tim 3,5. 15) and to the plural (1 Cor 11,16; 1 Thess 2,14; 2 Thess 1,4). For Paul the words *tou theou* are implied even when they are not specifically said. See K.L. SCHMIDT, «ekklēsia», 506-507.

[28] For an exegetical and theological study on the theme of building up of the Church see H. ALPHONSO, *Building up the Church.*

[29] Some scholars hold the view that each community represents the total community, the Church. To support this argument they give the examples of the Corinthian Church 1 Cor 6,4; 11,18; 14,23. The implication is that there is no difference between the universal Church and the local community. See K.L. SCHMIDT, «ekklēsia», 506-507. See also K. PIEPER, *Paulus und die Kirche,* 16-20; A. WILKENHAUSER, *Die Kirche als der mystische Leib Christi,* 6 ff; L. CERFAUX, *La Théologie de l'Église,* 90-97. 163-177.

such as «church», «churches», «churches of God» in no way affects his
real understanding of the Church. It is the Church of God. It is God who
assembles His own. It may be a liturgical assembly (I Cor 11,18;
14,19.28.34-35), or a local community (1 Cor 1,2; 16,1) or the whole
universal community of believers (1 Cor 15,9; Gal 1,13; Phil 3,6)[30]. This
biblical understanding of the Church would give us a better understanding
of relation between the universal Church and local Church[31.]

1.3 *The Relation between Universal Church and the Local Church*

As we have seen, especially in Acts and in the letters of Paul, the use
of words «Church» and «Churches» is interchangeable[32]. The Church in
each place is full in itself and it is one. The early tradition understood the
Church as «a people of God brought into unity from the unity of the
Father, the Son and the Holy Spirit» (*LG* 4). To express the universality
of the Church, Vatican II goes back to the time of Abel, the just one, to
the last of the elect[33]. The Fathers of the Church like Ignatius of Antioch,
Justin, and Irenaeus, had an extensive understanding of the Church. For
them Church is primarily a local Church[34]. According to *Lumen Gentium*

---

[30] The Church as liturgical assembly, local community or the whole universal
community of believers are inseparable. «"The Church" is the People of God that God
gathers in the whole world. She exists in local communities and is made real as a
liturgical, above all a Eucharistic, assembly. She draws her life from the word and the
Body of Christ and so herself becomes Christ's Body» (*CCC*, n. 752).

[31] The term «local Church», is understood as the diocese in the New Code of Canon
Law (*CIC*). It has got the same connotation of the particular Church. See *CIC*, 368. In
the Oriental Canon Law (*CCEO*) the terms Local Church and Particular Church are not
used To specify the Particular Church Oriental Code of Canon Law uses *Sui Iuris*. See
CCEO, ns. 27, 28.

[32] In Acts 5,11 the whole Church is identified with the Church of Jerusalem and in
Acts 16,5 the communities established by Paul are called Churches.

[33] See *LG* 2. Vatican II does not define the universal Church. But we could say that it
is the whole People of God which, under the guidance of the Roman Pontiff and the
college of bishops, is spread throughout the world. See *LG* 9. 13. 17. 22b; *CD* 10a, 23d;
OT 2e; *PO* 11b; *AG* 26b. See also G. GHIRLANDA, «Universal Church», 233-271.

[34] According to Ignatius of Antioch the universal Church is concretely present in the
local Church when it fulfills the liturgical action especially when the local assembly of the
faithful gathered under the bishop united with his priests (*presbyterium*) organized by the
service of the deacons. See ST. IGNATIUS OF ANTIOCH, «To the Ephesians», n. 5; «To the
Magnesians», n. 6; «To the Smyrnaens», n. 8 [H. DRESSLER, ed., *The Fathers of the
Church* I]. See B. NEUNHEUSER, «Chiesa Universale e Chiesa locale», 616-642. The
Church as universal is the well established conviction of the separated Churches too. See
L. BOUYER, *L'Eglise de Dieu*, 2-35.

a portion of the people of God is to be considered a Church when it is formed in the image of the universal Church[35]. The important point which we see in the development of ecclesiology is the mutual relationship between the universal Church and the local or particular Church[36]. For, the essentials of the Church are the same whether universal, particular or local[37].

1.3.1 Emergence of the Theology of the Local Church

Our study on the BECs, which are a source of «great hope for the life of the Church»[38], is rooted in the NT theology of the local Church. The Second Vatican Council does not give a full statement of a theology of the local Church[39] though it would have been difficult to develop such a theology without the Council[40]. The post conciliar Church also realized that the Church could not be a sacrament of salvation in the world in theoretical form. Its commitment to be «the light of humanity» (*LG* 1) and «the joy and hope»(*GS* 1) to the people are to be contextualized and concretized. The experience teaches that the Church's task for

---

[35] See *LG* 23a.

[36] «The universal Church, for its health, depends on the vitality of the member churches, each of which is expected to make a contribution to the life of the whole. Thus there is a kind of mutual indwelling, or circumincession, between the universal and the particular Church» (A. DULLES, *The Catholicity of the Church*, 134). See also H. DE LUBAC, *Les églises particulières dans l' Église universelle*, 29-69.

[37] G. Ghirlanda summarizes the essential elements of the Church as (1) an organic distinction between the members of the faithful although always in the unity of the Holy Spirit; (2) full acceptance of the authority of the visible Church and of all the means of salvation instituted within it, particularly the Eucharist; (3) union with Christ in the visible body of the Church through the bonds of profession of faith, sacraments, ecclesiastical government, and communion; and (4) the authority of the Supreme Pontiff and the bishops. See G. GHIRLANDA, «Universal Church», 233-271.

[38] JOHN PAUL II, *Redemptoris Missio*, n. 51.

[39] See D.E. LANNE, «L'Église locale», 481-511. See also J.J. VON ALLMEN, «L'Église locale parmi les autres Églises locales», 515-516.

[40] «senza il Vaticano II non sarebbe sorta la teologia della Chiesa locale come sta oggi davanti a noi. Il Concilio ha gettato le basi che la fondano ed ha stabilito i principi che la guidano. Soprattutto presentando la Chiesa come mistero di comunione in Cristo e come sacramento di salvezza per tutti gli uomini, "cioè come segno e strumento dell'intima comunione con Dio e dell'unità di tutto il genere umano" (*LG* 1). Qui è la primaria radice di una rinnovata visione teologica e non solo amministrativa della Chiesa locale» (J.VODOPIVEC, «La Chiesa Locale», 97-98).

contextualization and concretization as envisaged by the Council Fathers, is possible only in the local Church[41].

According to the Code of Canon law, «local Church» is considered as the diocese. The parish is a local Church in its relation to the diocese[42]. When we analyze the nature of the Church in the New Testament and the early traditions of the Church, we find that the concept of the local Church, because of its *diritto divino*[43], cannot be limited to the *diocese* alone. The existence of the local Church goes beyond the juridical boundaries of the diocese[44]. The diversification has been already realized by Vatican II. The Council says that the «Church of Christ is really present in all legitimately organized local groups of the faithful, which, in so far as they are united to their pastors» (*LG* 26). And again referring to the teachings of St. Augustine, the Council says that «though they may be often small and poor, or existing in the diaspora, Christ is present through whose power and influence the One, Holy Catholic and Apostolic Church is constituted» (*LG* 26). Referring to the role of priests, the

---

41 The frequent Synods after Vatican II are to be understood in the context of concretizing the vision of the Church envisaged by the Council Fathers. Every Synod was convened to find the ways and means to concretize the life of the Church envisaged by Vatican II. The New Code of Canon Law is also inspired by the theological vision of the Church. See *CIC*, n. 369.

42 «Each diocese or other particular Church is divided into distinct parts of parishes» (*CIC*, 374/1). In the post apostolic period also emphasis was given to the local Churches. «Wherever the bishop is, there let the people be; as wherever Jesus Christ is, there is the Catholic Church» (ST. IGNATIUS OF ANTIOCH, «To the Smyrnaens», n. 8).

43 «La Chiesa Locale nella vita concreta descritta dal Nuovo Testamento, vissuta dalla tradizione della Chiesa unita, intesa dalle Liturgie antiche, insegnata dai Padri, può essere compresa in tutta la sua determinante importanza, in tutta la sua attualità moderna, solo partendo dal presupposto ampiamente dimostrabile della sua realtà ultima: la Chiesa Locale é di diritto divino» (E. LANNE, «La Chiesa locale è dirito divino», 797). The bishop is not primarily the representative of his Church: he is their bond and very mediation. H.M. LEGRAND, «Inverser Babel», 323-346. See also K.L. SCHMIDT, «ekklēsia», 501-536.

44 See H.M. LEGRAND, «La realizzazione della Chiesa in un luogo», 147-333. See also J. LÓPEZ-GAY, «La missione come aiuto», 9-32; G. GHIRLANDA, «Universal Church», 233-271; H. DE LUBAC, *Les églises particulières dans l'Eglise universelle*; A. ANTON, «Iglesia universal, Iglesias particulares», 409-435; B. NEUNHEUSER, «Chiesa universale e Chiesa locale», 616-642; D.E. LANNE, «L'Eglise locale et l'Eglise universelle», 481-511; G. VODOPIVEC, «La teologia e la Chiesa locali», 38-76; A. AMATO, ed., *La Chiesa locale*; L. NEWBEGIN, «What is a local Church truly united?», 115-128; P. DE LETTER, «The Local Church», 3-29; J. DUPUIS, «Nagpur International Theological Conference», 458-471; Y. CONGAR, «The Need of Pluralism in the Church», 343-353.

Council again says that in local assembly of the faithful the priests represent in a certain sense the bishop[45].

As regards the liturgical life, the Council says that the Bishop is to be considered as the High Priest of his flock from whom the life in Christ of his faithful is in some way derived and upon whom it depends in some way[46]. The Council also accepts the fact that it is impossible for the bishop to preside over the liturgical celebrations always. So the Council speaks of the necessity of establishing the groupings of the faithful. Among these, parishes, set up locally under a pastor who takes the place of the bishop, are the most important, for in some way they represent the visible Church constituted throughout the world[47].

In the local Church, according to Pope Paul VI, one must recognize the *locus* of effective contact where one encounters Christ[48]. The Pope further exhorts the attitude that the faithful should have towards the Church. The Pope says that local Church should be loved as one loves the mother. For Paul VI, local Church means not only the diocese but also the parish and everyone ought to consider himself fortunate to belong to his own diocese and his own parish[49].

Pope John Paul II also accepts the plurality that exists within the local (particular) Churches. «No particular Church is the same as another, yet the one, holy, Catholic and Apostolic Church is present and active in each one. It is not as if the People of God were a loosely-linked international society or even a federation of particular Churches»[50]. In effect it is in

---

[45] See *LG* 26.

[46] See *SC* 41.

[47] See *SC* 42.

[48] «E nella Chiesa locale — e qui il pensiero dal perimetro diocesano, che per eccellenza definisce il carattere proprio d'una Chiesa locale, costituzionalmente riconosciuta come tale, si allarga e si ramifica nelle espressioni parocchiali e nelle altre particolari e legittime — noi possiamo riconoscere il punto di effettivo contatto dove l'uomo incontra Cristo e dove gli è aperto l'accesso al piano concreto della salvezza: qui il ministero, qui la fede, qui la comunità, qui la parola, qui la grazia, qui Cristo stesso che si offre al fedele inserito nella Chiesa universale» (PAUL VI, «L'Eucaristia centro di unità», 912).

[49] «La Chiesa locale come madre deve essere amata. Il proprio campanile dev'essere preferito come il più bello di tutti. Ciascuno deve sentirsi felice di appartenere alla propria Diocesi, alla propria Parrochia. Nella propria Chiesa locale ciascuno può dire: qui Cristo mi ha atteso e mi ha amato; qui l'ho incontrato, e qui io appartengo al suo Corpo mistico. Qui io sono nella sua unità» (PAUL VI, «L'Eucaristia centro di unità», 913).

[50] See JOHN PAUL II, «L'Omelia », 1542.

the parish that the Church is seen locally[51]. «In a certain sense it is the *Church living in the midst of the homes of her sons and daughters*»[52].

1.4 *Parish as the Local Church*

According to the Council documents[53] and the new Code of Canon law[54] the local Church means a diocese. A parish[55] is a local Church insofar as it is related to the diocese[56]. But the question is whether the Church as «universal», «particular», «parish» can become a sacrament of salvation in the world? Many a time, in the present state, a diocese or a parish, whether established in a mission area or in an urban area, fails to be «a sign of the presence of God in the world» (*AG* 15). For, as the Synod Fathers (1987) have pointed out, many parishes, whether established in regions affected by urban progress or in a missionary territory, cannot do their work effectively. The reason may be the lack of material resources or ordained men or the geographical vastness of the parish or other particular circumstances like exiles and migrants[57].

Since the Church's task in our day, according to John Paul II, is so great, its accomplishment cannot be left to the parish alone[58]. He confirms his vision of going beyond the parish and becoming the sign of the presence of God in the world when he says, «the evangelizing activity of

---

[51] See JOHN PAUL II, «L'Omelia », 1538-1545.

[52] JOHN PAUL II, *Christifideles Laici*, n. 26.

[53] See *UR* 14a. See also *LG* 23d, 26a; *AG* 19d, 27a.

[54] See *CIC*, ns. 368, 370, 370, 370 §1, 370 §2.

[55] The term «parish» was not used in the early Church as we mean today. For a detailed study on the term «parish» with its canonical (old Canon Law) implications see B.L. JOSE, *The Parish Council.* See also A. BLÖCHLINGER, *The Modern Parish Community.* ·

[56] For a broader meaning given to the parish see *LG* 28. See also JOHN PAUL, II, *Catechesi Tradendae*, n. 67; *CIC*, 515§ 1; JOHN PAUL II, *Christifideles Laici*, n. 26. Only once does the Council refer to the portion of the people of God under the care of a specific priest as a «local Church». See *PO* 6d. Y. Congar does not see the significance of the Church as a parish in a juridical terminology. The juridical emphasis will lead to the understanding that the priest, in a parish, has more responsibility to his bishop than to the faithful. «Canonically speaking, a parish is not a totality or society of faithful, it is not a moral person capable of rights; it is a certain territory over which the bishop has set a priest with cure of souls as his assistant; the parish priest depends on his bishop, not on his parishioners» (Y. CONGAR, *Lay People in the Church*, 260).

[57] See JOHN PAUL II, *Christifideles Laici*, n. 26. The inability of the Church to reach her full potential is also felt in the Synod for Africa. See JOHN PAUL II, *Ecclesia in Africa*, n. 89.

[58] See JOHN PAUL II, *Christifideles Laici*, n. 26.

the Christian community, first in its own locality, and then elsewhere as part of the Church's universal mission, is the clearest sign of a mature faith»[59]. The BECs have emerged in responding to the pastoral needs of the local Churches. It is in this context that we understand the significance and the theology of the BECs.

2. The BECs: New Forms of Being Local Churches

As a description we would say that the BEC is the smallest cell of the Church in terms of community. It is not just part of the whole. It is the whole Church in a concentrated form. Or to put it in another way, it is a germ or a seed which has within itself all the essential elements of the Church, and can truly bring that Church to birth. It is simple, supremely effective, and presents a radically new model of Church. It is the same Church, the *universal sacrament of salvation*, that continues the prophetic, priestly, pastoral mission of Christ, resulting in a community of faith, of worship and of love. It is another way of ecclesial expression[60].

BEC is really a local Church where people come together as the first Christian communities (Acts 2,42; 4,32). This is a realization of the universal Church in a given locality. It takes up the mission of Jesus Christ and bears the responsibility of carrying it out under the guidance of the bishops, in communion with the universal Church all over the world[61].

As the Vatican II opened the way to go to the early sources of the Church, people began to be more conscious about the concept of the Church and the relation between the universal Church and the local Church. This awareness helped to formulate a theology of local Church reaching out to the BECs. The emergence of BECs have also contributed toward understanding and appreciating a theology of local Church. The study of the phenomenon of BECs would show how the BECs have enriched the development of the theology of local Church within the last three decades.

---

[59] JOHN PAUL II, *Redemptoris Missio*, n. 49.

[60] See J. MARINS, «Comunità ecclesiali di base», 43. See also L. BOFF, *Church: Charism & Power*, 25-126; «AMECEA Plenary 1976: Building Christian Communities», 272-273; C. BOFF, «The Nature of Basic Christian Communities», 53-58.

[61] See «Report on the General Meeting of CBCI (Calcutta, 1974)», 127.

2.1 *The Phenomenon of BECs in the Church*

Small groups have always been recognized as the effective way of building Christian communities. This we notice everywhere in the world irrespective of countries or continents. The small groups[62] such as *L'Azione Cattolica, Movimento dei Focolari, Il Movimento Comunione e Liberazione, I Cursillos de Cristiandad, Il Movimento Luce-Vita, Le Comunità di Vita Cristiana, I Terz'Ordini Secolari e le Confraternite,* which originated before Vatican II, have been witnessing Christ and silently building Christian communities in Europe. Similar movements and groups can be named in the case of Asia as well as America. Movements that have very radical effects in the life of the Church are seen especially in Latin America and India[63]. The emergence of BECs is to be considered as *a gift of the present times* to live Church and to build Christian communities.

In English there are various expressions that denote the BECs, such as «basic communities», «base communities» or «grassroots communities», «spontaneous group», «under ground Church». It is modified as «basic Christian communities» or «basic ecclesial communities» to specify the religious character of communities in some contexts in order to emphasize the adhesion of the communities to the institutional Church[64].

The historical examination with regard to the development of BECs presents us with two main forms. The first one emerged in the developed countries as «base communities» as an outcome of dissatisfaction with an institutional Church and its hierarchical and its juridical structures and the second spontaneously developed in Latin America and widely spread in Africa and Asia[65]. The common phenomenon in both is the *new way of being the Church.*

---

[62] See B. SECONDIN, *Segni di Profezia,* 164-197.325-331. See also A. FAVALE, ed., *Movimenti ecclesiali.*

[63] In building Christian communities small groups such as *prarthanayōgam* (prayer meeting), *Kutumba yōgam* (family gathering), *vārdu yōgam* (ward meeting), *Kombriya Sabha* (a confraternity) have played an important role in Kerala, India. In the third chapter we will explain how these groups have helped to build Christian communities.

[64] See J. MARINS, «Comunità ecclesiali di base», 43-54. See also A. MÜLLER — N. GREINACHER, «Comunità di base», 17-23; J. EAGLESON, «Basic Communities», 80.

[65] Brazil, Chile and Panama are the first Latin American countries where this new way of being the Church through BECs originated See J. MARINS, «Comunità ecclesiali di base», 43-54. By 1965 BECs originated in Mindanao in Philippines. See W.C. GUBUAN, *The Basic Christian Communities,* 6-118.

One cannot date exactly the origin of BECs as it is now understood. In 1956, Agnelo Rossi, bishop of Barra do Pirai, Brazil, initiated an evangelization movement with the help of lay catechists for places not reached by pastors. The immediate reason which prompted Agnelo Rossi to the evangelization movement was the lament of one lady on his pastoral visit. She told him: «On the Eve of Christmas three Protestant Churches were illuminated and full of people. We could hear them singing [...] while our Catholic Church was closed without illumination, because we did not get a priest for the Mass»[66]. It was a challenge to the Bishop and he decided to train community coordinators in Barro do Pirai:

> to do everything a lay person can do in God's Church in the ecclesiastical discipline. At the least, these catechists will gather the people once a week for religious instruction. Normally they will also celebrate daily prayer with the people. On Sundays and Holy Days they will gather the people from all over the district for a «Massless Sunday» or «priestless Mass» or «Catholic worship» and lead them spiritually and collectively in the same Mass as is being celebrated by the pastor in the distant mother church. They will recite morning and evening prayers with the people, as well as novenas, litanies, May and June celebrations, and so on[67].

The catechesis became the centre of a community, and someone was responsible for religious life. Instead of chapels, meeting halls were built and then were used for school, religious instruction, sewing lessons, and meetings for solving community problems, even economic ones[68]. It is to be noted that already in 1956 there were about 372 catechists in the diocese. At this time the Archdiocese of Natal in Brazil introduced the «radio schools» along with the Movement for Basic Education[69]. Through

---

[66] «Nelle feste natalizie le tre chiese protestanti erano illuminate e molto frequentate. Abiamo ascoltato i loro canti [...] mentre la nostra chiesa cattolica era chiusa, senza illuminazione, perché non avevamo ottenuto un sacerdote per messa» (J. MARINS, «Comunità ecclesiali di base», 47).

[67] BRAZILIAN BISHOPS' CONFERENCE, *Plano pastoral de conjunto (1962-1965)*, 58 quoted by L. BOFF, *Ecclesiogenesis*, 3. See also A. ROSSI, «Uma Experiência», 731-37. This evangelization movement gave an impetus to the lay people to take active part in the life of the Church.

[68] See L. BOFF, *Ecclesiogenesis*, 3.

[69] According to M. De C. Azevedo, a theologian from Brazil, the great merit of the Movement for Basic Education (Movimento de educação de base) was that it was the first and most persevering programme of the grass-roots education in the context of the Church in Brazil, and indeed of the country itself. It started with the active role of the pupil in his or her own education, making education a process of consciousness-raising vis-à-vis the concrete reality in which one lived and the urgent need for its transformation. In that sense the *MEB*, from the very start, anticipated by two decades

this education programme the Church was trying to meet the human problems of poverty, illiteracy, epidemics, exploitation and injustice in the society. From 1958 on, the radio was used as the efficient method to have contact with the people. In 1963 there were 1410 radio classes in the Archdiocese of Natal alone. The radio schools taught the people to read and write and they were given religious instruction. On Sundays, communities without a priest would gather together by the radio and pray aloud the people's parts of the Mass being celebrated by the bishop and to listen to his homily[70]. Such communities spread all over the north-east and centre-west of Brazil.

Another important factor in the origin of BECs is the Better World Movement. This movement called for an urgent need to renew the Church. A team of fifteen persons travelled about the country for five years, giving 1.800 courses and stimulating all areas of the ecclesial life. Priests, bishops, religious, laity, and all experienced this renewal. This programme resulted in the Brazilian Bishops' Conference Emergency Plan, and the First Nationwide Pastoral Plan (1965-70), which said:

> Our present parishes are or ought to be composed of various local communities and «base communities», in view of their great extent, population density, and percentage of persons baptized and hence juridically belong to them. It will be of great importance, then, to launch a parish renewal in each place, for the creation and ongoing dynamics of these '«base communities». The mother Church will itself gradually become one of these communities, and the pastor will preside in all of them, because all are to be found in the portion of the Lord's flock with which he has been entrusted[71].

In the Nationwide Pastoral Plan the words used are «local communities» and «basic communities». Nevertheless, in the light of this Nationwide Pastoral Plan or Joint Pastoral Plan, theologians like R.B. Caramuru in 1967 and J. Marins in 1968 began to use the terms *Comunidade eclesial de base* (BEC) in their writings[72].

---

the concrete and thematic systematization of popular education in Brazil. See M. DE C. AZEVEDO, *Basic Ecclesial Communities*, 44.

[70] As M. De C. Azevedo observes, we could see the linkup of religion and life in this movement. In Barra do Pirai and Natal both movements were something new to the people. See M. DE C. AZEVEDO, *Basic Ecclesial Communities*, 27.

[71] P. DEMO, «Comunidades», ns. 3, 67-110 in L. BOFF, *Ecclesiogenesis*, 4.

[72] According to R.B. Caramuru the basic ecclesial community is not a re-edition in miniature of the present parish structure. It entails a whole new pastoral conception, certainly embodying the ecclesial awareness explored by Vatican II. See R.B. CARAMURU, *Comunidade ecclesial de base*, 61. See also M. DE C. AZEVEDO, *Basic Ecclesial Communities*, 41-56.

2.1.1 BECs in Latin America

In Latin America, the renewal of the Church through BECs was the major pastoral programme from the time of the Joint Pastoral Plan of 1965-1970 by the Brazilian Bishops' Conference. Thereafter BECs were becoming «effective laboratories»[73] to give a new image of the Church. The different Episcopal Conferences have repeatedly encouraged the movement with specific objectives. The notable feature in all the conferences is the progressive development in the ecclesiological vision of those local Churches. For example, the Brazilian Episcopal Conference for its pastoral plan for the years 1983-86 defined the role of BECs as the «dynamic reality of the life of the Church» and putting it as one of the important pastoral priorities for realizing «a new way of being the Church»[74]. And its steady and gradual development «opened a new chapter in the aspect of inculturation»[75]. Three conferences of Latin American Bishops (CELAM): the first at Medellin/ Colombia in 1968, the second at Pueblo/Mexico in 1979 and the third at Santo Domingo/ Dominican Republic in 1992, played a significant role. At the Medellin conference the bishops affirmed:

> the Christian [ecclesial] base community is the first and fundamental ecclesial nucleus, which on its own level must make itself responsible for the richness and expansion of the faith, as well as of the cult which is its expression. This community becomes then the initial cell of the ecclesiastical structures and the focus of evangelization, and it currently serves as the most important source of human advancement and development[76].

Together with the ecclesiology of the local Church initiated by Vatican II, the Medellin conclusions made it possible to proclaim *the new way of being the Church* through BECs. The Bishops' synod in 1974[77] and the Apostolic Exhortation of Pope Paul VI, *Evangelii Nuntiandi,* recognized the evangelizing power of BECs in the present world of anonymity[78]. The

---

[73] «efficaci laboratori» (B. SECONDIN, *Segni di Profezia,* 96).

[74] See B. SECONDIN, *Segni di Profezia,* 90-91. It is also important to note the theological reflections in the same book, 92-93.

[75] B. SECONDIN, *Segni di Profezia,* 97.

[76] «Joint Pastoral Planning», n. 10 in SECOND GENERAL CONFERENCE OF LATIN AMERICAN BISHOPS, *Conclusions,* 185. The Conference was held at Medellin.

[77] According to B. Secondin the Synod in 1974 was a legitimation for BECs. See B. SECONDIN, *Segni di Profezia,* 79. See also G. CAPRILE, *Il Sinodo dei Vescovi 1974,* 155-156.

[78] PAUL VI, *Evangelii Nuntiandi,* n. 58.

Pope's Exhortations became classic and became a point of reference in the subsequent documents on various types of BECs[79].

In light of the lived experience of the Latin American Churches since the Medellin conference in 1968, the Bishops Conference of Latin America was held at Puebla, Mexico in January/February 1979. This conference stressed the importance of communion, participation and option for the poor. It focused on the integral liberation of the people[80].It was followed by a series of national meetings of various kinds[81].

The Fourth General Conference of Latin American Bishops was held at Santo Domingo, the Domenican Republic, from 12-18 October, 1992, marking the anniversary of the landing of Colombus and the beginning of the first Evangelization five hundred years ago. The main thrust of the document was New Evangelization, Human Development and Christian Culture. However, the Conference also confirmed the importance of the BECs in the new evangelization, human development and Christian culture. The conference says that the Christian base community (CBC) is a living cell of the parish which, in turn, is understood as an organic and missionary community. The conference makes a universal appeal by saying: «We see a need to: Reaffirm the validity of basic Christian communities by developing in them a spirit of mission and solidarity and seeking to integrate them into the parish, the diocese, and the universal Church, in keeping with the teachings of *Evangelii Nuntiandi* (58)»[82].

According to M.de C. Azevedo[83], BECs were the result of the *consciousness-raising activity* of clergy and religious, who were helping the people *to see real elements of their life situation and historical situation.* The main reason for their rapid growth lies in the correspondence

---

[79] It is remarkable that *Concilium* brought out one full number of it 11/4 (1975) on the question of the influence of BECs in the Catholic Church. See B. SECONDIN, *Segni di Profezia*, 78-82.

[80] See B. SECONDIN, *Segni di Profezia*, 84-87.

[81] Following the Puebla Conference there were various meetings of BECs in different Latin American countries with particular themes. Among them the fourth meeting of BECs of Brazil at Itaicí (São Paulo) in April 1981 with the theme «Igreja: povo oprimido que se organiza para a libertação», the fifth meeting at Canindé (Ceará) in July 1983 with the theme CEB «Povo unido, semente de uma nova sociedade» and the sixth meeting in July 1986 at Tridande/Goiania (Goias) with the theme «Povo de Deus em busca da Terra Prometida» are important. These meetings helped BECs to have an enduring programme in the Latin American Church. See B. SECONDIN, *Segni di Profezia*, 87-92. See also L. BOFF, *Ecclesiogenesis*, 34-44.

[82] A.T. HENNELLY, ed., *Santo Domingo and Beyond*, 92.

[83] See M. DE C. AZEVEDO, *Basic Ecclesial Communities*, 35-36.

between the elements introduced by pastoral agents and the concrete needs of the people. To deny one of the two terms would be to succumb to a partial view of the situation. The work of the clergy and other pastoral agents was crucial in triggering the process and catalyzing the specific perspective of BECs. It gave them a body of ideas, a minimum of initial organization, and a guarantee of continuity, growth, and animation.

The social realities in which the BECs originated in Latin America is changing. A change in the method and functioning of BECs is inevitable, though the BECs today are acting like the woman who mixes a little yeast with three measures of flour and waits for the mixture to rise (Mat 13,33). The ecclesial consciousness reached by the people through BECs is not going to change in the near future[84].

2.1.2 BECs in Africa

The idea or ecclesiology behind the local Church became very effective after the Vatican II in the African continent. The theological vision and the missiological thrust moved the bishops to have their own pastoral planning quite different from the pre-Vatican style. The Church in Zaire had already initiated the programme of renewing the Church through basic communities before Vatican II[85]. The Churches in East African countries began to plan out their own methodology to deepen the faith and spread the Gospel message. An important milestone in their journey (cammino) was the decision taken by the bishops' conference of Eastern Africa (Association of Members of Episcopal Conferences of Eastern Africa- AMECEA) in 1973 to build small communities towards making the Catholic Church in Eastern Africa independent economically, pastorally and in its ministries[86]. The bishops of AMECEA, who assembled at the 1973 Plenary Assembly to «Plan for the Church in Eastern Africa in the 1980's» stated:

---

[84] See V. CODINA, «The Wisdom of Latin America's Base Communities»,71-80. According to a recent study conducted by the Bishops' Conference in Brazil shows that there are 80.000 communities with fifty people in each. See C. BOFF, «The Church in Latin America», 131-141. According to M. de C. Azevedo BECs are becoming the part of the culture of Latin America [personal interview with M. de C. Azevedo on 13-3-1995]. See also D. BARBÉ, Grace and Power; G. COOK, ed., New Face of the Church; K.C. ABRAHAM – B. MBUY-BEYA, eds., Spirituality of the Third World.

[85] See P.C. LEMBAGUSALA, «Approfondissement de la foi», 450-456. See also B. SECONDIN, Segni di Profezia, 101-115.

[86] See R. MEJIA, The Church in the Neighbourhood, 24.

We are convinced that in these countries of Eastern Africa it is time for the Church to become really «local», that is: self-ministering, self-propagating and self-supporting. Our planning is aimed at building such local Churches for the coming years. We believe that in order to achieve this we have to insist on building Church life and on basic Christian communities, in both rural and urban areas. Church life must be based on the communities in which everyday life takes place: those basic and manageable social groupings whose members can experience real inter-personal relationship and feel a sense of communal belonging both in living and working. We believe that Christian communities at this level will be suited to develop really intense vitality and to become effective witness in their natural environment[87].

In 1976, the bishops of Eastern Africa (AMECA) gathered at Nairobi in Kenya, with the theme «Building Christian Communities in the Eastern Africa»[88]. The Conference acknowledged the significant achievement of the BECs. It emphasized the need of systematic formation of BECs as its pastoral priority. The conference also made it clear that formation of BECs cannot be merely a personal activity, but it must be the activity of the Church. The conference gave freedom to each bishop to adopt the pastoral programme according to each situation[89]. In 1979, the Seventh AMECEA Plenary Assembly gathered at Zomba in Malawi and evaluated the implementation of the AMECEA Bishops' pastoral priority of building BECs[90]. They arrived at a conclusion that BECs are still the best means to renew the Churches in East Africa[91].

---

[87] «Planning for the Church in Eastern Africa in the 1980's», 9-10.

[88] See «AMECEA Plenary 1976: Building Christian Communities», The remarks of P.A. Kalilombe, bishop of Lilongwe, Malawi, is worth mentioning here. In the Position Paper titled «An Overall View on Building Christian Communities» he says: «Events following the 1973 Plenary prove that this resolve by the Church leaders in the AMECEA countries has not remained a dead letter». In between 1973 and 1976 «diocesan synods, Episcopal conference study sessions, and other pastoral study or planning meetings have been taking place in various parts of Eastern Africa. Among the major conclusions of these meetings one invariably finds the resolve to build Christian Communities. No wonder then that when AMECEA Documentation Service circulated a questionnaire in 1975 in order to find out how the Eastern African dioceses ranked their pastoral priorities, the results of survey indicated that "Building Christian Communities" was recognized as the highest priority in AMECEA. Logically then the Executive Committee decided to have this as the theme of the 1976 Plenary Assembly» («AMECEA Plenary 1976: Building Christian Communities», 262).

[89] See «AMECEA Plenary 1976: Building Christian Communities», 250.

[90] In the Seventh Plenary Assembly, the evaluation process continued in different parishes and dioceses. See D. KAMUGISHA, «The AMECEA Pastoral Priority», 138-141. See also N. KONINGS, «Christian Communities», 247-254; B. KIRISWA, «Small Christian Communities», 90-93; E.V. HUET, «Religious and the AMECEA», 265-268; M. FALEYE,

According to P.A. Kalilombe, it is through building BECs that the Church in a country can become «self-reliant» and become mature, truly local or «incarnated» Church[92]. For him the Church becomes incarnated or authentically localized in the measure in which the living and running of the Church life is actively and consciously assumed by the local Christians[93]. By «local church» he means the totality of all those who in a given area belong to Christ through faith and baptism[94].

The determined pastoral programme planned out in 1973 for the future Church is a sign of the great ecclesiological interest of the Churches in Africa. The African Churches had foreseen already in 1973 that the future of the Church in East African countries depended on the formation of BECs. The Sixth AMECEA Plenary Assembly in 1976, and the Seventh AMECEA Plenary Assembly are important milestones in the growth of BECs. For, it is through such basic or small communities that a Church could become «self-reliant» and mature, a sign and sacrament of salvation. However, in many dioceses the proposals of AMECEA remained only in words. Many priests, still did not see BECs as a new model of being the Church. Some were and still are very particular about the centralized parish structures. Despite these practical difficulties, the East African Churches have been able to clarify the ecclesiology of BECs which is basically Vatican II's renewed ecclesiology[95].

2.1.3 BECs in Asia

One of the important realities, perhaps the most important, that has emerged in Christian Churches in Asia in the past twenty years, is the grassroots ecclesial communities, or BECs, involving Christians where they are and as they are[96]. The Churches in Asia, after Vatican II, became more aware of the need to concentrate on vitalizing the local Churches. The origin of the Federation of Asian Bishops' Conference was one of the

---

«A Layman in a Small Christian Community», 343-346; V. OKEYO, «Small Christian Communities», 226-229.

   [91] J.M. MBINDA, «AMECEA Bishops' Consultations», 17-21.

   [92] See «Position Paper», [*AfER* 5 (1976)] 262.

   [93] See *AfER* 5 (1976) 264.

   [94] See *AfER* 5 (1976) 265.

   [95] See J.M. MBINDA, «AMECEA Bishops' Consultations», 21. See also J.V. KODA, *Small Christian Communities*, 23-46; M.I. AGUILAR, «An African Theology», 142-155.

   [96] See *FAPA*, xx. See also *CBCI Evaluation Report*, n. 632.

outcomes[97]. As a means of vitalizing the functioning of the Church, *the new way of being the Church* through BECs came to the Asian context as a «precious experience»[98], although the existence of similar groups is not a new phenomenon in Asia[99].

The *new way of being the Church* through BECs was not widely known and it could not make great impact in the universal Church because of the pluralistic nature existing in Asian countries[100]. In 1982 the Federation of the Asian Bishops' Conference made the decision to promote BECs[101]; most of the Asian Churches have given pastoral priority to the formation of BECs. It is to be noted that even before the FABC decisions, the bishops of Philippines had given pastoral priority to forming BECs. Bishop J.X. Labayen writes:

> I have promoted the growth of the BCCs in my area of pastoral ministry for over ten years now. I feel I have stumbled on a vein of gold. I have seen the faith of our people deepen, commitment to one another, narrow minds and

---

97 See *FAPA*, xxiii-xxx. See also T. BALASURIYA, «Contestation in the Church in Asia», 60-65.

98 B. SECONDIN, *Segni di Profezia,* 116. Already in the mid 70's the Asian Churches strongly felt the need of forming BECs. They realized that the existing parish structures were not helpful to intensive Christian life. However, the main concern of Asian Church has been dialogue, missionary dialogue with cultures (i.e., Inculturation), with the religious traditions (i.e., inter religious dialogue), and with the peoples, especially the poor multitudes in Asia (i.e., development/liberation).

99 See F. CLAVER, «Forms of Christian Community», 65-75. See also J. KAVUMKAL, «Christian Ashram», 68-78; J.P. PINTO, *Inculturation,* 182-233; G. BALI, «The Basic Features of Life», 8; B. SECONDIN, *Segni di Profezia,* 116-125. In Kerala, one of the Ancient Christian centres, different groups existed as an integral part of the parish structure. Even the idea of participatory church is not new to them. We speak about the Kerala Church in the third chapter while discussing the early ecclesial administrative structure which existed in Trivandrum.

100 See *FAPA*, xxvii - xxviii.

101 «small ecclesial communities at all levels of Church life be more widely and intensely fostered, characterized by their openness and outreach to society through evangelization, social service, dialogue, ecumenical and inter-religious cooperation with peoples of all faiths by their close union with their priests and bishops» (*FAPA*, 63). Already the Asian Colloquium on Ministries in the Church 1977 [prepared two years before] spoke about the growth of BECs in many parts of Asia and said that these groups are not the only way of participating in the life of the Church; still the Spirit seems to be moving the Church strongly in this direction. They even proposed to study the problem of providing the Eucharistic celebration for the BECs. See *FAPA*, 67-92. The Seminar on «Creative Ministries and Affirmative Action in Today's India», held at the National Vocation Service Centre, Pune from 5th to 12th February 1984 affirmed: «We are convinced that the formation and on-going animation of Basic Communities is a ministry of priority in the given situation of India» (A. D'SILVA, ed., *Creative Ministries,* 210).

hearts open up, prayer intensify community life form. However, it must be conceded that all is not perfect, but the BCC movement has touched our people's lives at a far deeper level than have any other of our church programmes in the past [102].

At present BECs exist in different names and forms in most of the Churches of Asia[103]. However, as the Church in Asia exists in a pluriform culture, the task of BECs is great and challenging. The task of BECs is great because the ecclesial life is to be felt in the day to day life. As BECs are lived in grass roots level it can easily dialogue with other religions, for, dialogue with other religions is the felt need of the Church in the pluralistic religious context of Asia. It is only through dialogue that one can explain more fully the truth that Christ is the one Mediator between God and humanity and the sole Redeemer of the world. It is through dialogue that one can show distinction between Christ and the founders of other great religions[104]. It is challenging because the BECs have to confront the evils of the society like caste system, dowry, corruption, exploitation.

2.1.4 BECs in the Developed Countries

In the development of an ecclesiology of the local Church the Churches in the developed countries too have had a role to play. Yet in applying the theology of the local Church into the common life of the people, the Churches in the developed countries, due to their strong *institutional impact*[105] could not achieve as much as in other developing countries. There were renewal movements which have given rise to many small groups or «intentional Christian communities» in North America and in

---

[102] J.X. LABAYEN, «Basic Christian Communities», 135-144. See also H. JANSSEN, «Ein Spannungsreicher Aufbruch», 532-536; E.S. DEGUZMAN, «Communiautés chrétiennes de base», 33-37; W.C. GUBUAN, *The Basic Christian Communities*, 65-118; A.L. PICARDAL, *An Ecclesiological Perspective*, 8-38.

[103] R. HARDAWIRYANA, – al., *Building the Church* . See also F. CLAVER, «Forms of Christian Community», 65-75. M. CAVALCA, «La Methode des Groupes», 496-500; L. MASCARENHAS, «Basic Christian Communities», 26-30; B. SECONDIN, *Segni di Profezia*, 116-125. 318-319.

[104] JOHN PAUL II, *Tertio Millennio Adveniente*, ns. 38, 52-53.

[105] K. Rahner in his evaluation of BECs says that Europe cannot simply imitate the BECs of Latin America. According to him Europe has a legitimate and meaningful hierarchically organized Church that is still important. The social reasons are also different from Latin America. K. RAHNER, «South American Base Communities», 148-154. See also B. SECONDIN, *Segni di Profezia*, 133.

Europe[106]. With the Second Vatican Council, many groups have been existing throughout western Europe with the intention of renewing the Church «consistently and radically». Many times they have arisen quite spontaneously because of dissatisfaction with the official Church's slowness or indifference with regard to concrete renewal[107].

The communitarian aspect of Christian life is very much stressed in the theological thinking and encouraging efforts are seen in the developed countries. The articles published in *Concilium* 11/4 (1975) and other studies[108] show that BECs are not a strange phenomenon to the developed countries, although the promotion of BECs still needs encouragement from the hierarchy.

In the Apostolic Letter *Tertio Millennio Adveniente* Pope John Paul II says: «In the history of the Church, the «old» and the «new» are always closely interwoven. The «new» grows out of the «old», and the «old» finds a fuller expression in the «new»[109]. This is also true with the growth of BECs. The existence of BECs is not a new idea born in someone's mind. It had been the original nature of the Church. Now it is being realized very effectively. The Christians come together and establish a Christian community. They support each other, love each other in a truly tangible way, help each other in need, and answer to each other[110]. Thus communion and *diakoinia* are experienced.

---

[106] See B.J. LEE – M.A. COWAN, *Dangerous Memories*, 33-58. See also B. SECONDIN, *Segni di Profezia*, 127-162; E.D. BALTZEL, *The Search for Community*; A. NESTI, ed., *L'altra Chiesa in Italia*; R. KEYES, *We the Lonely People;* O. SCHREUDER, ed., *Gemeindereform — Prozeß an der Basis*; AA.VV., *Le Organizzazioni Revoluzionarie*; J. LELL – F.W. MENNE, eds., *Religiöse Gruppen*. In the Diocese of Rotenburg-Stuttgart, W. Schmitt started *Familien Kreis* in Böfingen-Ulm in 1987 and it is spread out in many parishes in the Diocese. In the Diocese of Freiburg, Germany, through the «Bibel-Teilen» 7 Schritte zum Leben (7 steps method) renewal is taking place. Renewal through the «7 steps» method in the Diocese of Trivandrum will be discussed in the fourth chapter. See also M. HEBBLETHWAITE, «Earthing the Church», 11-12.

[107] R.J. BUNNIK, «Common-purpose Groups», 22-31. At the local level, there was insufficient collegial co-operation between bishops and their priests. Fear of difficulties with Rome still prevented bishops from encouraging active renewal. The critical groups rejected this timidity and insisted that the living Church had to change at least partly as the result of local experiment and not as the result of reforms imposed from above.

[108] See B. SECONDIN, *Segni di Profezia*, 126-157, 319-325. See also K. RAHNER, «The Future of Christian Communities», 120-133; R. SCIUBBA – R.S. PACE, *Le Comunità di base*; J. KERKHOFS, «Basic Communities», [1976] 23-26; «Basic Christian Communities», [1980] 30-36; A. FALLICO, *Chiesa – mondo*.

[109] JOHN PAUL II, *Tertio Millennio Adveniente*, n. 18.

[110] See K. RAHNER, «South American Base Communities», 148-154.

One feature which we notice in the development of BECs in different countries is that there is no uniformity in the functioning of BECs. The socio-cultural factors influence greatly their functioning. As every continent, country, diocese and parish is unique in itself the difference in the functioning of BECs also becomes inevitable[111]. The important point behind the BECs in any country is the contextualization of the theology of the local Church, a theology of communion and service.

BECs cannot be considered as mere prayer groups[112] or a ladder to achieve ecclesiastical or socio-political power. BECs have a prophetic role in the society. They, as the first cells of the Church, have to permeate the ecclesial life in the parish, diocese, the universal Church and in the whole of humanity.

3. Teachings of the Church on BECs

We have seen that the BECs have originated in Latin America and other developing countries. It is proving to be an effective means of renewing and revitalizing the life of the Church. It has become almost, one may say, the best means to carry out the Mission of the Church. As a *movement,* BECs have become universal due to three reasons. The first is that the context in which they emerged is existing throughout the world in different forms[113]. Secondly they are being encouraged by the papal teachings. Thirdly, they have a sound theological basis.

3.1 *Vatican II on BECs*

There is no explicit mention of BECs in the Council documents. Nevertheless, the conciliar and post-conciliar documents reiterated the need of Christian community building[114]. The council Fathers, while treating the hierarchical nature of the Church, affirms that the Church of Christ is really present in all legitimately organized local groups of the

---

[111] Even within the same country there are great difference between rural base communities and the base communities of the poor suburbs of the great cities. See V. CODINA, «The Wisdom of Latin America's Base Communities», 71-80.

[112] See K. RAHNER, «The Future of Christian Communities», 120-133.

[113] The social backgrounds may be different in each country, however, the spiritual needs of the people remain the same.

[114] The Popes of the pre-Vatican period also emphasized the communitarian aspect of Christian life. But there was no mention about the BECs. See K. POOVATHUMKUDY, *Missionary Task,* 37-38.

faithful, in so far as they are united to their pastors[115]. Speaking about laity the Council says that the apostolate of the laity is a sharing in the salvific mission of the Church. And it is through the laity that the Church can become the salt of the earth[116].

In speaking about the various fields of the lay apostolate the Council says that as participators in the function of Christ, priest, prophet and king, the laity have an active part of their own in the life and action of the Church. Their action within the Church communities is so necessary that without it the apostolate of the pastors will frequently be unable to obtain its full effect[117]. Again the Council affirms that the laity, according to their abilities, ought to cooperate in all the apostolic and missionary enterprises of their ecclesial family[118]. The Council document *Ad Gentes* clearly states that building communities of faith is not a clever ingenious invention of the Church. It is God who called the people from various origins to form them into a human family. It pleased God to share his life with men and women not as isolated individuals but as a community in Jesus Christ[119].

The need to reciprocate and interrelate is well noted in most of the Conciliar documents. In *Lumen Gentium* we read: «He has, however, willed to make men holy and save them, not as individuals without any bond or link between them, but rather to make them into a people who might acknowledge him and serve him in holiness» (*LG* 9). The Gospel proclamation demands a response from the hearers. Those who respond to the call of Christ need to be initiated to the community of believers. Thus «the Christian community will become a sign of God's presence in the world» (*AG* 15).

Although the Council documents do not explicitly mention the BECs in any of its documents, the vision about BECs is *implicit* in the ecclesiology of Vatican II. The Council has «*focused on the mystery of Christ and his Church and at the same time open to the World*»[120]. The BECs in effect are centered on the mystery of Christ and his Church. It is open to the world in a more practical and concrete way.

---

[115] See *LG* 26.
[116] See *LG* 33.
[117] See *AA* 10.
[118] See *AA* 10.
[119] See *AG* 2.
[120] JOHN PAUL II, *Tertio Millennio Adveniente*, n. 18.

3.2 *Post Conciliar Documents*

In our study on BECs we take only three post conciliar Papal documents namely, *Evangelii Nuntiandi, Christifideles Laici* and *Redemptoris Missio,* although various aspects of communitarian life are described in other documents like *Catechesi Tradendae, Familiaris Consortio* and in the various addresses of John Paul II[121].

3.2.1 *Evangelii Nuntiandi*

In the development of BECs no other Church document has contributed so much as the Apostolic Exhortation *Evangelii Nuntiandi* of Pope Paul VI. The Pope's exhortations on BECs is to be seen in the context of his special commitment to Evangelization especially «to make the Church of the twentieth century ever better for proclaiming the Gospel to the people of the twentieth century»[122].

In the introduction of the exhortation, the Pope affirms that his words come from the wealth of the Synod and are meant to be a meditation on Evangelization[123]. Speaking about the Ecclesial «communautés de base» Pope says: «The last Synod devoted considerable attention to these «small communities», or *communautés de base*, because they are often talked about in the Church today»[124]. He also recognizes that the nature of such communities differs from region to region and that they spring from the need to live the Church's life more intensely. One of the reasons the Pope finds for the emergence of such gatherings is the inability of living a true ecclesial life in the existing structure[125].

Appreciating the positive effects of the BECs, the Pope showed also the dangers inherent in the *basic communities*[126]. Again, pointing out the differences between basic communities and BECs, Pope Paul VI says:

---

[121] To have a general idea of the post Conciliar documents about the communitarian aspect see W.C. GUBUAN, *The Basic Christian Communities,* 119-157.

[122] PAUL VI, *Evangelii Nuntiandi,* n. 2.

[123] Already in 1973, in an address to the college of Cardinals Pope Paul VI had shown great concern to revise the methods of Evangelization. See PAUL VI, «Address to the College of Cardinals», 383. See also PAUL VI, *Evangelii Nuntiandi,* n, 3.

[124] PAUL VI, *Evangelii Nuntiandi,* n. 58.

[125] See PAUL VI, *Evangelii Nuntiandi,* n. 58.

[126] For Pope Paul VI the basic communities come together in a spirit of bitter criticism of the Church, which they are quick to stigmatize as «institutional» and to which they set themselves up in opposition as charismatic communities, free from structures and inspired only by the Gospel. Thus their obvious characteristic is an attitude of fault-finding and of rejection with regard to the Church's outward manifestations: her

The difference is already notable: the communities which by the spirit of opposition cut themselves off from the Church, and whose unity they wound, can be called *communautés de base,* but in this case it is a strictly sociological name. They could not, without a misuse of terms, be called ecclesial *communautés de base*, even if, while being hostile to the hierarchy, they claim to remain within the unity of the Church. This name belongs to the other groups, those which come together within the Church in order to unite themselves to the Church and to cause the Church to grow[127].

According to the Pope the BECs will be a place of Evangelization, for the benefit of the bigger communities, especially for the individual Churches. These communities could be a hope for the universal Church to the extent: (1) that they seek their nourishment in the Word of God and do not allow themselves to be ensnared by political polarization or fashionable ideologies, which are ready to exploit their immense human potential; (2) that they avoid the ever present temptation of systematic protest and a hypercritical attitude, under the pretext of authenticity and a spirit of collaboration; (3) that they remain firmly attached to the local Church in which they are inserted, and to the universal Church, thus avoiding the very real danger of becoming isolated within themselves, then of believing themselves to be the only authentic Church of Christ, and hence of condemning the other ecclesial communities; (4) that they maintain a sincere communion with the pastors whom the Lord gives to his Church, and with the *Magisterium* which the Spirit of Christ has entrusted to these pastors; (5) that they never look on themselves as the sole beneficiaries or sole agents of evangelization — or even the only depositories of the Gospel — but, being aware that the Church is much more vast and diversified, accept the fact that this Church becomes incarnate in other ways than through themselves; (6) that they constantly grow in missionary consciousness, fervour, commitment and zeal; (7) that they show themselves to be universal in all things and never sectarian[128].

These directives have made a great impact in the development of the BECs throughout the Church. The importance of the document is that it has become a point of reference for all the other documents concerning BECs[129].

---

hierarchy, her signs. Pope Paul VI uses strong words against such tendencies saying that they are radically opposed to the Church. See PAUL VI, *Evangelii Nuntiandi*, n. 58.

[127] PAUL VI, *Evangelii Nuntiandi*, n. 58.

[128] See PAUL VI, *Evangelii Nuntiandi*, n. 58.

[129] The Santo Domingo Conclusions, n. 63, also take *Evangelii Nuntiandi* as criteria for the functioning of BECs in Latin America.

3.2.2 *Christifideles Laici*

The teachings of *Christifideles Laici* must be seen in the context of the Synod of Bishops held in Rome from 1 to 30 October 1987[130]. The Synodal topic was «Vocation and Mission in the Church and in the World, Twenty Years after the Second Vatican Council»[131]. In the Synod the bishops spoke about the relevance of BECs in the present state of many parishes. According to Pope John Paul II many parishes, whether established in regions affected by urban progress or in missionary territory, cannot do their work effectively because they lack material resources or ordained men or are too big geographically or because of the particular circumstances of some Christians (e.g. exiles and migrants). Realizing the present day difficulties of the parishes to witness authentic *communion,* the Pope insists that the local authorities ought to foster small or basic or «living» communities. He also gives two directives: (1) adaptation of the parish structures according to the full flexibility granted by canon law, especially in promoting participation by the lay faithful in pastoral responsibilities; (2) small, basic or so-called «living» communities, where the faithful can hear the Word of God and express it in the service and love to one another; these communities are true expressions of ecclesial communion and centres of evangelization, in communion with their pastors[132].

3.2.3 *Redemptoris Missio*

The encyclical letter *Redemptoris Missio* of Pope John Paul II is intended to revitalize the missionary spirit among Christians. It is a

---

[130] It had been observed that there was no mention of BEC or BCC in the *Lineamenta* published in 1985 for the Synod. There was only one reference (n. 57) to BEC under the heading «The Laity and the Mission of the Parish», in the *Instrumentum Laboris* published in 1986. However, there were thirty seven spoken and written interventions on BECs. Although BECs received no mention in the *Lineamenta* and only a passing reference in the *Instrumentum Laboris*, the voice of bishops and representatives from around the world were heard loud and clear. See J.G. HEALEY, «BCCs in the 1987 Synod of Bishop's Documents», 74-86. See also C. DE WIT, «Viewpoint: Which way for the laity?», 962; MAURICE – M. MAGEE, «Which way for the laity?», 999.

[131] JOHN PAUL II, *Christifideles Laici*, n. 2. A remarkable feature of this Synod was the presence of qualified lay people from all over the world and whose valuable experience and suggestions were given more attention. See also PONTIFICIUM PRO LAICIS, *Lay Voices at the Synod*, n. 19.

[132] See JOHN PAUL II *Christifideles Laici*, n. 26. A comparison between *Evangelii Nuntiandi*, n. 58 and *Christifideles Laici*, n. 26 would show that *Christifideles Laici* does not show much anxiety over BECs.

challenge addressed to the whole Church and to the whole world to stand up to the demands of the Gospel[133]. Regarding the BECs, *Redemptoris Missio* holds the view of Pope Paul VI without showing any *ecclesiological anxiety* over the BECs. Under the sub-title «*Ecclesial Basic Communities*» as a Force for Evangelization» the Pope says:

> A rapidly growing phenomenon in the young Churches — one sometimes fostered by the Bishops and their Conferences as a pastoral priority — is that of «ecclesial basic communities» (also known by other names) which are proving to be good centres for Chrsitian formation and missionary outreach[134].

As a pilgrim Pope, visiting many countries, John Paul II could convincingly say that the «ecclesial basic communities» are proving to be good centres for Christian formation and missionary outreach. The Pope himself explains the nature of these «ecclesial» communities:

> These are groups of Christians who, at the level of the family or in a similarly restricted setting, come together for prayer, Scripture reading, catechesis, and discussion on human and ecclesial problems with a view to a common commitment. These communities are a sign of vitality within the Church, an instrument of formation and evangelization, and a solid starting point for a new society based on a «civilization of love»[135].

Mindful of the pastoral significance of the small communities, the Pope continues:

> These communities decentralize and organize the parish community, to which they always remain united. They take root in less privileged and rural areas, and become a leaven of Christian life, of care for the poor and neglected, and of commitment to the transformation of society. Within them, the individual Christian experiences community and therefore senses that he or she is playing an active role and is encouraged to share in the common task. Thus these communities become a means of evangelization and of the initial proclamation of the Gospel, and a source of new ministries. At the same time, by being imbued with Christ's love, they also show how divisions, tribalism and racism can be overcome[136].

Recalling Pope Paul VI's Apostolic Exhortation *Evangelii Nuntiandi*, *Redemptoris Missio* also says that every community must live in union

---

[133] See JOHN PAUL II, *Redemptoris Missio*, ns. 2, 92. See also M. ZAGO, «John Paul II's *Redemptoris Missio*», 59-66.

[134] JOHN PAUL II, *Redemptoris Missio*, n. 51.

[135] JOHN PAUL II, *Redemptoris Missio*, n. 51.

[136] JOHN PAUL II, *Redemptoris Missio*, n. 51.

with the Church's Pastors and *Magisterium*, with a commitment to missionary outreach and without yielding to isolationism or ideological exploitation[137]. Accepting the views of the Synod of Bishops in 1985[138], the Pope says:

> Because the Church is communion, the new «basic communities», if they truly live in unity with the Church, are a true expression of communion and a means for the construction of a more profound communion. They are thus cause for great hope for the life of the Church[139].

Papal teachings on BECs in *Evangelii Nuntiandi, Christifideles Laici* and *Redemptoris Missio* truly reflect the thinking of the world Church. The Papal Exhortations, *Evangelii Nuntiandi* and *Christifideles Laici* were written after the Synod of Bishops in 1974 and 1987 respectively. The encyclical *Redemptoris Missio* by Pope John Paul II was written with a rich experience of visiting many countries and meeting different peoples and cultures in different parts of the world. All the three Papal teachings speak about the relevance of BECs in the Christian formation. The potentiality of BECs in witnessing Christ in the living context is well expressed. The teachings of Popes remain as point of reference for discerning the functioning and growth of the BECs.

4. Theological Reflection on BECs

A remarkable achievement of the BECs is that they have developed a sound theology of the local Church. They have tried to re-discover the true nature of the Church in light of the Word of God and the official ecclesial teachings. In the new attempt to re-discover the nature of the Church they can formulate an ecclesiology shifting from *institutional model* to *communion model* leading to *servant model*[140].

4.1 *Covenant and Communion: Essential Elements of the Church*

God's intervention in the history of humankind and the human response to God's intervention is well expressed by the term communion

---

[137] See JOHN PAUL II, *Redemptoris Missio*, n. 51.

[138] Extraordinary Assembly of 1985, *Final Report*, II, C, 6.

[139] JOHN PAUL II, *Redemptoris Missio*, n. 51. See also Extraordinary Assembly of 1985, *Final Report*, II, C, 6; K. POOVATHUMKUDY, *Missionary Task*, 35.

[140] For various models of the Church see A. DULLES, *Models of the Church*. See also J. MARINS, «What are Basic Christian Communities?», 143-144; ID., «Comunità ecclesiali di base», 44-46.

(*koinōnia*)[141]. The word *koinōnia* is not very much used in LXX (only three times) as in the Greek world, although the use of the term expressing a close relationship between God and man is not unknown to the OT. To express the idea of communion, the OT uses the word covenant.

4.1.1 Covenant

A «covenant» (*bĕrît*) is an agreement enacted between two parties in which one or both make promises under oath to perform or refrain from certain actions stipulated in advance[142]. In the Sinai Covenant, God's divine intervention is very important[143]. It is God who elects the people of Israel. The initiative comes from God. It was gratuitous on the part of God (Deut 7,7-8). He liberates them from the bondage (Ex 19,5). And He makes a covenant (Ex 19,3-25). Before the ratification He imposes some stipulations which Israel has to observe. By observing the stipulations they are assured of divine blessing (Ex 19,5-6). Israel agreed to carry out what God has said (Ex 24,3). As a sign of ratification of the covenant blood was sprinkled (Ex 24,6-7)[144].

The effect of the covenant was that Israel became God's own people. They realized that their God is friendly. They became a community. This community, formed out of God's choice, has a great responsibility to others. The responsibility to others is also emphasized in the ten commandments. It is to be noted that seven commandments, out of ten,

---

[141] The word communion comes from the Greek word *koinōnia*. It is an abstract term, coming from *koinos* and *koinoneo* denoting participation and fellowship. In secular sense it is used especially of a close life participation. The word, in the ancient Greek, gives an idea of unbroken relationship of fellowship between God and humankind. See F. HAUCK, «*Koinos*», 789ff.

[142] There were pacts among groups or equal individuals who wanted to help one another. There are also unequal treaties, in which the latter engages himself to serve the former. For various types of treaties and their stipulations see G.E. MENDENHALL – G.A. HERION, «Covenant», 1179-1202. See also J. GIBLET – R. GIRAD, «Covenant», 93-98.

[143] God's plan over Israel was very clear when God manifested Himself to Moses. God wants to deliver Israel from Egypt to set her up in the land of Canaan (Ex 3,7-10.16); for Israel is «His people» (Ex 3,10), and He wants to give Israel the land promised to her ancestors (Gen 12,7. 13. 15). God has chosen Israel without merit on its part.

[144] «Blood, of course, was for the Hebrews the seat and sign of life and as such was reserved to God. Here Yahweh and people share in some sort of blood and hence the same life; they are members of one family» (D.J. McCARTHY, *Treaty and Covenant*, 255).

are directly related to the community (Ex 20,12-17). The social milieu in which the covenant was given is also important. God intervened in the life of a suffering people. And He liberated them and made a covenant with them. The theological implication of the covenant is that it was a preparation and figure of the new and perfect covenant which was to be ratified in Christ, and of the fuller revelation which was to be given through the Word of God made flesh[145]. The Church, as new people of Israel, participating in the covenant which was ratified in Christ, is expected to live in holiness and in communion[146].

4.1.2 Communion

Communion (*koinōnia*) in the NT is the dynamic expression of Christian life[147]. *Koinōnia* does not originate in the human person but in God. In Christ the communion becomes a reality, because he is himself God and man. Incarnation is the first moment of God's *koinōnia* with mankind. Christ has created a new openness among humankind introducing the concept of *koinōnia* as an open reality[148]. And the primitive Christians lived in that *koinōnia* (Acts 2,42).

Paul uses *koinōnia* for the religious fellowship (participation)[149]. This fellowship is the extension of the trinitarian God. For Paul, God the Father, His Son Jesus Christ and the Holy Spirit are intrinsically interrelated and form the basis of our Christian existence or the Church. So the Church is the explicit manifestation of the trinitarian God[150]. Paul,

---

[145] A new covenant becomes necessary because Israel was not faithful to the old covenant. They broke the covenant (Jer 31,32). But God was faithful in His promises. He promises a new covenant (Jer 31,33). This would be a permanent covenant. This covenant would bring a change of hearts and the gift of the divine spirit (Ezek 36,26ff). See *LG* 9.

[146] See *LG* 9.

[147] According to Pope John Paul II the words: «I am the true vine and my Father is the vine dresser [...] Abide in me and I in you» (Jn 15,1. 4.) reveal the mystery of communion that serves as the unifying bond between the Lord and his disciples, between Christ and the baptized: a living and life-giving communion through which Christians no longer belong to themselves but are the Lord's very own, as the branches are one with the vine. See JOHN PAUL II, *Christifideles Laici*, n. 18.

[148] G. PANIKULAM, *Koinōnia in the New Testament*, 140-141.

[149] See F. HAUCK, «*Koinos*», 804-809. See also D. SESBOÜÉ – J. GUILLET, «Covenant», 85-87.

[150] Paul was a staunch monotheistic believer. After the Damascus event his concept of God gets a new dimension. He began to call God as «Father of our Lord Jesus Christ». He understands Holy Spirit as the principle of Christian activity. Paul's use of trinitarian

in his exposition on *koinōnia* speaks more of *koinōnia* with the person of Christ. The Christians are called to fellowship with the Son (1 Cor 1,9). The participation in the person of Christ leads one to the participation in the Gospel (1 Cor 9,23). Paul uses *koinōnia* also for the fellowship which arises in the Lord's Supper. According to him those who partake in the Lord's Supper are Christ's companions (1Cor 10,16-22). Sharing in the fellowship of Jesus Christ means to participate in the life of Christ (Rom 6,8; 2 Cor 7,3), including suffering which will lead to glory (Phil 3,10-12)[151]. *Koinōnia* with Christ, according to Paul, necessarily leads to *koinōnia* with Christians. The *koinōnia* in Christ prompts one to help the other in spiritual or material needs (Rom 15,27).

The attitude of *koinōnia,* according to Paul, should be the guiding principle of Christian life. His analogy of body (1 Cor 12,12-30) is an example to show how a Christian community could live together[152]. A Christian community might transcend all local barriers to live in one Spirit so as to form one body[153]. It is to be noted that the Pauline concept of *koinōnia* has very much influenced the Fathers of the Second Vatican Council[154].

4.2 *BECs and Communion*

We have seen that *koinōnia* is the essential characteristic of Christian life. *Koinōnia* is concretely experienced in a community. It is manifested when two or three people are gathered in Christ's name. It is manifested

formula in epistles are also to be noted. See E.R. MARTINEZ, *La Vita Cristiana.* See also M. McDERMOTT, «The Biblical Doctrine», 64-77, 219-233; I.A. KAIGAMA, *The Trinitarian Implications.*

151 See F. HAUCK, «*Koinos*», 804-809; Paul uses mainly four prepositions: *dia* (through), *eis* (into), *syn* (with) and *en* (in) with «Christ» to show the intimate relation with Jesus. See J.A. FITZMYER, *Paul and His Theology,* 88-90.

152 Paul speaks in the context of the dis-unity among the Corinthian community (1 Cor 1, 10ff.).

153 See J.A. FITZMYER, *Paul and His Theology,* 95-97; For 1 Jn, *koinōnia* is a favourite term to describe the living bond in which the Christians stand. The word implies inward fellowship on a religious basis. To be a Christian is to have fellowship with God. This fellowship is with the Father and the Son (1 Jn 1,3. 7). This fellowship consisted in mutual abiding which begins in this world and reaches into the world to come, where it finds its supreme fulfillment. See F. HAUCK, «*Koinos*», 807-809.

154 See *LG* 2. 4. 8. 13-15. 18. 21. 24-25. See also *DV* 10; *GS* 32; *UR* 2-4, 14-15. 17-19. 22. «The ecclesiology of communion is a central and fundamental concept in the Conciliar documents. *Koinōnia* — communion finding its source in Sacred Scripture, was a concept held in great honour in the early Church and in the Oriental Churches, and this teaching endures to the present day» (JOHN PAUL II, *Christifideles Laici,* n. 19).

when the Word of God is proclaimed, listened to and lived in a community. It is manifested when the Eucharist is celebrated[155]. It is manifested when one shares the joy and sufferings of one's neighbours. And this kind of communion takes place better in small groups and in the full sense in BECs[156].

The people of a parish scattered in different sections of the parish cannot be formed into a communion through a liturgical service alone. The liturgy ought to be, rather, an expression of their living together in communion all the days of the week. Growing together in unity and fraternal love demands that people meet regularly in smaller groups in which close interaction and witnessing together are possible[157]. BECs make this journey to communion a reality[158].

Christian life is the participation in the trinitarian fellowship of God[159]. This fellowship of the Triune God invites and inspires the Church, which is the New Israel, the New People of God, to be united and interrelated in every ambient. This fellowship has a biblical basis: both in the OT and in the NT. The notion of communion was a central theme in the early Christian centuries, in the teachings of the great doctors of the Church like Augustine and in our age the Second Vatican Council[160]. The communion aspect is also highlighted in the ecclesiology of BECs. As people become more aware of their participatory role in the Church, a new ecclesial spirituality becomes the natural outcome. In the next section we discuss how a new spirituality has been evolving in the Church after the Second Vatican Council.

---

[155] JOHN PAUL II, *Redemptoris Missio*, n. 51.

[156] Basic Ecclesial Community is a *Church* in itself and it is in communion with the local and the universal Church. See G.K. KWAME, «Basic Ecclesial Communities», 160-179.

[157] Larger groups become too vast to experience communion. Family, though the basic unit of the Church and society, does not adopt a public value system and can remain internally oriented The membership in the family is by birth, while in an ecclesial community it is a matter of Christian commitment which comprises a mission. See D. CLARK, *Basic Communities*.

[158] When the people gather as a BEC they interact with the neighbours and witness Christ on a day-to-day basis. This ecclesial community gather together as the people of God and apply their talents and powers for the building up of the Body of Christ and its continual sanctification. See *LG* 33.

[159] See JOHN PAUL II, *Christifideles Laici*, ns. 18-20.

[160] See A. DULLES, *Models of the Church*, 47-62.

5. Evolving A New Ecclesial Spirituality

Spirituality[161] is a term that has not yet been defined, analyzed, or categorized to anyone's satisfaction. Spirituality being profoundly the inner experience of a person, it can not be measured quantitatively[162]. It is with Vatican II that spirituality became a subject not only of the selected few but also of the ordinary people. After Vatican II a shift in the traditional *systematization* in spirituality took place[163]. Our aim here is to show the changes that have taken place in the understanding of spirituality after Vatican II and its effects reflected in the BECs. This we do with a brief historical survey of the understanding of the concept of spirituality.

5.1 *Concept of Spirituality in the History of the Church*

The word *spiritualitas* first occurred in the 5th century in the writings of Pseudo-Jerome.[164] He used the word in Pauline sense. From 12th century a change has taken place in the use of the term[165]. St. Thomas

---

161 The word spirituality derives from the Latin *spiritualitas*, an abstract word related to *spiritus* and *spiritualis*, which were used to translate Paul's *pneuma* and *pneumatikos*. See A. SOLIGNAC, «Spiritualité», 1142-1143. «The Spirit is for Paul an "energizer", a Spirit of Power (1 Cor 2,4; Rom 15,13) and the source of Christian love, hope, and faith. It frees human beings from the law (Gal 5,18; cf. Rom 8,2), from "the cravings of flesh" (Gal 5,16), and from all immoral conduct (Gal 5,19-24). It is the gift of the Spirit that constitutes adoptive sonship (Gal 4,6; Rom 8,14), that assists Christians in prayer ("pleading along with us with inexpressible yearnings", Rom 8,26), and that makes Christians especially aware of their relation to the Father. The power of the Spirit is not something distinct from the power of the risen Christ: Christians have been "washed, consecrated, and have become upright in the name of our Lord Jesus Christ and in the Spirit of our God" (1 Cor 6,11)» (J.A. FITZMYER, *Paul and His Theology*, 57-58). See also W. PRINCIPE, «Toward Defining Spirituality»,130; ID., «Christian Spirituality - Terminology», 931.

162 The word spirituality can be treated from the experiential point of view and theological point of view.

163 See K. WAAIJMAN, «Toward a phenomenological definition of spirituality», 30-57.

164 PSEUDO-JEROME, Epist. 7; PL 30, 105-116: The letter was addressed to the recently baptized adults. «Quia tibi honorabilis et dilectissime parens, per novam gratiam omnis lacrymarum causa detersa est, age, cave, curre, festina. Age ut in spiritualitate proficias. Cave ne quod accepisti bonum, incautus et negligens custos amittas. Curre ut non negligas. Festina ut celerius comprehendas [...]. Dumtempus habemus seminemus in spiritu, ut messem in spiritualibus colligamus» (9, 11 4d-11 5a)» (A. SOLIGNAC, «Spiritualité», 1143).

165 See A. SOLIGNAC, «Spiritualité», 1144-1145.

uses the term in the Pauline notion[166], with an ascetical sense[167]. Later, persons exercising ecclesiastical jurisdiction were called the *spiritualitas*, or «lords spiritual», as opposed to those exercising civil jurisdiction[168]. From the 17th century different forms of the word like *choses spirituelles, livress spirituels, vie spirituelle* began to appear in French manuals of spirituality. In 1646 Jean-Baptiste Saint-Jure wrote *L'homme spirituel* (The Spiritual Man)[169]. The frequent use of the term «spirituality» comes in the late 19th or early 20th century in theological literature[170]. In English the word became common after 1950, especially with the translation of the classical works of Pierre Pourrat's four-volume «*La spiritualité catholique*» (1918-1928) and other French works. It is enough to compare the two major religious reference works published at the beginning of this century namely *the New Schaff-Herzog Encyclopedia of Religious Knowledge* (1912-1915) and *The Catholic Encyclopedia* (1912-1915), which contain no article on *Spirituality*. With *The New Catholic Encyclopedia,* published in the 70's containing eight articles which include the word *spirituality* in their titles and thirteen

---

[166] See R. BUSA, ed., *Index Thomisticus*, XXI, 86-111. See also W. PRINCIPE, «Toward Defining Spirituality», 130-31; A. MATANIC, «Spiritualità», 2383-2385.

[167] Thomas Aquinas does not treat spirituality as such. «Thomas d'Aquin prend surtout *spiritualitas* en un sens ascétique; il en distingue trois degrés selon que l'on triomphe plus ou moins de la *carnalitas*: celui des vierges, celui des veuves, celui des gens mariés (In Sent. IV, d. 49, q. 5, a, 2, sol. 3: le terme revient neuffois). Dans d'autres cas, le sens paraît plus général: le mot s'applique alors à des réalités qui relèvent de l'ordre de la grâce, du statut "spirituel" de l'homme, etc. Ainsi les péchés de l'esprit sont plus graves que ceux de la chair, en raison de la seule différence entre la *carnalitas* et la *spiritualitas* (Summa theol. 1 a 2ae, q. 73, a. 5); le mariage est le dernier des sacrements "quia minimum habet de spiritualitate" (3a, q. 65, a. 2, ad 1); le Christ comme homme n'eut pas à progresser, car en lui "a principio fuit perfecta spiritualitas" (3a, q. 34, a. 1, ad 1)». *Index Thomisticus, Concordiantia*, 1a, t. 21, Stuttgart, 1975, 111 quoted by (A. SOLIGNAC, «Spiritualité», XIV, 1146).

[168] W. PRINCIPE, «Toward Defining Spirituality», 130. See also ID., «Christian Spirituality - Terminology», 931.

[169] J. Baptiste Saint-Jure defines spiritual man like this: «L'Homme Spirituel n'est autre chose qu'un chrestien excellent, qui par consequent possède plus abondamment et plus profondament que les autres [...] ce qui constitue l'Homme Chrestien, a sçavoir l'Esprit de Jesus Christ» (A. SOLIGNAC, «Spiritualité», 1147).

[170] See A. SOLIGNAC, 1149-50. K. WAAIJMAN gives a chronologically ordered list of «introductions», to spirituality prepared in his article, «Toward a phenomenological definition of Spirituality», 14-30. It is specially noted that the books and articles of spirituality published after Vatican II are more than all the books and articles published from 1200 to 1965.

references to the word in its index, one understands the evolution and consequent acceptance of the term into theological circles.

It is in this historical context that we evaluate the development of the concept of spirituality. No wonder, after Vatican II, we find a lot of literature coming out in the field of spirituality in various languages including German[171].

5.2 A Change in the Concept of Spirituality

Soon after the Vatican Council, theologians have foreseen the development in the field of spirituality. A.M. Besnard wrote in 1965: «Everything Leads us to think that new forms of spirituality are taking shape in contemporary Catholicism»[172], and again he said that «the element of re-discovery is all the more evident because new members of the faithful are showing for the first time a desire for an authentic spirituality»[173]. This new way of understanding spirituality is evident in the various definitions scholars give to spiritual theology and spirituality.

C.A. Bernard defines spirituality as a theological discipline which, founded on the principles of revelation, studies Christian spiritual experience, describes its development and progress and explains its structures and laws[174]. L. Richard says that spirituality is the radical drive of the person toward self-transcending authenticity in knowing, naming and loving God. He argues that knowing, naming and loving are not only the basic structures of spirituality but also of theology. For it is the on-going task of the theologian to know, name and love the mystery in which, or better, on whom he or she is grounded[175]. K. Waaijman gives a phenomenological definition. According to him Spirituality is the on-going transformation which occurs in involved relationality with the

---

171 See B. SECONDIN, «Temi, problemi e Prospettive», 3. Treating spirituality like any other theological science is a new development. See C.A. BERNARD, ed., *La Spiritualià come Teologia*. See also J. ALEXANDER, «What Do Recent Writers Mean?», 247; W.. PRINCIPE, «Toward Defining Spirituality», 127-141.

172 A.M. BESNARD, «Tendencies of Contemporary Spirituality», 14-24. See also M. McDERMOTT, «The Biblical Doctrine», 64-77, 219-233.

173 A.M. BESNARD, «Tendencies of Contemporary Spirituality», 14-24. See also F. VANDENBROUCKE, «Spirituality and Spiritualities», 25-33 See also B. KANTROWITZ, «The Search for the Sacred», 38-41.

174 «La teologia spirituale è una disciplina teologica che fondata sui principi della rivelazione, studia l'esperienza spirituale cristiana, ne descrive lo sviluppo progressivo e ne fa conoscere le strutture e le leggi» (C.A. BERNARD, *Teologia Spirituale*, 70).

175 L. RICHARD, «Theology in need of Spirituality», 161-172.

Unconditional[176]. B. Secondin holds the view that spirituality is communitarian based on the renewed ecclesiological principle of «communion»[177].

According to S.M. Schneiders spirituality is that particular actualization of the capacity for self-transcendence that is constituted by the substantial gift of the Holy Spirit establishing a life-giving relationship with God in Christ within the believing *community*. Thus, Christian spirituality is trinitarian, christological, and ecclesial religious experience[178]. H. Alphonso sees spirituality as the way in which a person (or group of persons) animated by the living presence and action of the spirit of Christ acts and reacts habitually in accordance with his/her (or their) characteristic Christian gifts[179]. E.R. Martinez gives a trinitarian definition to Christian spirituality. According to him it is the mature and maturing relation to the Father, the Son and the Holy Spirit[180]. Spirituality, according to S. Galilea, means to live the Spirit according to the Gospel and to follow Jesus Christ with the help of the Church — whatever epoch, whatever the society, whatever the culture, whatever the personal circumstances[181].

F. Vandenbroucke understands spirituality in the socio-cultural milieu. He makes a distinction between spirituality and spiritualities. He defines spirituality as the science of the application of the Gospel to Christian life on the intellectual plane, on the ascetical plane and on the properly mystical plane, and spiritualities as the sum total of personalities and spiritual climates, characterized by a certain equilibrium among the various elements that are to be found in every Christian spirituality, such

---

[176] See K. WAAIJMAN, « Toward a phenomenological definition of spirituality», 4-57. The term «Unconditional» according to K. Waaijman, signifies that which is not bound to a specific time or place.

[177] In the renewed ecclesiological principle the personal and social dimension get important place as the divine aspect. «Oggi la spiritualità migliore tenta di coniugare maturità personale e coscienza collettiva, esperienza individuale del divino e dimensione interpersonale e sociale del divenire se stessi, angosce e speranze dei contemporanei e misteriosi percorsi dell'incontro con il Signore della storia» (B. SECONDIN, «Alla prova della nuova cultura», 680-752). See also ID., *Nuovi Cammini dello Spirito*, 195-204.

[178] See S.M. SCHNEIDERS, «Theology and Spirituality», 253-266.

[179] See H. ALPHONSO, *Placed with Christ the Son*, 151-162.

[180] «La spiritualità cristiana è una relazione matura e maturante con il Padre, il Figlio, e lo Spirito Santo» (E.R. MARTINEZ, *La Vita Cristiana*, 2).

[181] See S. GALILEA, «The Spirituality of Liberation», 186-194. J. Fuellenbach holds the view of S. Galilea in his understading of spirituality. See J. FUELLENBACH, *Hermeneutics*, 145-155.

as asceticism, mental or mystical prayer, liturgical prayer and the practice of virtues[182].

The above cited definitions and descriptions show the dynamic nature of spirituality. The words «a progressive development» (C.A. Bernard), «a radical drive» (L. Richard), «on going transformation» (K.Waaijman), «communitarian based on the renewed ecclesiology centered on «communion» (B. Secondin) «establishing a life-giving relationship» (S.M. Schneiders), «to follow Jesus Christ with the help of the Church» (S. Galilea), «living presence and action of the Spirit» (H. Alphonso), «mature and maturing relationship» (E.R. Martinez), «application of the Gospel to Christian life», and «sum total of personalities and spiritual climates» (F. Vandenbroucke) are very significant as regards the understanding of spirituality. The *fuga mundi*[183] attitude of religious experience is not seen in any of the definitions although C.A. Bernard, L.Richard, K. Waaijman, E.R. Martinez do not include the words like «community», «spiritual climates», group of persons. Nevertheless, in the descriptions on spirituality the authors give importance to the communitarian aspect.

B. Secondin, H. Alphonso and S. Galilea explicitly indicate the communitarian aspect in defining or describing spirituality. F.Vandenbroucke understands spirituality in the socio-cultural milieu. A trinitarian approach to the spirituality is seen in S.M. Schneider's definition with an *ecclesial* (believing *community*) bent. Whatever be the definitions or descriptions we find *a new interest* in spirituality.

One positive element we notice in all the understandings of Christian spirituality is that it is theological and related to the human person in the concrete situation.

5.3 *Spirituality of the BECs*

In the previous section, elucidating the views of various authors on the concept of spirituality, we tried to present the dynamic nature of spirituality. Such presentation helps us to understand better the spirituality of BECs. The Second Vatican Council reminds us that all Christians in any state or walk of life are called to the fullness of Christian life and to perfection of love, and by this holiness a more

---

182 See F. VANDENBROUKE, «Spirituality and Spiritualities», 27-28.

183 *Fuga Mundi* is a spirituality which posits both affective and actual flight from the world as the prerequisites for living a life of Christian perfection. See N. C. RING, «Fuga Mundi», 167-168.

human manner of life is fostered also in earthly society[184]. According to the teachings of the Council:

> The forms and tasks of life are many but holiness is one — that sanctity which is cultivated by all who act under God's Spirit and, obeying the Father's voice and adoring God the Father in spirit and in truth, follow Christ, poor, humble and cross-bearing, that they may deserve to be partakers of his glory. Each one, however, according to his own gifts and duties must steadfastly advance along the way of a living faith, which arouse hope and works through love (*LG* 41).

This exhortation has had a prophetic impact on the understanding of spirituality. Spirituality has become not the concern of a select few with their interior life in opposition to social, political, or secular life rather it has become the integration of all the aspects of human life and experience[185]. Such an integration of inner experience and social life has theological and practical effects. It involves a sacramental life. It begins with the sacrament of baptism. It is nurtured through the Word of God and the Eucharist, and is oriented towards the Kingdom of God. Regarding the sacrament of baptism the Council affirms:

> For those who believe in Christ, who are reborn, not from the corruptible seed, but from an incorruptible one through the word of the living God (cfr. I Pet 1,23), not from flesh, but from water and the Holy Spirit (cfr. Jn 3, 5-6) are finally established as «chosen race, a royal priesthood, a holy nation [...] who in times past were not a people, but now are the People of God (I Pet 2,9-10)» (*LG* 9)[186].

Through the reading of the Word of God and participating in the Eucharist the community grows. In reading the Word of God, one not only listens to the voice of God and but also is led to a privileged spiritual experience[187]. The community understands the value of the Eucharist

---

[184] See *LG* 40. See also M. O'NEILL, *God Hears the Cry*, 207-220.

[185] See S.M. SCHNEIDERS, «Theology and Spirituality», 265. See also the meaning given to the word «Spiritual», in Collins Cobuild English Language Dictionary published in 1990. It gives two meanings: (i) relating to people's deepest thoughts and beliefs, rather than to their bodies and physical surroundings (ii) relating to people's religious beliefs. The aspect of justice also becomes a prominent theme in spirituality. See M.M. THOMAS – J.H. CONE, «Spirituality, Culture and Justice», 176-183.

[186] The right to participate in the life of the Church comes from the sacrament of baptism. See K.J. BECKER, «The Teaching of Vatican II on Baptism», 47-99.

[187] B. SECONDIN, «Lectio Divina», 63-94. See also H.U. VON BALTHASAR, «The Gospel as Norm and Test of all Spiruality», 5-13.

through the Word of God[188]. It culminates in the Eucharist and extends to the community.

> The blessing-cup, which we bless, is it not a sharing in the blood of Christ; and the loaf of bread which we break, is it not a sharing in the body of Christ? And as there is one loaf, so we, although there are many of us, are one single body, for we all share in the one loaf (1 Cor 10,16-17)[189].

Oriented by the Word of God, the people will be led to an indissoluble union with Christ. This union is renewed day by day into ever more perfect union with God and each other.

The new ecclesial spirituality is oriented to the «Kingdom of God»[190]. In his Apostolic Letter in preparation for the third millennium, Pope John Paul II exhorts the Christians saying that they are called to prepare for the Great Jubilee of the beginning of the Third Millennium by *renewing their hope in the definitive coming of the Kingdom of God*, preparing for it daily in their hearts, in Christian community to which they belong, in their particular context, and in world history itself[191]. K.Rahner rightly observes that the Church is not identified with the Kingdom of God. It is the sacrament of the Kingdom of God in the eschatological phase of the sacred history which began with Christ, the phase which brings about the Kingdom of God[192]. In proclaiming the Kingdom of God the prophetic role of the Church continues. In effect it is the taking up of the prophetic role of Jesus Christ.

The prophetic role of the Church continues through witnessing Jesus Christ in the world. A spirituality that is prophetic is rooted in the social, economic, and political reality. It is not a theologizing of the past or speculating about the future but speaking the will of God involving in the contemporary world[193]. In the history of the Church we see that when the

---

188 See *SC* 48.

189 For further theological comments about the text see E.R. MARTINEZ, «"In Christ Jesus" Spiritual Experience in St. Paul», 45-62.

190 See JOHN PAUL II, *Redemptoris Missio*, n. 12-20. «whatever model of description one might propose for the Church, the Church must be seen first and foremost in the context of the Kingdom of God» (J. FUELLENBACH, *The Kingdom of God*, 285).

191 JOHN PAUL II, *Tertio Millennio Adveniente*, n. 46.

192 See K. RAHNER, «Church and World» 346-357. The BECs, as new model of living the Church aim at being at the service of the Kingdom of God. See G. DE LIMA, *Local Church*.

193 See *Instumentum Laboris: The Consecrated Life and its Role in the Church*, n. 64. See also B. HÄRING, «Profeti», 1271-1282; G.V. LEEUWEN, « Spirituality of II Vatican Council», 88-90; F.J. BALASUNDARAM, «The Prophetic Voices of Asia», 1-7.

official Church departed from the Gospel values it was the spiritual leaders, like the prophets of the OT, who came forward to renew the Church[194]. It is enough to look at the prophetic role played by saints such as Benedict, Francis of Assisi, Ignatius of Loyola, Theresa of Avila, Vincent Pallotti, Antonio Rosmini.

Another aspect of the new spirituality is its orientation to mission[195]. *Ad Gentes* is no more an appendix to theology but rather an important task of Christian life. The missionary spirituality is not a mere imitation of Jesus Christ in words, but it is the following of Jesus Christ in day-to-day life (Mk 8,34; Mt 16,24). It is not just copying the virtues and qualities of Jesus Christ, but giving concrete expression to Jesus Christ's action in today's world[196]. At this point a missionary realizes that he is sharing the vision and mission of Jesus Christ who came to announce the good tidings of God's eternal and everlasting love for humankind. He sees Jesus Christ not as an object of contemplation, but acknowledges his presence and companionship in the mission work. Pope John Paul II states that the nature of the missionary activity demands a specific spirituality, which applies in particular to those who are called to be missionaries[197].

The above mentioned factors are practised in a concrete way in the BECs. The baptized people come together for prayer, Scripture reading, catechesis, and discussion on human and ecclesial problems with a view to a common commitment[198]. They come together as children of God. They see the protecting hand of God in their lives. They strongly believe that Jesus Christ is the Saviour of humankind. The Saviour is present in and through them to redeem the whole humanity particularly and concretely in their creative reflection and application of the Word of God, co-operating with the Creator. They believe in the death and resurrection of Jesus Christ and the powerful presence of the Holy Spirit. They know that they are gathering as «Church».

---

[194] «Every great spirituality is connected with the great historical movement of the age in which it was formulated This linkage is not to be understood in the sense of mechanical dependence, but the following of Jesus is something that penetrates deeply into the course of human history» (G. GUTIERREZ, *We Drink*, 26).

[195] See JOHN PAUL II, *Redemptoris Missio*, ns. 87- 91.

[196] See JOHN PAUL II, *Redemptoris Missio*, n. 88. See also J.E. BIFET, *Spirituality for A Missionary Church*.

[197] See JOHN PAUL II, *Redemptoris Missio*, n. 87.

[198] See JOHN PAUL II, *Redemptoris Missio*, n. 51. See also J. FUELLENBACH, *Hermeneutics*, 137-143.

The Bible becomes the prayer book for everyone[199]. The people who come as ecclesial community read the Bible, meditate over it and share their own reflections. The Word of God becomes the touch stone of their day to day life. The Bible becomes no more a private transaction between God and some individuals, but the 'faith story' of a community of believers. Hence, the Bible belongs to the people of God as a community[200]. Prayer becomes very spontaneous. The people create prayers, compose new songs, use new symbols. There is no *liturgical restriction*.

The Word of God leads the people to the Eucharist. The Eucharist becomes the centre of ecclesial spirituality. It is the memorial of the great *diakonia* of *agapē* done on the day of the Last Supper and consummated on Good Friday. It is the greatest symbol of *covenant* and *communion*. In the communities, Eucharist may not be celebrated everyday. But whenever it is celebrated, it becomes part and parcel of the ecclesial community. It becomes an occasion to proclaim the passion, death and resurrection of Jesus Christ. Likewise, the community participation in the sacrament of baptism and marriage is assured. Nourished by the Eucharistic meal the communities take up new challenges in the world.

Since the communities are less structured, men, women, youth and children come together. They are not a crowd, but people who are responsible for each other and people who care for each other. There is no permanent house for the gathering. No economic or ethnic barriers affect such communion and communities. No more national or racial or sexist differences but only one fellowship exists. There may be pluralism in thought but there will be unity in action. For, the motivating force of this new ecclesial community is service. The people are united as a community, and actualize the words of Jesus Christ on service: «For the Son of man himself came not to be served but to serve, and to give his life as a ransom for many» (Mk 10,45). The incarnation of the «Church»

---

[199] «Many "basic Christian communities" focus their gatherings upon the Bible and set themselves a threefold objective: to know the Bible, to create community and to serve the people» (PBC, *The Interpretation of the Bible*, 125). «Before the invention of printing Scripture existed, but not Scripture as book for everyone. That is Scripture's purpose, although, on the conscious level, the Catholic Church has clearly grasped this fact only through a long laborious process, and said expressly, for the first time, in the Second Vatican Council that she wishes Scripture to be in everybody's hands. Formerly she treated Scripture almost like some secret writing that should be used only by experts in theology and in official preaching» (K. RAHNER, «Book of God», 223).

[200] See «Giving the Bible back to the Community» (VI All India Biblical Meeting, 4-8 December 1987), 78. See also E. MALATESTA, «Sacred Scripture», 64-78.

takes place in every house and in every family. The leadership becomes one of animation and service. A servant model of the Church becomes actualized[201]. In practice, in the BECs the Church exercises its prophetic, priestly and kingly role meaningfully.

As Pope John Paul II observes, there is a social commitment in the BECs[202]. The faithful come to know the needs of others. They discuss the social problems. They try to solve the problems in light of the Gospel and understand the Gospel in their life situation. They become more realistic. Their prayer life is not restricted to the time of prayer but is also extended to help their neighbours in the spirit of Christian fellowship. From such an attitude emerges a true ecumenism and dialogue both with the people and with the culture.

In the BECs there is an opportunity for dialogue with people who belong to other religions. In the salvific plan of God the Church is a universal sacrament of salvation even for the believers of other religions. The terms «ecumenism» and «dialogue» are not just theological jargon, rather they become a reality. A mutual relation with the brothers and sisters of other faiths becomes possible. In BECs, the Church becomes the «dynamic force in mankind's journey towards the eschatological Kingdom, and is the sign and promoter of Gospel values»[203]. Everybody tries to grow in love and in God experience. These communities respect and accept different cultures[204]. Thus truth, goodness, beauty, purity, and holiness will be a common patrimony.

From the practical effects it is clear that BECs are closely related to the people. One of the most important aspects of such communities is that each community bears the ethos of the place.

6. Conclusion

We are living in a world in which anonymity is prevalent. Modern technology has developed in such a way that anyone can cover the globe

---

201 See A. DULLES, *Models of the Church*, 88-102. See also J. NAVONE, *Self-giving and Sharing*, 35-44.

202 See JOHN PAUL II, *Redemptoris Missio*, n. 51.

203 JOHN PAUL II, *Redemptoris Missio*, n. 20. See also PAUL VI, *Ecclesiam Suam*, ns. 58-118. Dialogue at the grass root level will help to value what is good in other religions. See J. DUPUIS, «Dialogue and Proclamation», 165-172.

204 For a detailed study in the Indian context see J.P. PINTO, *Inculturation*. See also A. ROEST-CROLLIUS – T. NKÉRAMIHIGO, *What is So New?* ; F. WILFRED, «The Problem of a Valid Starting Point»; R. ESTEBAS, «Evangelization, Culture and Spirituality», 273-282; D. SMITH, «What Spirituality Can Resource», 183-191.

very fast. No continent is far away. No voice is unheard. No person is unseen. Yet the human person experiences loneliness. He is lonely in the crowd. This anonymity influences the Church too. One of the achievements of Vatican II is that the Council Fathers could read the signs of the time[205]. They tried to give guidelines in all aspects of the Christian life. The Council Fathers with an earnest desire to renew the Church could also make a dialogue with the world[206]. The spirit of the Second Vatican Council was so inspiring that the change that resulted in the life of the Church with the Council becomes irreversible.

Since BEC is the living cell of the Church in a locality we have attempted to explain the new dimensions of the local Churches. We analyzed the biblical concept of the Church and the relation between universal Church and the local Churches[207]. We have seen that BECs are rooted in a sound theology of the local Church. The concept of the local Church goes beyond the understanding of a diocese. With the support of the papal teachings we came to the conclusion that BEC is also a local Church in an analogical sense. A study on the phenomenon of BECs showed that though the small groups and associations have been existing in the Church, BECs can not be identified with the groups or associations. A BEC is not just part of the Church, it is the whole Church in a concentrated form[208].

We have seen that the BECs, *as new way of being the Church*, have originated in the Latin America, Asia and Africa with the Vatican II. In all these places the BECs were promoted and animated by the clergy and hierarchy. In the Church this *new way of being the Church* is contextualized in different forms even taking different names such as basic Christian communities, basic communities, small Christian

---

[205] See *GS* 4-10.

[206] See PAUL VI, *Ecclesiam Suam*, ns. 58-118.

[207] «We know that Churches existed at Jerusalem, at Antioch, at Corinth and at Rome, in the regions of Judea, of Galatia and of Macedonia. None of them claimed to be its own the entire Church of God, but the entire Church was really present in each one of them. Relations were established between the Churches: between Jerusalem and Antioch, between Churches founded by Paul and Jerusalem, to which the former sent the results of a collection, between the Churches to which the First letter of Peter is addressed and between those addressed in the Apocalypse. Paul writes that he bears the burden of all the Churches (2 Cor 11,28), and apostolic authority is recognized everywhere in the Church» (PBC, *Unity and Diversity in the Church*, 34). See also J. KOMONCHAK, «The Church Universal as the Communion», 30-35; H. DE LUBAC, *The Splendour of the Church*, 29-54.

[208] See J. MARINS, «What are Basic Christian Communities?», 142.

communities, grassroots communities, *Familien Kreis*. The papal teachings such as *Evangelii Nuntiandi* and *Christifideles Laici*, *Redemptoris Missio* have given new impetus to the growth of BECs. Two Popes, Paul VI and John Paul II, not only encouraged the BECs but also have given directives for better functioning of them, so that they would become a «great hope for the life of the Church»[209].

As we come to the theology of the Church, one sees that the Church is fundamentally based on the trinitarian communion of God. This makes the Church a community. This communion is seen in the BECs where people live together, know each other, share their joys and sorrows. With the Vatican II a shift has taken place in the concept of the life of the Church and the spirituality. The Council's understanding of holiness helps to re-define the nature of spirituality. Spirituality is no more an experience reserved for a few, but rather it is an experience obtained in the Church with the help of God in everyday life. This is a pilgrimage (*cammino*). This starts with the ecclesial awareness and social responsibilities, forming a new society based on the «civilization of love»[210]. It begins with the sacrament of baptism[211] and is nurtured by the Word of God and the Eucharist. It is oriented towards the Kingdom of God. It dialogues with the people of other faiths and cultures without losing the prophetic and missionary thrust.

The BECs, despite their widespread influence within the Church, have their limitations too. The BECs call for a basic change in the Church both on structural and personal levels. The social commitment of the BECs, unless supported by the *ecclesial* values, will tend to deviate from the mainstream of the universal Church. There is also a possibility to find self satisfaction in the «community», without the missionary vision of the universal Church. The BECs cannot remain satisfied with their progress or with the social commitment within themselves, but must carry the mission and vision of the Church[212]. The task still remains to transform

---

[209] JOHN PAUL II, *Redemptoris Missio*, n. 51.

[210] JOHN PAUL II, *Redemptoris Missio*, n. 51.

[211] See JOHN PAUL II, *Redemptoris Missio*, n. 48.

[212] L. BOFF, *Church: Charism and Power*, 135. See also B. SECONDIN, *Segni di Profezia*, 99-100; J. FUELLENBACH, *Hermeneutics*, 140-141; J. DUPUIS, «Lay People in Church and World», 347-390.

the Church[213] without forgetting the ecclesial principles for its discernment[214].

As our study is mainly on the spirituality of BECs in Trivandrum, the complexity of the social context in Trivandrum demands that we understand the socio-religious situation of the people in order to understand, to evaluate and to discern the spirituality of BECs in Trivandrum[215]. So in the next chapter we study the socio-religious context of the people of Trivandrum/ Kerala.

---

[213] See F. LOBINGER, *Towards Non-dominating Leadership*, 13.

[214] See PAUL VI, *Evangelii Nuntiandi* n. 58. See also JOHN PAUL II, *Redemptoris Missio*, n. 51; SCDF, *Instruction on Certain Aspects of the «Theology of Liberation»*; ID., *Instruction on Christian Freedom;* B. SECONDIN, *I Nuovi Protagonisti*, 142-147.

[215] According to Y. Congar human development, especially spiritual, is deeply conditioned by the milieu in which one lives. By milieu Y. Congar means the structures and institutions beyond one's social group, the totality of relations and involvements determined by the general set-up, laws, material conditions and social pressure. See Y. CONGAR, *Lay People in the Church*, 380.

CHAPTER II

The Socio-Religious Context
of the Diocese of Trivandrum

In the first chapter we have discussed the Spirituality of BECs in the theological and historical contexts. We have seen that socio-religious factors contribute to the development of BECs. The nature and function of BECs differ from country to country and from place to place due to the varying socio-religious factors even though the theological and ecclesiological principles remain the same. We have also seen the different dimensions of spirituality in relation to the BECs and have noticed that social and religious factors do influence the spirituality of the BECs, especially if it exists in a pluralistic culture.

In this chapter, therefore, we examine the socio-religious context of the Diocese of Trivandrum. The caste system and the different religions in Kerala with a special reference to Trivandrum[1] will be studied as they are important factors in understanding the genesis, nature, function and spirituality of BECs in Trivandrum.

---

[1] For the sake of brevity we do not treat politics as a section in this chapter. Different castes and religions play a significant role in the social make up of Kerala. No caste and no religion is free from political affinity. Fr. Joseph Vadakkan, who was one among the many Catholic priests who publicly denounced the governing communist party in 1957, took initiative to form a political party of farmers and labourers called *Karshaka Thozhilali Party* in 1967. For a detailed study See J.T. ERINGELY, *Coalition Game Politics*. See also P.T. CHACKO, «Towards a Theology of Politics», 12-28; S. KAPPAN, «Christian and the Call to Revolution», 29-45; A. KALLUNKALPURAYIDAM, «The Involvement of the Kerala Church in Politics», 61-71; M. KANJIRATHINKAL, «Christian Participation in Politics», 125-147; J. MURICKAN, *Religion and Power Structure*.

1. Trivandrum: A Short History

We look at Trivandrum from two angles: the secular and the ecclesiastical. Let us first see from the secular angle.

1.1 *The District of Trivandrum*

Trivandrum[2], Thiruvananthapuram (in Malayalam), is the southern most district of the Kerala State. The population of the district according to the 1991 census is 2.270.729, living in an area of 2.192 Sq. Km. Of the total population, around 69.80% are Hindus, 17.68% are Christians and 12.52% are Muslims[3]. The Trivandrum city takes its name from the deity of the celebrated Hindu temple of *Ananta* Sayanam (Sri Padmanabha)[4]. Trivandrum was the capital of the Princely State of Travancore[5], which

---

[2] It is bounded on the north by Quilon, Kottarakkara, and Pathanapuram taluks of Quilon district, on east by the Ambasamudram taluk of Tirunelveli district, on the south and south-east by Vilavancode taluk of Kanyakumari district of Tamil Nadu and on the west by the Arabian Sea. The district has four taluks (revenue unit of a district), namely, Chirayinkil, Nedumangad, Neyyattinkara and Trivandrum.

[3] The percentage of religion in Trivandrum is against the State average of Hindus 59.41%, Christians 21.05% Muslims 19.50% and others 0.03%. See DEPARTMENT OF ECONOMICS & STATISTICS TRIVANDRUM, *Statistics for Planning 1988*, 5. Of the total population of 2.270.729 there are 343.439 (11.90%) belonging to the Scheduled Castes and 16.181 (5.04%) belonging to the Scheduled Tribes. The Scheduled Castes and the Scheduled Tribes are the most depressed class of the Indian society. The literacy rate of Trivandrum is 89.22% against the State average of 89.81%. See DEPARTMENT OF ECONOMICS & STATISTICS THIRUVANANTHAPURAM, *Kerala at a Glance*, 6-12.

[4] The city is mentioned in ancient inscriptions as Sri Anantapuram or Tiru-Anantapuram. The exact date of the consecration of the idol in the temple is not known. The *Mahārājas* who reigned the state were very keen for its development. The foundation of the present *Gopuram* (tower) was laid in 1566. Trivandrum is regarded as the abbreviated English form Tiru-Anantapuram. During the closing years of the reign of Dharma Raja (1758-98) the capital of Travancore was shifted from *Padmanabhapuram* to Trivandrum. Thereafter Trivandrum continued to be the capital of Travancore, Travancore-Cochin and Kerala. See M. VIJAYANUNNI, *District Census Handbook*, 9. 24-25. Maha Raja Marthanda Varma (1729-58), after his victory over the Dutch at Colachal in 1741 and annexation of many neighbouring territories to his kingdom, dedicated it to his tutelary deity, *Sri Padmanabha*, on 5th *Makaram* 925 (3rd January 1750) and ruled the kingdom on his behalf in the assumed name of *Padmanābhadāsa*. *Padmanābhadāsa* means the servant of *Padmanābha*. See M. VIJAYANUNNI, *District Census Handbook*, 9.

[5] When India became free, Kerala was made up of two princely states, Travancore and Cochin, and Malabar which was under the direct administration of the British. One of the first steps taken by independent India was to amalgamate small states together so as to make them viable administrative units. In pursuance of this policy the Travancore and Cochin States were integrated so as to form Travancore — Cochin Sate on 1st July 1949. But Malabar remained as part of the Madras Province. Under the States Re-organization

was ruled by Hindu Kings and Queens, and it continues to be the state capital of the present day Kerala.

Trivandrum, like any other coastal districts, had been in commercial contacts with many countries from ancient times. The people were of the Dravidic origin[6]. The history of Trivandrum or rather Travancore comes with the *Sangam* age which comprised the first five centuries of the Christian era[7]. From the *Sangam* age Trivandrum was under different Kingdoms. There was no caste distinction in the early period. Hinduism was the religion and Sri Padmanabha temple marked the religious symbol of the people.

In the post *Sangam* Age (after 500 A.D.), Kerala was on the threshold of feudalism. The increased inflow of Aryans[8] from North India and the consequent Aryan colonization of Malabar ushered in a new era marked by significant socio-economic and political changes in Kerala. With Aryanisation, caste distinctions entered into society, dividing it into many castes. Towards the end of the 12th century A.D., Kerala became a full-fledged feudal society with its peculiar socio-religious institutions,

---

Act of 1956, Travancore — Cochin State and Malabar were united to form the State of Kerala on 1st November, 1956. In the re-adjustment Kerala lost to Tamil Nadu the taluks of Thovala, Agasteeswaram, Kalkulam and Vilavancode in the far south and Shencotta in the east, while it gained the Malabar district and Kasargode taluk of South Kanara district in the north. See *Manorama Year Book –1986*, 637-638. Geographically, Travancore is the territory lying between the Malabar Coast and the Western Ghats and its southern and northern boundaries are Cape Comerin and Paravur respectively.

[6] The name Dravidian is applied to the people of south and central India and to those of parts of Ceylon where a Dravidian language is spoken. Dravidians are the early settlers in India. Their origin is traced back to 3rd millennium B.C. Recent archaeological discoveries of the Indus valley proves a pre-Aryan civilization and religion which were practically absorbed by the Aryan immigrants. See D. ACHARUPARAMBIL, «Hinduism», 256-265.

[7] The name *Sangam* denotes the renowned Tamil Academy, established by the Royal house of the Pandiyan Dynasty at Madurai, where the Tamil poets from different parts of Tamil Nadu assembled and performed great literary activities of historical and cultural importance. See V. PERUMAL, *Glimpses of Tamil Culture*, 1-2. Kerala at the time of *Sangam* age was not a separate cultural entity. It was part of Tamilakam. See A.S. MENON, *Social and Cultural History*, 45-46. During the Sangam age Kerala was part of Tamilakam of which the Southern Kerala was under the Ay Kingdom. See M. VIJAYANUNNI, *District Census Handbook*, 9. Vizhingam one of the harbours of Kerala and one of the big Catholic parishes in the Diocese of Trivandrum was the capital of the Ay dynasty. See G. WOODCOCK, *Kerala: A Portrait*, 65.

[8] Aryans, (from Sanskrit *ārya*, «noble»), are the people who came to India from central Asia towards 2nd millennium B.C.

customs and usages[9]. The spread of Christianity and Islam added many divisions in the society, though Trivandrum as such has never been under a foreign ruler[10].

1.2 *The Diocese of Trivandrum*

Trivandrum[11] is one of the nine Roman Catholic (Latin Catholic) dioceses of Kerala[12]. The present Diocese was carved out of the Dioceses of Cochin and Quilon on 1 July 1937 by Pope Pius XI[13]. It consists of the entire Trivandrum civil district of the Kerala State and a part of Kanyakumari district of Tamil Nadu[14]. There are 11 Vicariates of which Anjengo, Pudukuruchy, Pulluvila, Thoothoor, Valiyathura, are situated on the coast[15], and Chullimanoor, Kattakode, Neyyattinkara, Undencode, Palayam, Vlathankara are inland[16].

---

[9] «The janmi system is the Kerala prototype of European feudalism with its manifold forms of infeudation and subinfeudation. As in Europe, so too in Kerala the system was the outcome of the anarchic and unsettled state of affairs prevailing in early society which enabled the landlords of the day to grab more land and compelled the weaker sections to surrender the lands in their possession and to accept the benign protection of the stronger ones» (A.S. MENON, *Social and Cultural History*, 76). See also L. LOPEZ, *A Social History*, 1-12.

[10] It is natural that the political independence that the people enjoyed from the very inception of the Kingdom influences the socio-religious life of the people.

[11] The existence of Christianity, before the coming of the Dominicans and Franciscans in the 14th century, in Trivandrum is doubtful though the possibilities can not be ruled out. The absence of historical evidences should not damage the historical facts. If at all there existed a Christian community in Trivandrum it was either powerless or without proper shepherds. At present the Diocese consists of around 400.000 Catholics.

[12] In Kerala there are three Liturgical rites namely Latin (nine dioceses), Syro-Malabar (eleven) and Syro-Malankara (three). The Syro-Malabar Church is a *Sui-Iuris* Church.

[13] See PIUS XI, *In Ora Malabarica*, 90-92. When the Diocese was erected the area covered was only of the revenue district of Trivandrum except those parishes which were under the Cochin Diocese. Archbishop Benziger proposed the division of Quilon Diocese into three — Quilon, Kottar, Trivandrum — in 1929. See A. BENZIGER, *Division du Diocèse, AGOCD*. It is remarkable that more than 5.500 BECs are functioning within the old geographical boundary of the Diocese of Quilon.

[14] There are seven parishes in the coastal strip from the Kannyakumari district of the present Tamil Nadu remain with Trivandrum. As the Dioceses of Cochin and Quilon had jurisdiction in Tamil speaking area we find an interaction between the people and dioceses.

[15] Most of the parishes in these Vicariates were visited by St. Francis Xavier. Anjengo was once the residence of Cochin Bishop when he was not able to reside at Cochin because of the Dutch rule (1663-1795). «In 1745 Dom Clemente Jose Colaso Leitao, S.J. became Bishop of Cochin. His residence, however, was in Anjengo, and so was his Cathedral Church, for the Dutch would not allow a Portuguese Prelate in the Capital»

The Diocese had been closely associated with the Dioceses of Quilon which is one of the early centres of Christianity in Kerala[17]. It was the first Catholic Diocese erected in India by a Roman Pontiff. The Diocese of Quilon was erected on 9 August 1329 by Pope John XXII, while the Pope was in Avignon, with a decree *Ad perpetuam rei memoriam*. The first bishop was Iordanus Catalani of Sévérac[18]. Since no bishop is known to have succeeded Bishop Catalani we find a historical gap in the ecclesiastical history of Quilon. Therefore a new beginning took place

---

(D. FERROLI, *The Jesuits in Malabar*, II, 112). See also V.A. PASCAL, *The Latin and Syrian Hierarchies*, 117; L.M. PYLEE, *St. Thomas Christians*, 197.

[16] The inland Vicariates were the result of missionary works after the coming of the Portuguese. It is possible that people who came out from the coastal side lived a Christian life and influenced the Nairs, the Nadars and the Izhavas. The parishes like Karakkamandapam, Balaramapuram, Neyyattinkara, Amaravila, Parassala have become the first inland centres of Christianity.

[17] According to tradition St. Thomas, the Apostle, converted people to Christianity in Quilon along with other centers of Kerala. For a discussion on the early tradition of Christianity in Quilon see E.P. ANTONY, «Hierarchy and the Community», 355-357. It is from the thirteenth century we get a clear picture of Christianity at Quilon. Monte Corvino, a Franciscan friar, visited Quilon in 1291 and stayed for thirteen months in South India. See K.J. JOHN, «Emergence of Latin Christians» 350. The French Dominican priest Jordan Catalani of Sévérac visited Quilon in 1321 as part of a Roman Catholic mission. See J. C. DE SÉVÉRAC, *Mirabilia Descripta*, 19-39. Some hold the view that Nicholas of Pistoia, an Italian missionary came to Quilon in 1292. Odoric of Pordonone (1286-1331), an Italian born in Friuli also visited Quilon in the same period. The next Franciscan (bishop since 1338) to visit Quilon was the Papal Legate to China John of Marignoli (from Florence). Marignoli's delegation included many friars; they set out from Naples in 1339 and reached Khanbaliq by 1342. After spending three years there, Marignoli, on his return to Europe, landed in *Quolon* (Quilon) in March 1346. During his stay in the St. George Latin Church, Quilon, he visited Cape Comorin. He spent sixteen months in Quilon and Cape Comerin. See G.T. MACKENZIE, «History of Christianity», 135-148. See also G.J. MULAKARA, *History of the Diocese of Cochin*, 41-48. Marignoli, before leaving India, set up a pillar at Cape Comorin (Kanyakumari), the extremity of the Indian peninsula. See G.M. MORAES, *A History of Christianity*, 80-105. See also A.M. MUNDADAN, *History of Christianity*, 1, 126-144; L. ROCHE, «The Latin Catholics», 599-606. It is very likely that the Franciscans and Dominicans, who evangelized Quilon in the thirteenth century, much earlier than the arrival of the Portuguese who came in the 16th century, worked in Trivandrum. It is also reasonable to believe that two Churches namely the Holy Ghost Church at Mampally and St. Antony's Church at Valiathura have pre-Portuguese origin. See M. NETTO, «The Diocese of Trivandrum», 374. See also C.M. AGUR, *Church History*, 197-199. Here also tradition takes over history.

[18] See A. MERCATI, «Aloysii Mariae Benziger», 1-11. See also the letters written by Pope John XXII to Bishop I. Catalani between 9 August 1329 to 31 March 1330 in ID., «Aloysii Mariae Benziger», 12-29. See also A.J. ROSARIO, *Kollam Kristiānikal* (The Christians of Quilon); S. PIMENTA, «La nostra Chiesa», 7.

when the Portuguese missionaries came to India in the 16th century and established a dioceses in Goa in 1533 and its sufragan in Cochin in 1558[19]. Thus the Christian centres of Quilon and Trivandrum came under Portuguese Padroado administration. In 1838 the Diocese of Cochin was suppressed and annexed to the Diocese of Verapoly[20]. In 1886 the Diocese of Quilon was *re-erected* dividing the Verapoly Diocese[21]. Thus the Diocese of Trivandrum is also related to the early Dioceses of Goa, Cochin and Verapoly along with Quilon.

Despite the early traditions of Christianity in Quilon and Trivandrum (South Travancore) a real evangelization in a mass level took in south Travancore only with the arrival of the Portuguese missionaries and St. Francis Xavier in the 16th century. The Portuguese Missionaries in the

---

[19] It was because of the successful Portuguese missionary endeavour Cochin Diocese was erected on February 4, 1558. The ecclesiastical territory of Cochin at the time of the Portuguese mainly comprised of the Cochin coast from Cannanore to Purakkad, the Travancore coast from Purakkad to Cape Comorin, the Fishery coast from Cape Comorin to Tuticorin, the Coromondol coast from Tuticorin to San Thomé, and the Ceylon coast from Jaffna to Colombo. For a detailed description with sufficient charts of the ecclesiastical territories see G.J. MULAKARA, *History of the Diocese of Cochin*, 19-22. 65-93. See also ID., «Portuguese Missionaries in Cochin», 69-94. Cochin had the ecclesiastical jurisdiction over all these areas because of the Royal Patronage known as *Padroado* given to the Portuguese King by the Pope for the great service rendered to the Church in spreading the Christian faith. Through the Royal Patronage the Portuguese King had the right to nominate a bishop in its territory. See *FX*, II, 144-146. The Royal Patronage in the course of time became a hindrance to the free growth of the new missions.

[20] When the Diocese of Cochin was suppressed in 1838 by Pope Gregory XVI (*Multa Praeclara* 24 April 1838), all the parishes of the present Trivandrum came under the jurisdiction of Vicariate Apostolic of Verapoly which was under the *Propaganda*. The Portuguese authorities did not welcome the suppression. The Portuguese claimed that the decrees which were not issued through their primates of Portugal were not binding and that they enjoyed juridically every right and privilege. This gave occasion to «double Jurisdiction». The result was very far-reaching because the clergy and the laity in the whole diocese were split into two sections i.e., *Propaganda* and *Padroado*. The impact of this double jurisdiction is reflected also in the Diocese of Trivandrum. In 1886, when the Diocese of Cochin was restored, the coastal parishes from Pallithura to Thengapattanam were attached to Diocese of Cochin. In 1950 the *Padroado* privileges were suppressed by the Holy See and in 1955 again those parishes were attached to the present Diocese of Trivandrum. The history of «double jurisdiction» is a black mark in the history of Kerala Church. See T. PUTHENVEETIL, «The Diocese of Cochin», 404-412. See also C.J. COSTA, «A Missiological Conflict», 131-160.

[21] When the Diocese of Quilon was re-erected, the parishes except Pallithura to Thengapattanam came under the new Diocese. Quilon and the southern part of Travancore were already entrusted to the Belgium Discalsed Carmelites from 1845. See J. FERNANDEZ, «The Diocese of Quilon», 382-391.

beginning, were more engaged in the affairs of the Syrian Church in Kerala. The system of preaching Christ to all was set on foot by the celebrated missionary St. Francis Xavier who, unlike Robert de Nobili of Madura, chiefly evangelized the depressed classes of Travancore and Fishery coasts[22].

It was to speed up the mission work in India that the Diocese of Cochin was erected by Pope Paul IV in 1558. It then comprised of the entire west coast and practically the whole of India except for the territory of the Archdiocese of Goa which was founded in 1533. In 1601 the Jesuit province of Goa was divided and the province of Malabar was erected with its headquarters at Cochin. It speeded up the evangelization work in Trivandrum[23]. The report to the Jesuit General prepared by Fr. Andre Lopez, S.J. of the Malabar Province in 1644 sheds light on the successful mission carried out by the Jesuits in the beginning of the 17th century in Trivandrum[24].

It took still fifty years to spread the Gospel in the agricultural areas of Trivandrum. In 1701 the Provincial of the Malabar province complained that the efforts at evangelization were confined to the coastal belt, that the interior places were completely neglected[25]. Therefore some Jesuits with native dress (dressed as *Pandārasvami*) came to a village called Nemam.

---

[22] See C.M. AGUR, *Church History*, 207.211. St. Francis Xavier spent most of his missionary life in Travancore and especially in the areas of Trivandrum, Kottar and Tuticorin.

[23] The evangelization work in Trivandrum was not easy. Despite the religious toleration of the Travancore *Rājas* (Kings), there was persecution between 1600 and 1604. More than 20.000 Christians were dispersed and many Churches were destroyed. The Jesuit Rector of Coulam (present Quilon or Kollam) Padre Nicolao d'Espinola, endeavoured to calm the anger of the *Rāja*. See D. FERROLI, *The Jesuits in Malabar*, II, 96.

[24] The letter reads as follows: «At a distance of five leagues from *Coulao* along the sea-shore is the residence of Mampulium. The patron of the Church is the Assumption of Our Lady. There are 540 Christians; 40 children daily attend Christian doctrine; 20 the school». It reveals the educational vision of the Jesuits in these areas. The description of A. Lopez also points out the life and attitudes of the people. He says that the people at Raithura gave much trouble to the priests because of their wealth. He speaks of the difficulties to instruct the people at Anjengo while they were living in the midst of Moors (Mohamedans). See A. LOPEZ, *Translated Extracts*, 9-11.

[25] The Jesuits should have known the nature of the people in the inland as they had successfully converted the Nadars at Vadakkankulam. In 1680, the first congregation of Nadars was started at Vaddakankulam with a conversion of a Nadar woman and a church was built in 1685. A permanent mission was established in 1701. There were more than four thousand Christians in the Vadakkankulam parish and most of them were Nadars. See R.L. HARDGRAVE, JR., *The Nadars of Tamilnad*, 43.

They aimed to convert thousands of high caste Hindus[26]. The conversion of Neelakanda Pillai, the first Christian Martyr of Travancore, was also connected with the Nemam mission under taken by the Jesuits[27]. However, the missionaries found it difficult to convert the higher castes like Brahmins and thus they turned to the people of Nadar caste who according to the missionaries are of humble tribe. The missionaries realized that it was easy for the Nadars to receive the Gospel. According to the missionaries it was easy for the Nadars to keep commandments: «Their women are naturally chaste. The men climb coconut trees and cultivate the fields. This keep them busy and makes them avoid idleness, which is the origin of all vices»[28]. Although many Nadars were converted, the missionaries and the converted Christians had to face opposition from the Hindu Nadars[29].

The conversion work in Trivandrum suffered a great set-back in the subsequent years. The Dutch dominance over the Portuguese at Cochin[30], the suppression of the Jesuit Order in Portugal and in its colonies, the disappearance of Nemam mission, unsatisfactory work of the priests who succeeded the Jesuits, the suppression of the Cochin Diocese, the schism that crept into the Church because of the non-acceptance of the Papal Bull by the Goan priests, and the unhealthy competition of jurisdictional power of the *Padroado* (representing the Diocese of Cochin) and

---

[26] See D. FERROLI, *The Jesuits in Malabar*, II, 355-372. It seems that some of the missionaries had the false assumption that they could easily convert the low caste people when they convert the higher castes. Actually the early missionaries failed to understand that the low caste people had also their own religious practices beyond the philosophical religion of the Brahmanic caste. However, the effort of missionaries to build Churches and appoint catechists has to be appreciated. Already in 1716 there were five Churches and twelve catechists at Nemam.

[27] Neelakanda Pillai was holding high office at the Padmanabhapuram Palace. He was given Catholic instruction by De Lanoy. Neelakanda Pillai was Martyred on 13th January 1752. See D. FERROLI, *The Jesuits in Malabar*, II, 364-372. See also C.M. AGUR, *Church History*, 279-286; L.M. ZALESKI, *The Martyrs of India*, 231-255.

[28] D. FERROLI, *The Jesuits in Malabar*, II, 363.

[29] See D. FERROLI, *The Jesuits in Malabar*, II, 355-370.

[30] See B. SOBHANAN, «Glimpses into the Disputes», 223-231. See also M. NETTO, «The Diocese of Trivandrum», 376-378. It was during Dutch dominance that Clemente Jose Golaso Leitao S.J., as bishop of Cochin, resided at Anjengo. See D. FERROLI, *The Jesuits in Malabar*, II, 112. See also E.P. ANTONY, «Hierarchy and the Community», 374.

Propaganda (Verapoly) were some of the major causes for the set-backs in mission work in the area[31].

A new phase of missionary enterprise took place with the re-erection of the Diocese of Quilon in 1886 and especially with the arrival of A.M. Benziger as the Bishop of Quilon in 1900[32]. The primary concern of Bishop Benziger was the propagation of faith. Many from Nadars, Izhavas and from other lower castes called Dalits were converted to Christianity. Together with Bishop Benziger, the most celebrated Carmelite missionary, Fr. John Damascene, spent 48 years in Neyyattinkara Taluk with a dedication to love and to serve the poor[33]. The conversion work in Nedumangad taluk started only during his period. The Diocese of Quilon then comprised of the whole of the civil districts of Quilon, Trivandrum and Kanyakumari excluding those old *Padroado* parishes which were still under the Diocese of Cochin. In 1929 Bishop Benziger, because of the vastness of the Diocese, asked the Holy See for the establishment of the Diocese of Trivandrum. It materialized only on 1st July 1937 and Bishop Vincent V. Dereere (V.V. Dereere) became the first bishop of Trivandrum. In 1953 the narrow strip of coastal parishes, covering the region from Pallithura to Eramainthura in the Trivandrum Portuguese mission, was temporarily attached to the Diocese of Trivandrum. In 1955 Bishop V.V. Dereere received an auxiliary in the person of Bishop Peter Bernard Pereira (P.B. Pereira); in the same year the territory was permanently integrated into the Diocese of Trivandrum[34].

---

31 See E.P. ANTONY, «Hierarchy and the Community», 329-362.368-384. See also A.J. PANACKAL, «The Archdiocese of Verapoly», 355-360; M. NETTO, «The Diocese of Trivandrum», 374-381; J. FERNANDEZ, «The Diocese of Quilon», 382-391; T. PUTHENVEETTIL, «The Diocese of Cochin», 404-412. There are differences of opinion regarding the missionary work of Jesuits in Malabar. Nevertheless, the suppression of the Jesuit Order did affect the evangelization work in Kerala. See D. FERROLI, *The Jesuits in Malabar*, II, 488-614. It may be true that the Jesuits did not understand the St. Thomas Christians in the early Portuguese period. See J. KOLLAPARAMBIL, *The St. Thomas Christians' Revolution*, 3. A critical study will reveal that both the old Christians and the new Christians were patronized by something of foreign elements: either *Syriackaisation* (Syriac-isation) or *Latinisation*.

32 For a study on the contribution of A.M. Benziger see F. KILIYAMPURAKAL, *Aloysius Maria Benziger*.

33 See D. FERNANDEZ, «Spanish Carmelite Missionaries», 175-197.

34 See E.P. ANTONY, «Hierarchy and the Community», 375-376. See also M. NETTO, «The Diocese of Trivandrum», 374-381. P.B. Pereira was the first indigenous bishop of Trivandrum.

Bishop P.B. Pereira was one of the pioneers of social work in the Catholic Church of Kerala. The TSSS, which started before the Second Vatican Council, and the Marianad Project, the brain child of the Bishop, which captured the attention of the Kerala Government, are some of the events in the history of the Diocese of Trivandrum. Bishop P.B. Pereira played a significant role in the deliverance movement against the Communist Government which stood against the welfare of the Catholic Church in Kerala (1957)[35]. In 1966 Bishop V.V. Dereere resigned and Bishop P. B. Pereira took the reins of the Diocese until his death on 13th June 1978.

On 7th October, 1979 Bishop Jacob B. Acharuparambil, O.F.M. Cap., (A.B. Jacob) was consecrated Bishop of Trivandrum. The fishermen's agitation of Kerala in the '80's took place during his time[36]. It was also during his time that the Diocese celebrated its Golden Jubilee. The «Living Together», which we will discuss in the third chapter, of all the priests of Trivandrum with the Bishop under the leadership of the late Indian theologian Fr. D.S. Amalorpavadass was held as the part of Jubilee celebration which was the beginning of the renewal in the Diocese. The renewal of the Diocese took a new dimension when M. Soosa Pakiam (M.S. Pakiam) became the Co-adjutor bishop of Trivandrum on 2nd February, 1990. With the coming of Bishop M.S. Pakiam, BECs in the Diocese marked a new phase in the history of the Diocese and in the history of the Kerala Church.

2. The Social Background: Caste Impact

No historian or a socio-religious scholar can ignore the impact of caste system in India[37]. Although caste system is one of the by-products of Aryanisation in Kerala[38], the good and evil effects continue up to now

---

[35] See M. NETTO, «The Diocese of Trivandrum», 374-381.

[36] The fishermen's agitation was one of the important events in the history of the Diocese of Trivandrum. This agitation caused an ideological rift in the Diocese among the clergy. We will discuss the cause and effect of the fishermen's agitation in the third chapter.

[37] The Indian Hindu society is divided into four main castes namely the *Brahmanas* (Brahmins), the *Kṣatriyas*, the *Vaiśyas* and the *Śūdras*. See N.K. DUTT, *Origin and Growth of Caste*, I, 2-3. Caste is also a religious institution. See *Travancore Census Report*, 615-629. All the political parties base their strength on the basis of a particular caste. See D.M. MENON, «Prospects in Kerala», 40-41.

[38] The caste system did not exist in ancient Kerala society. It was introduced by the Aryans who came from outside. Although the caste system with its rigours of social

marking the differences of life, dress, food, rites and ceremonies[39]. The presence of castes in the former Travancore state and the present day Trivandrum district[40] reveals that it is not easy to eliminate the caste feeling easily «unless some powerful religious influence were brought to bear upon the people in its place»[41].

We see people of different castes in Trivandrum. To have a general understanding of the impact of the castes we give a short description of the most important of them[42].

---

exclusiveness had not crystallized itself during the early Sangam age, the later Sangam period witnessed the rudimentary beginnings of social stratification. See A.S. MENON, *Social and Cultural History*, 65-66. According to E.K. Pillai, the caste system was unknown in Dravidian society. See E.K. PILLAI, *Studies in Kerala History*, 311. The story of the castes as originating from different parts of the body of *Prajāpati* (creator) or the explanation of the caste system in terms of the *Karma-samsāra* doctrine (a series of re-births according to one's good or evil deeds) are post-factum legitimization of an already existing order rather than the origin of the system. See M. AMALADOSS, *Becoming Indian*, 46-48.

[39] See *Travancore Census Report*, 621-627. According to Prof. S. Menon the caste rules operated in the most irrational manner. The triple social evil of un-touchability, un-approachability and un-seeability was observed by people at all levels of Hindu society. See A.S. MENON, *Social and Cultural History*, 66. Already in ancient times Buddha and Jaina and in the modern times Vaikunda Swami, Sri Narayan Guru, Mahatma Gandhi and Ambedkar have opposed the evils of caste system.

[40] According to 1891 Travancore Census Report there were 578 subcastes. At present there are 68 Scheduled Castes and 35 Scheduled Tribes in Trivandrum district. See M. VIJAYANUNNI, *District Census Handbook*, 5-6. Caste and communalism play a vital role in Kerala even now. See M.G. RADHAKRISHNAN, «Kerala: Lessons to Learn», 98-99. In Kerala the caste elements dominate even among the Marxists. See D.M. MENON, «Prospects in Kerala», 40-41.

[41] See *Travancore Census Report*, 624.

[42] «The average Indian Christian is a staunch observer of castes» (L.K.A., AYYAR, *Anthropology of the Syrian Christian*, 218). See also G. KOILPARAMBIL, *Caste in the Catholic Community*; J.W. GLADSTONE, *Protestant Christianity*; D.A. FERNANDEZ, «Search and Fidelity», 222-231; M. KALATHIL, «Caste Discrimination», 196-202; J. KANANAIKAL, «Caste Discrimination», 529; E.J. THOMAS, «Caste and the Syrian Rite», 227-233. «The most dominant characteristic and chief contributing factor of inter-caste tensions in the Kerala Church is the exclusiveness of the Syrian Christians as a distinct caste and their apparent determination to perpetuate this» (K. NINAN, *Caste in the Kerala Churches*, 51). «Though theoretically there is no caste system within Christianity, it is soaked with this evil and Christians of all status — the laity, sisters, brothers, priests, and even Bishops — are part of this unjust system. Sometimes, this practice is more blatantly prevalent among priests and sisters than among lay Christians» (*CBCI Evaluation Report*, n. 715). In the Diocese of Trivandrum population-wise the important castes are the Mukkuvar, the Nadars, the Izhavas and the Dalits. The castes like Goldsmiths, Anglo-Indians, Bharathar and other castes which are not mentioned in the study carry the ethos of one of the castes discussed in this chapter.

2.1 *The Brahmins*

The Brahmins, known in Kerala as Nambudiris, the priestly class of the Indian society, though numerically less, were politically and economically the most powerful caste in Travancore. According to E.K. Pillai, a historian of Kerala, the kings were mere servants of the Brahmins. Because of the extraordinary control they exerted over the Kings, they influenced even the politics of the State[43]. The Kings of Travancore regarded it their sacred duty to please the Brahmins erecting *ūṭṭupura,* feeding the Brahmins on the days of *Murajapam* and *Hiranya Garbha*[44] and ruled the country in accordance with the advice of the Brahmin scholars. They were not only given privileges but also deified in such a way that: «His word is law; his smile confers happiness and salvation; his power with heaven is unlimited; the very dust of his feet is purifying in its nature and efficacy. Each is an infallible Pope in his own sphere»[45].

The Brahmin women were given the privilege to cover their body; no woman of lower castes was permitted to cover her breasts. But in Brahmanic practice women have no ritual status and are considered inferior in society. They are subject to all sorts of impurities[46]. A proper education was often denied to them. With regard to the family life the Brahmins had a peculiar system. Only the eldest son of the family was permitted to enter into a marriage relationship. The other male members of the family used to have concubinage with Nair women, and children born from this relationship had no right to inherit from the father and the children became the integral part of the Nair community. The Brahmins

---

[43] E.K. PILLAI, *Studies in Kerala History*, 195. Among the Brahmins the non-Malayali Brahmins had upper hand in the administration. The beginning of «Malayali Sabha» and «The Malayali Memorial» movement among the Nairs in the 19th century was against the domination of non-Malyali Brahmins. See J.W. GLADSTONE, *Protestant Christianity*, 224-231.

[44] *Ūṭṭupura* (free inns) are the places where the Brahmins are fed at the expense of the State. *Murajapam,* a feast celebrated at Trivandrum every sixth year for forty days, was indeed a festival of feeding the Brahmins and giving them gifts. *Hiranya Garbha* is a feast in which the Brahmin priest declares the king as a twice born. The Brahmins are called 'Twice Born' and as a mark of that all the male members wear a sacred thread. This they start to wear at the age of eleven when the religious rites are performed. See S. MATEER, *The Land of Charity,* 158-188. See also R. JEFFREY, *The Decline of Nayar Dominance,* 3-13.

[45] S. MATEER, *The Land of Charity,* 31-32. The people of Travancore have high respect for the priestly class including the priests of Christian religion.

[46] In the Sabarimala Temple women between the age of ten to fifty are not allowed to enter and worship. See M.G. RADHAKRISHNAN, «Sabarimala Temple», 117.

also practised child marriage, and the re-marriage of widows was strictly prohibited until the end of the 19th century[47].

It is an undeniable fact that the presence of Brahmins and their religious practices in the temples have given the natives of Trivandrum a sense of religion. The people were tolerant towards the priestly class despite the *inhuman* attitude of the priestly class towards the lower castes. The respect and awe given to the Absolute by the learned class has inspired the lower castes to search for the Absolute in their own way. The success of missionaries, including St. Francis Xavier could be attributed to the atmosphere that existed in the state. With the emergence of lower castes and the change in the social systems in Kerala the Brahmins are losing their ground in the contemporary society though they are still known for their Hindu religious fervour[48].

2.2 *The Nairs*

The Nairs, known as *Sūdras*, were subordinate to Brahmins.[49] The scholars are of the opinion that the Nairs are those people who were ready to serve the Brahmins[50]. The Nairs, according to R. Jeffrey, were by no means a monolithic, egalitarian group. There were different sub-castes. All Nairs followed the *Marumakkattāyam* (matrilineal) system of inheritance, based on the matrilocal joint-family called *taravād*. All members of a *taravād* were descended from a common female ancestor, but the management of *taravād* affairs was vested in the eldest male

---

47 See K.P.P. MENON, *History of Kerala*, III, 67.74.

48 See «Row over Sabarimala priest's church visit» [The Hindu], 16

49 They were originally the lowest of the four castes, and are still a degraded caste in North India. See S. MATEER, *The Land of Charity*, 34-35. In Trivandrum and in Kerala the *varna* model of caste did not enter along with Brahmins.

50 See E.K. PILLAI, *Studies in Kerala History*, 314. The relation between Brahmins and Nairs is also legendary. According to the Brahminical tradition, the creation of Kerala resulted from the banishment from India of the God of Parasurama. Having nowhere to live, he won the permission of Varuna, the god of the sea, to reclaim all the land within a throw of his axe. Parasurama threw his axe from Cape Comorin to Gokarnam, the sea receded and Kerala was formed. To populate the new area, Parasuram introduced a special race of Brahmins, the Nambudiris, and gave to them the ownership of all land and unique customs which prevented their return to India on the other side of the Western Ghats. Next, he brought *Sūdras* — the Nairs — to act as the servants and body guards of the Nambudiris. He bestowed on the Nairs the *marumakkattāyam* or matrilineal system of the family and inheritance, and decreed that Nairs should have no formal marriage and that their women should always be available to satisfy the desires of the Brahmins (Nambudiris). See R. JEFFREY, *The Decline of Nayar Dominance*, xv.

member, the *kāranavan*; the system was matrilineal and not matriarcal. The property and assets of the *taravād* were held in common by all members, and no individual could claim his share of the joint property[51]. Connected with the system of *Marumakkttāyam,* there was *sambandham* and *talikeṭṭukallyānam* uprooting the family values[52]. However, they had a greater portion of the land and were owners of slaves[53]. They were also the dominant ruling class[54].

The systematic oppression of lower classes by Nairs and their unhealthy attitude towards those missionaries[55] who worked for the uplifting of the lower castes are still a living legend in Trivandrum. The political and social status of Nairs were being questioned by the emergence of lower castes in the 19th and 20th century. However, a revival in the Nair community began in 1877 when a few Nair young men, with English education, formed themselves into an organization. The organization was enlarged and extended to «Malayali Sabha» and later to «The Malayali Memorial»[56]. It was supported by Chattambi Swamikal, a native of Trivandrum and the social reformer of the Nair

---

[51] According to *matrilineal* system the heir to the throne was the son not of the King, but of his eldest sister. See A.L. BASHAM, *The Wonder that was India,* 94. See also R. JEFFREY, *The Decline of Nayar Dominance,* 14-16. According to historians *Marumakkattāyam* was not known in Kerala before 10th century. The first foreign traveller to mention the system was Friar Jordanus. See A.S. MENON, *Social and Cultural History of Kerala,* 83-101. See also E.K. PILLAI, *Studies in Kerala History,* 292-323; L. LOPEZ, *A Social History,* 13-21. The system caused instability in the Nair families. The system of *Marumakkttāyam* came to an end through Western education.

[52] *Sambandham* was only a marriage alliance and *talikeṭṭukallyānam* was a mock marriage. Some historians hold the view that *talikeṭṭukallyānam* was a real marriage. See L. LOPEZ, *A Social History,* 27-28. The problem connected with Matrilineal system (*Marumakkttāyam*) is discussed in J. PUTHENKALAM, *Marriage and the Family.*

[53] See R. JEFFREY, *The Decline of Nayar Dominance,* 23-26. See also L. LOPEZ, *A Social History,* 33-39. Slave system existed till the coming of the missionaries from England.

[54] See S. MATEER, *The Land of Charity ,* 35.

[55] See WHITEHOUSE, «To Tidman, Seminary Report», CWMA. See also R.S. SINCLAIR. «To Foster, Report of the Parachaley Mission», CWMA; H.T. WILLS, «To Rev. F. Lenwood, Letter (Foreign Secretary of, LMS)», CWMA; J.W. GLADSTONE, *Protestant Christianity,* 61. 284-289; J. TOMBÉR, *Led by God's Hand,* 15.

[56] See J.W. GLADSTONE, *Protestant Christianity,* 224-231. It is interesting to note that with the coming up of the lower class in the social life, the Nairs felt that they were neglected by the non-Malayali Brahmins who dominated the government services. Paradoxically they sought moral support from Izhavas and Syrian Christians against the Non-Malayali Brahmin dominance.

community[57]. With the establishment of the Nair Service Society in 1914 for the exclusive development of Nairs, the community became a powerful institution in Kerala.

The Nairs had already established a status in the social life of Trivandrum and Kerala. All are basically associated with Hindu religion but need not be worshippers of the same God. Conversion to Christianity is a remote possibility due to caste identification though there are exceptions. Even if some like the Gospel message it is extremely difficult for them to receive baptism, for the reception of baptism creates another caste identification[58]. At the same time a good number of the Nairs have great respect for the Christians and even visit Churches. It may be paradoxical that the first martyr in South Travancore was a Nair convert called Neelakanta Pillai who took the name Devasahayam Pillai after his baptism[59].

2.3 *The Mukkuvar*

The Mukkuvar (plural of Mukkuva), probably a few among them, were the first to receive the Christian faith from the Apostle Thomas or at least the first Christian community in Trivandrum[60]. They were the fishermen and descendants of Dravidians who settled in South India before the coming of Aryans[61]. The name is very much related either to the sea based occupation or of geographical identity. In Tamil «Mukku» means «the tip» or «the corner». According to K. Ram, at least from the

---

[57] See L. LOPEZ, *A Social History*, 113-116.

[58] The possibility of a «non-baptized Christian» in the Indian context becomes relevant in this context. For a theological reflection see H. STAFFENER, *Jesus Christ*. See also M.M. THOMAS, *The Acknowledged Christ*.

[59] The historical facts regarding the conversion of Neelakanda Pillai and his martyrdom are given in detail by the famous Church historians. See C.M. AGUR, *Church History*, 279-286. See also D. FERROLI, *Jesuits in Malabar*, II, 367-372; E.P. ANTONY, «Hierarchy and the Community», 370-373. If the Jesuit Mission was not suppressed there would have been many converts from the Nair community. See *FX*, 337. Regarding the death of Neelakanda Pillai, although another version is given in the Travancore State Manual, the historical evidences show that it was a martyrdom. See V.N. AIYA, *Travancore State Manual*, II, 129-130.

[60] See M. ARATTUKULAM, «The Latin Catholics», 111-119.

[61] See E. THURSTON – K. RANGACHARI, eds., *Castes and Tribes*, V, 107. According to some «Mukkuva» is a tribe which lives near the sea-coast of Malayala, to the inland parts of which they seldom go, and beyond its limits any way they rarely venture. *Ibid.*, 106. In the context of Trivandrum we can say that all the Mukuvar are mostly Latin Catholics with the exception of a few who joined the Protestant denominations in this century. Though numerically less, there are Muslim fishermen and Hindu fishermen.

folk etymological point of view, «Mukkuvar» denotes the people who occupy the very tip or edge of the land mass[62].

In society, the Mukkuva community belongs to the lower class, despite their identification with the Catholic Church[63]. Nevertheless, like any other community in Kerala they had their own prestigious past identity. There exists sub-classes among the Mukkuvar themselves[64]. The majority of the Catholics of the present Diocese of Trivandrum is from the Mukkuva community. They have been faithful to the Catholic Church. Their faith supersedes their suffering, poverty and starvation.

> The Church is the central institution within the community and in a way the *raison d'etre* of the entire community. The priest is the ex-officio leader of the village. Despite the fact that indigenous leaders do exist, no major decisions in the village can be taken outside the priests authority. This also accounts for the internal organization of the community. The Church has a dominant say in the political, economic and social life of the people. By using the pulpit on Sundays the priest is both the spiritual and ideological leader. He has not only the monopoly of interpreting the Word of God but also of determining the social ethics of the community, telling its members what they can or cannot do[65].

---

[62] K. Ram gives the etymological meaning in the context of Kanyakumari district. But Kanyakumari was under Travancore till 1956. According to Thankkappan Achari, a fisheries scientist, there are lots of similarities among the Mukkuvar of Kanyakumari and Trivandrum and Quilon districts [Personal interview with Thakkappan Achari, Former Joint Director Kerala State Planning Board]. This term is commonly used in Trivandrum district also. According to A.K. Iyer the word «Mukkuvar» and «Moger» in Canarese come from the same root, which means «to dive». See K. RAM, *Mukkuvar Women*, 1.

[63] For centuries Mukkuvar have been looked down with contempt by caste Hindus as well as the caste Christians. See K.J. JOHN, «Emergence of Latin Christians», 347-354. There is no doubt that the missionaries, whether from Portugal or from Goa, who worked among them did not do much for their social emancipation. They failed to understand the cultural identity of the people and the intellectual calibre which St. Francis Xavier himself had realized. The changes that are taking place from 1960 need special mention. See J. ALBARIS, *The Trivandrum Latin Diocese*. After the fishermen's agitation, starting from 1972, we see a new awakening among the Mukkuvar community. See J.J. KALEECKAL, *Oru Samara Katha* (History of a Struggle). See also N. NAYAK, *A Struggle within the Struggle*.

[64] The cultural differences existing between the neighbouring parishes like Poothura and Anjengo, St. Andrew's and Puthenthope, St. Andrew's and Fathimapuram, are typical example of such cultural complexities. Although they live within a distance of one mile having the same occupation, same social status in relation to other communities, and the same faith under the same diocese, there are no inter marriages.

[65] F. HOUTART – N. NAYAK, *Kerala Fishermen*, 6. This book sheds light on the different socio-cultural and religious aspects of fishermen belonging to Catholic, Hindu and Muslim communities in Kerala.

It is true that some of the traditions introduced among the people by the missionaries hindered their social uplift. The concern that St. Francis Xavier had for them and the vision the subsequent Jesuit missionaries carried out in the 17th century were shattered by the suppression of the Jesuit order in Kerala. The lack of concern for the people by the succeeding clergy added to the social situation existing in the society made their situation *worse* than that of Dalits of Kerala.

2.4 *The Nadars (Shānārs)*

The next major caste in the Diocese of Trivandrum is Nadars, who were known as shānārs. They are widely found in the States of Tamil Nadu and in Kerala. Most of the Nadars are settled in Trivandrum[66]. As in the case of most of the Hindu castes in India, the Nadars have their own legendary divine origin[67], and practice Hinduism in their own way[68]. The hereditary occupation of the Nadars was that of cultivating and climbing the palmyra palm, the juice of which they boil into a coarse sugar. They claim that they are the descendants of Chera, Chola and Pandya kings, though sociologist like R. Caldwell and R.L. Hardgrave do not agree with their claim. Neverthless, in the social structure, the Nadars occupied «a social limbo somewhere between the Sūdras [Nairs] and the out-caste untouchables»[69]. This «social limbo», was not accepted by most of the Nadars and even the Nadar women revolted[70] against the higher caste in the beginning of the 19th century under the leadership of Muthukutty

---

[66] Many Nadars hold the view that they had come to South Travancore at the invitation of Travancore King probably in the sixteenth century when the Travancore King held control of the southern region of Tinnevelly, including the sandy wastes of Manadu. See R.L. HARDGRAVE, JR., *The Nadars of Tamilnad*, 56.

[67] See R.L. HARDGRAVE, JR., *The Nadars of Tamilnad*, 19-20.273-274. See also E. THURSTON – K. RANGACHARI, *Castes and Tribes*, VI, 363-378.

[68] In a typical Shānār house, a room on the south-western part is always kept separate as a sacred place with a basket containing ashes in it. The senior male member of the family alone can enter into it. This leads to an inference that the head of the family originally acted as the family priest. See V.N. AIYA, *Travancore State Manual*, II, 393-398.

[69] R.L. HARDGRAVE, JR., *The Nadars of Tamilnad*, 21.

[70] The Nadar women revolted in 1859 for the right to wear *Melmundu* (upper cloth) as any other Brahmin women. The revolt was known as *Melmundu Samaram* or *Canar lahala* (Upper cloth revolt). According to social historians this was the first agitation against the inequality existing in South India. For a detailed study on the revolt see R.N. YESUDAS, *A People's Revolt.* See also N.K. JOSE, *Cānar Lahala* (Shānār Revolt or Upper Cloth Revolt).

Swami, who founded the *Samattuva Samajam* (an association to establish equality), which in turn influenced the Izhava caste and Kerala renaissance under the leadership of Sri Narayana Guru (1856-1928)[71].

There also exist sub-castes within the same caste mainly based on one's profession[72]. The social set up of Nadars is very peculiar that even the missionaries who worked among the Nadars could not understand them[73]. R. Caldwell writes:

> In some respects the position of the Shanars in the scale of castes is peculiar. Their abstinence from spirituous liquors and from beef, and the circumstance that their widows are not allowed to marry again, connect them with the Sudra group of classes. On the other hand, they are not allowed as all Sudras are, to enter the temples; and where old native usuages still prevail, they are not allowed even to enter the courts of justice, but are obliged to offer their prayers to the gods and their complaints to the magistrates outside, and their women, like those of the castes still lower, are obliged to go uncovered from waist upwards. These circumstances connect them with the group of castes inferior to the Sudras; but if they must be classed with that group, they are undoubtedly to be regarded as forming the highest division of it[74].

The peculiarity in social life is reflected in religious life both in Hinduism and in Christianity. In their Hindu religious practices, the Nadars were very much influenced by Brahminical Hinduism but not the

---

[71] Muthukutty Swami took the name Vaikunda Swami and erected a temple at Santhithope near Kannyakumari. See R. PONNU, «Vaikunda Swami», 186-199. In the religious history of Travancore the emergence of a new sect devoted to Muthukkutti, the first social reformer in South Travancore, was also remarkable. Muthukutti claimed that he is the incarnation of Viṣṇu. The religious practice, according to S. Mateer, is a combination of Hinduism and *demonolatry*. Since the death of Muthukutti (1848), he has been worshipped by his followers as a manifestation of the Supreme God. See S. MATEER, *The Land of Charity*, 222-223.

[72] In olden days the caste was divided into the palm climbers, the agriculturists and the businessmen. See R.L. HARDGRAVE, JR, *The Nadars of Tamilnad*, 252. *Karukku-pattayār, Kalla, Natāti, Kodikkal, Mēl-nātar* are some of the sub-divisions seen in Tamil Nadu. See E. THURSTON – K. RANGACHARI, *Castes and Tribes*, VI, 376-377.

[73] The observation made by a Protestant missionary in 1856 is remarkable: «They wish to be Christians, but they wish also to be allowed to follow as much as possible the customs of their Fathers. They wish to be Christians, but they lack the courage boldly, consistently, and constantly to carry out their Christianity in all things, among their relations and before the heathens» (JAMESTOWN, *1856 A General Description*, CWMA). The missionaries, however, had high regard for the values that the Nadars have given to marriage. «The heathen Shanars regard the marriage relationship as sacred and permanent» (S. MATEER, *Pareychaley Report*, CWMA).

[74] R. CALDWELL, *Lectures on the Tinnelvelly Mission*, 44-45 quoted by R.L. HARDGRAVE, JR., *The Nadars of Tamilnad*, 22.

«orthodox one»[75]. They are not religious fanatics though the Hindu revivalism throughout India under the political power of Bharathiya Janatha Party, influences the Nadar Hindus at present. A glaring difference is seen among the Hindu Nadars[76], Catholic Nadars and Protestant Nadars[77]. With the advent of the Catholic and Protestant missionaries a good number of Nadars embraced Christianity[78], without leaving their caste identity and social customs. This caused a formation of complex culture within the same caste[79], which in turn calls our attention to the importance of dialogue and ecumenism. The ecclesial life of the Catholic Nadars also deserve special study as it was the major Catholic community in the Diocese of Trivandrum till the annexation of the old *Padroado* portion of the Cochin Diocese to Trivandrum in 1955.

---

[75] R. CALDWELL, *The Tinnevelly Shanars*, 5. The Nadars considered themselves to be called a priestly class. The priests are the elders of the family. See V.N. AIYA, *Travancore State Manual*, II,395. They worshipped male and female deities. *Mādan* is one of the important deities which the Hindu Nadars worship with great fear because they believe that it can harm human beings and animals. *Bhadrakāi* is the tutelary deity of the Nadars. See J.G. GLADSTONE, *Protestant Christianity*, 27-31. *Bhadrakāi* was worshipped also by the Mukuvar. See *FX*, 465.

[76] Many Hindus were converted to Christianity. At present conversions are a few, but Christian fellowship attracts the Hindu Nadars to Christianity. Often Hindu Nadar girls do not find it difficult to marry a Christian. And often the converted Christians are more *fervent* in Christian religious practices. See S.B. HARPER, «Ironies of Indigenization», 13-20.

[77] Until recently, from the religious point of view, there was no healthy relation between Catholic Nadars and Protestant Nadars. This was mainly due to the general attitude of Catholic Church and Protestant Churches. A typical example is one with regard to marriage. Though the Catholic Church allows mixed marriages in principle, in the concrete situations priests do not recommend it in the Catholic Church at least in Kerala and in Tamil Nadu. The present Church of South India (C.S.I.) Bishop Samuel Amirtham, the former Vice-Chairman of the World Council of Churches is ready to have an ecumenical solution to the problems regarding the marriages between Catholics and Protestants of Nadar, Izhava and communities of Dalit castes. This issue may not be very relevant among the other Latin or Syrian dioceses of Kerala [Personal interview with Bishop S. Amirtham on 10-6-1994].

[78] For further study see P. DEVADAS, *Kālpāṭukal* (Footprints [Social & Church History]). See also F. KILIYAMPURAKAL, *Aloysius Maria Benziger*.

[79] One of the characteristics of the Nadar families is the presence of Hindus, Catholics, and Protestants in the same family. It is an undeniable fact that Christianity has greatly influenced the social emancipation of the Nadar castes. After the period of St. Francis Xavier, it was among this caste that many conversion works had taken place in Travancore.

2.5 *The Izhavas*

The Izhavas like the Nadars and Mukkuvar were also one of the suppressed castes in the Kerala society. K.P.P. Menon, a Kerala Historian, supported by the famous ethnologist E. Thurston, who made an extensive study on the South Indian castes, traces the origin of the Izhava community to Ceylon (Sri Lanka)[80]. Wherever be their origin, as a single caste, Izhavas are the major caste in the State of Kerala. If Nadars were palmyra climbers by profession, Izhavas were coconut palm climbers. There are also weavers, boatmen and traders among the community[81]. They occupied more or less the same social position in the northern districts of Kerala which the Nadars occupied in the southern districts. As far as religion is concerned they were not allowed entry into the Hindu temples though they themselves were Hindus. The religious practices were also very similar to the Nadars at least up to the time of Nanu Samy, who became known as Sri Narayana Guru. Sri Narayana Guru, the spiritual and social leader of Kerala renaissance, played a significant role in the uplift of the Izhava caste in the society[82].

Although Izhavas are a minority group in the Diocese of Trivandrum, the Izhava Catholics have contributed remarkably well to the growth of the local Church of Trivandrum without losing their caste identity[83]. They received the Christian faith two centuries ago. Their faith in the Catholic Church was so strong that they remained in the Catholic Church even during the adverse situation of the Hindu revival movement initiated by Sri Narayana Guru. It is because of their strong faith in the Catholic Church that Sri Narayana Guru got the insight to say, *Matam Etāyālum*

---

[80] See K.P.P. MENON, *History of Kerala* III, 424. See also E. THURSTON – K. RANGACHARI, *Castes and Tribes*, VI, 376-377; ID., *Castes and Tribes*, VII, 37; V.T. SAMUEL, *One Caste, One Religion, One God*, 24-42.

[81] See S. MATEER, *Native Life in Travancore*, 83-91.

[82] See V.T. SAMUEL, *One Caste, One Religion, One God*, 29-42.

[83] Throughout Travancore the Catholic and Protestant missionaries converted Izhavas into Christianity simultaneously in the 19th century. Many of the Izhava converts lost their caste identity and took on western names and life style. The Izhavas of Kamukincode and nearby places kept up the caste identity and accepted Christianity. It shows that the Izhavas at Kamukincode were culturally in an upper position. The inborn talents of the people in Astrology, Ayurvedic Medicine and literature are examples of their cultural heritage. See A. PETER, «Yuvākale Unarū» (Youth Wake Up!) [no page numbering]. A. Xavier, a writer from the same community, holds the view that Izhavas should rise above the caste feelings. See A. XAVIER, «Kamukinkōdum miṣanarimārum» [no page numbering].

Manuṣan Nannāyal Mati (Whatever be the religion, it is enough that man becomes good)[84].

The Izhavas, although they are a minority in the Diocese of Trivandrum there are vocations to the priesthood and religious life from among them. A deep understanding of this caste is needed because of the socio-religious problems the community faces today especially in the case of marriage. As caste dominates over religion in South Travancore, to get a partner from the same caste having the same faith becomes a great problem. Like the Nadars, Izhavas are divided into different religions and denominations though the majority are Hindus. Many girls who are born and brought up in strong Catholic faith may find it difficult to get a bridegroom from the same community, professing the same faith. As the Hindu revival movement is at its peak the Izhava community calls the attention of the Church to have a meaningful initiative as regards ecumenism and dialogue.

2.6 *The Dalits*

The most oppressed castes in the society are called the Scheduled Castes and Scheduled Tribes. The Pulayas, the Pariahs, the Kuravas, the Vedas, the Kanikars are some of them. Though all these castes were the most oppressed by the caste dominated society of Kerala a close study reveals that all of them had a glorious past[85]. According to some historians the Pulayas are the earliest inhabitants of Kerala. The Pariahs had higher position in the society before the coming of Brahmins[86]. In the cast

---

84 When Sri Narayana Guru had enthroned Śiva, the Hindu God, at Aruvippuram (1888), an act that could never be imagined from a lower caste Hindu in the last century, the Izhavas of Kamukincode approached the Guru with a request of re-converting the Izhava Christians to Hinduism. Most probably it was in that context that the Guru had said *Matam Etāyālum Maṇṣan Nannāyāl Mati* (Whatever be the religion it is enough that man becomes good). See K.G. VIJAYAKUMAR, «Kerala Samskārattinu Oru Anubandhanam» (An Appendix to the Kerala Culture)» [no page numbering]. See also M. NETTO, «Kamukinkode Idavaka Caritram» (History of the Kamukinkode Parish).

85 There is a belief in Trivandrum that there was a Pulaya king who had a fort. From the etymology of the place Pulayanar Kotta, the Fort of the Pulayan, it is reasonable to accept the tradition of the Pulaya king in olden days. See J.W. GLADSTONE, *Protestant Christianity*, 33-44. «[...] we should not forget the fact that in all communities there have been honourable persons who were an asset to the nation» (D.T. SWAMI, *History of Hindu Imperialism*, 9-10).

86 The *Pariahs* also claim that they enjoyed a higher position in Kerala before the coming of Brahmins. «It has been traced that in many traditions and customs there are

ridden society they were mainly treated as slaves for a long time[87]. Mahatma Gandhi called the most oppressed caste in India «Harijans», which means children of God. B.R. Ambedkar, one of the main architects of India's constitution, preferred to call the lowest class as «untouchables»[88]. Now the oppressed classes call themselves Dalits. There are 103 sub-divisions in the oppressed castes in the Trivandrum district[89]. S. Mateer wrote regarding the situation of the slave castes in Travancore like this:

> Could we depict in true and vivid colours the miseries and woes of the Pulayas and other slave population of Travancore, the hearts of readers would melt with pity and compassion for their temporal sufferings and spiritual danger. Mention can only be made of some of the bare facts as to how the inhuman system of caste affects the poor Pulayan in his person, his house and family, his business, his religious worship, and, in short, throughout the whole of his wretched life[90].

In the social history of Travancore the Dalits were not only oppressed by the caste Hindus but also by the caste Christians whether they were Catholics or Protestants[91]. R. Jeffrey writes:

---

many points of similarity or connection between the Parayas and the Brahmins» (J.W. GLADSTONE, *Protestant Christianity*, 37).

[87] The condition of slaves in Travancore is said to have been like this: «In former times slaves were let or transferred at the choice of the owner, were offered as presents to friends or as gifts to temples, and were bought, sold, or mortgaged in the same manner as the land on which they dwelt or as the cattle and other property of their owners» (S. MATEER, *The Land of Charity*, 44).

[88] B.R. Ambedkar himself was born in a untouchable family. See B.R. AMBEDKAR, *Slavery and Untouchability*. See also J. MALIEKAL, *Caste in India Today*, 80.

[89] See M. VIJAYANUNNI, *District Census Handbook*, 6.

[90] S. MATEER, *The Land of Charity*, 44.

[91] Archbishop Menzes of Goa was interested in the Dalits and he wanted to propagate Christianity among them and even sent a few priests to work among them. However, their work among them was not successful. See E. THURSTON – K. RANGACHARI, *Castes and Tribes*, VI, 376-377. See also ID., *Castes and Tribes*, IV, 390. Many missionaries thought that if they could win over the caste Hindus, it would be easy for them to convert the oppressed class. See B.R. AMBEDKAR, *Christianizing the Untouchables*, 26-81. Some missionaries in principle loved the Dalits and worked for them but influenced by the systems of Travancore they could not consider the Dalits as equal. When one of the pioneers of the Protestant missionaries Charles Mead wished to marry a Dalit woman, after the death of his wife, other Protestant missionaries raised strong objection. It was unthinkable for some missionaries that a Missionary marry a native woman belonging to Pariah caste. It was paradoxical that most of the missionaries were at the same time preaching for inter caste marriages. See C. MAULT, *To C. Mead*, Letter, CWMA. See also RUSSEL – LEWIS – WHITEHOUSE, *To C. Mead*, Letter, CWMA; *Correspondence*

Conversion [of slave castes] to Christianity was their only road to improvement; but they had so little to offer — their resources both of status and of material things were non-existent — that some missionaries were reluctant to accept them. They saw that slave-caste converts would lower the prestige of the mission and make it difficult for them to retain Syrian Christians or to convert members of higher castes[92.]

Following the Nadars in the early 19th century and Nairs and Izhavas in the last quarter of 19th century the Dalits also became aware of their depressed situation and entered into the arena of social reform under the leadership of Ayyan Kali (1863-1941), from the Pulaya caste, a native of Trivandrum[93]. His persistent effort to reform the community was crowned with continuous success. He fought for the right to use the public roads and established the right to enter markets. He realized that the redemption of backward class was possible only through education. He represented to the government that the Pulaya children should be given admission in government schools and in 1904 he himself started a school at Venganoor. When the Izhavas joined with the Nairs against Pulayas, Ayyan Kali sought the support of Sri Narayana Guru[94]. In 1905 he organized *Sadhu Jana Paripalana Sangam* (Organization for the Welfare of the Poor) like that of *Sree Narayana Dharma Paripalana* (SNDP) organized by Sri Narayana Guru and Dr. Palpu. As a result of the strenuous struggle carried on by the backward and depressed classes against caste discriminations by the high castes, there was a gradual change in the attitude of the governments of Travancore. It was decided to give representation to these classes in the Sri Moolam Assembly by nominating a representative[95].

Regarding Mr. Mead's marriage to a native woman, CWMA; C. MAULT, *To the Directors of LMS*, CWMA; J.W. GLADSTONE, *Protestant Christianity*, 191-194. The higher caste Christians did not foster the conversion of the oppressed class for the fear that they would not get slaves to work in their fields. See S. MATEER, *The Land of Charity*, 43.

[92] R. JEFFREY, *The Decline of Nayar Dominance*, 25.

[93] For a detailed description of the role played by Ayyan Kali for the awakening of the Backward castes see L. LOPEZ, *A Social History*, 162-167. See also J.W. GLADSTONE, *Protestant Christianity*, 265-305.

[94] See L. LOPEZ, *A Social History*, 163.

[95] See L. LOPEZ, *A Social History*, 165. Already in the last decade of the 19th century both British administration and the Travancore government began to take more interests in the education of the lowest class. See D. DUNCAN ESQ., *To the Chief Secretary to Government*, CWMA. The English missionaries played an important role to convince the Travancore government to support the lowest class in various ways. See *Minutes of the Travancore District Committee*. It was in 1912 that Ayyan Kali represented his community in the Assembly. He continued to be a nominated member for 28 years.

It was through the representation in the Sri Moolam Assembly that Ayyan Kali could raise his voice for the needs of the community before the government. The Christian missionaries also could not do justice to them as the missionaries were very much concerned about the higher class. No wonder that Ayyan Kali turned against Christians[96]. In the Riots of 1914-15 the Hindu Pulayas and Christian Pulayas joined together against the Nairs[97]. Following the riots Ayyan Kali instructed the Pulaya women not to wear their traditional chains with a kind of stone beads and glass pieces which symbolized the lower class and servitude. Instead, he asked them to dress decently covering the upper part of their body, as in the case of any other higher castes. These social changes introduced among the backward class had a great influence in society. This was the beginning of the change in the concept of *right for the upper class* and *duties for the lower class*.

The social situation of the Dalit Christians in the Diocese of Trivandrum is to be understood in the above mentioned background. In the Diocese of Trivandrum there are about 20.000 Dalit Christians[98]. Since the government takes repressive measures against the Christian Dalits many cannot profess the faith publicly[99]. In comparison with the early period of this century we notice that there is a decline in the number of Dalit Christians in the Diocese of Trivandrum. There are

---

[96] See H.T. WILLS, *Trivandrum City-1914*, CWMA. According to the missionaries the government favoured the Pulayas to keep them in Hinduism. See J.W. GLADSTONE, *Protestant Christianity*, 294.

[97] R. SINCLAIR, *To Foster, Report of the Parachaley Mission*, CWMA. See also J.W. GLADSTONE, *Protestant Christianity*, 284-289. Here also the caste dominates over religion.

[98] Report on the Dalit Christians prepared by Devadas [TSSS, 1994]. A report of Fr. Ildaphonse O.C.D., a missionary who worked in the Diocese of Trivandrum, lists twenty *Dalit* Churches in the *Summarium Relationum Annualium Districts Trevandrum – Neyyattinkara a 1 Juli 1931- ad 30 Juni 1932, AGOCD*.

[99] In Kerala the government takes various measures to uplift the Dalits. However, they are only for the Hindu Dalits. Because of the unhealthy attitude of the government towards the Christians, many Dalits even leave the Church. In the present social situation to be a Dalit and Christian is a challenge. How far the Catholic Church in Kerala succeeds in fighting for the rights of the Dalit Christians is questionable. «A problem that is getting more and more serious is the situation of the so-called *Dalit Christians*. We have a large number of them in our Regions — in Andhra, in Kerala, and in the Western Region, who on being converted to the Faith lose, by Civil law, the financial aid and other benefits that the Hindu Dalits get» (S. PIMENTA, «La nostra Chiesa», 7). For the social problems that the Dalits are bearing after conversion see J. KAIMLETT, *An Evaluation of the Protective Legislation*, 51-91. See also V.R.K. IYER, *Justice in Words*; J. KANANAIKIL, *Scheduled Castes in Search of Justice*.

socio-political reasons for the decline in the number of Dalits in the Church but the Diocese has to understand the Dalits also in the context of other Christian denominations in Trivandrum[100].

The ritual status of a caste carried its privileges or disabilities which we may regard as «resources» of a kind. Similarly, in the changing economic and social situation which developed in Travancore from the 1850s, a caste's traditional customs and occupations could be an advantage or a drawback[101]. In light of the contemporary situation there is no possibility of abolition of castes in the near future. And it is in this caste ridden social situation that we discuss the religious background of Trivandrum. For it is in the religious context that we can understand better the culture of the people whether Brahmanic or non-Brahmanic, Islamic or Christian[102].

3. The Religious Context

Kerala became a meeting place for all the Indian religions and philosophical systems at a very early period of its history. Foreign religions such as Christianity and Islam are well rooted in Kerala adding to the multiplicity of native religions which included Jainism, Buddhism and Hinduism. Generally there is religious *harmony* among the religions. Neverthless, there is a lot of change in the attitude towards religion, as religion in Kerala at present is becoming more of a cultural inheritance rather than the fact of one's conviction[103]. In this section we first discuss Buddhism and Jainism because of their profound influence at least indirectly in Kerala and in India. It will be continued with the discussion of the important religions like Hinduism, Islam and Christianity which pertain to our study directly.

---

100 The Dalits, when they accept Christianity, lose privileges, especially in the field of education and employment. The Church on the other hand failed to extend a helping hand to the Dalits like that of Muthukutty Swami for Nadars, Sri Narayan Guru for the Izhavas and Ayyan Kali, for the Pulayas. Till the «Living Together» of the priests of Trivandrum, no substantial work was done for the uplift of the Dalits. See X. ALEXANDER, ed., *Report of the Commission*, ADT. We will describe the «Living Together» of priests of Trivandrum in the third chapter.

101 See R. JEFFREY, *The Decline of Nayar Dominance*, 9. See also A.S. MENON, *Social and Cultural History*, 65-75.

102 To understand the inner dynamism of culture in the Indian context see M. AMALADOSS, *Becoming Indian*, 20-37.

103 J.T. ERINJERY, *Coalition Game Politics*, 15.

3.1 *Jainism and Buddhism*

Both Jainism and Buddhism originated as a reaction to Brahmanical authority and its ritualistic religiosity. They are known as *śramaṇa* or *nāstika* against *āstika* (Brahmanic) religions. They followed a set of ethical principles and admitted into their communion the common people notwithstanding the caste and creed[104].

Jainism[105] was probably introduced into Kerala in the 3rd century B.C. It had a religious impact on the people before the Christian era. The central virtue of Jainism is *ahimsa* or non-injury to living beings, which has much influenced the non-violent policy of Mahatma Gandhi. It was with the *Saivite* and *Vaiṣṇavite* movements[106] that Jainism declined in Kerala. The ascetic severity was also one of the reasons for its unpopularity[107]. According to historians, Jainism had influenced the architecture of temples and mosques of Kerala[108].

Buddhism[109] was brought to South India by the Buddhist missionaries, probably during the reign of Ashoka in the 3rd century B.C.[110] Buddhism rejected the appeal to revelation and in particular Brahmanical claims for

---

[104] See AA. VV., *The Cultural Heritage of India*, I.

[105] Jainism is both a religion and a philosophy. The name Jainism derives from the term *jina* (conqueror or victor) applied to the 24 great religious persons on whose examples the religion is centred, and its followers are known as Jainas or Jains. Jainism arose about the 6th century B.C. in protest against the orthodox Vedic ritualistic cult of the period. Jainism was founded by Vardhamana Mahavira (599-527 B.C.).

[106] *Vaisnavism* is a creed, within the Hindu fold, based on the authority of the four Vedas. The term Śiva stands for auspiciousness and *Śaivism*, is the school of thought which adores the Auspicious Being. In effect the the followers of *Vaisnavites* are those who worship Visnu as their personal God and *Śaivites* are those who worship Śiva as the personal God. See M.D. CHATURVEDI, *Hinduism*, 167-173.

[107] The Jain ascetics wear masks so that they do not inadvertently inhale insects and harm them. See N. SMART, *The World's Religions*, 68-71.

[108] See W. LOGAN, *Malabar Manual*, 1, 185-186. See also A.S. MENON, *A Survey of Kerala History*, 88-89; V.T. SAMUEL, *One Caste, One Religion, One God*, 12-13.

[109] Buddhism is an Indian religion founded by Sidhartha Gautama, who was born about 563 B.C. and died between 486 and 473 B.C. Sidhartha, in his search to remove suffering from the world, became the enlightened, the Buddha. The Buddha emerged as the leader of a band of the followers who pursued the «Middle Way» between extreme asceticism and worldly life. See A.L. BASHAM, «Jainism and Buddhism», 37-202. See also AA. VV., *The World's Great Religions*; V.T. SAMUEL, *One Caste, One Religion, One God*, 12-13.

[110] A.S. MENON, *A Survey of Kerala History*, 92.

the Vedas[111]. In contrast to Brahmanical teachings, the Buddhist teaching was simple and ethical[112]. Together with the ethical principles and its eight fold paths[113], Buddhism created a profound impact on the people. The Buddha preached against animal sacrifices and pleaded for mercy towards all living being. His earnest exhortation for practicing righteousness and self-renunciation, his message to the people in their own vernacular language and his exhortation for abolition of castes made his religion more popular. However, Buddhism faded in Kerala as a religion, though the doctrines are very much appreciated[114]. Among all his teachings, perhaps the practice of Yōga has influenced the people both in the east and in the west the most. From the Christian point of view, a good understanding of Buddhism is required even to dialogue with the Hindus.

Although both Jainism and Buddhism have not many followers as such in Trivandrum/ Kerala, the doctrinal impact of these religions contribute to the cultural growth of the place.

---

[111] According to Buddha a true Brahmin was not the one born into a priestly class, but the person who followed virtue and self-control. See N. SMART, *The World's Religions*, 56-67.

[112] According to Buddhism, our actions should be controlled by the Five Precepts: One should refrain from taking life, from taking what is not given, from wrong sex, from wrong speech, and from drugs-substances which obstruct self-awareness. See N. SMART, *The World's Religions*, 63.

[113] The eight fold paths are: Right belief, Right attitude, Right speech, Right bodily action, Right livelihood, Right effort, Right self-awareness, and Right meditation.

[114] The failure of Buddhism is also attributed to the corrupt religious practices and rigid rules which existed in the course of time. «Gross idolatry in practice, formal atheism in doctrine, a regular army of monks and nuns everywhere eating up the substance of the industrious and charged with the worst evils of decayed monasticism, were only a few of its bad features» (See V.N. AIYA, *Travancore State Manual*, II, 44). It is also reasonable to think that since caste system was the general rule of the region, the idea of casteless society was unthinkable to the people. Moreover the Hindu revivalism through the Vedic interpretations by Sri Sankara (788 – 820 AD.), the native of Kerala, gave a new impetus to the Brahmanic class which also caused the decline of Buddhism in Kerala. For a detailed study on Sri Sankara see A. THOTTAKARA, «Sankara», 35-68. According to N. Smart, a major reason for of Buddhism's success was its cultural adaptability and that in a sense too was the cause of its demise in India since it merged so successfully with Hindu culture that the latter took it over. See N. SMART, *The World's Religions*, 71.

3.2 *Hindu Religious Influence*

Hinduism is a very comprehensive term and has many shades and degrees of varying forms in it ranging from Brahmanism, the highest, the purest and the most philosophical form of theism, to the fetish worship of the aboriginal castes, which is the religion of the crudest type imaginable[115]. Hinduism is not the proper and original name. This was the name given to it by foreigners. The original and more suggestive name is *Sanātana Dharma*, which stands for the eternal spiritual truths enunciated by the Vedic Seers. In the past, the river *Indus* formed the north western boundary of India. It was then called Sindhu. The Persians pronounced it as «Hindu» and therefore began to designate the Aryans living on the side of the river as Hindus, and their religion Hinduism. The name possessed nothing more than a territorial significance and conveyed no hints or suggestions about the religion of the people to whom it was applied. With the passage of time the word Hinduism supplanted the original name *Sanātana Dharma*.[116] Despite the complexities of religious practices it is admirable that Hinduism has its own concepts about the present life which in turn calls for the personal responsibility of each person.

According to Hinduism the present life is explained by the previous one. Hence, human life is called *karma-samsāra,* a cycle of birth and rebirth determined by the law of retribution[117]. Hinduism is professed by more than two-thirds of the entire population of India and has exerted a profound influence on its culture, philosophy, arts and architecture, literature, laws, politics and sociology in the past and continues to mould at present the lives of millions from birth to death. It would not be an

---

115 V.N. AIYA, *Travancore State Manual,* II, 39.

116 See J.P. SUDA, *Religions in India,* 44. See also D. ACHARUPARAMBIL, «Hinduism», 256-265; M.D. CHATURVEDI, *Hinduism,* 1-10.

117 See M.D. CHATURVEDI, *Hinduism,* 100-106. The only means to break the cycle of birth and rebirth and thus attain the final liberation from bondage is knowledge (*jñana*) See A. THOTTAKARA, «Sankara», 35-68. «The main justification of belief in rebirth is to account for life's perennial problem of evil, inequalities, suffering, etc. It says that each one is responsible for one's fate; God is not partial to anybody. This idea enables people to face the trials of life with a sense of resignation and security. Obviously belief in rebirth is incompatible with Christian faith which upholds the unicity of human life ruled by the law of grace» (D. ACHARUPARAMBIL, «Hinduism», 260-261). See also ID., *Spiritualità e mistica indù.*

exaggeration to say that without Hinduism India would be a geographical expression of the past, a dim memory of a perished glory[118].

The characteristic feature of Hinduism is that a Hindu is born not made. Unlike Christianity and Islam, Hinduism does not convert anybody. It does not oppose the progress of any other system. It has no difficulty in including all other religions within its all-embracing arms. Adaptability to the infinite diversity of human characters and human tendencies is one of its important characteristics[119]. As a term of religious significance the word «Hindu» is restricted to those who believe in the Vedas[120]. After Vedas, *Puraṇās* and *Itihāsas* clarify the Hindu *dharma,* religious doctrine. Hinduism, in short, may be understood as the sum total of the religious beliefs, doctrines, rites, and codes or rules of conduct contained in the Vedas, *Purānas* and *Itihāsas* — Ramayana and Mahabharata[121]. The Gīta, the song divine in the Mahabharata, is a unique work which not only represents the philosophy of Hinduism but also reveals certain definite schemes by which every individual can work out his own self-improvement[122].

Apart from the philosophical explanations, the crux of Hinduism lies in the worship of the Supreme Being. *Ekameva Advatīyam Brahma*

---

[118] See J.P. SUDA, *Religions in India*, 44.

[119] «It has its highly spiritual and abstract side suited to the metaphysical philosopher — its practical and concrete side suited to the man of affairs and the man of the world — its aesthetic and ceremonial side suited to the man of poetic feeling and imagination — its quiescent and contemplative side suited to the man of peace and lover of seclusion. Nay, it holds out the right hand of brotherhood to nature worshippers, demon worshippers, animal worshippers, tree worshippers and fetish worshippers» (V.N. AIYA, *Travancore State Manual,* II, 41-42).

[120] The term «Veda» is defined as knowledge or sacred lore embracing a body of writings the origin of which is ascribed to divine revelation. The foundation of Veda is called *sruti* (revelation), that which is heard. The walls of Veda is called *Smṛiti* (memory) that which comes down through the ages from memory. The Vedas are four: (i) the *Rgveda* (Veda of hymns), (ii) the *Yajurveda* (*mantras* relating to sacrificial rituals to God, (iii) *Sāmaveda* (Veda of music) and (iv) the *Atharvaveda* (Veda dealing with spells and incantations, sciences, such as the medical science, biology and its attainment through *mantra*). Each Veda consists mainly of three parts: (i) *Samhitā,* a collection of hymns addressed to various gods and goddesses (composed some time between 2000 B.C.and 1000 B.C); (ii) *Brāhmaṇa,* the liturgical texts ((1000-800 B.C.); and (iii) *Upaniṣad,* the philosophico-mystical texts (800-300 B.C.) See M.D. CHATURVEDI, *Hinduism,* 11-29. See also D. ACHARUPARAMBIL, «Hinduism», 257; V.N. AIYA, *Travancore State Manual,* II, 45-49; K. SIVARAMAN, ed., *Hindu Spirituality,* 5-85.

[121] For a further study on Hinduism see M. DHAVAMONY, *Classical Hinduism*; D. ACHARUPARAMBIL, *Induismo.*

[122] See M.D. CHATURVEDI, *Hinduism,* 51-53.

(Brahman alone exists without a second)[123]. The one Supreme Being is worshipped in three aspects as Brahma, Viṣṇu and Siva, representing respectively the threefold function of creation, preservation and destruction *(Sṛṣṭhi, Stiti and Samhāra)*. According to higher conceptions of Hindus, all three are equal, no one taking precedence over the other. Their functions are sometimes interchangeable so that each may take the place of the other[124]. On the popular level all the prerogatives of the Supreme Reality are attributed to personal gods: Visnu *(Vaisnavism)* and Śiva *(Śaivism)*[125].

3.2.1 Hinduism and Its Influence in Trivandrum (Travancore)

Hinduism is the major religion in Trivandrum and in the whole of Travancore[126]. It has been sustained and supported by the State with all its power, wealth, and social influence. This had been so because of the socio-religious importance that Travancore inherited from time immemorial. According to S. Mateer, who studied the native lives of the people, Travancore retains the observance of most of the laws and institutions of Hinduism in their primitive form and obligation[127]. Viṣṇu, the second deity of the Hindu triad, is worshipped as the national deity of Travancore[128].

---

[123] Candaogya Upaniṣad Vi. 2-1 quoted in M.D. CHATURVEDI, *Hinduism*, 82.

[124] M.D. CHATURVEDI, *Hinduism*, 88-91. See V.N. AIYA, *Travancore State Manual*, II, 47-49.

[125] See D. ACHARUPARAMBIL, «Hinduism», 259. The differences between *Vaisnavism* and *Śivism* are not glaring in Kerala as in other parts of India. See A.S. MENON, *Social and Cultural History*, 188.

[126] As Travancore was one of the most important kingdoms of the present Kerala, reference to Travancore is applicable to the whole of Kerala. Since the Diocese extends over Kanyakumari district (now in Tamil Nadu) which was under Travancore till 1956, the mention about Travancore is reasonable. «Travancore is perhaps the only kingdom in India which preserves its original caste, religion, customs, manners, institutions» (P.S. MENON, *History of Travancore*, vii).

[127] See S. MATEER, *The Land of Charity*, 158-188.

[128] According to Hindu concept Brahmā is the creator, Viṣṇu is the redeemer and Śiva is the destroyer for renewal. The legend of the Viṣṇu Temple is the result of the vision of Viṣṇu to a Pulaya woman. Paradoxically the low castes were not allowed to enter the temple. See S. MATEER, *The Land of Charity*, 161-162. Viṣṇu has *Avatāras*. Nine times he has incarnated and descended on the earth. At his tenth advent, all things, it is said, are to be consummated, and the world resolved into himself. For the explanations on *Avatār* see F. DAY, *The Land of the Perumals*, 277-282. Viṣṇu is worshipped in different forms

3.2.2 Hindu Spirituality in Praxis in Trivandrum

The Hindus have a high concept of the Supreme Being. The Hindu spirituality cannot be distinguished from one's life and religious practices. In whatever manner they worship God or whatever be the prayers they recite and whatever be the festivals they celebrate, everything is aimed at the worship of the Supreme Being. The fear which they had to approach the Supreme Being was expressive in their various ceremonies including the coronation of the King. The spirituality of the *native people* is to be understood in the context of celebration of different festivals, their veneration of nature, *Pūjas* (offering) and *Mantravāta* (recitation of prayers) and different worships including *devil worship*.

3.2.3 Festivals: An Expression of Hindu Spirituality

The Hindu spiritual life is expressed in the celebration of different feasts. In addition to the special ceremonies occurring at occasional intervals, periodic festivals are observed at least once a year in connection with almost every temple, and are regarded as an essential part of Hindu worship; much merit being attributed to their bountiful and punctual celebration[129]. One of the popular festivals in Trivandrum is *Araṭu*. The «Arattu» or bathing festival, occurs twice a year, April and October. A festival, regarded as having much importance, and celebrated at great cost is called *Murajapam* or customary prayer. This occurs at intervals of six years, and is supposed to be eminently conducive to the defense of the kingdom and the people, the procuring of a regular supply of rain, and the general safety and prosperity of the country. It is also to atone for any imperfection, or sins of ignorance and omission, in other religious observances[130].

---

such as Vamana, Varaha, Parasurama, Sri Krishna, Narasimha, Sri Rama. Other major gods and goddesses are Siva, Bhagavati, Subramania, Sasta and Ganapati.

[129] See S. MATEER, *The Land of Charity*, 183. Without any scrupulosity they spent money for the celebration of festivals. The festivals celebrated in the Hindu Temples have, to a large extent, influenced the extravagant celebration of feasts in the Christian parishes in Kerala.

[130] Some of the important Hindu festivals are: 1. *Ponghal* (The boiled Rice Feast); 2. *Śrādha* (Funeral Offerings to deceased ancestors); 3. *Śiva Rāṭṛi* (Śiva's Watchful Night); 4. *Bharani* (in honour of *Kali*, wife of Śiva — originally a feast in honour of spring); 5. *Sri Rāma Navami*, (commemoration of the birthday of Rama); 6. *Viṣu* (astronomical new year); 7. *Ōṇam* (the most popular festival of Kerala). During the continuance of these festivals the Brahmins are supposed to be constantly engaged in offering special prayers

Another phenomenon we see in the spiritual practices of Hindus is the pilgrimage to Sabari Mala. A unique fellowship is experienced by the pilgrims during the time of penance and pilgrimage. Here women of ten to fifty years of age are not allowed to enter the temple. During the time of preparation for the pilgrimage they forget all caste distinctions[131].

3.2.4 Worship of Animals and Plants

Eco-spirituality is a new development in the Western world[132]. For a Hindu, all organic life is sacred. *Ahimsā parama dharma* (Non-violence is the greatest virtue) is his basic belief. A true Hindu, especially of the higher class, abhors the idea of killing any animal even for his sustenance. Even plants are respected and some are regarded with special reverence as the abode of or as being sacred to particular deities[133]. The cow is *Kamadhēnu*, the giver of all things[134]. Among the plants and trees the *Asvatha,* the *Bilva* and the *Tulasi* are important. The *Tulasi* is sacred to Viṣṇu. It is a domestic divinity worshipped daily by the women. Its wood is used for making rosaries which are worn round the neck and used for ejaculatory prayers[135].

---

for the sovereign and the kingdom at large. See S. MATEER, *The Land of Charity,* 167.184-188. See also F. DAY, *The Land of Perumals,* 285-290.

[131] See M. AMALADOSS, *Becoming Indian,* 31. See also A. NAMBIARPARAMBIL, «From the "SARANAM" of Sabarimala Pilgrimage», 227-232.

[132] See S. SPINSANTI, «Ecologia», 440-460. See also B. SECONDIN, *Nuovi cammini dello Spirito,* 271-274; A. THOTTAKARA, ed., *Eco-Spirituality.*

[133] The animals that are regarded as objects of worship are the cow, the serpent, the bull and the garuda. The serpant is worshipped as *Ādiesa* who supports the earth and is the cot of Maha Viṣṇu. No orthodox Hindu would dare to kill or otherwise hurt a snake especially a cobra, for it is a very common belief that those who accidentally or willfully kill a cobra will be punished in this life and in the next either by childlessness, leprosy or ophthalmia. A *Sarppakkavu* (special place dedicated to snakes as their abode), is very common throughout Travancore. However, the expansion of population causes to clear up many *kaus.* The bull is Śiva's vehicle and Garuda is *vāhanam* (vehicle) of Viṣṇu. See V.N. AIYA, *Travancore State Manual,* II, 57-62.

[134] To be born of a cow in a future birth is a high honour and a privilege. The five products of the cow (milk, curd, butter, urine and dung) are the elements of a composition the most efficacious for purification known to the Hindus. See S. MATEER, *The Land of Charity,* 170. See also V.N. AIYA, *Travancore State Manual,* II, 58.

[135] See V.N. AIYA, *Travancore State Manual,* II, 58.

3.2.5 Worship, *Pūja* and *Mantravāda*

Worship is the expression of love for the Supreme. Worship is called *Upāsanā* (to sit near the Lord). *Upāsanā* includes many forms of worship like meditation, *sandhya vandana* (worship at evening twilight)[136]. The *pūja* is a daily worship of a Hindu. Usually it is done by a Hindu priest called *Pūjari* or *pōtti*[137].Personal cleanliness and purity are scrupulously expected of him. He is also expected to live close to the temple. He is to do temple service for a period of six years during which, he is not to leave the temple or his dwelling - home called a *Matam*[138]. During the days of *Pūja,* he is not to allow himself to be touched by any one, not even by other Brahmins in which case he should have a fresh bath for resuming the *Pūja.* Such scrupulous observance of personal purity is one of the characteristic features of all the West Coast temples[139].

Mantravāda is practiced mostly by Brahmins. *Mantravāda* is not merely to propitiate the evil spirits but also to control it by spells, incantations, and penances. The method of worship is not by animal sacrifices but by *hōmams* (sacrifices) and *japams* (prayers) as in the worship of Siva and Viṣṇu. Some *Mantrams* (*japams* or *homams* used for *Mantravādam*) are supposed to have great efficacy, and by constant repetition with necessary ceremonial, the worshipper is believed to acquire the power of controlling the actions of the spirits[140].

3.2.6 Spiritual Praxis of the Lower Castes

The popular Hindu religion in Travancore is not philosophical[141]. Probably when the worship of major gods of Vedas or of Sanskrit tradition were forbidden by the Brahmanic castes, the suppressed castes

---

136 For different ways of worship see M.D. CHATURVEDI, *Hinduism,* 157-191.

137 In the Patmanabha Swami Temple in Trivandrum the Hindu Priest is called *Nambi Pōti.* See V.N. AIYA, *Travancore State Manual,* II, 74.

138 In Kerala the house of Religious women is called *maṭham* and the house of Religious men is called *Āśram.*

139 See V.N. AIYA, *Travancore State Manual,* II, 74, 84-85.

140 See V.N. AIYA, *Travancore State Manual,* II, 63. See also S. MATEER, *The Land of Charity,* 170.

141 This is true with all the great religions. For a theological reflection on the subject see M. AMALADOSS, *Becoming Indian,* 20-37. «Official religion, as a religion of the elites, stands challenged by the people's religiosity which today by its inner force and vitality is breaking down everywhere the barriers of conventional forms» (F. WILFRED, «Faith without "Faith"?», 594-613).

turned to gods of lower status. The religious practices were based on fear and ignorance. The popular religious practices are very much connected with demon worship, sorcery, witchcraft and magic[142]. Human and animal sacrifices to gods and goddesses were not uncommon. *Mādan*, *Kāli*, *Pattirakāli* are some of the popular gods[143].

The striking phenomon as regards the Hindu religious practices in Trivandrum is the clear distinction existing between the upper castes and the lower castes. Most of the great festivals were conducted by the higher caste Brahmins for their welfare. It is said that during the festivals the multitudes of Brahmins visited the capital to witness the performances. Police forces were also stationed to prevent the low caste people from entering or approaching the fort of the temple[144].

Religion is the human's fundamental option for God. Although the social systems objected to the lower castes worshipping the vedic gods, the lower castes had their own way of worshipping gods. In their worship we see the sign of the original Dravidic worship. The *demon worship*, as attributed by the higher castes and the missionaries, is one among them. Since most of the converts are from the *demon worshippers* we give some space to the description of *demon* worship in Travancore.

Many natives of Travancore (most of the parts of South India) worship «devils»[145]. The existence and prevalence of disease and suffering of every kind were, by the original inhabitants of India, ascribed to the agency of wicked spirits, and these spirits they thought it wise to propitiate by whatever offerings and acts of worship which appeared to them calculated to effect this purpose. Probably instinctive fear of

---

[142] See A.S. MENON, *Social and Cultural History*, 162-212. See also S. MATEER, *The The Land of Charity*, 158-229.

[143] *Mādan* is said to strike men and oxen with sudden illness. *Pattirakāli* is said to molest and kill women during the period of pregnancy. So the gods and goddess are worshipped in order to placate them. See S. MATEER, *The Land of Charity*, 194-195.

[144] See S. MATEER, *The Land of Charity*, 174. After a long agitation and interventions of people like Gandhi the low castes were allowed to enter the temple only on 12th November 1936. This event in the history of Kerala is known as «Temple Entry Proclamation». Gandhi remarked this event as «the modern miracle in Travancore» (*Complete Works of Mahatma Gandhi*, LXIV, 27). The fear of the conversion of people from low castes to Christianity was one of the important reasons for the «Temple Entry Proclamation». See J.W. GLADSTONE, *Protestant Christianity*, 403-413.

[145] Demonology is confined only to the lower orders and is absolutely unconnected with the higher forms of Hinduism, but a belief in the power for mischief possessed by the devils is widespread and even the Brahmins are not free from it. See V.N. AIYA, *Travancore State Manual*, II, 55-69. See also M. SEBASTIAN, *Kānikārute Lōkam* (The World of Kanikar).

departed souls is also one of the elements of this worship[146]. A personal experience given by S. Mateer shows how the devil worship is deeply rooted even among some of the Christians, though not common. He narrates:

> Yohannan [John] had been a steady and apparently consistent member of the church, and an elder in his congregation, for about twenty-five years. Most of his relatives remained in heathenism, and when he was attacked with serious illness they persuaded him that he had been bewitched, and that this illness had been caused by devil. Notwithstanding the protestations and advises of the catechist, Yohannan consented to the celebration of the usual ceremonies, and sent for devil [worshipping] priests to dig up the ground in front of his house, in search of the supposed hidden charm which had caused his illness. On hearing of this, I immediately sent two of our best native preachers to warn and exhort him, but their visit was in vain. He certainly denied having consented to the heathen rites, and assented to all that our catechists advanced, but the very next day these ceremonies were performed. [...] The fear of the demons is the last superstition that leaves the native mind[147].

Most of the new converts belonging to different castes joined Christianity with the above mentioned background. Even now, a good number of them have at least relatives who follow such practices. In contemplating the moral influence of the *devil* worship it is evident that it hardens the heart and increase cruelty, covetousness, worldliness, and other evil passions[148].

As an assessment we may say that the Diocese of Trivandrum is in many ways related with believers of Hinduism. Most of the Latin Catholics of the Trivandrum Diocese in Trivandrum district are converts from Hinduism and a good number of those converts still keep up the Hindu customs in their day to day life[149]. The characteristic difference is only in faith.

---

[146] See S. MATEER, *The Land of Charity*, 191-192.208. The Diamper Synod exhorted its clergymen from the superstitious and Heathen Exorcism taking words out of an impious and prohibited book called *Parisman* for casting out Devils. See M. GEDDES, *The History of the Church*, 299-302.

[147] S. MATEER, *The Land of Charity*, 212.

[148] See S. MATEER, *The Land of Charity*, 225.

[149] For example during the house blessing, digging wells, marriages, funerals, many people give importance to particular time considered auspicious in the Hindu calendar.

3.3 *The Muslims and Islam*

Muslims, account for 20% of the population and its own political party plays a vital role in the socio-religious context of Kerala[150]. The advent of Islam in Kerala, like that of Christianity, is not recorded and tradition takes the place of history[151]. But since traders from Arabia were sailing to the Malabar coast through out the period when Mohammed was carrying out his great conversions, one can assume that Muslims were living there as merchants no later than the middle of the 7th century[152].

The organized Islamic worship was first established in the merchant communities[153]. Many Arabs frequenting the Malabar coast took native women as wives or concubines, and the offspring of these unions were among the first *Moplahs* or *Mapillas*, as the native Muslims were called[154]. Islam, in the early period, did not come to Kerala as a conquering religion[155] as in the case of North India[156]. A change in the attitude of Muslims took place with the arrival of the Portuguese[157]. The real challenge (spread) of Islam in the land of Kerala took place with the coming of Hyder Ali and Tippu Sultan from Mysore. In 1757 Hyder Ali

---

150 According to S. Mateer they are an industrious and thriving people, principally engaged in trade and agriculture, and some are amongst the wealthiest of the inhabitants. The females are not secluded as in strictly Muslims countries. See S. MATEER, *The Land of Charity*, 227.

151 Like the Christians and Jews of Kerala, the Muslims believe Crangannore has been the first place where their religion was taught.

152 See G. WOODCOCK, *Kerala: A Portrait*, 130-131.

153 Ibn Batuta, the 14th century traveler, refers to the five mosques which stood as an ornament to the noble emporium of Quilon and bestows high praise on the generosity and power of its Hindu sovereigns. See K.P.P. MENON, *History of Kerala*, II, 532-563.

154 See G. WOODCOCK, *Kerala: A Portrait*, 130- 131.

155 The Arab merchants were fully supported by the native Kings as the Arabs who had a commercial relation with Kerala. G. Woodcock remarks that Arab Merchants never allowed religious fanaticism to spoil the smoothness of their relations with the Zamorines and the Nairs. See G. WOODCOCK, *Kerala: A Portrait*, 134.

156 F. DAY, *The Land of Perumals*, 355-373. Already in the 14th century Islam was a threat to Christianity. The Dominican Friars Peter of Sienna, Thomas of Tolontino, James of Padua were killed by Muslim leaders. See G.M. MORAES, *A History of Christianity*, 80-105.

157 Portuguese writers of the 15th and 16th centuries used the term «Moors» to denote all Malabar Muslims and this practice has been followed by the Dutch and the English. The word, as used by the Portuguese referred to religion only and implied no nationality. See K.P.P. MENON. *Kerala History*, II, 532. See also G. WOODCOCK, *Kerala: A Portrait*, 135. There was a conflict between Jesuits and Muslims near Vaipincotta in 1584 and the Church and the Jesuit residence were burned down. See J. KOLLAPARAMBIL, *The Thomas Christians' Revolution*, 76.

was a local Muslim commander in the service of the Hindu King of Mysore. His attention turned to Malabar and in 1763 he conquered territories on the northern boundaries of Malabar[158]. In 1766 he entered Kerala without much resistance from the small principalities of the Northern territory. However, he did not reach Travancore. His son and successor, Tippu Sultan, entered the northern part of Travancore and formed settlements in convenient places of Kerala. As a result Muslims spread over the coastal area.

Many of the Muslim pockets in Trivandrum are close to the Latin Catholics of the Diocese. Bheema Palli, Vizhinjam, Perumathura, Poovar, Pozhiyoor are the most important places where Catholics and Muslims live very close. At Vizhingam and Bheema Palli, the Muslims also are engaged in fishing like the Mukkuvar community of the Diocese of Trivandrum.

Socially the Muslims hold a high position in the society, though educationally they still need to develop. The Muslims in Trivandrum, like in any other place in Kerala, are large businessmen. In Trivandrum especially at Poovar[159] the Latin Catholics were exploited by the Muslims. The study conducted by J. Murickan at Poovar depicts the relation between the Muslims and the Catholics of the Trivandrum Diocese especially in the coastal area. J. Murickan writes:

> Moslems [Muslims] not only dominated the marketing system by way of exploiting the Christian fishermen but also propagated the «Jenmi Kudiyan» system. The fishermen were the tenants of Moslem landlords. A system of rules and regulations determined the fishermen's relations to the landlords. If a fisherman wanted to thatch his house, he had to inform his owner and offer him a gift of Rs. 15. Otherwise, there involved the risk of being harassed by the «Jenmi» [landlord]. Even repairs of one's house had to be compensated with gifts to the landlord[160].

The *Kuttaka* system (rate of payment charged on fish landings), which existed been in most of the coastal parishes in Trivandrum was also an

---

[158] When Hyder Ali conquered the northern part of Malabar he secured a neutral attitude from the English East India Company's officials at Tellichery in case he should attack Calicut. See G. WOODCOCK, *Kerala: A Portrait*, 175-176.

[159] See J. MURICKAN, *Religion and Power Structure*, 43-45. The study of J. Murickan sheds light also to the religious practices of Catholic fishermen of the Dioceses of Trivandrum and Quilon. The Muslims of Poovar have the same pattern of life at Pozhiyoor and Vizhinjam.

[160] J. MURICKAN, *Religion and Power Structure*, 45.

occasion for exploitation[161]. The mode of exploitation multiplied through buying the fish at cheaper rate from the fishermen, which caused the deterioration of relations between the Muslims and Christians. The three communal riots in 1968, 1972 and 1981 originated in Poovar and spread over other parts of the coastal villages, were «essentially a protest movement of the exploited class»[162]. In spite of the occasional communal riots there is a growing mutual understanding between both communities. It is to be noted that often lack of understanding between the Muslims and Christians causes many clashes. When governments have a leaning towards a group for political motive, the gap between the two communities widens. The Vizinjam incident which caused the death of two Muslims and four Catholics in May and July 1995 is a typical example of this sort of clashes.

3.4 *Christianity*

Our knowledge about the history of Christianity in Kerala till the arrival of Portuguese depends on the post Portuguese findings and studies. The traditional belief is that Christianity in India has its beginning with two Apostles, namely, St. Thomas and St. Bartholomew[163]. Although the historicity has always been called into question, no one can rule out the possibility of the Apostolic connection with India, as India was not at all unknown to the Western or Mediterranean world[164]. Moreover, there is a strong living tradition that St. Thomas the Apostle came to India, especially to Kerala, and preached the Gospel[165]. The traditional belief is that St. Thomas founded seven Christian communities at Palayoor, Cranganore, Parur, Kokkamangalam, Kollam (Quilon), Niranam and Chayal[166]. It is also the traditional belief that there existed from the early time of Christianity some kind of relations between the Christians of Kerala (Malabar) and the Church of Persia[167]. A new phase in the history

---

[161] In some parishes the *Kuttaka* system still exists.

[162] J. MURICKAN, *Religion and Power Structure,* 51.

[163] See Roman Missal, July 3 and August 24. See also G.M. MORAES, *A History of Christianity,* 13-79; A.M. MUNDADAN, *History of Christianity,* I, 65-66.

[164] See G.M. MORAES, *A History of Christianity,* 13-79.

[165] See G.M. MORAES, *A History of Christianity,* 1-79. See also A. M. MUNDADAN, *History of Christianity in India,* I, 21-64.

[166] See V.C. GEORGE, «The Seven Churches», 179-181.

[167] See A.M. MUNDADAN, *History of Christianity,* I, 78-89. It is difficult to determine the exact year in which the Chaldean Bishops were in charge of the Christians of Kerala. However, the post Portuguese period gives light to strong Chaldean relations existing

of Christianity begins with the coming of Thomas of Cana who landed in Kerala in the 4th century[168]. According to one tradition Thomas of Cana strengthened the Christians in Malabar[169]. It is from the time of Thomas of Cana we find a better contact between the Christians of Kerala and the Persian Churches[170]. From the 10th century to the 16th century we do not find many documents about Christianity in Kerala except those reporting of Western missionaries in the 14th century[171]. A historical shift took place in the life of Christians of Kerala with the coming of Portuguese missionaries in the beginning of the 16th century especially with the Synod of Diamper (Udayamperur) in 1599[172]. Despite its various positive effects, the Synod of Diamper gradually led the Syrian Christians into various Churches and denominations.

At present there are more than 20 Churches and denominations[173]. Some of them have the Syrian liturgical tradition. The most obvious

---

with the Syrian Christians of Kerala at least from the 4th century. For a detailed study see J. KOLLAPARAMBIL, *The St. Thomas Christians' Revolution*. See also ID., *The Archdeacon of All-India*.

[168] According to A.M. Mundadan, Thomas of Cana and the Persian Christians who had come with him allegedly played a great role in the organization and building up of the Church and the community of Cranganore and apparently exerted a very great influence in the whole Christian community of Kerala. See A.M. MUNDADAN, *History of Christianity*, I, 90-98. The Christians of Southists among the Syrian Christians believe that they are the descendants of Thomas of Cana through his legitimate wife. Even now they keep a separate caste identity having a diocese (Kottayam) with personal jurisdiction. It is also believed that the Archdeacon system in Kerala was instituted with the coming of Thomas of Cana. See also J. KOLLAPARAMBIL, *The Archdeacon of All-India*, 80.

[169] See C.M. AGUR, *Church History*, 29.

[170] See A.M. MUNDADAN, *History of Christianity in India*, I, 98-115. About the Catholic doctrines and religious practices of the Christianity which existed in Kerala we do not have much evidence. It is also natural that the ordinary Christians were least bothered about the subtle theological problems.

[171] See G.M. MORAES, *A History of Christianity*, 1-79. See also C.M. AGUR, *Church History*, 39-40; G.J. MULAKARA, *History of the Diocese of Cochin*, 44-48. There are some historical references regarding the presence of Christianity in the Syriac literature. See M. APREM, «The Nestorian Church», 37-47.

[172] There is a lot of literature about the events that led to the Synod of Diamper. There are positive and negative impacts of the Synod on the Church of Kerala. For reference see A.M. MUNDADAN, *History of Christianity*, I. See also C.M. AGUR, *Church History*, 39-40.

[173] The prominent denominations besides the Catholic Church with three rites are: (1) Malankara Orthodox Syrian Church, (2) The Malankara Jacobite Syrian Church, (3) The Mar Thoma Church, (4) Chaldean Church or Nestorian Church, (5) Church of South India: (5a) Anglican Church, (5b)London Mission Church, (5c) Basel Mission, (5d) Wesslian Methodist Church, (6) The Kerala C.M.S. Church, (7) Yooyomayam or

division among the Syrians are those caused by ecclesiastical obedience. The division among Syrian Christians varied according to the alliance to the ecclesiastical heads: to Rome, under Chaldean or Antiochian rites, to the Patriarch of Antioch or to Catholicos of the East, to the Mar Thoma Church or to the Church of South India (former Anglicans)[174].

3.4.1 The Syro-Malabar Catholics

The Syro-Malabar Catholics[175] are said to be the first Christians in Kerala claiming the Apostolic Tradition of St. Thomas the Apostle[176]. They are also known as St. Thomas Christians with a *Chaldean* liturgical

---

Anchara, (8) The Thozhiyoor or Anjoor Church, (9) St. Thomas Evangelical Church of India, (10) Russel Church, (11) Brethren Church, (12) Viyojitha Church, (13) Salvation Army, (14) Pentecost Church, (14_a) Pentecost Church of God, (14_b) Indian Pentecost, (14_c) Assemblies of God, (14_d) Ceylon Pentecost, (14_e) Apostolic United Pentecost, (14_f) Saron Pentecost, (14_g) Independent Indian Pentecost, (14_h) Backward Pentecost, (14_i) Philadelphia Pentecost, (14_j), Pentecost Gospel Society, (15) Seventh day Adventists or Sabbath Church, (16), Revival Centre, (17) «Jesus for India Society», (18) Berarch (House of Worship), (19) The Church of God. It is to be noted that most of these denominations have at least a few centres in Trivandrum. See M.A. THOMAS, *An Outline History of Christian Churches.* Now a new denomination called «Church of Christ» is also spreading in Trivandrum. Whether all the denominations could be called Churches is doubtful. Many a time they function like sects.

[174] Among the traditional Syrian Christians we find a socio-cultural identity. See L.W. BROWN, *The Indian Christians*, 174-175.

[175] The Syrian Christians as a whole had the same patrimony and ethnic identity at least till the time of the Portuguese. The division of Syrian community into different Churches and denominations started with the Synod of Diamber in 1599, except the «Southists», who claim that they are the descendants of Thomas of Cana. See L.K.A. AYYAR, *Anthropology of Syrian Christians*, 50-69. It is to be noted that some of the Latin Catholics of Kerala are also the descendants of those who received baptism from St. Thomas the Apostle. See E.P. ANTONY, «Origin and Growth», 19.

[176] Christian historians like Mundadan, Podipara and E.P. Antony hold the view that St. Thomas came to Kerala in 52 A.D. and the Syrians in Kerala are the children of those who received baptism from St. Thomas himself. Some historians like C.M. Agur and G.M. Rae (*The Syrian Church in India*) do not agree with this claim. Secular historians like A.S. Menon and others take it for granted that Christianity had set root in the first century itself. Dr. Radhakrishnan says: «the Syrian Christians of Malabar believe that their Christianity is apostolic, derived from the apostle Thomas. They contend that their version of Christian faith is distinctive and independent of the forms established by St. Peter and St. Paul in the West . [...] What is obvious is that there have been Christians in the west coast of India from the very early times» (S. RADHAKRISHNAN, *East and West*, 34).

rite[177]. They are mainly concentrated in the central part of Kerala and some of them have migrated to the northern parts of Kerala. Their role in Kerala ecclesiastical history is very significant[178]. As a community, very rich in vocations, the St. Thomas Christians of the Syro-Malabar Rite contribute the lion's share in providing missionaries all over India and abroad. In the caste ridden society of Kerala they have been identified with the upper castes like *Brahmins* and Nairs. They have kept a long distance away from the lower castes[179].

The Travancore kings were said to be tolerant[180] towards the Christians (Syrian Christians) though, the latter were not employed in the government offices[181]. A close study of the socio-religious history reveals

---

[177] The Syro-Malabar Church had its own Chaldean Liturgy till the coming of the Western missionaries in the 16th century. With the overpowering of Western missionaries they lost the original Chaldean Liturgy. For a detailed study see J. KOLLAPARAMBIL, *The St. Thomas Christians' Revolution*.

[178] Among the Syrian Christians of Kerala, Malabar Syrian Catholics (*Sui Iuris Church* with Major Arch Bishop and eleven dioceses in Kerala), Jacobites, Orthodox Syrian Christians, Marthoma Syrian Christians and Malankara Syrian Catholics (Metropolitan Church) are influential in every respect.

[179] Syrian Christians also had slaves. Once they were also against the lower castes' joining into Christianity. For, if people from lower castes join Christianity, Syrians together with Nairs were afraid that they would lose the slaves who were working in their farms. See L.K.A. AYYAR, *Anthropology of the Syrians Christians*, 205-219. See also S. MATTER, *The Land of Charity*, 43. J.W. GLADSTONE, *Protestant Christianity*, 143.

[180] One of the important reasons for the toleration of the *Rājāhs* of Travancore towards the Syro-Malabar Christians was due to the influence of the Italian missionaries over the *Rājāhs* of Travancore. The *Rājāhs* preferred the Italian Carmelite missionaries to the Portuguese. «They gave special protection to the Italian priests of Verapoly. On more than one occasion the Rajahs received from their hands, with all courtesy and honours, presents and letters from the Pope, and sent in return presents and letters to Rome; thus showing an outward friendship» (C.M. AGUR, *Church History*, 20).

[181] «There are no instances of Syrians occupying positions of trust in the Travancore Government prior to the advent of the British. It was Colonel Munro, who for the first time, employed a few in the Sirkar [Government], in the judicial and some other departments» (C.M. AGUR, *Church History*, 18). See also N. KOSHY, *Castes in the Kerala Churches*, 18-20. R. Jeffrey makes a remark in this regard. «Having been associated with the English missionaries from 1816, Syrians had the earliest and widest contacts with the new rulers of India. From the 1820s the missionaries made available English education, Malayalam printed books and a wide circles of connections» (R. JEFFREY, *The Decline of Nayar Dominance*, 19). During the Indian independent struggle most of the Syrian Christians also supported the British rule. «During the struggle for independence in Kerala at one stage our bishops under the leadership of Mar Ivanios supported Sir C.P. Ramswamy Aiyer. This was against the wishes of the majority of the lay people in Travancore» (See K.T. SEBASTIAN – S. ZACHARIA, «The Role of the Laity», 208-218).

that among the Syrian Christians, the Syro-Malabar Catholics were becoming powerful in the Kerala society when they got their own proper dioceses and indigenous bishops[182]. The fast growth of the Syro-Malabar Catholics is well described thus: «By 1890 even the most numerous, wealthy and educationally backward section, the Romo-Syrians, were beginning to establish western style schools. Education was to lead to demands for more equitable representation in the government service»[183].

The Syrian Christians are the first to speak strongly about participatory Church in Kerala[184]. The remarkable position achieved both in the secular and in the ecclesiastical field by the Syro-Malabar Catholics through indigenous bishops have moved the Latin Catholics to ask for indigenous bishops[185]. This was fulfilled only in 1932. The history of Christianity shows that a rapid growth in developments have taken place among the Syrian Catholics with the indigenous bishops[186]. The history of the Syro-Malabar Church also reminds us of the importance of religion in the socio-educational development of a community in the context of Kerala[187]. This also reveals the fact that religion plays a significant role in the social development of the people of Kerala.

---

[182] In 1896, the Holy See erected three Vicariates Apostolic, namely, Trichur, Ernakulam and Changanacherry, under the Propaganda Fide. The bishops were also indigenous. And «under indigenous bishops, the Syro-Malabar Catholics began to make fast progress in all fields» (J. KURIEDATH, *Authority in the Catholic Community*, 12). See also P.J. PODIPARA, *The Thomas Christians*, 195-203.

[183] R. JEFFREY, *The Decline of Nayar Dominance*, 118.

[184] The Syrian Catholics always desired to have participation in their ecclesial life. One of the important reasons for the conflicts with the Portuguese missionaries was based on the question of the participation in the ecclesial administration.

[185] Seeing the development of the Syrians Catholics, the Latin Catholics, who were under the strict control of the European missionaries, also aspired for indigenous bishops. They even submitted a memorandum in 1922, stating that the Syrian Catholics had progressed a lot because of indigenous prelates and that the Latin Catholics had remained backward. It was also stressed that the movement was causing bitter enmity towards foreign missionaries. The first indigenous bishop for the Latin Catholics was appointed in 1932. See L.M. PYLEE, *St. Thomas Christians,* 384-388. See also E.P. ANTONY, «Hierarchy and the Community», 343-349.

[186] See J. KURIEDATH, *Authority in the Catholic Community,* 12. The social growth among any community whether Syrian Catholics in the central and North Travancore or Protestant Christians in the South Travancore, helped the growth only of their own communities. It did not help directly any other lower castes.

[187] For a detailed study on the role of the Church in the development of a community in the context of Kerala see F. HOUTART – G. LEMERCINIER, *Church and Development in Kerala.*

The Syro-Malabar Church, being a *sui juris* Church, has jurisdiction in the territory of Trivandrum Diocese, as Catholics from the Syro-Malabar rite settled in Trivandrum for better prospects. It is the right of the Syro-Malabar Church to meet the pastoral needs of its own people. But before the Syro-Malabar Church had jurisdiction in Trivandrum revenue district it was the Latin Diocese of Trivandrum that met the pastoral needs of the Syro-Malabar Catholics in this region. Many Syro-Malabar Catholics who were holding top offices in Trivandrum were active members of the St. Joseph's Cathedral parish, Palayam of Trivandrum Diocese. Justice Joseph Thaliath's letter to I.C. Chacko reveals that the former was even proud of being identified with the Palayam parish. J.Thaliath writes:

> As for the question of jurisdiction, I am not very much interested in it. Personally I feel no doubt that I am a parishioner of St. Joseph's, Trivandrum. Three children were born to me after I came to Trivandrum, and they were all baptized in St. Joseph's. One of them died, and that one was buried in the cemetery attached to St. Joseph's. I am quite happy and contented to remain where I am[188].

3.4.2 The Syro-Malankara Catholics

The Syro-Malankara Catholic Church, with its Metropolitan See in Trivandrum and with its reputed educational institutions, plays an important role in Trivandrum. The Syro-Malankara Catholics are those Syrian Christians who were separated from the Catholic communion in 1653 and joined with the Antiochene Jacobite Patriarch and formed themselves into an autonomous Church[189].

On 30 September, 1930 one group of Jacobites[190] under the spiritual leadership of Mar Ivanios, the Metropolitan of Bethany, later known as

---

[188] J. THALIATH, *Letter to I.C. Chacko, AGOCD*. The rite conflict in India calls the attention of theologians to think about the formation of one Indian rite. As Kerala being the centre of Christianity in India the attempt initiated after Second Vatican Council by Cardinal Parecattil is praise-worthy. His vision of an Indian Church cannot be utopian. It is remarkable that a secular historian of Kerala has appreciated the attempts of the Cardinal. See A.S. MENON, *Social and Cultural History*, 208-210. See also J. PARECATTIL, «Adaptation», 186-191; A.M. MUNDADAN, ed., *Cardinal Parecattil*. The CBCI Evaluation committee has also given sufficient attention to the problems existing between different rites in India. See *CBCI Evaluation Report*, ns. 684-693.

[189] For a detailed history of the Malankara Catholic Church see C. MALANCHARUVIL, *The Syro-Malankara Church*. See also C.M. BASELIOS, «The Reunion Movement», 308-315.

[190] The separated Syrians who affiliated with the Jacobite Patriachate of Antioch had a number of disputes mainly about the jurisdiction of the Antiochian Patriarch over the local

Archbishop Mar Ivanios and Mar Theophilos came to communion with the Catholic Church. One of the important desires of the Catholic Church was to bring back the upper class Jacobites, who were ready also to come back to the Catholic communion[191]. However, re-union of the Jacobites with the Catholic Church did not have the expected result[192] when Archbishop Mar Ivanios began to admit the people from lower castes of South Travancore into the Malankara Catholic Church. Within two years of the reunion, Mar Ivanios was appointed as the «Archbishop of Trivandrum»[193] instead of «Titular Archbishop of Phasi»[194]. Although the erection of a new diocese and multiplication of Catholic liturgical rites caused scandal among the new converts in Trivandrum[195], it was an important event in the life of the Syrian Catholics — both of the Syro-Malankara rite and Syro-Malabar rite — to have an indigenous bishop in

---

community. The dispute ended with the division of Orthodox Church which claimed complete autonomy to the local Church in all administrative matters leaving only spiritual leadership to the Patriarch. Another group of the Jacobite Church favoured a close link with the patriarchate. See J. KURIEDATH, *Authority in the Catholic Community*, 13-14.

[191] Archbishop Benziger of Quilon was the inspiring personality behind the reunion movement. He had kept good contact with the Jacobites who were settled in Mavelikkara. To know the original plan followed by the re-union movement it is enough to go through the speeches of Archbishop Mar Ivanios and reports about the re-union movement in those days inside and outside India. See F.A. DE STE-MARIE, «Vers la fin d'un long Schisme», 509-514. See also «Jacobite Conversions in Malabar», 442-443; «La Conversione dei Giacobiti in India», 1; B. GUDGEON, *Mar Ivanios and the Jacobites*, *AGOCD*; «Premier Anniversaire de la Conversion des deux Eveques Jacobites», *AGOCD*; M. IVANIOS, *Christmas Message*, *AGOCD*.

[192] Many Jacobites from Pakudy of Muthukolam, Chathanur and Thevalakara desired to join the Catholic Church during the re-union of Archbishop Mar Ivanios with the Catholic Church. Since Archbishop concentrated his attention among the lower castes the Jacobites did not join the Syro Malankara Church at least in the early period. See BERNARDIN, *Muthukolam Conversion*, *AGOCD*.

[193] The erection of the new Diocese and making Mar Ivanios as the Archbishop of Trivandrum was «surprising and astonishing» to Archbishop Benziger and it caused displeasure among the clergy and laity of the Quilon Diocese. See BERNADIN, *To Fr. Herman*, Letter, *AGOCD*. The erection of the Diocese also caused surprise and something strange to Angel Mary O.C.D. the then Archbishop of Verapoly. A. MARY, *Letter to Bernardine*, *AGOCD*. The main reason for the surprise of the Latin bishops was that already in 1929 Bishop A.M. Benziger of Quilon had proposed the erection of a Latin Diocese in Trivandrum along with the erection of the Diocese of Kottar. See A. M BENZIGER, *Division du Diocèse de Quilon en trois*, *AGOCD*.

[194] See A. M. BENZIGER, *Copie d'un lettre*, *AGOCD*.

[195] See ILDAPHONSE, *Letter to Right Rev. Mgr. Bernardine*, *AGOCD*. The scandal was mainly due to the re-baptism and re-marriage.

Trivandrum which helped them to have socio-political hold in the capital city of Travancore[196].

The Syro-Malankara Catholic Church follows the Antiochene Liturgy. The Syrian Catholics of the central and northern Travancore are familiar with this liturgy. In the context of Trivandrum where the vast majority are familiar with Latin liturgy there is a cultural difference between the people who come from the Jacobite tradition of central Travancore and the new converts of South Travancore. As a matter of fact the three liturgical rites in one place can create only tensions and often it causes unhealthy competition in putting up churches. The competition becomes a scandal to the faithful, though the variety of Rites are part of the spiritual tradition of the Church.

3.5 The Protestant Churches

The effects of the Protestant Revolution in Europe began to be seen in Kerala when the missionaries of London Missionary Society and Church Missionary Society entered Travancore at the beginning of the 19th century[197]. Within a short span of time the Protestant Church (Churches) gained unprecedented success and progressed at a comparatively more rapid stride[198]. William Tobias Ringeltaube was the first Protestant missionary (London Missionary Society) to arrive in South Travancore in 1806. At the same period John Munro, a British Resident from 1810, decided to revive the Jacobite Syrian Christians with the help of Church Missionary Society and even invited the clergymen of the Church of England[199]. The missionaries Norton, Bailey, Backer, and Fenn thus came

---

[196] «The choice of Trivandrum, the Capital of Travancore and the most important city in Malabar, as the seat of our Metropolitan Archbishop, is calculated to facilitate this consummation, as Trivandrum already contains a large settlement of influential Syrians from all parts of Travancore and is frequently visited by many others brought hither for purposes of education, governmental business and other attractions of a metropolis» (THE CLERGY AND THE LAITY OF THE TRIVANDRUM PROVINCE, Letter to His Excellency, AGOCD. The appointment of Archbishop Mar Ivanios and the erection of the Archdiocese of Trivandrum has indirectly affected the socio-educational growth of the Latin Catholics in Trivandrum who represent the depressed class of the Trivandrum district.

[197] In Tamil Nadu (South India) the Protestant missionaries began their work already in the 18th century.

[198] See C.M. AGUR, Church History, 423

[199] J. Munro had two motives: first as a Christian philanthropist he wished to renew the Syrian Church. Second he thought that the missionaries would help for the stability of the British supremacy in Travancore. J. Munro wrote a letter on August 7, 1815, to M. Thompson, Secretary of the newly formed «Madras Corresponding Committee of the

and worked among the Jacobite Syrians. The Syrian *Metrān* (bishop) and the priests also worked along with the missionaries and even allowed them to preach in the Syrian Churches. Some reforms had also taken place within the Jacobite Syrian Church[200]. But it did not last long. The Syrians stopped all the official connection with the missionaries with the Synod of Mavelikara in 1836[201]. A small but significant group that had been associated with missionaries left the Syrian Church and formed the *Anglican Church* in Travancore in 1937[202].

The London Missionary Society (LMS) on the other hand concentrated in South Travancore and carried out successful missionary activities. Since there are many cultural similarities between the people of LMS Church in Trivandrum and the Latin Diocese of Trivandrum a short description of LMS is also necessary to understand the socio-religious context of Trivandrum.

3.5.1 The London Missionary Society

The founder of LMS mission in Travancore is William Tobias Ringeltaube. Paradoxically for the Christian tradition of Travancore, the first introduction of the Protestant religion into Travancore was

---

CMS» like this: «I am more anxious than ever to attach a respectable Clergyman of the Church of England to the Syrains in Travancore; and I should wish that Mr. Norton might be sent to me» (quoted in J. W. GLADSTONE, *Protestant Christianity*, 62-68). See also S. MATEER, *The Land of Charity*, 253-256. Colonel Munro's interest is a typical example to show how religion and political power were interrelated in the history of Kerala Church.

[200] Together with the reformation of the Syrian Orthodox Church the missionaries' main idea was to disseminate the Protestant ideas among the members of the Orthodox Church. See M.A. THOMAS, *An Outline History*, 126-129.

[201] For the events which led to the Synod see L.W. BROWN, *The Indian Christians of St. Thomas*, 132-140. See also J.W. GLADSTONE, *Protestant Christianity*, 65-68.

[202] The *beginning* of Anglican Church in North Travancore also helped the missionaries to work among the lower castes. See J.W. GLADSTONE, *Protestant Christianity*, 68. See also S. MATEER, *The Land of Charity*, 254. Though there were many conversions from the Hill Arrians and Pulaya castes, the missionaries tried to please the Syrians who were with them. Some of the high officials of Travancore government was in favour of the uplift of the lower castes. The approach of the Old Christians was different. It is enough to look at an instance to know how the Syrian Christian community was prejudicial to the lower castes. «The only instance of a Pulayan being admitted to the CMS College resulted in such a commotion that the boy was obliged to leave for the North, where the feeling is less strong. He was there educated by the German Missionaries and became an ordained Minister» (*Industrial School for Pullayan*, Kottayam, 1892, Church Missionary Society Archives quoted by J.W. GLADSTONE, *Protestant Christianity*, 124-125).

associated with the personal conversion of Maha-Rasan, a man from a lower caste, of Mylaudy in South Travancore. He was a devotee of Śiva[203]. After his conversion to Christianity he was known as Vedamanickam[204]. Soon a mission was started at Mylaudy[205]. When Ringeltaube left Travancore in 1816, Vedamanickam was appointed as the pastor and superintendent of the Mission which he founded[206]. The mission founded by Ringeltaube was given a strong footing by the subsequent missionaries[207]. The LMS missionaries unlike the Church Missionary Society missionaries worked among the lower castes such as Nadars, Izhavas, Pulayas, Parayas and Hill Aryans. The missionaries not only baptized the people from lower class but also educated them[208]. The importance given in the field of education was remarkable. J.W. Gladstone writes:

> The educational endeavors of the missionaries exploded the myth that only the higher castes were destined to learn. It also laid strong foundation for the «cultural renaissance» which had been taking place in the society. The mission schools provided in many places the depressed classes of people with the opportunity to educate their children and the missionaries made special efforts to bring them to the schools. The «commercial value» which the English education secured, helped to popularize it among all sections of people[209].

---

[203] S. MATEER, *The Land of Charity*, 260-282. See also J. YESUDASAN, *Maha Rasan Vedamanickam*, (Biography of Vedamanickam), 14.

[204] See RINGELTAUBE, *Letter*, CWMA. It was Maha Rasan who invited Ringeltaube to Travancore. The life of Maha Rasan also sheds light on the life, belief and ability of the lower castes in Travancore in the 19th century.

[205] To support the mission Mrs. Munro, the Resident's wife, at her cost, regularly sent from the Residency, bread and wine required for the sacrament of the Lord's supper in the Church at Mylaudy. And it is reported that in 1816 Vedamanikam administered the Lord's supper to 108 members of the Church. See C.M. AGUR, *Church History*, 632.

[206] See *Authorization by Rngeltaube to Vedamanikam*, CWMA.

[207] C. MEAD was a founder of Nagercoil and Neyoor Mission and known as the Father of the South Travancore Mission. See C.M. AGUR, *Church History*, 647.

[208] The Church Missionary Society missionaries began to work among the lower castes mainly after the Synod at Mavelikara in 1836. The mottoes of Protestant missionaries were *Pallikalum Pallikūtaṅgalum* (churches and schools). The Catholic missionaries taught the people Christian doctrine but did not promote secular education to the extent that the Protestant missionaries did.

[209] J.W. GLADSTONE, *Protestant Christianity*, 71-72. See also «Report of the Nagercoil Station for the year 1844», CWMA; MATTHIAS, *Review of the History of the College*, CWMA.

The missionaries were very keen to educate girls too. Their concept was that liberation in the society would be possible only through the education of women. The Gospel message that the Protestant missionaries have preached to the lower castes and the education that they have imparted to them, attracted many to receive Christianity[210]. The Christian religion actually had a liberative effect in Travancore already in the 19th century. Christianity gave a new social awakening to the oppressed class among both men and women. The oppressed class began to claim more freedom in social life. They also insisted that they should not be compelled to do forced labour and work on Sundays nor should they be forced to supply food to temples and government institutions free of cost. On account of their defiant and rather rebellious conduct, many Christian converts of the South were arrested, imprisoned and beaten to death. Some of the mission sheds were burned[211].

The *negative* impact of the social awakening among the lower class through the reception of Christianity was well understood by the higher castes[212]. They insisted that the change of religion does not imply a change in the established customs, caste rules and in its social relationships[213]. The Nairs and the people who were in authority took it as a privilege to make the lower castes do labour on Sundays, and what the lower castes had been doing even after the conversion to Christianity. On the other hand the Nadars and Izhavas claimed equal rights like any other Christians in Travancore. In short the social awareness among the lower and suppressed class became so vibrant that it had been showing the signs of Renaissance in Kerala[214]. The Upper Cloth Revolt of South Travancore by the Nadar women had its own socio-religious impact in Trivandrum and in the history of modern Kerala.

---

[210] Most of the new converts were from Nadar caste. Already in 1820 nearly all of the three thousand who had received instruction were Nadars. See R.L. HARDGRAVE, JR., *The Nadars of Tamilnad,* 43-70. Most of the Nadars joined Christianity destroying their own Hindu shrines and temples. «[...] 3.000 persons, chiefly of the Shānār (Nadar) caste placed themselves under Christian instruction, casting away their images and emblems of idolatry, and each presenting a written promise declarative of his renunciation of idolatry, and determination to serve the living and true God» (S. MATEER, *The Land of Charity,* 269).

[211] L. LOPEZ, *A Social History,* 106.

[212] Conversion to Christianity from the Izhava caste meant a material loss to the Nairs and to the Syrian Christians. See J.W. GLADSTONE, *Protestant Christianity,* 143.

[213] *Report of the Nagercoil Station,* January-June (1829), MS, India Odds, Box 16, CWMA. See also C. MEAD, *To Rev. Clayton,* Letter, CWMA.

[214] L. LOPEZ, *A Social History,* 105.

3.5.2 The Upper Cloth Revolt of 1859 (*Melmundu Samaram*)

In Travancore the caste system had imposed certain traditions even with regard to dress, wearing of ornaments, wearing of sandals. The women of higher castes used to wear a light piece of cloth across the breast and over the shoulder. That piece of cloth was called the upper cloth. By tradition in Travancore, the breast was bared as a symbol of respect to those of higher status. The Nairs, for example bared their breasts before the Nambudiri Brahmins, and the Brahmins did so before the deity[215]. The Nadar women and Izhava women were desirous of having the freedom of dress. They were not permitted this by caste rules supported by government regulations[216]. The Nairs complained to the government about the Nadars regarding clothes. The government issued an order in 1813 allowing the Nadars and Izhavas to wear jackets called *Kupāyam* like the women of Christians, Shonagas and Moplas[217]. However, the Nadars were not satisfied with that proclamation. Under the leadership of Muthukutty known as Vaikunda Swami[218] and the Christian missionaries, they fought for the right to wear upper cloth like any other women in the higher castes[219]. This was resented by the high-caste Nairs who took the law into their own hands and used violence against those who infringed the long standing custom and caste distinction[220]. In December 1828 the Nairs organized themselves and attacked the Nadar Christians[221]. In 1829 again the *Rāni* (Queen) made a proclamation saying that the Nadar women have no right to wear upper cloth[222].

---

215 See R.L. HARDGRAVE, JR., *The Nadars of Tamilnad*, 55-70. See also A.S. MENON, *Social and Cultural History*, 111-112; MATEER, *Native Life in Travancore*, 230; R.N. YESUDAS, *A Peoples' Revolt* .

216 See J.W. GLADSTONE, *Protestant Christianity*, 82-85. See also V.N. AIYA, *Travancore State Manual*, 1, 525-531.

217 See the translation of a circular order from Colonel Munro, Dewan, dated at Baleamporam the 7th *Ydavam* in the Malayalam Year 989 (1813 A.D), regulating the dress of Christain women in C.M. AGUR, *Church History*, LIII. See also J.W. GLADSTONE, *Protestant Christianity*, 83.

218 N.K. JOSE, *Cānar Lahala*, 49-51.

219 The Hindu Nadar women also began to imitate the Christian Nadar women. It also shows the affinity existing among the Nadar community despite the religious differences.

220 See V.N. AIYA, *Travancore State Manual*, I, 525-531. See also J.W. GLADSTONE, *Protestant Christianity*, 83.

221 The Nadar Christians were more a threat to the Nairs than the Hindu Nadars.

222 See «Translation of a Proclamation by Her Highness the *Rani* (Ranee) of Travancore», CWMA.

Encouraged by the Christian missionaries, the Nadar women showed remarkable courage resisting the social restrictions imposed on them by the customs of antiquated society. The government authorities could not stop the fight of the Nadars for their social emancipation and the tension continued and reached its climax in 1858 when violence took place in many parts of Neyyattinkara, Neyyoor and Kottar. The police force could not control the situation. And on 26th July 1859, under the pressure of the Madras Governor, the *Mahārāja* (King) issued a proclamation granting the Nadar women the right to wear the upper cloth on the condition that they should not imitate the same mode of dress appertaining to the high caste[223].

The upper cloth revolt by the Nadar women brought a new incentive for the Nadars to join Christianity[224] destroying their own Hindu temples. And many congregations could maintain their own catechists[225]. The success of the upper cloth revolt in 1859 reflected in the subsequent revival movements in Travancore[226]. The backward communities began to agitate for the equality before the law. The success of the upper cloth revolt supported by the missionaries[227] was a great incentive for the orthodox Hindu Nadars, and their children began to attend the schools run by the missionaries.

Paradoxically, the Nadars, when they got an upper hand in the Protestant Mission through education and social awakening, failed to recognize the human rights of other downtrodden castes[228]. They were no better than the Syrian Christians of Central and North Travancore[229]. There was no social integration of Nadar Christians with Pulayas and Parayas. There were strong oppositions from Nadars Christians in giving

---

[223] This was not a satisfactory solution to the missionaries for the right to wear upper cloth was still forbidden to the Izhava and other backward castes.

[224] See C. MEAD, *To Burder* Letter, (April 4, 1818), CWMA. See also ID., *To Burder*, Letter, (August 10, 1819), CWMA.

[225] J. COX, *Report of Trevandrum* , CWMA.

[226] The Malayali Memorial, Ezhava Memorial, Vaikom Satyagraha are some of them. Even Sri Narayana Guru was very much inspired by the upper cloth revolt.

[227] We have to remember that the missionaries were only a moral force behind the upper cloth revolt. It is through their mediation that much bloodshed was avoided.

[228] When the Missionaries turned their attention to the Pulayas and Parayas the Nadars did not welcome the approach of the missionaries. See J.W. GLADSTONE, *Protestant Christianity*, 101.

[229] The division among the non-Catholic Syrians was also caused by the caste problem. See J.W. GLADSTONE, *Protestant Christianity*, 123-136.

permission to the Pulaya converts to enter their churches[230]. The suppression and the lack of integration within the mission caused many Pulaya and Paraya Christians to join the Salvation Army[231]. J.W. Gladstone comments on the situation of the depressed class during the period of mass movements in the Protestant Church:

> The history of the mass movements among the depressed castes in Kerala tells us that, it is not money or effort that matters, but what matters is being accepted into the community of the people of God. The conversion of the Pulayas and Parayas, as in the case of any other castes was motivated by the hope of their socio-economic and religious emancipation and it was part of their struggle for their own progress. They had suffered all the humiliations as non-Christians, as slaves. But the discovery of the existence of caste inside the mission shattered their hopes and was too much for them to bear[232].

3.6 *The Latin Catholics*

The term *Latin Catholics* is generally identified with the *powerful European and American Church* that follows the Latin Liturgy. Its liturgical rite is of the Roman Church. In Kerala, the Latin Catholic community is considered as one of the backward classes[233]. From a sociological point of view, Latin Catholics, in Kerala, have a social identity of backwardness. They are composed of St. Thomas Christians who embraced the Latin Rite during the Portuguese regime, Anglo-Indians, the converts from Hinduism such as Mukkuvar, Nadars, Izhavas,

---

[230] See S. MATEER, *To Duhie* (Secretary, TDC), Letter, CWMA. See also J.W. GLADSTONE, *Protestant Christianity*, 136.

[231] J. COX, *To R.W. Thompson, Letter*, CWMA. See also ALLEN, *To R.W. Thompson*, Letter, CWMA; J.W. GLADSTONE, *Protestant Christianity*, 138.

[232] J.W. GLADSTONE, *Protestant Christianity*, 138. The situations described above have not changed completely even now in the Protestant Churches. The Nadar Christians are not yet disposed to accept the Pastors from the Dalit community. However, the Dalit Christians are happy with the approach of Bishop Samuel Amirtham, a Nadar by caste, who had been the Vice-Chairman of the World Council of Churches. From my interview with Bishop S. Amirtham of Trivandrum CSI Church on 10th June 1994 I realized that the Bishop is committed to liberate the Dalits.

[233] The backwardness of the Latin Catholics is based on the economic conditions and employment in the government services. In 1939 there was not a single Latin Catholic drawing over Rs. 100/- though their population in Travancore was nearly 4 hundred thousand. The community's representatives in the Legislature continued their fight. So, the Travancore Public Service Recruitment Rules were passed on March 4, 1940 according to which out of every 51 appointments the Latin Catholics were granted 4 seats. See E.P. ANTONY, «Hierarchy and the Community», 329-459. See also L. LOPEZ, *A Social History*, 174-181.

Dalits. All these castes in the Latin community are categorized as the Other Backward Class (OBC) by the Kerala Government[234].

In Kerala the identification of the Latin Catholic Community with the backward class is important more from the socio-educational point of view than from the *ecclesiastical point of view*. The social identity of Latin Catholics is often ignored or misunderstood by the civil authorities[235] and Christians other than Latin Catholics. E.P. Antony[236] writes:

> Even today, the caste of the Latin Catholics is not properly recorded in the school registers and SSLC, etc. In the Trivandrum diocese, the parishioners of St. Antony's Church, Kamukincode, and St. Peter's Church, Kochupally, call themselves Ezhava [Izhava] Latin Catholics and are recorded as such. Many from Trivandrum diocese have their castes shown as Nadar Christians and both in Trivandrum and Quilon dioceses many show their castes as Bharatha Christians. Again there are many who are shown as Pulaya and Paraya converts. The Latin Catholics of Vijayapuram diocese are seen as Cherama and Samabava Christians. Further, those Latin Catholic educational institutions headed by priests and nuns of the Syrians Catholic Community, do not show them as Latin Catholics in the records, and had also been apathetic towards them in the matter of admission. Due to these anomalies the population of the community remains deflated and also lose their reservation benefits in the matter of recruitments to public services[237].

Another reason for the social backwardness of the Latin Catholics was lack of ecclesiastical leadership. As the Latin Church has a centralized

---

[234] The caste identification in the category of Other Backward Class (OBC) is important in Kerala. For, the caste identification also gives privileges in the government employment through reservation.

[235] The census reports do not give a correct number of the population of Latin Catholics. Often the employees who do the census work do not know the distinction between the Syrian Catholics and Latin Catholics. It is interesting to note, for example in the Secondary School Leaving Certificate (SSLC) book, if a student of Latin Catholic writes near the column of religion Roman Catholic (R.C.), he or she would be considered as the Syrian Catholic and the effect would be no privilege due to the lower castes. In 1995 Bishop M.S. Pakiam, has called the attention of the government highlighting the problems of the Latin Catholics of different castes. See M.S. Pakiam, *Thiruvanthapuram Latîn Kattōlikka Rūpata Bodhipikkunna Apēkṣa* (Memorandum submitted by the Latin Catholics of Trivandrum), ADT.

[236] E.P. Antony was a History Professor at St. Albert's College under the University of Kerala and later became a member of the Kerala Public Service Commission. He specially mentions the problem of the new converts of Trivandrum.

[237] E.P. Antony, «Origin and Growth», 19-20. See V.N. Aiya, *Travancore Census Report,* 99-100.

administrative system the lay participation in the ecclesial life was not encouraged. E.P. Antony writes:

> Though individuals of the community have made outstanding contributions in politics, stage, screen, music etc. they were branded delinquents and discouraged by the Church and the community failed to recognize them or encourage them. Naturally they could not capitalize their leadership qualities and resource base. Latin Catholics are the pioneers in printing and journalism and the first man to own ships in Kerala hailed from the community, but the repressive ecclesiastical and regressive educational policies, opposition of the foreign Prelates to organize lay associations, lack of sincere and concerted efforts for the community's general welfare and the silent internecene [internecine] bickering and the consequent weakening of its association and thereby its political influence, etc., have added to its backwardness. However, the indigenous Prelates who have taken over the administration are struggling to improve the lot of the community[238].

In the context of Trivandrum, the Latin Catholics represent the poorest section of the society. Poverty, illiteracy, lack of primary needs, are some of the problems facing the community[239]. The unsolved problem of the dowry system makes many families poor. The social status of women has not yet risen as in other communities. Most of the people in the fishing villages are very clustered and densely populated. Nevertheless, it was these fish workers who mobilized and took onto the streets of the Trivandrum city to oppose the communist Government of 1957 when it was a threat to the educational institutions of Kerala. Ironically the community remained illiterate. Alcohol has become the curse of the society. Some Christian centres became notorious for illicit distillation[240].

---

[238] E.P. ANTONY, «Origin and Growth», 20. See also C. LOPEZ, «Latîn Kattolikkaruṭe Sāmūhika Munnēttam?», (Social Revival of Latin Catholic Community?) December, 1993, 41-48; January, 1994, 8-9.14; February, 1994, 14-16.

[239] A report of the «Benchmark Survey of Slums under Urban Basic Services for the Poor (UBSP) Programme in Thiruvananthapuram May – October 1993» shows the slow education growth among the fisher folk. The report throws light also to the problem of housing, water supply, health and sanitation. The report is to be understood in the context of Trivandrum. The rural areas would be still worse. «It is a phenomenon found common in most of the slum areas specially among the fisher folk, that their children drop out from schools before they complete their fifth standard» (LOYOLA EXTENSION SERVICES, *Report* , 67). In 1990 the Kerala government had initiated an intensive literacy programme. However, it did not reach out to the people. For example in one of the fishing villages there were more than 1263 illiterates out of the total Catholic population of 6479 in 1993.

[240] The Diocese of Trivandrum is fighting a crusade war against alcoholism. See M.S. PAKIAM, «Thapasukāla Sandēśam» (Lenten Message), 1-6. Some of the social problems in Kerala are attributed to alcoholism. «The state (Kerala) has 3.000 illegal liquor shops.

The entire life of the Christian fishermen revolves around the Church as an institution. In the fishing villages like Poovar, Vizhinjam, Pulluvila, Poonthura and Anjengo, the density of population is as high as 4.000 to 6.000 persons per sq. km. Churches are crowded on Sundays, devotions are plenty, pious associations are many. The rule of Sabath is strictly maintained. Normally no one goes to the sea for fishing and no woman to the market on Sundays. Their stability as a community depends on their church. Church committees that are dominated by the educated, and the well-to-do men (*Pradhāni*)[241] in the village play the role of the *gram sabha* (village assembly) and are the reference point in the village. The Church played a traditional role in the eradication of poverty through alms giving and charity. In spite of all, the people are poor and educationally backward[242].

Among the new converts like the Nadars, the Izhavas, the Dalits, etc., too the social situations are not better. For example in Nedumangad taluk though the missionaries had sowed the seed of faith in the areas as early as 1914, there were few persons to care for them. The pioneers lacked a long term pastoral plan towards the integral development with the concerted effort[243]. The fall in number of Dalit Christians is conspicuous. It is learned from the recent study conducted by the Trivandrum Social Service Society that 15% of the total Catholic families of the Chullimanoor Vicariate are Dalits and twelve mission substations are mainly of the Dalits. The policy of governments has pulled the Dalits out of the Church, and lack of plan and concern from the part of the Church has enhanced this pulling out.

Some blame the state Government for encouraging consumption to fill its coffers. Revenue from liquor sector has risen from just Rs. 3 crore in 1962 to Rs 300 crore in 1993» (V. ABRAHAM, «Between brew and blue water», 24-26). See also R. KRISHNAN, «Kerala: A Fall from Grace», 116-117.

[241] The system of *Pradhāni* will be discussed in the next chapter.

[242] See PCO, *Ripples and Repercussions*, 1-16. According to the report of the Theology Students of Trivandrum, 50% of the Latin Catholics of Trivandrum are below poverty line. See S. KUMAR – RAJADAS, *The Report of Pastoral Exposure Programme*, TSA. The Pastoral Exposure Programme was conducted by the Loyola Extension Services, Sreekaryam in 1994 under the guidance of Joy James, Lecturer, Social Work Department, Loyola College, Trivandrum.

[243] According to a survey conducted at Chullimanoor Vicariate, animated by Fr. R.P. Lean and the animators of BECs, between 24th July to 24th August 1994, 28.64% families have less than ten cents of land and only 14.87% have got more than fifty cents of land and 157 families do not have houses. See JESSINA, *A Study of Chullimanoor Forane*, PAC. See also Reports on each Vicariate conducted by the Trivandrum Social Service Society in 1992-93.

No real social uplift has taken place among the Latin Catholic women. The male domination was one of the major reasons for it. The male domination was mainly felt in the Church activities. In most of the pious associations women take an active part and in the parish administration the male members dominate. Many parishes did not have even one woman representative in the parish council[244]. The spirituality of the parish was centered on the rituals. The difference of approach in evangelization by the Protestants and the Catholics is also to be noted. In this connection, the question remains: why do the disturbances — which arose in connection with the spread of Protestant Christianity in Travancore — did not occur between Roman Catholics and heathens? The reason according to S. Mateer is that there is, in the first place, less difference between *Romanists* (Roman Catholics) and Hindus than between Protestants and Hindus. The *Romanists* are by no means so well instructed, either in scriptural or secular knowledge, such as the Protestants. The native *Romanists* are admitted much more readily to baptism and communion with the Church than are those others who apply to the Protestant Church[245].

4. Conclusion

In our investigation of the socio-religious background of Trivandrum we came to know that Trivandrum symbolizes the pluriform culture of Kerala and Indian society. In general we could say that each caste has created its own culture. The religions have a great significance on every caste.

As our scope of the study is to understand the spirituality of BECs in the context of Trivandrum we analyzed the most important aspects of

---

[244] In the same social background we find ordained women in the Protestant Church in Trivandrum.

[245] S. MATEER, *The Land of Charity*, 275-276. What S. Mateer says is not completely true. However, it shows two approaches of evangelization to the same people. The caste and culture are the same. Because of the difference of approaches in the field of Evangelization, a section of the community advanced in spiritual and social development. A close study on the nature and functioning of the two Churches would show that in the Protestant Church more participation is given to the lay people. In the Catholic Church, on the local level, the aspect of lay participation has not been encouraged. According to various reports we know that even parish councils are not functioning in many dioceses in India. See *CBCI Evaluation Report*, n. 652/15. As the future of the Church of Asia depends on the laity the participatory Church envisaged through the BECs is going to play an important role. «Il futuro della chiesa in Asia dipenderà in gran parte dall'impegno che sapranno i laici» (A.D. OSTO, «La Chiesa guarda all'Asia», 19-21).

social life namely caste and religion, which give a general background of the social situation of Trivandrum. The description of the socio-religious context of Trivandrum is not only a key to understand the spirituality of the BECs in Trivandrum but also a means to understand any diocese in Kerala and to a certain extent in India and to go deep into the hidden realities of the society, which is a pre-requisite for preaching the Gospel effectively.

Our study reveals the fact that caste system and religion play a vital role in the society. There is no doubt that the caste system which crept into the Kerala society through the Aryan colonization, is one of the evils of Kerala and Indian society in general. The influence is seen in every walk of social life in Trivandrum[246]. No religion is free from it. In the case of new converts caste dominates over the established religion. In this regard the Christian mission needs to surmount all ethnic barriers which block the proclamation of the Gospel and our relation to God and to human beings. It is true that the Church is not against the good values of any culture and religion. At the same time as ohn Paul II reminds, «Church never ceases to proclaim that *Jesus is "the way, and the truth, and the life"*(Jn 14, 6), the One in whom the fullness of religious life is found and in whom God has reconciled all things to himself»[247]. It is in this context that the BECs, as they function in the existential situations of human beings, can become a leaven of Christian life[248].

The Brahmins, once the aristocratic caste of Trivandrum, are loosing their prestige in the changing society. The present day society is not disposed to tolerate all the unnecessary customs of the society just to please the Brahmins. However, the presence of Brahmins and their priestly services in the Hindu temples would be acceptable even in the changing society. Although the Nairs have lost the old prestige in the society with the social awakening of the low castes, they hold an upper position in the Kerala society[249]. The study on the Nair community

---

[246] A.S. Menon writes: «It is true that inter-caste barriers in Kerala have broken down and caste consciousness is less pronounced in the minds of the people of the present generation, but it is doubtful whether the caste system can be said to have died out completely» (A.S. MENON, *Social and Cultural History*, 75).

[247] Pope's homily in Sri Lanka on 21 January, 1995. See *OR* (E) 1 February 1995, 6-7. See also *NA* 1-2.

[248] JOHN PAUL II, *Redemptoris Missio*, no. 51.

[249] If we look at the political history of Kerala we could see that from 1957 most of the time the Chief Ministers were from higher castes though the majority of the people belongs to the lower class. See E.J. THOMAS, *Coalition Game Politics*, 30-70.

reveals the fact that moral decadence in the family is the beginning of social decadence. Their courage to renew the social system is an inspiration for others to change any kind of unhealthy social systems. The renewal started with the Chattambi Swamikal in the 19th century and continued by M. Padmanabha Menon in the 20th century contributed a stable position to the Nairs in the social life. As the Nairs have constant contact with the Christians in manifold ways, especially through education, the Catholics have a field of evangelization among them. As the Christians and Nairs are living as neighbors throughout Trivandrum as in any other parts of Kerala, the Church has an important role to witness Christ before them. It is practically impossible to have contact with them in the traditional way of the functioning of the Church.

The Mukkuva community is the largest caste group in the Diocese[250]. The faith of the Mukkuva community is proverbial: *patrosinte pāra poleyulla visuāsam* (the strong faith like that of St. Peter). However, the community has been systematically oppressed by all social and religious institutions[251]. They were untouchables to caste Hindus and caste Christians. Most of the priests did not work for the integral development of the people[252]. The Latin Catholics of *Ezhunūtticar* (Seven Hundreds) and *Anjūtticar* (Five Hundreds)[253], in their constant effort to identify with St. Thomas Christians, kept the Mukkuvar community of Trivandrum at a distance. The children of the fishermen were not admitted for priesthood even though they were ready to serve the Church[254]. From the social

---

[250] The Mukkuva community in Trivandrum is still divided into many subdivisions. A real ethnographic research is needed to understand the origin of these divisions in Trivandrum itself.

[251] See E.P. ANTONY, «Origin and Growth», 100c.

[252] The writings of St. Francis Xavier himself confirms that at least some of the missionaries did not come with good intentions. See *EX*, I, 278-282. See also E. JONES, «Work among Fishermen», CWMA.

[253] *Ezhunūtticar* and *Anjūtticar* are probably related with the reception of baptism. But in the Latin Church of Kerala this division has created a lot of tensions. For a detailed study see M. ARATTUKULAM, «The Latin Catholics», 126-328. See also V.N. AIYA, *Travancore State Manual*, II, 119-121.

[254] It is a fact that most of religious congregations (men and women) have not fostered vocations from the native Christians of Trivandrum till recently. It is true that men and women religious have been working for the people and even played a prophetic role during the fishermen's agitation. But whether they worked with the people, accepting the people in their religious fellowship is questionable. Encouraging vocations to priesthood and religious life from the local Church is a sign of the growth of the Church. Already in the beginning of this century Popes have exhorted to encourage native vocations. One of

point of view some Christian missionaries failed to do justice to the people as they deserved[255].

Participation in the ecclesiastical offices was not possible to the people of the Mukkuva community[256]. Since the major part of the parishes of the Mukkuva community was under the Diocese of Cochin till 1953 there was a great break between civil authorities and ecclesiastical authorities[257]. The administrative system of the *Padroado* created some *pradhānis* who were acting like that of any other secular leaders of the Hindu system. The system is deeply rooted at least among the few who still find it difficult to digest the idea of a participatory Church and the new ecclesiological vision which emerged after Vatican II. Nevertheless, the recent social awakening starting with the time of Bishop Peter Bernard Pereira is remarkable. The fishermen's agitation has made the awakening faster.

The Nadars, the Izhavas and the Dalits are called new converts. Though there were random conversions among these castes before the 18th century, the real conversion work started with the arrival of the Carmelite missionaries such as Archbishop Benziger, the Bishop of Quilon, Fr. John Damasceno and Fr. Ildaphonse in this century. These Carmelite missionaries, who had not experienced the scene of the caste Christians of Syrian Catholics and Latin Catholics, preached the Gospel invariably to all. They organized prayer meetings which may be said to be an early form of BECs in Trivandrum. They trusted the natives. They appointed catechists and promoted native vocations. Today the presence of more than fifty priests from the new converts in the Diocese shows the vitality of Christian faith among them.

---

the basic reasons for the foundation of the *Propaganda Fide* was also to promote native vocations.

[255] Once even the Hindu King Rama Varma complained about the Portuguese parish priests of the coast of Travancore and asked the Bishop of Verapoly to supply priests from Missionaries of the Sacred Congregation for the Propagation of Faith. See P.S. BARTOLOMEO, *India Orientalis Christiana*, 261.

[256] The problem is well described with the support of documents in M. ARATTUKULAM, «The Latin Catholics» 189-192. One of the reasons for the conflict between Syrian Christians and Missionaries in the pre-Diamber era was due to the conversion of Mukkuva community to Christianity. See J. KOLLAPARAMBIL, *The St. Thomas Christians' Revolution*, 42.

[257] In Kerala, and in most of the parts of India, religious leaders play a very important role in the development of its community. Among the Mukkuva community of Trivandrum the social development through religious leaders was also not easy since they were politically under Travancore Kingdom and ecclesiastically they were under the Diocese of Cochin.

The conversion work was mainly carried out in the agricultural areas. Numerically, the Nadars are the majority among the new converts and still they keep their caste identity. Their economical and social backwardness, compared to their own people in the neighbouring Protestant Churches, shows that the Catholic Church had less vision than the Protestants in uplifting its own people. The Nadars and the Izhavas have a pluriform religious culture. A meaningful dialogue and ecumenism in concrete level would be the major tasks of BECs.

The social reforms undertaken by the Pulaya caste under the leadership of Ayyan Kali, and the unhealthy policies of the government towards the backward caste, obstruct any possibility of conversion of this caste to Christianity. To be a member of a backward caste and to be a Christian is a real challenge and a living martyrdom in Kerala. The Church in Kerala and in India also *has failed* to understand the suffering of the voiceless[258]. It is also to be noted that the backward classes are even ready to sacrifice all their privileges at least if they are recognized in the Church[259].

Since a peculiar social system is existing among the new converts due to their pluriform religious culture, it is difficult to have a social integration with the traditional Latin Catholics or Syrian Catholics. So, a new pastoral approach is to be sought out. Probably the greatest problem concerning the new converts is with regard to marriage. The pastoral laws envisaged for the traditional Catholics may not be suitable for the new converts. It demands a broader understanding of other Christian denominations and Hinduism[260]. Nevertheless, a social integration is also an important factor. The Church is communion. As St. Paul exhorts the Christians of Corinth, they should not be divided. It is in this respect we find more meaning in the formation of BECs. For, BECs help not only to

---

[258] It is true that the Church takes different measures to get equal rights for the Christian Dalits as Hindu Dalits. It is not enough. The Dalit movement in India at present is an indication that the Christian Churches are still lagging behind in their work with the Dalits. See M. AZARIAH, *The Un-Christian side*. See also F. WILFRED, *From the Dusty Soil*, 124-134.

[259] The backward classes find themselves more comfortable in other denominations such as Salvation Army and Pentecostal Churches than in the Catholic Churches. At present the Indian Church can not blame the western missionaries because most of the missionaries are of Indian origin.

[260] The principles of ecumenism and dialogue given by Second Vatican Council might be given serious attention as the Church is preparing for the celebration of the Jubilee Year of 2000 AD. See JOHN PAUL II, *Tertio Millennio Adveniente*, n. 20. See also *UR; NA; GS* 90; PAUL VI, *Ecclesiam Suam*, ns. 58-118.

have religious integration but also social integration respecting the values of other cultures and traditions[261].

In the religious context we find that Hinduism, Islam and Christianity play a vital role in the life of the people of Trivandrum[262]. Though no follower of Jainism and Buddhism is seen in Trivandrum, the principles of these religions influence the people. Hinduism is the major religion in Trivandrum. Many new converts are related to Hindus not only culturally but also ethnically. The influence of Hinduism is not going to diminish. But there will always be renewal. The renewal initiated by Vaikunda Swami (*Samatva Samājam* — all are equal) and Sri Narayana Guru (*Oru Jati Oru Matam and Oru Daivam* — One Caste, One Religion and One God) influence many Hindus and Christians. The renewal within the Hindu religion is also a challenge to the caste ridden Christian communities. The division due to the liturgical Rites without geographical boundaries in the tiny State of Kerala become incomprehensible. Hence the real mission of the Church is also threatened.

The Muslims are becoming an important socio-religious power in Kerala. It is a fact that there cannot be a government in Kerala without a Muslim representation. A large number of the Muslim centres are very close to the thickly populated Catholic communities of Trivandrum. Fellowship has to be maintained between these two communities not only to avoid communal riots but also to live in religious harmony. A broader understanding of Islam is a need of the time[263]. The importance of forming the basic human communities from BECs will help the dialogue

---

261 See *GS* 58-60.

262 The observation of R.E. Miller regarding dialogue in the presence of three religions deserves special attention. See R.E. MILLER, «Trialogue», 47-63.

263 «Over the centuries many quarrels and dissensions have arisen between Christians and Muslim. The Sacred Council now pleads with all to forget the past, and urges that a sincere effort be made to achieve mutual understanding; for the benefit of all men, let them together preserve and promote peace, justice, liberty, social justice and moral values» (*NA* 3). The description about Muslims by S. Mateer is worth mentioning. He writes: «Our native agents are often positively afraid to address them on the subject of Christianity, as their fierce and fanatical character sometimes leads to violence. With a few of them, however, we have been personally on the most friendly terms, and such individuals readily hear and freely converse with us. One amiable old gentleman, possessed of large estates, who used occasionally to send us presents of native dishes, and come to drink coffee with us, generally taking a small quantity of ground coffee home with him in a paper, was on terms of almost affectionate intimacy with the writer» (S. MATEER, *The Land of Charity*, 228). In my personal interviews with lay people in the Diocese I came to know that in many parishes there exists good relation between Muslims and Christians.

to be more meaningful. It can remove the prejudices both religions cultivate against each other.

Trivandrum being the «headquarters» of many dioceses and denominations, Christianity has an important role to play in the society. The Syro-Malabar Church because of its *Sui Juris* power can establish churches any where in Trivandrum. The Syro-Malankara Catholics also have good institutional basis and a Metropolitan See. But the natives of Trivandrum are not familiar with the Syrian language or Syrian spirituality. These Churches have to identify with the people. Moreover whether the multiplicity of liturgical Rites in Trivandrum without cultural integration would help the growth of the Church is another serious question[264]. Often the multiplication of Rites will only contribute to divide the family relations of the lower castes, who inherited good family values even before accepting the Christian faith.

Trivandrum is the largest Diocese in Kerala. Although Latin Catholics, who, in comparison with all the other Christian Churches, are numerically very significant in Trivandrum, spread out in four taluks of Trivandrum and Kanyakumary districts, socially they represent a large crowd of backward classes. The historical error done to the Latin Catholics of Kerala on the basis of false prestige by a group of powerful Latin Catholics has made the social situation of the community worse than that of lowest class of the Kerala society[265].

The Latin Catholics who have always supported the Congress party were disregarded by the political parties who are known for their *coalition games*. Because of the cultural differences among the Latin Catholics the disunity is also projected in all their attempts to have a common political party. Even the Fishermen's agitation could not unite the people on a common platform for a long time. The problem of fishermen is still unanswered or unsolved.

From the study we could also discover that the social life of the people of Trivandrum is woven with complex realities. The multiplicity of castes in Trivandrum had created enough tensions in the past. The religions also played an important role to foster this tension. The feasts, celebrations, and pilgrimages, though they are occasions of true spiritual experience, need not change the attitude towards the fellow human being. Christianity

---

264 What is important is to preach the Gospel to all people. A liturgy imposed by means of *Latinisation* or *Syriachaisation* may not be suitable to the Church of Kerala. See V. KARUNAN, «Expert Committee», 7. It is a sad story that because of the liturgical multiplicity there is no uniformity even in the verses of «Lord's Prayer».

265 See E.P. ANTONY, «Hierarchy and the Community», 433.

was not an exception to it. At the same time it was through Christianity that many social changes like abolition of slavery, right to wear upper cloths, liberation of women, have taken place in the society. Neverthless, Christianity remained an established religion of a few castes without reaching out to the people of the region. It did not incarnate properly into the cultural situation of the people. It is to be noted that in spite of the intensive mission work carried out for the past five hundred years less than 20% have become Christians.

The situation of un-touchability and un-seeability has changed at present in conceptual and legal level. But the question whether the age-old sentiments of caste and religious feelings have changed, must still to be answered in the negative[266]. What is on the conceptual and legal level has to be incarnated. In the processes of incarnation a methodological shift is inevitable. A new methodology of dialogue or trialogue is a historical necessity[267]. The study also revealed the intimate relationship between social life and spiritual life. The social reformers like Vaikunda Swami, Sri Narayana Guru and Chattambi Swamikal were real charismatic leaders who were born in the social milieu of Trivandrum or South Travancore. The life and activities of these charismatic leaders also show that the native leadership is an important factor for renewal or re-formation[268].

The entire life of Christians in Trivandrum, especially that of the fisher folk, revolves around the Church as an institution. As a good number of the Catholics of Trivandrum are ethnically belonging to the Hindu culture and other Christian denominations, a new approach to ecumenism and dialogue is to be envisaged at grassroots level. As the Church is preparing herself for a new millennium with its Gospel commitment (Mt 28,16-20), she can never remain idle in proclaiming the uniqueness of Christ even in a pluralistic culture. This is not possible with *borrowed identities* or with imposition of a foreign culture[269]. A

---

[266] The attempts to form basic human communities by the Hindu leaders also cannot be ignored. See V. ABRAHAM, «Neighbours in Love», 14-17.

[267] «The state of Kerala provides a unique history of trialogical relationships, a kind of laboratory even within multi-religious India. Kerala is the only place in the world where Hindus, Muslims, and Christians live together in such numerical equilibrium. According to 1981 Census Hindus comprise 58 percent, Christians 21 percent and Muslims 21 percent of the population» (R.E. MILLER, «Trialogue», 48).

[268] See J.W. PICKETT, *Christian Mass Movements*, 319-320.

[269] «The earlier the Indian Church gets rid of the stigma of an imported religion, the better will be her prospects of penetrating Hindu minds» (D. ACHARUPARAMBIL, «The Problem of Presenting Christianity», 162-182). According to L. Freeman among many

methodological shift in the functioning of parish, therefore, becomes inevitable. Already in 1977 the Asian Bishops have realized that the existing parish structures sometimes were not conducive to intensive Christian life[270].

In the present day of fast changing culture, we see a break up in the traditional cultural units. Social problems, like alcoholism and separation of families, are increasing day by day. The traditional way of living the Church is not satisfactory and lacks pastoral vision in keeping with the culture of Trivandrum. And *a new way of being the Church* through the BECs is a felt need of the people of God in the Diocese of Trivandrum. The BECs, as they grow from the grassroots, can carry the ethos of the people. They may work as a leaven in the society. The afore-mentioned socio-religious context helps one to understand the background to the emergence of the BECs in the Diocese of Trivandrum.

---

ordinary Christians in India there remains a deep fear and ignorance of their country's spiritual culture. And because of western conditioning the Indian Christians are strangers in their own land. See L. FREEMAN, «A Hindu saint», 173-174. See also *FAPA*, xxiii-xxx; J.A.G.G. VAN LEEUWEN, *Fully Indian;* A. ROEST-CROLLIUS – T. NKÉRAMIHIGO, *What is so New*; A.R. CROLLIUS, *Teologia dell'Inculturazione*; M. DHAVAMONY, «The Christian Theology of Inculturation», 1-43.

270 See *FAPA*, 76. The Workshop on «Pastoral Life» in 1969 has expressed the need of a structural change in the parish. See CBCI, *All India Seminar*, 423-431.

CHAPTER III

The Emergence of Basic Ecclesial Communities
in the Diocese of Trivandrum

In the second chapter we discussed the various aspects of the socio-religious context of Trivandrum. We have seen that Trivandrum is geographically a small region of Kerala with a population of 2.270.729 living within the area of 2.192 sq. Km. The geographical size has never been a reason to keep its cultural diversity which is the characteristic feature of the Indian sub-continent. Trivandrum is a city of complex socio-religious culture with different castes and multiplicity of religions. It is from this cultural background that most of the leaders like Sri Narayana Guru, Chattambi Swamikal, Ayyan Kali of modern renaissance emerged in Kerala. They did not separate spirituality from social development; religion from culture. They proved that spiritual renewal is the basis of social renewal in the Hindu context.

Christianity, with an eschatological orientation, has been in existence in Trivandrum from the 16th century as a part of the people's faith and culture[1]. The Christian message had a social and spiritual effect on the people. The people were proud of being Christians in a caste ridden society. More than any material benefit, the message of the Gospel, which was expressed through the devotional prayers and Christian doctrine became part and parcel of their very existence[2]. The very fact that they

---

[1] «The church also appeased the poor with bible texts that God will look after tomorrow and that suffering in this life will be rewarded in the next» (N. NAYAK, *A struggle within the struggle*, 4).

[2] What Fr. Mark Stephen says of the Catholics of Kodimanai in the Diocese of Kottar is also applicable to Trivandrum. He says: «They have been Catholics for almost four hundred years. Even now they are ready to shed their blood and die for their faith» (S.H.M. STEPHEN, «Basic Community» 60). A comment made by the first Protestant missionary W.J. Ringeltaube in 1813 also testifies the strong faith of the people. He says

did not go for work on Sundays even at the time of extreme poverty shows how they were emotionally attached to the teachings of the Church.

In this chapter our study aims at investigating the genesis of BECs in Trivandrum. We begin this with a description of the early forms of the ecclesial communities in the particular situation of Trivandrum and the role played by St. Francis Xavier and the Carmelites. Then we discuss the changes that have taken place in the ecclesial life of Trivandrum after the Second Vatican Council. Finally we give a detailed description of the theological and sociological factors that prompted the beginning of BECs in Trivandrum as a diocesan pastoral programme.

1. Earlier Forms of Ecclesial Communities in Trivandrum

We have seen in the second chapter that already from the time of Portuguese missionaries Christianity has been spread all over the Travancore Coast. The whole geographical area was under the «Ecclesiastical territory of Cochin» though the ecclesial life was not deeply rooted in the life of the people. However, there had been constant effort on the part of some of the missionaries to build up ecclesial communities in the region[3]. Among all the missionaries in the region, St. Francis Xavier played a significant role in this endeavor. His life and teachings are still a paradigm in Trivandrum. Although there had been missionaries before him the ecclesial life and the spirituality of the region

---

that the people whom St. Francis Xavier converted form a powerful and unconquerable body. They have been brought up in that religion and they like it. Regarding the conversion of Catholics to the Protestant Church he says: «It remains to be seen whether we shall get many converts from the Church of Rome» (W. RINGELTAUBE, *Journal from January 7, 1813 to January 20,* CWMA). As regards the faith of the new converts, Bishop V.V. Derrera writes in his report to Peter Cardinal Fumasoni-Biondi, the Prefect of the Sacred Congregation of the Propagation of faith in 1939: «I am glad to say that our new converts disappointed totally the Hindu Mission promoters. They were offered pecuniary help and reduction of school fees for their children on condition to return to Hinduism; but they all refused the offers although they are miserably poor, and remained faithful to God. I am awfully proud to have such good and faithful converts, and I thank God for having given them strength and courage to resist. Some 2 months ago the Secretary of the Hindu Mission told one of my secular priests: We do not understand your new Catholic converts. We promise them a lot if they come back to Hinduism, but they do not want it; Protestant-converts on the contrary easily come over, we get as many as we like. Why should we uselessly spend more time in trying to reconvert your new converts? We are not going to molest anymore. — This is surely a nice testimony coming from our opponents!» (V.V. DEREERE, The «Status Missionis», AGOCD).

[3] For a short description of the missionary activities in the region before the coming of St. Francis. Xavier see M. D'SA, *History of the Catholic Church* I, 27-69. See also D. FERROLI, *The Jesuits in Malabar,* I, 140-142.

depends to a large extent on the saintly personality of St. Francis Xavier. He remains *a point of reference* and *a point of departure* for further ecclesial growth.

1.1 *The Contribution of St. Francis Xavier*

At the time of the arrival of Francis Xavier in Goa on 6th May, 1542, Goa was the largest Diocese in Christendom though, it had only 13 parishes. The bishop was Frey Juan de Albuquerque to whom Francis Xavier paid his first visit[4]. After spending a few months in Goa due to the unfavourable climate for traveling to Fishery Coast, he sailed to Fishery Coast at the end of September crossing through the Cochin and Travancore Coasts. He landed at Manapad in October 1542. From there he walked by foot to Tuticorin, the main town of the Fishery Coast[5]. There he spent four months from October 1542 to February 1543[6]. As it was the time for the people to go for the great Pearl Fishery near Mannar (Ceylon), Francis Xavier began to visit the interior villages from Tuticorin to Manapad and from there to Cape Comerin until September 1543[7].

In October 1543 Francis Xavier returned to Goa after a short visit to Colombo and remained there till December 21, 1543[8]. On December 21, 1543 Francis Xavier, with his friends, set out from Goa to Cochin, the most established Christian centre, and reached Cochin on 1st January, 1544. There he visited Pedro Gonçalves, who entrusted the task of Christianization of Tuticorin in the Fishery Coast to Francis Xavier and the Franciscans[9]. From Cochin Francis Xavier and his friends started out

---

[4] Francis Xavier informed the bishop that His Holiness, Pope Paul III, and His Highness, the King of Portugal, had sent him to India to help the Portuguese, to instruct the new converts, and to labour for the conversion of the infidels. At the same time he presented the bishop with the papal briefs appointing him nuncio, which he had received from the king; and he declared that he was surrendering them to His Lordship and would not use them in any other way than that approved by him, the bishop. See *FX*, II, 154-156.

[5] See *FX*, II, 279-282. 285-286.

[6] See *FX*, II, 303-311.321. It was at Tuticorin that Francis Xavier translated the most important prayers and truths of the catechism into the language of Paravas (Tamil) and taught them to both children and adults.

[7] From the villages Francis Xavier could also understand the superstitious beliefs of the people. See *FX*, II, 334-359.

[8] See *FX*, II, 360.

[9] Before the coming of Francis Xavier, Franciscans were working in the coast. See *FX*, II, 405. As the ships to Portugal were to leave Cochin, Francis Xaviers' main work

to Fishery Coast and when they reached Quilon, Francis Xavier had to interrupt his journey to pay a visit to Ceylon[10]. From Ceylon Francis Xavier returned to the Fishery Coast and began to organize the work of missions[11].

1.1.1 St. Francis Xavier's Mission in Travancore

It was only in November-December 1544, visiting the coast from Punnalkayal to Cape Comerin that Francis Xavier could come to the Travancore Coast that extended from Cape Comorin to Quilon and plan for a general conversion[12]. Francis Xavier entered into the Travancore Kingdom after a rich mission experience at the Fishery Coast. Though there was a large population of *infideles* living outside the coast Francis Xavier tried first to convert the people of the coast[13]. Regarding the conversion work of Francis Xavier, C.M. Agur, who wrote the voluminous Travancore Church History, says:

> The progress of the Roman Catholic Mission from Quilon to Cape Comerin is a remarkable record. The permanent results of the early work of the early labourers are still seen. When Quilon was occupied by the early Jesuits, they formed three congregations there, and attached to them they also erected a

---

in Cochin was to prepare his letters to Europe. See also M.J. COSTELLOE, *The Letters and Instructions*, xvi.

10 Francis Xavier thought that he could convert Bhuvaneka Bahu, the ruler of Ceylon. But he did not succeed in doing so. See *FX*, II, 411-424.

11 Francis Xavier divided the Fishery Coast into three regions. He entrusted Manapad to Mansilhas, Tuticorin to Lizano (Liçano) and reserved Punnaikayal for himself as it was centrally located in between Tuticorin and Manapad. During this time Francis Xavier kept up an active correspondence with his confreres. See *FX*, II, 425-427.

12 The inhabitants of the Travancore coast were mainly of Mukkuva caste. On 18th December 1544 Francis Xavier wrote to Mansilhas from Cochin: «A 16 do mês de Dezembro cheguei a Cochim. Antes que chegasse baptizei todos os macuás, pescadores que vivem em o reyno de Travancor» (*EX*, I, 244). See also *MX*, II, 350-354. During this period he visited the following villages namely: Pūvar (poovar), Colancor (Kollankod), Valevalé (Pallavilatura: now it is known as Vallavilaithura), Tutur (Tuttûrturai), Puduturé (Putturai) Temguapatão (Taingapatam) União (Injam), Morála (Midalam), Vaniacur (Vanniakudi) Coléche (Kolachel), Careapatão (Kadiapattanam), Calmutão (Muttamtura) Palão (Pallam). It is also reasonable to believe that Francis Xavier had visited places beyond Pûvar (Poovar) especially Vilinjam (Vizhinjam). See *MX*, II, 375. See also *FX*, II, 463-467.

13 He had least hope for the conversion of the Brahmins. Moreover it was in the interest of the Portuguese, who were engaged in trade through sea, that the fishermen be converted. See D. FERROLI, *The Jesuits in Malabar*, I, 124-126. However, Francis Xavier had contact with the Brahmins. His contact with the Brahmins are described in his letter on 15 January, 1545 to his companions in Rome. See *EX*, I, 272-278.

monastry [monastery] and a chapel and adorned them. They are also said to have founded a distinct Christian Village along the sea-shore for their fishermen converts and surrounded it with a wall mounted with cannon. From Quilon they extended southward towards the Cape and easily occupied the whole coast «sacred ground to them from its having been the scene of Francis Xavier's labours». The first Churches built by Xavier at Mampully and Kottar were very modest and humble buildings. In fact all the early Churches were built of palm trees and leaves surmounted by a simple cross[14].

1.1.2 Formation of Ecclesial Communities

One of the greatest achievements of Francis Xavier's mission in the Fishery Coast and in the Travancore Coast was the establishment of ecclesial communities. As the number of Christians increased he was concerned about the construction of the churches[15]. But he gave more importance to building up ecclesial communities emphasizing the spiritual aspects of Christian life. This he did through the deepening of Christian doctrine.

1.1.3 Christian Doctrine: Basis of Ecclesial Communities

As a pre-condition for the formation of ecclesial communities Francis Xavier was very particular to teach Christian doctrine. According to G.Schurhammer, Francis Xavier adapted himself to the mental capacities of his listeners[16]. His method was very simple but profound. When Francis Xavier reached a village, he brought all men and boys together[17]. He then preached to them and explained the chief articles of the Christian faith in their native language[18]. He made the sign of the cross and asked his hearers repeat three times their acknowledgment of one God in three

---

[14] C.M. AGUR, *Travancore Church History*, 279.

[15] «Far-me hás a saber novas vossas e dos christãos de contino, e dai-vos pressa a fazer igreja; e quando for acabada, far-mo heis saber» (*EX*, I, 205).

[16] See *FX*, II, 218-224. His stay at Goa for some days helped him to understand the mind of the people of India. From there he formulated his own methodology to preach the Gospel to the people of India.

[17] Sometimes the villagers themselves invited Francis Xavier to the village and expressed their desire to become Christians. «quando llegava en los lugares de los gentiles, los quales me mandaron llamar para que los hiziesse chiristianos [...]. En otra tierra a cinquoenta legoas desta donde ando, me mandaron dezir los moradores della que querían ser christianos [...]» (*EX*, I, 273-274 ff).

[18] Francis Xavier wrote down the prayers and Commandments in Latin and with the help of someone it was translated into Tamil. Francis Xavier might have learned the prayers by heart to teach the people. See *FX*, II, 308. See also *DI*, 1, 286.

divine Persons: «In the name of the Father, and of the Son, and of the Holy Spirit». He then put on a sleeveless white surplice of the kind worn by Portuguese priests and recited the *Confiteor*, Creed, Commandments, Our Father, Hail Mary and *Salve Regina*. Then all, both young and old, had to repeat for sometime what he had said.

He gave an explanation, also in Tamil, of the articles of the Creed and of the Commandments. Then all, who wished to become Christians, publicly asked pardon from God for the sins of their past lives. At the end he asked all, both young and old, if they believed. He then recited for them in a loud voice one article of the Creed after another, and after each article he asked them if they believed it. All would then cross their arms over their breast and reply that they believed. After this he baptized them with the simple formula, «I baptize you in the name of the Father, and of the Son, and of the Holy Spirit», without further ceremonies. Each one received a palm-leaf strip on which the *kanakapula* (an accountant) had written his new Portuguese name in Tamil. The men then went home and sent their wives and the rest of their households; and these too, after being prepared in the same way, received the sacrament of baptism[19].

1.1.4 Role of Priests in the Ecclesial Communities

Francis Xavier converted the people of Travancore Coast *en masse*. After giving baptism to the people of a village, he passed to another. In the process of great Evangelization he did not get sufficient help from secular or religious priests. So he wrote to St. Ignatius in Rome and Fr. Simon Rodrigues in Lisbon, urging them to send more priests[20]. In his

---

[19] See *FX*, II, 470-471. See also *EX*, I, 271-278. Francis Xavier persuaded Gasper Coelho, a native priest, to translate the *Explanation of the Creed* into Tamil and to make numerous copies of it so that it could be distributed and explained to the women in the churches on Saturdays and Sundays. He also ordered his *Explanation of the Apostles' Creed* and his *Christian Doctrine* to be taught in other villages of India. See *EX*, I, 348-370.

[20] See *EX*, I, 255-260. Francis Xavier even invites S. Rodrigues to come to India but strongly tells him that he should not send any of his friends. Francis Xavier, by this time, might have heard of the evil deeds of many Portuguese. «Nenhum amigo voso consentais vir à India com carregos e oficios d'El-Rey, porque deles propriamente se pode dizer: «Deleantur de libro viventium et cum iustis non scribantur». Por muyto que de sua virtude confieis, se não for confirmado en graça como forão os apostolos, doutra maneyra não espereis que farão o que devem; porque o de quaa estaa tanto en costume de fazer o que não se deve, que não vejo cura nenhuma, porque todos vão para o caminho de rapio, [rap]is. He stou spantado como os que de lá vem achão tantos modos, tempos e participios a este verbo cuytado de rapio, [rap] is; he são de tam boa presa os que de lá

letter to Fr. Francisco Mansilhas, who was at the Fishery Coast, he gives admonition to take special care of the newly converted Christians of Travancore[21]. In his letter, dated 8th May, 1545, to Master Diogo and Fr. Micer Paulo in Goa, Francis Xavier writes that since Mansilhas and the Malabar priests were in Cape Comerin his service was not that much required[22]. He, however, had shown special concern towards the new converts by asking the priests who came from Europe to go to Cape Comerin[23]. And in his letter on 22 October, 1548 he encourages Fr. Francisco Henriques[24] to continue in Travancore inspite of the anti-conversion approach of the king. For, Francis Xavier was quite sure of the result of F. Henrique's work[25].

Among all the instructions to priests, his instruction in February 1548 is prophetic. It is called a «Missionary Testament»[26]. He instructs the priests to visit the houses under their care and be diligent in giving baptism to the newborn children[27] They should be diligent in teaching

---

vem despachados com estes cargos, que nunqua alargão nada do que tomão» (See *EX,* I, 281-282).

[21] «E vizitareis os christãos que se fizerão em a praya de Travancor, repartindo por todas essas terras, como melhor vos parecer, estes Padres malavares; olhareis [que vivam] muito bem e castamente, trabalhando em serviço de Deos, dando bom exemplo de sy» (*EX,* I, 286).

[22] See *EX,* I, 288-294.

[23] Francis Xavier writes to Ignatius of Loyola and the Companions in Europe that the missionaries should be sent from Europe even if they are not scholars. See *EX,* I, 298-301, 307-310. 397-400.

[24] F. Henriques (1547-1551) joined the Society of Jesus at Coimbra in 1545 and came to India in the following year. From 1547 to 1548 he worked in Travancore and then from 1550-1551 at the Madre de Dios College at Cochin. See *DI,* I, 47*. (The particular page numbering in *Documenta Indica* is of editors). For short biographical notes on the Jesuit missionaries who excelled in their services see G. J. MULAKARA, *History of the Cochin Diocese,* 85-88. See also *DI,* I, 43*-52*; II, 6*-8*.

[25] «Nam vos descomsoleis em ver que não fazeis tamto fructo com eses christãos como desejais, por serem elles dados a idollatryas, e ell-rei ser comtra os que se fazem christãos [...]. Oulhai Irmão meu Efrancisco Amriquez, que fazeis nese regno de Travancor mays ffructo do que cuidais; e oulhai, depois que vós estays nese regno, quantas crianças baptisadas são mortas e estão aguora na gloria do paraisso, as quaes não gosarão de Deus [76v]se vós lá não estiverês!» (*EX,* I, 466).

[26] See C. VARKEY, ed., *St. Francis Xavier,* 132.

[27] «A ordem que haveis de ter para servirdes a Deos hé a seguinte, na qual vos occupareis com muita deligencia: 1. Primeiramente vos occpareis com muita deligencia, nos lugares que vizitardes ou tiverdes a cargo, de baptizar as crianças que nascem, por ser este hum feito mayor que nestes partes ao prezente se pode, hindo de caza em caza pelos lugares que andardes vizitando, preguntando se ahi há alguma criança para baptizar, levando comvosco alguns meninos do lugar para vos ajudarem a preguntar. 2. E não

Christian doctrine to the children and should know whether the people attend regularly on Sundays and whether they recite the prayers which were taught. Francis Xavier also reminds the priests to give explanation of the prayers which they recite and tells them to condemn the vices of the people[28].

According to Francis Xavier, the priests also should be instruments of peace. He says that the priests should enquire about any quarrelling in the villages and should help the people to become friends when they come to the church on Sundays and the women on Saturdays[29]. Though Francis Xavier was concerned very much about the salvation of souls he had special care for the sick and the needy. He instructs the priests to exhort the faithful about their obligation to inform them when someone is sick in

---

confieis em meirinhos nem em outras pessoas, que vos vierem dizer quando alguma criança nasce, pelo descuido que nestes cabe, e perigo que corre[m] as crinaças de morrerem sem baptismo» (*EX,* I, 426). Francis Xavier tells the priests about reading the Gospel, when they give baptism to infants. «Quando baptizardes crianças, rezai-lhes primeiro hum evangelho de S. Marcos ou o Credo, e depois o [s] baptizarês com a intenção de o [s] fazerdes christãos, dizendo as palavaras essenciaes do baptismo, que são: «Ego te baptizo in nomine Patris et Filii et Spiritus San [c]ti» lançando agoa quando dizerdes as palavras; acabando-as de baptizar, lhe direis hum evangelho ou huma oração, segundo for vossa devoção» (*EX,* I, 432). However, H. Henriques, one of the succesors of Francis Xavier had his reservations regarding the ceremonies of infant baptism proposed by Francis Xavier. See *DI,* I, 600.

[28] «Occupar-vos heis muito em os lugares onde estiverdes, ou lugares que vizitardes ou tiverdes cargo, de fazer ensinar aos meninos a doutrina christã, fazendo com muita deligencia ajunta-llos, e emcommendando aos moradores que os ensinem com muita deligencia, e que façã,o seu officio; tomando-lhe conta de quantos sabem as oraçoens, para quando outra vez o[s] vizitardes, acheis mais fruito, sabendo elles a conta que lhes haveis de pedir: e este fruito dos meninos' hé o principal. 4. Aos domingos, no lugar ou lugares que tiverdes o cargo de vizitar, fareis que vão os homens à igreja dizer as oraçoens; e [n] os lugares em que òs domingos não fordes, pedireis conta ao meirinho se os patangatins do lugar vão à igreja, e assim as outras pesoas do lugar. No lugar em que vos achardes, depois de ditas as oraçoens, lhas declarareis, e reprehendereis os vicios que entre elles há com exemplos e comparaçoens claras, procurando sempre de lhe fallar tão claro a que vos entenda [m], dizendo-lhe que não se emmendando, que Deos os há de castigar nesta vida por doenças, e abreviando-lhes os dias da vida por tirannias de tigares e rey, e depois de sua morte hindo ao inferno» (*EX,* I, 427-428).

[29] «Emformar-vos heis dos que no lugar se querem mal, e ò domingo trabalhareis de os fazer amigos quando se ajuntarem na igreja, e outro tanto fareis aos sabbados com as molheres que se querem mal» (*EX,* I, 428). According to Francis Xavier problems of little importance must be settled by the «patangatins» (village leader) of the village. «e as demandas houver no povo, as que não forem de muita importancia, ao domingo, depois de acabadas as oraçoens, dareis ordem como se despachem com os patangatins do lugar» (*EX,* I, 430-431).

the village[30]. His *option for the poor* is well reflected in his sensitivity to the poor and the needy. He says that the alms which the priests receive from men and women on Sundays and Saturdays and what is offered in the church or promised by the sick, should be distributed among the poor[31].

Francis Xavier was so particular that the adults, both men and women, also should be taught Christian doctrine in their own language. Regarding the Christian doctrine he wanted that his successors should follow what he had left in writing[32]. The pastoral concern of Francis Xavier also extended to those who die. For Francis Xavier, funeral services also were to become occasions for exhortation to think about the future life[33]. Reminding himself of the Gospel episode (Mk 10,13-16), Francis Xavier had special concern for the children. He exhorted the priests to show much love for the children who come to the prayers, and avoid offending them, overlooking the punishments which they deserved[34].

---

[30] «Os que estiverem doentes vizita-llo[s] heis, dando-lhe lugar e ordem como vos venhão dizer quando alguem estiver doente; e nesta vizitação fa-llo[s] heis dizer a confissão geral e Credo, e preguntando se crem em cada artigo verdadeiramente; e para isto levareis hum menino que saiba as oraçoens porque as diga, e rezareis hum evangelho; e amoestareis aos homens e molheres aos domingos e sabbados que vos fação saber quando alguma pessoa adoecer, avizando que, se vo-llo não fizerem saber, que os não haveis de enterrar na igreja, nem adonde enterrão os christãos» (*EX*, I, 427-428). Francis Xavier's concern for the poor and sick is seen even in his voyage to India. See his letter to Rome written on 1st January, 1542 at Mozambique. See *EX*, I, 91-93.

[31] «E as esmollas que derem, assim homens como molheres, aos domingos e sabbados, ou esmollas que offerecem nas igrejas, ou promessas de doentes, destribuhir-se hão todas aos pobres, de modo que não tomemos nenhuma couza para nós outros» (*EX*, I, 428). During the four months of stay in Tuticorin, Francis Xavier was called from all sides to the homes of the sick so that he might pray over the sick and over the others in the house. See *FX*, I, 310.

[32] «Aos sabbados e domingos quando se ajuntarem na igreja os homens e molheres declarar-lhes heis os artigos da fé pela ordem que vos deixo escripto ao P. Francisco Coelho, para que do portuguez os mude em malavar; e acabados de mudar, fareis como por elles o tenho escripto, para que cada sabbado e domingo os façais ler na igreja em que estiverdes e tiverdes cargo de vizitar» (*EX*, I, 429).

[33] «Quando morrer [alguem], enterra-llo heis, hindo a sua caza com huma cruz e meninos dizendo as oraçoens pelo caminho, e em chegando a sua caza direis hum responso, e levando depois [a] enterra-llo, e todos os meninos dizendo as oraçoens; quando [o] houverdes de enterrar, outro responso. E acabado de enterrar, aos que estão prezentes em breves palavras lhes fareis huma exortação, fazendo-lhes lembrança que han de morrer, e que para isso se emcommendem com bem viver se querem hir ao parazio» (*EX*, I, 429-430).

[34] «Aos meninos que vem às oraçoens mostrareis muito amor, e guardai-vos de escandalizar, dessimulando com os castigos que merecem» (*EX*, I, 434). Francis Xavier

The ecclesial communities which Francis Xavier envisaged were not based on mere devotional prayers. Though, many a time, Protestant missionaries criticized the method of keeping the Catholics ignorant of the Gospel, the exhortation of Francis Xavier testifies that the Gospel was given due importance in his time[35]. He knew very well that without the help of native Christians an ecclesial community could not be fostered. Out of this conviction he appointed *kanakapula* or catechists whose presence still continue in many of the parishes of the Diocese of Trivandrum. In the absence of priests they played an important role.

1.1.5 Lay Participation in the Ecclesial Communities

When the missionaries came to Travancore they sought the help of the natives[36]. Lay *participation* in the ecclesial matters in Kerala is not a new phenomenon[37]. The appointment of *kanakapula* by Francis Xavier is evidence of his attitude towards the laity in that period. In Trivandrum the *kanakapula* had much influence in the ecclesial communities.

1.1.6 *Kanakapula* in the Coastal Villages

In his mission work, Francis Xavier was assisted by local laymen. They were called *kanakapula*, in Tamil *kanakkapillei*, whose duty was to teach catechism[38], assist as sacristan, assemble the people for prayers, administer baptism in case of necessity, keep register of births and enquire about impediments of marriages[39]. Francis Xavier also asked his

---

had forseen the potentiality of children in evangelization. So he took more care to instruct the children. See *EX*, I, 285. In the present day context, John Paul II's concern for the children in 1994 (*Letter of the Pope to Children*) deserves special mentioning.

[35] «Exorta-llo heis aos sabbados e domingos aos homens e molheres que, quando algum menino estiver doente, que o tragão à igreja para lhe dizerem o Evangelho; e isto para que os grandes tenhão fé e amor à igreja, e as crianças se achem melhor» (*EX*, I, 430).

[36] Unlike other Portuguese missionaries Francis Xavier brought together the most learned individuals of the place and sought out individuals who had some knowledge of Portuguese in addition to their own native speech. There were three seminarians who accompanied him from Goa. See *FX*, II, 308.

[37] See J. KOLLAPARAMBIL, *The Archdeacon of All-India.*

[38] It was the desire of Francis Xavier that the Christians be taught catechism in fixed localities. See *EX*, II, 69-80. The term *kanakapula* denotes only an accountant. In the coastal villages the *kanakapula* had been very influential people.

[39] «With the four thousand *fanams* which M.A. de Sousa had generously given him for each year of his term of office, Master Francis Xavier could appoint a *kanakapula*, or catechist, in each village, who would teach Christian doctrine twice a day, one hour in the

successors to continue his method. In his letter to F. Mansilhas on 18 December, 1544, Francis Xavier even mentions a particular *kanakapula* called Mateus, who helped Francis Xavier in his missionary work[40]. Francis Xavier gave specific instructions to the catechists called *kanakapula* in 1545. He reminds them that if they would follow his instruction well, they could also gain many souls for the glory of God[41]. What Francis Xavier carried out 450 years ago sheds light on his vision of lay participation in the ecclesial communities. However, since *kanakapula* had acquired a hereditary status, the system was also not free of errors[42]. Since the people of coastal villages lived so close to the Church and the parochial house, the role of *kanakapula* became functionary.

1.1.7 Confraternities

The emergence of confraternities in the history of the Church goes back to the Middle Ages especially during the time of Francis of Assisi and St. Dominic[43]. In India they became a part of the Christian religious

---

mornings to the boys and a second in the evening to the girls. The *kanakapula* also acted as sacristan of the Church» (*FX*, II, 425). «He wrote to the king and queen about his first experiences on the India mission and about the four thousand *fanams* which M.A.de Sousa had been willing to allot during his period of office for the support of the *kanakapulas*, and he asked that this grant might be confirmed in perpetuity» (*FX*, II, 406).

[40] «Trareis comvosco Matheus e o meirinho que andava comigo de Viravãodepatanão, e vossos mossos, e algum canacapula comvosco que saibão escrever para em cada lugar deixar as oraçoens escriptas» (*EX*, I, 247). See also *FX*, II, 474.

[41] See *EX*, II, 304-307. See also *FX*, II, 219-222.

[42] Hacker, a Protestant Missionary, writes about the Vallavila Parish in 1886 like this: «A work which has taken up a good deal of my time one way and another during the past two years and a quarter is a new work among the fishermen on the seashore. These fishermen have been Roman Catholics for centuries; but so far as I can see they have benefited little from their connection with Rome, and at times being ground[ed] down by priests and their kanakans turned against them» (HACKER, *Printed Report, 1886*, CWMA). In some places *kanakapula* became only a *kanakan* doing the work as an accountant. See BERNARDIN, *To Rev. Fr. Damascene: Parassala*, PAP.

[43] See F. VANDENBROUCKE, *A History of Christian Spirituality*, II, 319-327. A confraternity is defined as a sodality that has been established as a moral person and has as its purpose the promotion of public worship. The worship may assume any one of the many practical forms: assistance at the Mass, nocturnal adoration, procession, public recitation of the rosary. The purpose of a confraternity is often indicated by its title, which may also refer to the attributes of God, the mysteries of the Christian religion, the Feasts of Our Lord or His Blessed Mother, or the saints. A confraternity has a distinct habit or insignia. Its male members may not take part in public sacred functions unless

culture when two secular priests and Portuguese missionaries Michael Vaz and Diogo de Borba (1537-1553), introduced them on 24th April, 1541 in Goa. M. D'sa writes:

> Michael Vas and Diogo de Borba, both secular priests, both eminent in learning and sanctity, both very zealous for the propagation of faith, consulted with each other to find out the best way of propagating Christianity in Goa and the surrounding countries and after many conferences came to the institution of a confraternity under the protection and direction of men who possessed influence and zeal, whose work would be the persecution of idolatry and propagation of the Catholic religion. They informed Bishop Albuquerque and the principal civil officials of their resolution and, with their approval, statutes were drawn up of a new confraternity, that of Santa Fé or Holy Faith. On Sunday, the 24th April 1541, Diogo de Borba, with his wonted eloquence published [announced] to the assembled nobility and gentry of Goa from the pulpit of the Church of Our Lady of Light (N. Sra. da Luz) the establishment of the confraternity[44].

One of the important results of the confraternity was that people liked it so much that soon plenty of alms began to pour in for the benefit of the new converts. It influenced both the Latin and the Oriental Christians of Kerala. Within a short period it was spread throughout all the Christian centres. The presence of different confraternities existing already from the time of Francis Xavier is a sign of their popularity[45]. Despite many shortcomings, the confraternities helped the ecclesial life to be very active[46].

The confraternities had been fostered throughout the universal Church and the Portuguese and the Carmelite fostered them in Kerala. In the old Cochin parishes these confraternities are known as *combria sabha*. A short experience in the coastal villages of Trivandrum would reveal how much the people were taken up by the confraternities in their religious life. The confraternity promises to abide, obey and practice everything

---

they wear it. Women may be enrolled in confraternities only for the purpose of gaining the indulgences and spiritual favours granted to the members. See F. LOMBARD, «Confraternities and Arch-confraternities»,154.

44 M. D'SA, *History of the Catholic Church* I, 65-66. The establishment of the Seminary of Santa Fé which gradually developed into the College of St. Paul was aimed to establish a confraternity of men of good conduct and zeal. See D. FERROLI, *The Jesuits in Malabar*, I, 130-131.

45 See *FX*, II, 401. See also M. D'SA, *History of the Catholic Church*, I, 65-66.

46 See *FX*, II, 219.

which is ordered by Canon Law specially what is contained in the second book 3rd part of Canon 684-725 of 1917 Code[47].

No one leading a scandalous or unchristian life was ever to be admitted into the confraternity. And the members of the confraternity had privileges[48] and duties[49]. The president of the confraternity has a respectable position in the society[50] and he would meet the expenses of the celebration of the annual feast of the confraternity. The feast was an occasion to show one's prestige and he became a debtor. When one becomes a president of a confraternity he will ever be called *Prisenti or Prasidenti*[51].

2. Role of Carmelites in the Formation of Ecclesial Communities

The presence of Carmelites in Kerala forms part of the history of the 17th century Catholic Church in Kerala. The important mission of the

---

[47] Though a number of Canons are quoted in the norms, the people were not given instruction about what is said in the Canons. The significance of confraternity in the old Cochin Diocese could be understood from the norms given to the «Comprimsso» of the Confraternity of Our Lady Mother of Doloures established in the Mullavalappu Chapel in 1936. See «*Comprimssio» of the Confraternity O. L. Mother of Doloures established in the Mullavalappu*, (1936), AC. The establishment of the confraternity was in response to the request of 22 lay people. In the Diocese of Trivandrum at least some priests consider that the emergence of BECs cause the decline of confraternities.

[48] The members shall wear as their uniforms violet *mureas* as their emblem over white *opas*. The confraternity in a body will take part in the funeral of the members free of the fees except for the cross and *chamador*. The office bearers of the confraternity had also special privileges. Women were not entitled to be elected as office bearers.

[49] The members and specially the office bearers are bound to attend the funeral procession of the members of the confraternity and others for which the confraternity is invited lawfully. Gradually it led to *expensive funerals*. «They wanted to make the funeral rites grand, and were ready to spend money on them. Showy funerals and expensive Church ceremonies are a matter of social prestige for families and relatives. A living person seems to be of less value than his corpse and a lot of ceremonial around the corpse. The Church does not seem to have a different value to convey, and this adds to the painfulness of the situation» (T. KOCHERY, «The Cross Now and Here», 241).

[50] The presidents are called *prisenti*, in Trivandrum. They have a respectable position in the coastal parishes. It is also tragic that many a time with a celebration of one confraternity feast, called *Kombriya Perunāl*, the *prisenti* becomes poor. Only *reputation* remains!

[51] It is beyond doubt that the confraternities played a significant role in the religious life of the people. It gave a special security to its members within the association. However, the relevance of confraternities were being questioned. The *CIC* does not deal with the confraternities like that of old Code of Canon Law. See B. SECONDIN, *I Nuovi Protagonisti*, 66-67.

Carmelites was to bring back the separated Syrian Christians to the Catholic faith. Within a short period of time they made a great impact on the ecclesial life of the people of Kerala[52]. In the Diocese of Trivandrum, as with Francis Xavier, the Carmelites made a missionary harvest especially working among the non-coastal villages, converting the Nadars, the Izhavas and the Dalits to Christianity[53]. The main concern of the Carmelites, like that of Francis Xavier, was the salvation of souls. In order to save souls by converting the Hindus to Christianity, the Carmelites adopted a method different from Francis Xavier. The approach of Francis Xavier was first baptism and then catechism or instruction. The Carmelites' approach was first instruction and then baptism.

Among all the Carmelite missionaries Bishop Benziger (1864-1942), who had been the Bishop of Quilon from 1905 to 1931[54], and Fr. John

---

[52] The Carmelites had established themselves in Goa in the year 1620. In 1634 Fr. Jose Elias along with another Carmelite from Goa came to Malabar to study the possibility of establishing a residence in the Diocese of Cochin and the Archdiocese of Angamaly. Despite the objection from the Jesuits to have a residence, the Carmelites established a Confraternity of the Scapular of Carmel at Kuravilangad. It is reasonable to believe that the happy and pious memories which the Carmelites had left behind by the establishment of the Confraternity at Kuravilangad caused the St. Thomas Christians to desire to have the Carmelites settle problems connected with the power interests between Archbishop Garzia and Archdeacon Thomas, which led to the *Coonen Cross Oath* on 3rd January, 1653. And in 1655 Pope Alexander VII appointed the Carmelites Fr. Jose de Sancta Maria (Sebastiani) and Fr. Jacinto of St. Vincent as Apostolic Commissaries. And on 3rd December 1659 a new Vicariate Apostolic was erected under the name of the Vicariate Apostolic of Malabar and ever since the Carmelites have played a significant role in the Kerala Church. For further study See V. SANMIGUEL, *Three Century Kerala Carmelite Mission*. See also ID., *Carmelite Seminaries*; L.M. PYLEE, *St. Thomas Christians*, 144ff; D. FERROLI, *Jesuits in Malabar*, II, 117-139. For a study on the problems leading to the *Coonen Cross Oath* see J. THEKKEDATH, *The Troubled Days of Francis Garcia*; J. KOLLAPARAMBIL, *The St. Thomas Christians' Revolution*.

[53] One of the reasons for the successful missionary endeavor of the Carmelites was that already in 1845 the Quilon mission was entrusted to the Belgian Discalced Carmelites (Flanders). They were away from the scene of most of the ecclesiastical confrontations which existed in central Travancore as a result of the *Coonen Cross Oath*. «When the Catholic Syrians were separated from Verapoly in the latter part of the last century, the apostolic action of the Carmelite took a more vigorous turn» (V. SANMIGUEL, *Three Century Kerala Carmelite Mission*, 54).

[54] Though there will be difference of opinion about the socio-educational policies, the pastoral vision of Bishop Benziger has contributed a lot for the conversion of many Hindus to Christianity. He was a good administrator too. Nothing concerning the welfare of the Diocese had been considered too small to claim his notice. He was well informed of the diocesan matters. He also reformed the way of Pastoral Visits. First he cut short all unnecessary expenses in connection with Pastoral Visits. His visit in a mission district

Damascene had remarkable success in missionary work[55]. The establishment of the Malabar Province by the Belgian Carmelites in Trivandrum speeded the missionary work in Trivandrum[56]. The Carmelite missionaries, who made a considerable contribution in the formation of native clergy in India, promoted native vocations to priesthood and worked along with the native clergy in Trivandrum. It was through their spiritual support and co-operation that native priests like Msgr. Manual Anpudayan, Fr. Joseph Rayappan, Fr. Jeremias and Fr. Paul Avarthan could succeed in their missionary endeavor. Msgr. Manual Anpudayan was one among the notable native missionaries to conduct *Prarthanayōgaṅgal* (Prayer meetings) in Trivandrum, which had a communitarian effect among the Christians prior to Vatican II[57].

---

lasted two to three days. And he personally instructed those to be confirmed, personally examined all the parochial books. Till his time Pastoral Visits of the parishes were not frequent. For further study on the pastoral vision of Bishop Benziger see M. BENZIGER, *Archbishop Benziger*. See also F. KILIYAMPURAKAL, *Aloysius Maria Benziger*.

[55] Fr. John Damascene worked in Trivandrum for 48 years. According to D. Fernandez, John Damascene is the most celebrated Carmelite missionary of India. See D. FERNANDEZ, «Spanish Carmelite Missionaries», 175-197. According to V. Sanmiguel Fr. John Damascene administered the greatest number of baptisms in the history of the missions in India. See V. SANMIGUEL, *Three Century Kerala Carmelite Mission*, 52-55. Other celebrated missionaries of the Carmelite Order who made remarkable impact on the people of Trivandrum are Fr. Brocard, Fr. Gerald, Fr. Norbert, Fr. Ildaphonse and Fr. John Baptist. Fr. Ildaphonse started forty-four mission centers in Nedumangad Taluk. Unlike the other Portuguese who worked in the coastal villages, the Carmelites tried to educate the people starting primary schools. Compared to the Protestant missionaries who worked in the same area, the Carmelites had a limited vision regarding the integral development of the people in those days. But most of them led a simple and holy life.

[56] The presence of two prestigious Carmelite institutions are typical example of the influence of Carmelites in Trivandrum. One is the Carmel Hill Monastery of Trivandrum, which was blessed on 13th May 1906 by Bishop Benziger. The other one is the Holy Angels' Carmelites, Trivandrum, established in 1880. See V. SANMIGUEL, *Three Century Kerala Carmelite Mission*, 68-69. 81-82. It is beyond doubt that the major part of missionary work of the Diocese of Trivandrum is accredited to Carmelite Missionaries. Whether *indigenous Carmelites* have met the aspirations of the natives of Trivandrum is questionable.

[57] Usually prayer meetings were conducted in one of the houses in a village. Msgr. M. Anpudayan used to conduct prayer meetings after visiting the nearby houses without making any distinction between Hindus and Christians. The prayer meetings were also an occasion for him to teach Christian doctrine. He also taught the people about savings, education and health. He made use of such meetings to have dialogue with Protestants and Hindus. Msgr. S. Thomas and Msgr. A. George were very much influenced by Msgr. M. Anpudayan in their pastoral activities [Personal interview with Msgr. A. George on 6-6-1994].

The formation of ecclesial communities in the non-coastal villages was not that easy, for the people were scattered. Moreover, they had a pluriform culture inherited with all the multiplicity of the Hindu religion. However, the missionaries, because of their holy life inspired the natives. They visited the houses constantly and through better contacts with the people many embraced Christianity. Fr. J. Damascene alone baptized 4.655 people within a short span of eleven years in Trivandrum. The constant support of Bishop Benziger for building churches also speeded the growth of the missions[58]. And the missionaries appointed *upadēsi* (catechists) from the locality and promoted lay participation in the Church.

2.1 *The Upadēsi (Catechist) in the Non-Coastal Villages*

The catechist in Trivandrum is known as *upadēsi*[59]. The literal meaning is the one who gives counseling or teaches wisdom. In the Diocese of Trivandrum the catechists played and still play an important role as evangelizers[60]. Since there were not enough priests to look after the faithful, especially the new converts, the missionaries appointed catechists in the new missions[61]. As the people were scattered, the

---

[58] There were three stages for the establishment of a Church. According to Bishop Benziger the beginning should be modest. He instructed the priests to start with single individuals or one family. The missionaries were instructed also not to hasten to build churches but rather put up a small catechetical school, thatched with coconut leaves in the house of the catechist. When the catechumens were ready to receive baptism they were given baptism at an appointed time. Only when the new converts demanded, a hut chapel was enlarged. The third stage was the deepening of the faith of the new converts. Only then a church would be constructed. See F. KILIYAMPURAKAL, *Aloysius Maria Benziger*, 81-86. Bishop Benziger was willing to construct a church for the people if there were five hundred new converts. See D. SELVARAJ, ed., *Platinum Jubilee Smaranika* (Platinum Jubilee Souvenir).

[59] In Kerala itself the function of catechists differs from place to place. In some dioceses, the catechists are only Sunday school teachers. For a further study on the role of catechists see S. KUNNEL, *Family-centered Catechesis.*

[60] At present there are 238 catechists, of which only twelve are working in the coastal Vicariates. Most of the catechists are from the new converts namely Nadars, Izhavas and Dalits. The role of catechists and *kanakapula* was basically the same in the beginning and a change has taken place in course of time. At present the catechists play an important role in the animation of BECs.

[61] The catechists, being natives, were able to help the missionaries. The missionaries were also careful to appoint proper catechists according to the cultural situation of the place even considering the caste aspect. «In each Mission the Missionary had to have permanent catechists, to help him in the work of Evangelization. While the Missionaries traveled from place to place, the catechists were to remain in each village, where they had

missionaries had to adopt a different methodology in forming ecclesial communities. Many a time it was done through the *upadēsi*. There was no fixed time for recruiting the candidates but exemplary life was expected of an *upadēsi*[62]. The great success of Fr. John Damascene and other missionaries at the end of the 19th century and in the beginning of the 20th century in evangelizing the major part of Neyyattinkara and Nedumangad Taluks in Trivandrum is because of the assistance the missionaries received from the *upadēsi*[63]. The missionaries took more care also to teach Christian doctrine to *upadēsi*. And the latter were further entrusted with the teaching of Christian doctrine to the catechumens[64].

Compared to the *kanakapula* of coastal parishes the *upadēsi* were more concerned about the teaching of Christian doctrine and visiting homes[65]. In the coastal parishes, because of the *kuttaka* system[66], *kanakapula*

---

to instruct the children, watch over the conduct of the villagers, gather them every Saturday or Sunday into the Church for prayers» (D. FERROLI, *The Jesuits in Malabar*, I, 139). For the relevance of catechist in the Indian context see THE CAPUCHIN MISSION UNIT, *India and Its Missions*, 224-233.

[62] When Fr. J. Damascene converted about 600 people at Aira «ex caṣta Nadars and infina casta», the Apostolic Administrator Msgr. Bernardine of Quilon gave special instruction to Fr. J. Damascene to appoint one or two catechists. «You may therefore appoint one or two catechists, as you thing[k] best, for which purpose we shall sanction a sum of Rs. 8/- per month» (BERNARDIN, *To Rev.& Dear Fr. J. Damascene*, PAP). See also F. KILIAYAMPURAKAL, *Aloysius Maria Benziger*, 156.

[63] For the role played by the catechists along with some of the missionaries see D. SELVARAJ, *Platinum Jubilee Smaranika*. In the mission areas women also worked as catechists. See P. DEVADAS, *Kālpadukal*, 153-157.

[64] We find a clear distinction in the approach of the *Padroado* missionaries in the 16th century and the Carmelite missionaries (*Propaganda*) in the 19th and 20th centuries. The difference is well reflected in the people of the Diocese. The *Padroado* missionaries need not be from Portugal. There were indigenous missionaries too under the *Padroado*.

[65] Missionaries like Adeodatus used to offer special classes for the catechists every week. See T. JAMES, «Adeodatusacan Oranusmaranam» (Fr. Adeodatus: A Reminiscence).

[66] The Portuguese missionaries introduced the custom of giving 1/10 of the income to the Church in the coastal parishes. The Church directly collected this share-collection from the people. In course of time due to practical problems a contract system was introduced by which the contractor collected the amount during a specific period. Usually the richest man of the locality was given the contract. In case more people contended, an auction of *kuttaka* was held. The first installment was supposed to be paid to the Church on the spot and the rest of the two installments to be deposited later on. The parish priest and the *pradhāni* controlled the funds. And the *kanakapula* also plays an important role as accountant or as the contractor of the auction. In each parish the amount paid to the Church was different. Though in the beginning it functioned well with the intention of making the Church self-supportive, in course of time many evils crept in. For a study on

became the *watchmen* of the temporalities of the parishes. In the non-coastal villages the conversion was not as a village but as individuals or families. As we have mentioned in the second chapter even in one family the members may be following different religious faiths. And for the missionaries to know the full background of a family some help of a *upadēsi* was also inevitable in earlier days.

2.2 *Popular Devotions and Pious Associations:*
   Vitality of Ecclesial Communities

Already from the time of Jesuit missionaries popular devotions and pious associations were rooted in the Kerala Church. The Carmelites missionaries gave a new vitality to popular devotions and pious associations[67]. The Sacred Heart devotion, May devotion (devotion to the Blessed Virgin Mary in the month of May), the devotion of the Brown Scapular and Rosary devotions are some among them. These devotions have influenced the Kerala Church in forming its Christian culture.

In most of the parishes in Kerala devotion to Sacred Heart captured much attention. As a part of this devotion one can note that the first Fridays have better participation for the Holy Mass than in other week days. One of the most powerful religious expressions of the Catholics throughout Kerala is the solemn enthronement of the Sacred Heart picture in the house and the evening family prayer in front of the picture[68].

---

the positive and negative effects of *Kuttaka* see J. MURICKAN, *Religion and Power*, 62-68. After the Second Vatican Council a few priests tried to stop this system. Often the *pradhāni* were against stopping this system. The role of *pradhāni* will be discussed later.

[67] The Carmelites believed that if there are pious associations people also would be obedient. In connection with some problems regarding accounts, the Vicar General of Quilon writes: «Please therefore instruct the people and start to organize some pious associations, so that they become more pious and more obedient and ready to give the Church contribution with good will» (BERNARDIN, *Accounts & Church contribution*, PAP).

[68] As regards the evening prayer among the fishermen community in Trivandrum N.Nayak says: «Night prayers are the only moments when the whole family is together and in restful peace. Observing the men and women with closed eyes, imploring the almighty, is a sign of their trust in a power beyond and an absorber of the day's trials and tribulations. No psychiatrist can offer a better couch for the gut expression of the day's experience. They are confident that He listens to them and whatever be His answer, it is His will and hence their total resignation to it» (N. NAYAK, *Struggle within the Struggle*, 10). Bishop Benziger encouraged very much the Sacred Heart Devotion in the whole of Quilon Diocese in the early part of this century. See also J.V. FERNANDEZ, *A Quarter Century of Progress*, 18-19. This trend in spiritual matters started by Bishop Benziger was continued by Bishop V.V. Dereere. «The yearly renewing of the Consecration of the Diocese and of every Parish in the Diocese to the Most Sacred Heart of Jesus will be

The devotion to Blessed Virgin Mary is manifested in different ways. St. Francis Xavier was very particular to teach Marian prayers too. The Rosary devotion is a long established practice of the Kerala Church. Another popular devotion is the brown scapular. As the Diocese of Quilon has been entrusted to the Order of Carmelites, the missionaries also spread this devotion throughout the Diocese. In 1907 there were 70 confraternities of the Scapular of Our Lady of Mount Carmel in the Old Quilon Diocese. In 1950 Bishop V.V. Dereere, then Bishop of Trivandrum, exhorted the priests to spread the devotion to every parish[69]. Even now the devotion continues especially among the women. The month of May is dedicated to Blessed Virgin Mary, Queen of Heaven. People used to express their devotion to the Blessed Virgin Mary the Queen of Heaven through prayers and hymns[70].

The popular devotion created a sense of religion among the people. And a sense of fellowship was achieved through pious associations.

2.2.1 Sodalities (Christian Life Communities)

The Jesuit Sodalities are known all over the world[71]. Already in the seventeenth century the Sodalities were founded in India. There were sodalities at Cochin, Quilon, Tuticorin, San Thome and elsewhere[72]. From the Annual Letter of Jesuits in 1633 we learn of the martyrdom of a member of the Sodality of Our Lady in Cochin[73]. The Carmelite missionaries encouraged the Sodalities. Bishop Benziger introduced the

---

done in our Cathedral Church, Trivandrum on the 1st of January during the Pontifical Benediction and in all the churches of the Diocese on the following Sunday, 4th January 1942 during the Benediction» (V.V. DEREERE, *Consecration of the Diocese*, ADT).

[69] «This year, on the 700th Anniversary year of the miraculous institution of the devotion to the Scapular of Carmel. [...] During these last centuries the devotion to the Scapular was spread all over the world. Everywhere confraternities of the Scapular of Our Lady of Mount Carmel were erected by so far that the brown Scapular of Carmel became the distinctive mark of the Catholic Faith» (V.V. DEREERE, *Reverend Fathers*, ADT).

[70] For a detailed study on popular devotions see P. PUTHENANGADY, ed., *Popular Devotions*. In the particular context of South Travancore see J.V. FERNANDEZ, *A Quarter Century of Progress*, 18-22.

[71] The Sodalities are now called *Christian Life Communities*. The characteristic feature of it is the act of consecration to the Virgin Mary. In Italy the Sodalities are called *Le comunità di Vita Cristiana*. See B. SECONDIN, *I Nuovi Protagonisti*, 69-71.

[72] For the pastoral work of the Jesuits between 1600-1650 see D. FERROLI, *The Jesuits in Malabar*, I, 398-429. The presence of Sodalities also helped priests in settling hatred and quarrels among the people.

[73] See D. FERROLI, *The Jesuits in Malabar*, I, 446.

Christian Doctrine Sodality through out the Diocese. The purpose of it was to give an occasion to teach Christian doctrine[74]. In Trivandrum there were separate Sodalities for boys and girls. The object of the sodality was personal sanctification. For that, attendance of Holy Mass, reception of Holy Communion and recitation of prescribed prayers were encouraged. The sodalists also took active part in the adoration of the Blessed Sacrament and teaching Sunday Catechism classes[75].

2.2.2 Legion of Mary

The first *praesidium* (unit) outside the British Isles was started in Madras in 1931. Fr. Ildaphonse, the then parish priest of Palayam, wanted to begin a unit of the Legion of Mary at Palayam in 1931 itself[76]. It was realized only in 1939[77]. In Trivandrum, at present, there are 5.000 members in the Legion of Mary. Although they have a *rigid* way of religious practices, the Legionaries have a tradition of dedicated service in forming faith communities. As a lay pious association their service in the local Church of Trivandrum is by no means negligible. Their activities include visiting of sick people in the hospitals, jails and asylums. Their participation in the renewal programme in the Diocese is notable. Many leaders of the Legion of Mary work as animators of BECs. They also take part in the fight against social evils[78].

The pious associations played a significant role in the faith formation. It created a fellowship among the members. However, since the parish

---

[74] See also J.V. FERNANDEZ, *A Quarter Century of Progress*, 15-22.

[75] See A. PEREIRA, ed., *The Sodalist*, II, 11-14. See also J.V. FERNANDEZ, *A Quarter Century of Progress*, 13-22. For further study on Christian Life Communities see J. OCHAGAVIA, *The CLC World Community*, ; KERALA REGIONAL CHRISTIAN LIFE COMMUNITY YEARLY PROGRAMME — 1992; B. Mc LOUGHLIN, «Christian Life Communities», 87-90.

[76] See ILDAPHONSE, *Legion of Mary*, AGOCD.

[77] Justice Joseph Thaliath, though belonging to Syro-Malabar rite, was proud of being a member of Palayam Parish and was the first president of the Legion of Mary in Trivandrum.

[78] Around 65 *Curia* office bearers attended a seminar on BECs from 22nd to 24th January 1993 at Vellayambalam. For further studies on Legion of Mary see B. SECONDIN, *I Nuovi Protagonisti*, 78-80. See also F. DUFF, *The Spirit of the Legion of Mary*. Other pious associations in the Diocese are *Little Way Association, Mission League, Franciscan Munām Sabha* (Franciscan Third Order) and *Vanita Samājam* (Women's Association). *Little Way Association* functions as a continuation of *Crusaders* and *Snéhasēna* (Army of Love).

priests were the directors of these associations, the growth of these associations depended on the interest of the priests.

2.3 *Catholic Action*

The origin of Catholic Action derives from a lay movement (*Azione Cattolica Italiana*) in the last century in Italy[79]. In its later development Catholic Action has become one of the means to assure lay participation in the Church. With Papal approval and encouragement it became one of the best means of vitalizing the Church with lay participation[80]. In the Diocese of Trivandrum Bishop V.V. Dereere, insisted that all the priests establish Catholic Action in every parish. The main purpose of the establishment of Catholic Action was re-christianization of parishes. But the *re-christianization* according to the Bishop was obedience to the hierarchy. He exhorts: «my dear Catholic Faithful, respect and revere your Parish Priest, be obedient to his directions, remain all united with your Parish Priest and offer him whole heartedly your co-operation»[81].

Together with Catholic Action, St. Vincent de Paul Society has been working in the Diocese for a long time. Compared to the pious associations where women dominate, in St. Vincent de Paul Society we can see the laymen in charitable works[82]. The Carmelite missionaries gave special attention to the youth also. The Catholic Young Men's Society was started at Palayam in 1911[83], the first of this type in Kerala is a typical example.

In most of the pious associations women's participation exceeded that of men. But in the ecclesial administration women did not have any voice.

----

[79] See B. SECONDIN, *I Nuovi Protagonisti*, 75-78.

[80] The Second Vatican Council gives special reference to the Catholic Action when it speaks of the Apostolate of the Laity. The Council also gives four characteristic principles by which Catholic Action now functions. See *AA* 20.

[81] V. V. DEREERE, *Advent and the Erection of the Catholic Action*, ADT. Together with the Pastoral Letter the rules were given which had been approved by all the parish priests on 8th November 1949.

[82] The report of the working of the St. Joseph's Conference of St. Vincent De Paul's Society for the year 1935 gives a picture of the activities of the Society in Trivandrum. See. A. PEREIRA, ed., *The Sodalist*, 111-115.

[83] From the twenty fourth annual report of the Catholic Young Men's Society in 1935, we understand that in the beginning the organization had only a limited scope of friendly meetings and recreations. In 1935 the organization was in the process of making an effective form of Catholic Action. See A. PEREIRA, ed., *The Sodalist*, 97-102. The Malabar Catholics Students' League and the Malabar Catholic Youth League are of later origin. See M. THOMAS, *The Catholic Youth Movement*, 100-122.

And in many cases the power and authority was vested in the hand of priests and *powerful* men of the parishes. This has been the phenomenon in the Syrian Church too.

3. Ecclesial Administrative Structures

The Church of Christ, as A. Dulles writess, could not perform its mission without some stable organizational features[84]. The stable organizational features are visibly seen in parish pastoral councils, though canonically they have only a consultative vote[85]. It is through the parish pastoral councils that the laity express their services in a visible and meaningful manner. It is in the parish pastoral councils that the laity also exercise their right which they derive from baptism. In Trivandrum and in Kerala the administrative structures have been in existence from the beginning of the formation of ecclesial communities. Although the ecclesial administrative systems were meant to help the people experience the love of God, often it turned out to be similar to secular and temple administrative system where *yōgam* decided everything.

3.1 *Yōgam (Assembly)*

From the ancient times, the *Rājās* (Kings) followed a system which gave the representatives of the people some responsibility. The *Rājā* was the supreme ruler of the country[86]. In all the religious matters everything was determined by the assembly of Brahminic priests called *yōgam*. Anything which had any remotest connection with the religion is brought before the *yōgam* and discussed by the *yōgam*. The decision of the *yōgam*

---

[84] For a theological reflection on the «Church as Institution» see A. DULLES, *Models of the Church*, 34-46.

[85] «Si, de iudicio Episcopi dioecesani, audito consilio presbyterali, opportunum sit, in unaquaque paroecia constituatur consilium pastorale, cui parochus præest et in quo christifideles una cum illis qui curam pastoralem vi officii sui in parœcia participant, ad actionem pastoralem fovendam suum adiutorium præstent» (*CIC*, 536 -§1). «Consilium pastorale voto gaudet tantum consultivo et regitur normis ab Episcopo diœcesano statutis» (*CIC*, 536-§ 2).

[86] The local administration was entrusted with hereditary chiefs called *Mādampi* (Lord). The kingdom was divided into *nāds* (districts) and *dēsams* (villages). There was a chief in every village called *Dēsavāsi*. The village was usually the private property of the chief. His office was hereditary. The civil, religious and military affairs vested in the same person. In the village the basic assembly was the *sabha* or *yōgam* which was concerned with all the matters relating to the village including the criminal cases. See C. ACHUTHAMENON, *The Cochin State Manual*, 47-48.

was absolute. The King never gave his vote till the Brahmins had sufficiently examined the case before them and delivered their opinions[87].

In Trivandrum the administration of Sri Padmanabha Swami Temple was managed by a committee known as *E ttarayōgam* (literally an assembly of 8 1/2), composed of eight Brahmin *Jenmies* with one vote each and the *Mahārāja* who had only a half a vote[88]. Even in the royal temple the King had less participation than the other Hindu community. It is in this background that we understand better the *Edavaka Yōgam* that existed in the Syro-Malabar Church during the time of Portuguese and the *ūrukūttam* (the gathering of the village) that developed among the Latin Catholics of Trivandrum[89].

3.2 *Edavaka Yōgam (Parish Assembly)*

One of the important contributions of the Syro-Malabar Church is that it was the pioneer in introducing the *Edavaka Yōgam* (parish assembly) in the administrative structure of the Church[90]. As *Yōgam* was the

---

[87] The system of *yōgam* has influenced the Syrian Christians also. «Tutti i punti di religione decidonsi dai soli Brahmani, ai quali presiede il *Sarvavèda* o il loro Pontefice. Il Re, come della tribù dei Kshetria, reale e militare, non vi dà il suo voto se non dopo che la questione o lite è decisa da' Brahmani. Il consesso o la comunità che decide si chiama «Yòga». Tutti danno il loro voto, e quest' usanza passò nelle comunità ecclesiastiche de'Cristiani di S. Tommaso, a cui presiede il Vescovo, od il Missionario, o l'anziano tra li Sacerdoti chiamato *Mùppen*, ossia l'anziano, il *più vecchio*. I Brahmani nelle loro adunanze tengono il medesimo ordine. Quel che fu deciso dal Yòga si prende per inviolabile, e quasi infallibile sentenza. Chi ricalcitra, è escluso dalla communità, e cessa di essere membro del *Yòga*. In queste radunanze si tratta de'sposalizj matrimonj, doti, colpe e pecati contro la religione, o contra la tribù. L'odio, l'inimicizia, *aborti* ovvero sconciature, bastonate senza effusione di sangue, cattivi tratamenti de'genitori, ed altri punti appartenenti alla tribù, famiglie, religione, pagodi o tempj, sono riferiti a questo tribunale. Ciascuno può difendersi parlare, opporre, portare i suoi testimoni, ed avvocati senza obbligazione di fare scriture e regali. Il presunto reo rimane in piedi, e la communità od il *Yòga* sede sopra le store tessute de'fili di *Ananas* Silvestre, o di foglie di palma» (P.S. BARTOLOMEO, *Viaggio alle Indie Orientali*, 256).

[88] See V.N. AIYA, *Travancore State Manual*, II,84. In Kerala, the Hindu temples are administered by a special committee called the *Dēvasvam* (belonging to God). But the Sri Padmanabha Swami Temple does not come under the administration of *Dēvaswam*.

[89] Though the basic structure is the same there is a change in the form of *Edavaka Yōgam* after the Second Vatican Council. In some of the dioceses in Kerala *Edavaka Yōgam* is converted into a parish council with more representation of the people.

[90] P. S. Bartholomeo calls the system a kind of *Christian Republic*. See *Viaggio alle Indie Orientali*, 137. For an extensive discussion on *Edavaka Yōgams* in various Churches in Kerala and the role of *Kaikār*, the treasurer of the *Yōgam* see B.L. JOSE, *The Parish Council*, 263-306. See also J. KURIEDATH, *Authority in the Catholic Community*, 77-104; G. NEDUNGATT, «The Spirituality of the Syro-Malabar Church», 4-39.

general administrative pattern of the temples and the secular society in Kerala, the *Edavaka Yōgam*, giving more participation to the laity, had a significant role to play in the parish. A brief account of the *Edavaka Yōgam* would also help us to understand the democratic nature of the people of Kerala in religious matters.

The *Edavaka Yōgam* (parish assembly) traces its origin back to the Hindu temple administrative system[91]. The *Edavaka Yōgam* was the most important administrative body among the St. Thomas Christians[92]. P. S. Bartolomeo in the 18th century writes: «The gathering or community that decides is called *Yōgam*. All give their votes and this usage passed also to the ecclesiastical communities»[93]. The *Yōgam* constituted of the *respectable* members of the parish or the seniors of the bazar as members or «all the male members of the parish»[94]. J. Kuriedath holds the view that it was a body exclusively of male and most seniors (elders) of aristocratic families *(taravād)*[95]. Apart from the aristocratic way of functioning of *Edavaka Yōgam* it is evident that the lay people had a decisive role in the parish administration and the lay people did not leave the parish matters to priests alone[96]. However, from the history we understand that many a time justice without mercy was the prevalent

---

[91] See V.N. AIYA, *Travancore State Manual*, II, 71-72. Today the temples are managed by *Dēvasvam* Board.

[92] There were three grades of *yōgam*: *Edavaka Yōgam* (parish assembly), *Prādēṣikayōgam* (regional Assembly), and *Potu Yōgam* or *Sabhāyōgam* (General Assembly). Delegates from *Prādēṣika yōgam* formed the members of regional and general *yōgam*. The local *yōgam* had priests and lay people as members. The eldest priest of the locality presided over it and all other priests of the parish attended it. The general assemblies were presided over by the Archdeacon. See P.J. PODIPARA, *The Hierarchy of the Syro-Malabar Church*, 106. See also J. KOLLAPARAMBIL, *The Archdeacon of All-India*, 192-205. *Edavaka Yōgam* exists in different forms in the Latin Catholic Church and in other non-Catholic Churches. See B.L. JOSE, *The Parish Council*, 267-276.

[93] «Il consesso o la comunità che decide si chiama *Yòga*. Tutti danno il loro voto, e quest' usanza passò alla comunità ecclesiastiche[...] » (P.S. BARTOLOMEO, *Il Viaggio alle Indie Orientali*, 256).

[94] See J. KURIEDATH, *Authority in the Catholic Community*, 92. See also P.J. PODIPARA, *The Thomas Christians*, Bombay, 1970, 96.

[95] See J. KURIEDATH, *Authority in the Catholic Community*, 92-93.

[96] The reason for such less influence of the priests in the *Edavaka Yoōgam* would be the under qualification of priests in those days. The priests were ordained at the age of 17 to 18 and often they did not receive any formal and systematic theological education or any secular knowledge. See M. MUNDADAN, *Traditions*, 150. The Portuguese missionaries could not digest the idea of *Edavaka Yōgam* with executive powers.

practices in the *Edavaka Yōgam*[97]. And that would be the reason why, added with the Western influence, the Bishops controlled (diminished) the power of *Edavaka Yōgam* and more power was given to the clergy[98].

3.3 *Ūrukūṭṭam (Village Assembly) and Pradhāni*

Parallel to the *Edavaka Yōgam* in the Syrian Churches, in Trivandrum there existed a system called *ūrukūṭṭam* (Village assembly) in most of the coastal parishes[99]. In Trivandrum it represented the general assembly of the parish. To understand the significance of *ūrukūṭṭam* in Trivandrum we have to understand the role played by the *pradhāni* in the parish. The word *pradhāni* in Malayalam means an important person. In the coastal villages the *pradhāni* played a prominent role. Although the system was introduced by the European missionaries[100], the Mukkuvar, like any other community in Kerala, had a *well established* administrative system in their villages[101]. As soon as Christianity was rooted in the soil they

---

[97] Sometimes the decisions on the culpable members had excommunicative effect. «A questi scomunicati si nega la confessione e l'Eucaristia, il *castùri* o la *pace* dopo la Messa; i preti non possono andare in casa loro; non amministrano il Sagramento del Matrimonio nè in chiesa nè in casa; non vanno all *Ciàta* cioè per gli anniversarj dei loro defunti parenti, che si fanno in casa. Essi non hanno voce e voto nella communità, nè possono mettersi a sedere nel circolo del *Jògam*, cioè nel circolo della communità o *congregazione* adunata de' Cristiani d'una Parrocchia» (P.S. BARTOLOMEO, *Il Viaggio alle Indie Orientali*, 137). There was a felt need of the more participatory character of *Yōgam* in the Syro-Malabar Church after Second Vatican Council. At present the people prefer parish council to *Edavaka Yōgam*. See J. KURIEDATH, *Authority in the Catholic Community*, 195-237.

[98] See B.L. JOSE, *Parish Council*, 270-274.

[99] Unlike the *Edavaka Yōgam*, women participated in the *ūrukūṭṭam* . However, the major decisions were made by men. The system of *ūrukūṭṭam* prevailed till recently in the coastal parishes. With the emergence of BECs, the system of *ūrukūṭṭam* is not much felt though some priests hold the view that the system of *ūrukūṭṭam* has a more democratic aspect than the BECs.

[100] See J. MURICKAN, *Religion and Power Structure*, 54.

[101] «The old caste organization seems to have persisted to the present day among the Mukkuvans to an extent which can be paralleled amongst few other castes. They have assemblies (rājiams) of elders called Kadavans, or Kadakkōdis, presided over by presidents called Arayans or Karnavans, who settle questions of caste etiquette, and also constitute a divorce court. The position of the Arayans, like that of the Kadavans, is hereditary. It is said to have been conferred by the different Rājas in their respective territories, with certain insignia, a painted cadjan (palm leaf) umbrella, a stick, and a red silk sash. The Arayans are also entitled to heads of porpoises captured in their jurisdictions, and to presents of tobacco and *pānsupari* when a girl attains puberty or is married. Their consent is necessary to all regular marriages. The Mukkuvans have their

adopted their inherited administrative system in the parishes. St. Francis Xavier had already appointed *Kanakapula*. But for a better functioning of the ecclesial communities the later missionaries adapted the then existing administrative system of the place and assigned special qualities to them.

A *pradhāni* was expected to be a man of knowledge, spirituality and ability. People with better economic and social position and leisure time came to hold these positions. They were the informal *conventional leaders* of the parish and their main task in the parish was to act as mediators between the parish priest and the people especially when parishioners could not directly approach the priest. In the initial stages this system worked well and proved useful in the functioning of the parish especially when priests were quite unfamiliar with the local culture and customs.

Gradually they became an important factor in the decision making process of the parish. The festivals in the parish were organized with their help. And they supervised the temporal goods of the parish[102]. Since the *pradhāni* system was hereditary, many unworthy and unfit elements crept into it leading to the deterioration of this institution. The *pradhāni* indulged in drinking, feuds and misappropriation of the Church funds. It had been commonly said that priests also joined with the *pradhāni* in the misappropriation of the Church funds and the imposition of extra taxes on the people[103]. However, the early structure of the parishes gave a protection from unnecessary external interference[104].

---

oracles or seers called Ayittans or Attans; and, when an Arayan dies, these select his successor from his Anandravans, while under the influence of the divine afflatus, and also choose from among the younger members of the Kadavan families priests called Mānakkans or Bānakkans, to perform pūja in their temples» (E.THURSTON – K. RANGACHARI, *Castes and Tribes* V, 108). Since there is an established system, the punishments imposed on people were often unproportionate. See N. NAYAK, *Struggle within the Struggle*, 9.

[102] See J. MURICKAN, *Religion and Power Structure*, 54-64. See also T. KOCHERY, «The Cross Now and Here», 240-246.

[103] «Nel 1783 alcuni Parrochi della costa *Travancor* avevano imposte alcune pene pecuniarie alli pescatori Cristiani loro parrocchiani. Questi ricorsero al Re, che stava allora a *Padmanàburam*, e volevano che fossero mandati via tali curati. Il Re scrisse una lettera a Monsig. *Carlo di S. Corrado* Vescovo e Vicario Apostolico, e gli dava ad intendere, che voleva staccare 75. Chiese Cristiane dal Vescovado di *Coccino* e consegnarle al Vicario Apostolico, acciocchè le facesse dirigere dai suoi Missionarj di Propaganda Fide. In conseguenza voleva che il Vescovo venisse a *Patnam* per esaminare i delitti di questi curati Portoghesi di Goa; che mandasse via i colpevoli; e prendesse possesso delle chiese. Il Vescovo era ammalato, e toccò a me il andar a *Padmanàburam*» (P.S. BARTOLOMEO, *Viaggio Alle Indie Orientali*, 127). For different aspects of problems regarding the collection of money for the parish see J. MURICKAN, *Religion and Power Structure*, 62-68. The introduction of election for Church committee from the *ūrukūṭṭam*

In the non-coastal parishes also the *pradhāni* system existed. The important function of the *pradhāni* was primarily to superwise parish feasts, and to collect the annual contribution of the people of the parish. They acted like the members of the present parish pastoral council without any responsibility for the administration of the parish. Priests used to consult the *pradhāni* only for some important matters concerning the parish. The role of these *pradhāni* was totally different from the *pradhani* in the coastal parishes[105].

4. A New Way of Being the Church after Vatican II

The impact of the Second Vatican Council began to be experienced throughout the country with the *All India «Church in India», Seminar* held at Bangalore in 1969. One of the aims of the seminar was to enable the Indian Church to make a breakthrough in the process of its renewal. This was achieved to a certain extent by an extensive self evaluation. The subjects dealt within the Seminar show that the Church in India was really an emerging Church responding to the challenges of the time. The seminar gave a new vision to spirituality, Catechesis, Indian Culture, Liturgy, Dialogue with other religions, Evangelization, Education, Socio-Economic Activities, Health and Social Services, Labour, Social Communications, Media, Civic and Political Life, Family, Leadership, Ecumenism, Pastoral Life, Personnel and Resources. It was an opening to the principle of co-responsibility within the Church and openness to the world[106].

Already before the National Seminar, the Diocese of Trivandrum had set up an Orientation Centre in 1968[107]. The scope of this was to train catechists and lay leaders in the local Church. The participation of the

---

became a threat to the *pradhāni*. The members of the Church committee were concerned about the material affairs of the parish life instead of having a holistic approach to the ecclesial life.

[104] Normally the police does not enter directly into a coastal (Catholic) village without the permission of the «petty Raja of the Mukkuvars» (K. RAM, *Mukkuvar Women*, 29).

[105] See P. DEVADAS, *Kālpāṭukal*, 157. At present the *pradhāni* do not have any administrative role in the non-coastal parishes.

[106] To concretize the decisions of the Seminar, the formation of pastoral councils, though a consultative body, was given high priority. See J. THALIATH, «The Thought of the Seminar», 511-542.

[107] See L. ROCHE, «Diocese of Trivandrum», 81-83. The regional Pastoral Orientation Centre (POC) also began to function in 1968. It has been publishing literature and conducting Seminars for the people of Kerala. See POC, *First Three Years*. See also J. KARIYIL, *Rajata Jubili Aghōṣikunna POC*.

Diocese in the regional and national programmes in connection with the renewal of the Church deserves special attention[108]. But in effect renewal has taken place in the liturgical, catechetical and social field.

As a part of liturgical renewal, the Holy Mass began to be celebrated in the local vernacular. The people welcomed the liturgical renewal especially in celebrating the Mass facing the people. To assure active participation in the liturgy community singing, offertory processions, etc., were introduced. The people of Trivandrum appreciated the renewed liturgy. For them it was not only meaningful and relevant, but also in tune with their age-old cultural traditions. The faithful, however, felt that the progress in the implementation of the liturgy was rather slow[109].

4.1 *A Change in the Social Vision*

We have seen in the second chapter of our study that religion and social development are closely related in Kerala. For the Christians, the Church has been the agent of social development. Among the Latin Catholics, the social development began to take place mainly with the coming of indigenous Bishops. In Trivandrum, P.B. Pereira, the first indigenous Bishop, began to launch a social development programme in 1960. It gained new impetus with the Second Vatican Council[110]. The main reason for the Bishop to enter into social work was the suffering of his own people. The «Marianad Community Development Programme» was his first experiment to alleviate the sufferings of the people and which was

---

[108] A lay representation (Mr. Nesan T. Mathew) in the «Church in India Today» seminar from the Diocese of Trivandrum along with Bishop Peter Bernard Pereira and two other priests from the Diocese shows that the Diocese was really interested in the renewal. See CBCI, *All India Seminar*, 3. 502-508. 578. 606.

[109] L. ROCHE, «Diocese of Trivandrum», 81-83. The different conferences conducted by eminent liturgists like D.S. Amalorpavadass and P. Puthanangady in Trivandrum manifest further the desire of the Diocese to welcoming the renewal.

[110] It was in 1960 the TSSS, a charitable organization, was organized and registered. The aim of the society was the socio-economic up-lift of the poor and oppressed sections of the society. See J. ALBARIS, *The Trivandrum Latin Diocese*, 22. Following the registration of TSSS, the Diocese of Kottar also formed Kottar Social Service Society. See J. TOMBÉR, *Led By God's Hand*, 37. The appointment of Fr. T. Kochery, who has been playing a significant role for the welfare of the fishermen, as a parish priest in a fishermen's parish was also a typical example of the social vision of the Bishop. «The Bishop took me to different coastal parishes, and persuaded me to take charge of Poothura parish for a while and win the trust and friendship of the people before trying out my longing to live in a hut right in the midst of the fisher people without any kind of office, power or privilege» (T. KOCHERY, «Where I met Jesus», 187).

well appreciated by the sociologists; even the Kerala Government projected the programme as a model[111]. He made an option for the poor. In 1962 Bishop P.B. Pereira also initiated a «self-help project» at Kunnukuzhy for the construction of a full village of about 100 fishing families[112]. Together with further housing schemes in the various parishes many self employment schemes were also introduced[113].

Bishop P.B. Pereira, initiated social work in the Diocese, aware of the poverty and social situations of the poor. However, this initiative lacked a scientific approach. It was not an outcome of a common vision of the Diocese. A close analysis of the mode of social work undertaken during his period would show that most of the efforts were on the part of the Bishop and the priests who were interested in social work. The role of laity in socio-religious life of the Church was not yet achieved. Even the registration of Trivandrum Social Service Society was declared as defunct by the Registrar of Societies. The Diocese of Trivandrum was not an exception to the general phenomenon of the Kerala Church in not sharing power with the lay people. To put it in the words of Fr. V. Sanmiguel:

> Too many priests have not realized at least in Kerala their duty of organizing laymen and entrusting them with responsible work in the church. Such

---

[111] Marianad is a Catholic parish where Bishop P.B. Pereira introduced his first experiment of a housing project in 1960. By introducing a housing project the people were brought from the thickly coastal villages. The bishop's intention was to give a holistic formation to the people. With that end in view a co-operative society was formed. The system introduced by the bishop at Marianad inspired also the Kerala Government. «The experience of Marianad Malsya Ulpadaka Cooperative Society, Puthen Curichy near Trivandrum is an eye opener to the fishermen cooperatives in Kerala. [...] Cooperative education class and seminars are organized periodically with a view to building up leadership from within the fishermen rank and file. Dedicated leadership, and the felt-in-need of the fishermen rank for united action against the exploitation by the middlemen could be reckoned as the contributing factors for the dynamic outlook of Marianad» (GOVERNMENT OF KERALA, *Economic Review*, 45-46). See also J. KURIAN, *Fishermen's Cooperatives*; N. NAYAK, *A Struggle within the Struggle* [J. Kurian and N. Nayak are sociologists who have been closely associated with the «Marianad Community Development Programme»].

[112] According to Fr. V. Sanmiguel, the former Professor of Sociology at Pontifical Seminary, Alwaye and Director of Kerala Social Action, the scheme of Bishop P.B. Pereira would be a model for low income housing projects in well to do parishes of India and especially of Kerala. See V. SANMIGUEL, *Parish Welfare Orientations*, 140-143.

[113] Weaving school at Vattavila, St. Jude Weaving Centre at Chamavila, St. Xavier's Technical Institute are some among them. For further information about the social work see J. ALBARIS, *The Trivandrum Latin Diocese*, 44-116. For a comparison of the different projects in relation to other Latin Catholic dioceses or Syro-Malabar dioceses see F. HOUTART – G. LEMERCINIER, *Church and Development*, 75-78.

priests seem to think that the laity has no special mission to fulfill in Church because they lack the power of jurisdiction and orders, as if their only role in the Church consisted in receiving spiritual help-sacraments etc., — from the clergy... Priests in India particularly in Kerala feel great disinclination to grant real authority to the laity. It is because they fear, and at times they are right, that laymen will abuse their position and meddle with parish affairs that are beyond their competence. This happens because the laymen themselves are not properly educated on lay apostolate doctrine concerning their rights and duties in the Church and especially in the Parish[114].

According to Fr. V. Sanmiguel it was unjustifiable to keep the lay people away from the mainstream of the administration of the Church, while the laymen in Kerala have had traditionally so much say in the administration of finances of the parish. He says:

As a matter of fact in Kerala, at least, priests are very elusive to the educated laymen and parishioners, because they think that if laymen are allowed to have their confidence by giving them some positions they will take advantage of them, for example when they are appointed president of a committee with a good deal of freedom *to build* a hospital, a school or a chapel in a cottage etc. But priests in India should put away a bit of their superiority complex and become more accessible to their educated parishioners, for the priests must understand that the success of parish lay apostolate depends on their mutual understanding and cooperation. The priest who is willing to work with the lay apostles and take them seriously and inspire them by their example is truly a parish priest with zeal and real modern priestly outlook[115].

---

[114] V. SANMIGUEL, *Parish Welfare Orientations*, 109. Even after 30 years there are parishes in many dioceses in India without parish pastoral councils. At present lay participation is minimal. In many places there are no pastoral or parish councils. Membership in these bodies is by nomination. Even at the national level, membership in bodies like the Catholic Council of India is nominated, not elected. See «Final Consultation on CBCI Evaluation», 2.

[115] V. SANMIGUEL, *Parish Welfare Orientations*, 110. What V. Sanmiguel said in 1963 has not changed much in the subsequent years. The studies carried out by F. Houtart and G. Lemercinier deserve special attention. The authors argue that most of the development programmes are oriented toward the betterment or increase of private property, with little collective organization or representation. And many of the Church's projects are not reaching out to the people for whom the project is intended. See F. HOUTART – G. LEMERCINIER, *Church and Development*, 317-348. The study carried out in the Syro-Malabar Church also speaks of the centralization of authority. See J. KURIEDATH, *Authority in the Catholic Community*. «The Church in India is exceptionally clerical; lay persons hardly play any role. People from other countries are often surprised to see how many "secular", worldly posts and functions are held by priests and religious» (J.A.G.G. VAN LEEUWEN, *Fully Indian*, 118-132). «For many Christians, the Church is a

As social factors are essentially associated with the life of the Church no wonder that the lay people, who are enlightened by the teachings of Second Vatican Council and the socialistic ideologies obtained through education and political interactions within the society, began to evaluate critically the traditional role of the Church in the changing society. Many young priests who came out of the Seminaries with a new vision of the Church, with the Second Vatican Council, were unable to digest the traditional way of functioning the Church. This gradually led to the ideological tension in the Diocese.

Many priests and religious began to be involved in social action beyond the traditional role of the Church. Often their actions were a threat to the Church institutions and traditional systems. The activities of Kerala Catholic Youth Movement (KCYM) and All India Catholic Students Federation created a new momentum in the Diocese. The members were criticized for having association with communism. The fishermen's agitation, fasting unto death by priests and religious (men and women) were also some of the external expressions of the tensions which existed in the Diocese. The caste and cultural differences broadened the tension. But all these factors have indirectly contributed to the formation of BECs in the Diocese.

5 The Formation of BECs in the Diocese of Trivandrum

The formation of BECs in the Diocese of Trivandrum was not an outcome of a sudden decision of a bishop or of a few priests. A continuous theological research, study, self-evaluation and struggle of the people of God could be seen behind it. The influential factors are manifold. Of these, the most important is the theological awareness of the Church as «People of God». The impact of the theological understanding of the Church as «People of God» had its effect in many of the parishes, both in the coastal and non-coastal areas, though the traditional parishes were reluctant to accept changes. The contributions of D.S. Amalorpavadass, Bishops A.B. Jacob and M.S. Pakiam are very important. And the Golden Jubilee Celebration of the Diocese in 1987 was the point of departure for the formation of BECs.

---

body that is meant for the welfare of the Catholic community only, instead of being a community that has been entrusted with a mission» (*CBCI Evaluation Report*, n. 794).

5.1 *Theological and Social Background*

Ever since the Second Vatican Council a change has taken place in the overall thinking pattern of the priests and lay people. The spirit of renewal has been reflected in many corners of the Diocese, though some have not welcomed changes. With the introduction of vernacular language in the liturgy people began to take part in the liturgy actively. The notion of the Church as «People of God» assured the role of lay people in the Church[116]. The establishment of a Orientation Centre at Trivandrum in 1968 was aimed at training the catechists and lay people of the Diocese[117]. The beginning of parish pastoral councils immediately after two weeks of the «Church in India Today Seminar» manifests the theological awareness of the clergy to share the power of the parish administration with the laity[118]. In 1972 itself a diocesan by-law for the Parish Council was promulgated[119].

The formation of *Kerala Catholic Youth Movement* (KCYM) in 1976 in Trivandrum gave another boost to the theological reflection of the youth[120]. Though it started with twenty-five members in 1976, within a short period eighteen units were formed in the Diocese. With a formal

---

[116] In parishes study classes were conducted about the teachings of Vatican II for catechism teachers, youth and adults.

[117] In 1968 the Diocese started an Orientation Centre. Fr. Augustine Xavier, a member of the KCBC Commission for Pastoral Orientation, was appointed as the Director of Orientation Centre at Trivandrum in 1968. He also participated in the «All India Seminar: Church in India Today» at Bangalore in 1969.

[118] The first parish council was established in 1969 at the St. Joseph's Cathedral Church, Palayam. See B.L. JOSE, *The Parish Council*, i.

[119] The aims of the parish council were: (1) increase the religious knowledge and awareness in the parish, (2) promote the missionary spirit, promote the Holy Scripture reading, improve the participation of the parishioners in liturgical functions, (3) co-ordinate, according to need, the activities of the pious associations like Sodality, Legion of Mary, Society of Vincent de Paul, (4) promote educational uplift and cultural progress of the parishioners, (5) make use of all efforts for the financial uplift, social work, care for the needy, food and clothing for the poor, financial help for the poor girls towards their marriage, (6) work for peace in the parish and peaceful settlement of the quarrels, (7) evaluate by discussion the financial running of the parish and submit suggestions for the next financial year, (8) participate and co-operate in the diocesan undertakings, (9) send members to the diocesan pastoral council and to co-operate with it, (10) relate with other parishes; relate with other Christians and communities. The by-law of the parish council was promulgated in June 15, 1972. See B.L. JOSE, *The Parish Council*, 131177.

[120] It was in the context of the restrictions imposed by the Kerala State Government over the private Colleges in 1972 that the KCBC planned to organize the Catholic youth under the KCYM. For further study see M. THOMAS, *The Catholic Youth Movement*, 149-166.

organization the KCYM members got an opportunity to come together and discuss various problems related to the Church and society. Various seminars, symposiums and camps were conducted for the youth. One of the themes selected for the youth in 1976, for the youth of the Kattakode Vicariate was «Change the Church through my Parish»[121].

The *All India Catholic University Federation* (AICUF) even at the moment of its identity crisis, starting with its *Poonamalee Seminar*[122], Trivandrum Region had better results. Within a period of two years (1971-73) they conducted one orientation camp on «The Task and Response of the AICUF to Indian Reality», a leadership camp to experiment «Leadership Training through Social Awareness», a «live in exposure» programme, a one-day seminar on «The Approach of Political Parties to Indian Reality». They also organized a study group to analyze the situation of a fishermen village of Poonthura. A group of AICUF volunteers spent almost one week with the poor fishermen of that area to study their living conditions. The abject poverty, the exploitation of the middlemen who get the fish from the poor fishermen at a very low price and sell it for a high price, illiteracy and other daunting problems of those people were studied.

Further, the AICUF formulated a policy of direct involvement and the students of that region, mostly from the same parish (Poonthura), began to be in frequent contact with the people of that area. They gave free tuition to the poor students, conducted family gatherings and organized women workers. However, the programmes arranged by AICUF at Poonthura created a lot of unrest in the coastal area[123].

---

[121] See J. PARAMKUZHY, «KCYM working Report 1976-1991» (No page numbering). Already in 1967-68 Fr. A. George, who later became the Vicar General of the Diocese, had begun to animate the youth. The formal recognition of KCYM gave a new awareness of the Church and its role in the changing world. From 1968 Fr. D. Elias also began to conduct *study classes* on Council Documents for the catechism teachers and for the youth at Utchakkada.

[122] As *aggiornamento* became the catch word after the Second Vatican Council, the AICUF leadership was trying to read the signs of the time and update the movement. And in light of this, at Poonamalee, the AICUF conducted a seminar from 28 December to 2 January 1971. The seminar concentrated on a scientific analysis of the society of India and led to radical decisions including exposing the students to all currents of thought including the Marxist modes of thought. Thereafter there was a strain in the relationship between bishops and the leaders of AICUF. See M. THOMAS, *The Catholic Youth Movement*, 144-149. See F. HOURTART – G. LEMERCINIER, *Church and Development*, 341.

[123] D. GOMAS, «Pōnturayil Oru Mahāyañam», 95-100. See also M.THOMAS, *The Catholic Youth Movement*, 206-212.

It was during this time that a team of young priests, ordained after 1970, inspired by the theological vision of Vatican II, began to gather together and animate the youth and lay people in some of the non-coastal parishes[124]. The priests, who could be described as a *mutual supportive group*, began to introduce changes in the liturgy in their respective parishes[125]. In their attempt to have a meaningful celebration of the liturgy, Holy Masses were celebrated in the villages (*vards*) where people could gather[126]. They emphasized the role of the laity in the parishes. A change in the traditional way of celebrating parish feasts also took place[127]. The introduction of the parish council system was a set back to the traditional leaders[128].

The Priests had theological discussions and began to join with the poor in their struggle against injustice. In their *option for the poor* they even joined with other religious and secular action groups in the region[129]. The active participation of the Trivandrum clergy in the fishermen agitation is to be seen in this context of theological enlightenment. In most of the cases they stood for the development of fishermen and paradoxically

---

[124] M. NICHOLAS, *Letter*, PPn.

[125] Already in 1969 Holy See had approved the 12 points of adaptation proposed by the CBCI. See D.S. AMALORPAVADASS, ed., *Post-Vatican Liturgical Renewal*, 444-445. The execution of it was left to the local hierarchies.

[126] In the non-coastal parishes people are scattered. The priests after visiting the neighbouring houses used to gather all the people and celebrate Holy Masses. Though the missionaries had celebrated Holy Mass in houses in the early days, the new attempt of young priests re-vigourated the Christian life in many parishes. The new attempt of young priests brought criticism also.

[127] In most of the parishes the patron's feasts were celebrated most solemnly. The success of the parish feasts was dependent on external celebrations such as processions, fire works, cultural programmes. Some of the traditions were inherited from the Hindu Temple feasts. With a new theological thinking, priests gave more importance to the Scripture, prayer and reflection. A *new community* conscience has been formed through various seminars and study classes in connection with parish feasts.

[128] In Poovar, for example, the parish council could be introduced only in 1981. See J. MURICKAN, *Religion and Power*, 57-58. Many a time parish priests are afraid of being controlled by people on ecclesiastical matters. See R.B. SELVARAJ, *Report of the Animation Seminar*, ADT.

[129] Some priests were closely associated with the Programme for Community Organization and Students Christian Movement in Trivandrum. Some were associated with *Dynamic Action Group* of Kerala. See J.P. PINTO, *Inculturation*, 224-225. A Protestant Theologian M.M. Thomas and Paulose Mar Paulose, Bishop of Syrian Orthodox Church, were also closely associated with these priests in their fight for the poor.

some of the priests working in the coastal parishes labeled such priests as communists.

The changes that were taking place throughout the world especially in the Latin American countries both in the ecclesiastical life and in secular life had also greatly influenced the thinking of the clergy of Trivandrum. The Synod of Bishops in 1974 followed by the Apostolic Exhortation *Evangelii Nuntiandi* in 1975 also gave a new awareness and mission of the Church. In 1974 one of the prominent socialist leaders, Jayaprakash Narayan, a disciple of Mahatma Gandhi, called for a «Total Revolution» in India to fight against injustices. The emergency declared in 1975 and a change to a non-Congress Government in the centre in 1977, and a political polarization throughout India, were some of the factors which contributed to challenge the existing system and the role of the Church towards these changes.

Another phenomenon that has made a spiritual revolution in the Kerala Church is the Charismatic Movement. Ever since the first Charismatic retreat was held at Alwaye, Kerala, in 1976, a change has been taking place in the Christian life. Active participation of Bishop Jerome Fernandez of Quilon eased many anxieties of priests, nuns and lay people about its *orthodoxy*, though there were lot of criticisms. The Charismatic Movement in Kerala appealed to a good number of lay people of every walk of life. Lay people who had professional security — advocates, doctors, engineers — began to be involved as full-time members[130].

In many places lay people animated by priests took much initiative to conduct prayer meetings, retreats and conventions. The Charismatic meetings gave more importance to the Word of God. The style of praying was changing. Oftentimes Charismatic retreats attracted more people than the traditional retreats. It was a blessing for the Church of Kerala already *disfigured* by the Rite issues. People began to find more meaning in praying the Bible and came forward to preach the Word of God. They also interpreted the Scripture. Together with the lively liturgical celebrations, the healings attracted thousands[131]. The influence of the Charismatic movement still continues in Kerala.

In the theological development, the NBCLC has played a significant role. From the very inception of the centre, priests and lay people were participating in the various seminars which gave a general awareness

---

130 See D.S. AMALORPAVADASS, «Meaning and Role», 92-93.

131 «The rise of the charismatic movement is interpreted by many as a kind of religious desertion in reaction to the turbulence of ecclesiastical politics» (L. FREEMAN, «A Hindu Saint: a sign to Indian Christians», 174).

about the happenings of the world and the Church. D.S. Amalorpavadass always incorporated some particular themes in the beginning of any Seminar conducted in the NBCLC[132]. And the NBCLC has also been emphasizing the role of the local Church in India[133]. Following the «Asian Colloquium on Ministries in the Church» of FABC, held at Hong Kong, February 27 - March 5, 1977[134], the Second Bishop's Institute for Missionary Apostolate (BIMA II) of the Federation of Asian Bishops' Conference held in Trivandrum from November 20-30, 1980 having the

---

[132] According to D.S. Amalorpavadass the participants of any seminar, before entering into their particular subject, have to become aware of the two most powerful determinants of the contemporary Indian reality — the social and cultural reality of India and our mission there — and analyze them in the light of the new vision. The general scheme is: A. *General Introduction and background:* (i) Our Christian World Vision: The Old World Vision (Model 1), The Biblical/New World Vision (Model 2); (ii) The Church's Mission as Prophetic and Hermeneutical (Revelation and Faith); (iii) Practical Conclusions and Obvious Consequences of a new understanding of our Christian World Vision, Revelation and Faith for our Pastoral and Spirituality; B. *The struggle for and commitment to social Justice:* (iv) Tools to understand the Indian reality (social analysis); (v) The Indian situation analyzed with the above tools and a case study to work with the tools of social analysis; (vi) The Church, social change and liberation; C. *The right to and need for:* (vii) Cult, culture and Indian culture; (viii) History and theological bases of inculturation; (ix) Inculturation of all aspects of Christian life, i.e. worship, spirituality, theology and life-style; (x) A new understanding of our relationship to other world religions and evangelization. See J.A.G.G. VAN LEEUWEN, *Fully Indian*, 105-106. No wonder the clergy of Trivandrum, despite their theological differences, agreed to invite D.S. Amalorpavadass to animate them for the «Living Together» in 1987.

[133] According to D.S. Amalorpavadass the Church becomes Church when it is incarnated in a place and this localization is called the Local Church. The Church can fulfill its mission only by being local and incarnated. See D.S. AMALORPAVADASS, *Gospel and Culture*, 22-23. The influence of NBCLC in Trivandrum could be seen from the personal sharing of Msgr. S. Thomas, the Vicar General of Trivandrum. He writes: «I got the idea of prayer meetings from Msgr. Manual Anpudayan. House visitings which I did regularly was one of the means of reaching the people. In ward meetings we discussed informally but openly the various areas of the pastoral and other needs of the parish. I could organize those meetings meaningfully and with better results after a four month's course in Bangalore in 1971» (S. THOMAS, *Letter*, PPn). In the Diocese of Trivandrum most of the non-coastal parishes were divided into different wards similar to the present day BECs.

[134] The participants of the Colloquium were convinced of the urgent need of forming BECs in Asia. In the conclusion, the participants said that in some parts of Asia today the need for forming BECs is becoming more strongly felt. According to them though BECs are not the only way of sharing the life of the Church, the Spirit seems to be moving the Church strongly in that direction. They were convinced that the existing parish structures sometimes are not conducive to intensive Christian life. The participants were also convinced of the possibility of shared and participative leadership in BECs where consultation, dialogue and sharing become a reality. See *FAPA*, 67-92.

theme as «The Christian Community as the Bearer of the Good News», discussed the growing phenomena of BECs in Asia. The conference recognized the potentiality of BECs in revitalizing and rejuvenating the Asian local Churches[135]. In its understanding of the local Church, the practical experience of the Latin American Church also inspired the Indian Church. In 1981, a team from Latin America led by Jose Marines, one of the pioneers of the BECs, conducted a seminar at the National Centre[136]. It also gave new theological and pastoral awareness about BECs.

5.1.1 Renewal in the Neighbouring Diocese

In the renewal process we see a mutual influence and many innovations in the Dioceses of Trivandrum and Kottar[137]. The geographical proximity and the cultural similarity of Trivandrum and Kottar have been mutually helping the priests to form a theological vision of *a participatory Church*. In the neigbouring parishes like Kanjampuram and Pacode of the Diocese of Kottar Fr. C. Amirtha Raj was implementing certain renewal

---

[135] «Among us Catholics, communion must prevail in each local individual Church at the various levels, such as diocese, parish and other forms of community at which the mystery of the Church is present. Given the nature of the Church as communion, various new forms of community, such as those usually referred to as "basic Christian communities", within which interpersonal relationships are fostered, the life of faith and the missionary commitment are shared, need to be encouraged and nurtured. Their ecclesial character requires, however, that they remain open to the larger community of the parish which in turn they will greatly contribute to rejuvenate and revitalize» (*FAPA*, 98-99).

[136] See J. MARINS, ed., *Basic Ecclesial Community*. See also J.P. PINTO, *Inculturation*, 175-176.

[137] Except for the language, there is a cultural similarity between the two dioceses. In Kottar, Fr. J. Tombér had already launched renewal programmes in the very nearest parishes of Trivandrum even before Vatican II. One of the renewals is the construction of a Church in a Hindu Temple Model at Parakunnu. And Holy Mass was celebrated also facing the people. «I was particular that the church should have some connection with Dravidian architecture and art. This was something new for the people, but they agreed [...]. The altar should be in the centre of the "*Vimana*" (the dome), which symbolizes the sacred presence of divinity. The altar was to be placed in such a way that Mass could be said facing the congregation on special occasions. This was 8 years before the Second Vatican Council. The pillars were to be in a similar Dravidian style decorated by bunches of plantains, symbols of fertility and abundance. For the baptismal font, we proposed a lotus flower emerging from the water, which should be situated at the entrance of the church» (J. TOMBÉR, *Led By God's Hand*, 16). See also F. WILFRED, «In Service and Fellowship, 125-230. The best example of the mutual relation between priests of two diocese is the management of St. Jude's College at Thoothoor, which comes under ecclesiastical Jurisdiction of the Diocese of Trivandrum, in Tamil Nadu.

programmes in the light of Vatican II and «Church in India Today Seminar» of 1969 at Bangalore[138]. Fr. J. Edwin, born in the Diocese of Trivandrum, was pioneering the BEC programmes at Kodimanai in Kottar from 1978. The people of Kodimanai are traditional Catholics. They have been Catholics for almost four hundred years. Their attitude towards religion has been described as:

> Even now they are ready to shed their blood and die for their faith, but they do not know who Christ is. The abysmal ignorance of the «person of Christ», could be shocking to many. They know little about the Gospel Values proclaimed by Jesus Christ. There seems to be an un-bridgeable gap between their life and liturgy[139].

Though the priest had to act like social worker, policeman, and judge, because of the social structures, the people were exploited by the middle men. Police cases were common. When Fr. Edwin took charge of the parish there were three hundred police cases[140]. Realizing the socio-religious situation of the parish Fr. Edwin divided the whole parish into eighteen groups. Each group consisted of roughly thirty families. The functioning of these groups is described as follows:

> The groups gather twice a week. They worship together and spontaneously praise and thank the Lord, offer petitions to God asking for what they need. Then a passage from the Gospel is read. One of them shares with his group his ideas, experiences and reflections in connection with the situation prevailing in the village. In a way he unfolds the loving goodness of Jesus Christ by giving his interpretations and explanations. This seems to be a powerful tool for them to establish a healthy and loving relationship with their neighbours, to share the joys and sorrows of those who are around them and help them with well-ordered charity. After the shared prayer, the problems concerning their community and misunderstandings that exist among them are discussed. People are also informed of the causes or the evil forces that are behind such alienation or strain in their relationship. Naturally people discuss problems. This discussion that follows their shared prayer enlightens people, broadens their vision and helps to promote harmony and social responsibility[141].

Despite the developmental attempts and the theological awareness of some priests and lay people, the Diocese of Trivandrum could not

---

138 See C.A. RAJ, «Creative Ministries», 47-56.

139 C.A. RAJ, «Creative Ministries», 60-61.

140 When Fr. Edwin was transferred from the parish there were only five *issue* based cases [Interview with Fr. Edwin at Thengapattanam on 10-6-1994].

141 S.H.M. STEPHEN, «Basic Community», 57-69.

envisage a holistic vision of its own to the people. The lay participation in the ecclesial life also has not improved substantially. Multiplication of groups among the priests based on ideology, difference based on the ecclesiastical traditions like *Padroado and Propaganda* and the cultural differences caused by the caste system disfigured the image of the local Church of Trivandrum. There was a strong demand for the division of the Diocese[142]. The most important among all the problems was ideological. The ideological differences were well reflected when priests and religious took active part in the fishermen's struggle.

5.2 *The Fishermen's Agitation*

The most important social movement that captured the attention of the Catholic Church in Kerala after the Second Vatican Council is the fishermen agitation that took place in 1981 and 1984. The chief protagonists of the agitation were the Latin Catholic fishermen, priests and religious, both men and women. Picketing of government offices, undertaking mass hunger strikes and Gandhian methods of *Satygrāha* formed part of their agitation that opened in 1981 and reached its peak in 1984. The role played by priests and nuns annoyed the bishops and civil authorities. The reaction of the bishops was severely criticized by a good number of priests, nuns and laity, who had maintained a submissive attitude towards the hierarchy.

To understand the implications of the agitation some background information is necessary.

5.2.1 *Background of the Fishermen's Agitation*

The social systems in Kerala denied any opportunity for the development of the fishermen. The only protector from the clutches of the social evil was the Catholic Church. The Catholic Church as such could not respond to the basic needs of the people. However, in light of the spirit of Vatican II a *silent revolution* had been taking place among the fishermen community[143]. By the mid 70's, the effects of «Community

---

142 One of the major problems of the Diocese has been regarding the mode of the division of the Diocese. Added to the caste differences — Mukkuvar and Nadar — the bad effects of two ecclesiastical traditions namely *Padroado* and *Propaganda* played an important role in the procedure of the mode of division of the Diocese into two.

143 In the early 60's Bishop P.B. Pereira, with the help of Claire and Gaetane, French Canadian women and experienced social workers, and Lauretta, an Italian nurse began to work among the fishermen community at Marianad. This was the initiation of

development Programme» initiated at Marianad began to show its impact in other fishermen villages of Trivandrum[144]. In 1977 the official organization, «Programme for Community Organization» (PCO) was registered with headquarters in Trivandrum. The team of social workers, formerly working under the auspices of the Trivandrum Latin Diocese, became autonomous[145]. By this time priests like Paul Arackal in Alleppey, Albert Parisavila in Quilon, and Cletus Gomes and Tom Kochery in Trivandrum had organized the fishermen and they were fighting for the just and basic needs of the fishermen[146].

---

development work among fish workers of Kerala. See N. NAYAK, *Struggle within the Struggle*, 25. The later development of Programme for Community Organization traces its origin to the Bishop Periera's Marianad Project. For a description of the historical development of fishermen's struggle see J.J. KALEECKAL, *Oru Samara Katha*.

[144] «When the co-operative began to stabilize and returns from fishing proved lucrative, there was an inflow of people into Marianad who came as seasonal labour. Such workers came to learn of what was taking place in Marianad and then began to ask for a similar set-up in either villages. Simultaneously, in an effort to share the experience learnt, the team decided to organize various kinds of training programmes so that young educated people from other areas could see the meaning of taking up leadership for change in their villages. There was a five month residential camp for youth. It was these young men and women who tried to respond to requests from the fishermen and women in their villages while the team of Marianad stood by offering the guidance when required. New members who began to join the team after 1975 took up residence in other villages to try to respond to needs as they arose. It was in these ways that organizational work gradually evolved in other areas of the district with new approaches and new experiences» (N. NAYAK, *Struggle within the Struggle*, 26).

[145] See N. NAYAK, *Struggle within the Struggle*, 26 After 1977 Bishop P.B. Pereira also could not carry out his social work because of ill health. And he died on 13 June 1978. Another important factor is that most of the social workers had to confront the existing social systems in the coastal parishes. Many a time the social workers were accused of being communists and non believers. The social workers, animated by some priests and sisters, were scientifically analyzing the socio-economic situation of the places. The social workers had direct contact with the people. They gave special training to children, youth, women, and fish workers. Without the Church's official approval they formed *Mahilā Samājam* (women's association) and *Anganwādis* (Integral Child Development Centers). See PCO, *Annual Report*. According to the CBCI Evaluation Report the laity are more in touch with the day-to-day realities of life than the hierarchy. Even among the lay people, those who are poor and those who are really committed to the cause of the poor are closer to the realities of life. See *CBCI Evaluation Report*, n. 646. See also J.P. PINTO, *Inculturation*, 224-226.

[146] See J.J. KALEECKAL, *Oru Samara Katha*, 13-65. See also J. MURICKAN, *Struggle for Justice*, 10.

5.2.2 Fishermen's Agitations in 1981 and 1984

Ever since the introduction of the mechanization of boats in the fishing industry the livelihood of traditional fishermen was threatened[147]. There were no norms for fishing for the traditional fishermen and mechanized fishermen in Kerala till 1980, when the Left Democratic Front (LDF) government of Kerala passed the Marine Fisheries Regulating Act (KMFR Act). As per the Act there was banning of purse seining within twenty-two kilometres of the coast, banning of mechanized boats and trawlers within twenty kilometres and banning of trawling during the months June, July and August. But within six days of passing the Act the Government had suspended its enforcement in Neendakara succumbing to the pressure from the mechanized fishing sector.

Following the inability of the Kerala Government to implement the vital clauses of the 1980 KMFR Act, especially banning of trawl fishing in June, July and August, the fishermen's organizations launched their first struggle in 1981 with protests, demonstrations and *dharnas*. Fr. Tom Kochery, who was working among the fishermen in Trivandrum and Joychan Antony, of Thumba parish, started an indefinite hunger strike in front of the Kerala State Secretariat on 25th June 1981 and this was continued by other priests and lay people[148]. The agitation came to an end on July 14, 1981 when the Government was ready to set up the Babu Paul Commission with 13 members[149]. The Commission submitted its report in July 1982.

By this time the United Democratic Front (UDF) government came into power but the situation of the fishermen remained the same. The Kerala Independent Fishermen's Federation launched a second struggle in 1984. They put forward seventeen demands[150]. From May 15 to 22nd of

---

[147] 90% of the fishermen in Trivandrum are Latin Catholics.

[148] During the fasting days there had been further demonstrations and picketing. Picketing of all the village offices of the coastal area, Trivandrum Airport, Kadakkavoor Railway Station, and Indian Space Research Organization on different days gave a momentum to the struggle. The fisherwomen with headloads of the fish made a *dharna* in front of the Secretariat. On 1st July, 25 priests observed a one day fast in support of the hunger strike at the Secretariat gate. See J.J. KALEECKAL, *Oru Samara Katha*, 66-75. See also TRIVANDRUM DISTRICT FISHERMEN'S UNION, *Facts and Reflections*, 1-18. See also T.W. JOHN, *Malsyatozhilāli Samarangalum, kristiānikalum* (Fishermen's Agitation and Christians). In general the priests of the coastal parishes were supporting the fishermen.

[149] See J.J. KALEECKAL, *Oru Samara Katha*, 66-75.

[150] The demands were to ban trawling during June, July and August; to ban night trawling; to ban purse seine boats fully; to ban trawlers from within 20km; to introduce pension for fishermen; to offer educational concessions for fishermen's children; to

June 1984, intense agitation was organized all over Kerala with picketing and fasting in Calicut, Quilon, Alleppey and Trivandrum. The agitation picked up momentum and spread throughout the state within two weeks. In Trivandrum itself Fr. James Culas, former Youth Director of the Diocese, Srs. Philomin Mary, Patricia Kuruvinankunnel, Therama Prayikulam and Elsy participated in the hunger strike[151]. The Hindu and Muslim fishermen sectors also joined and took part in the hunger strike. The agitation was suspended on 22nd June after the Chief Minister agreed to all their demands except the ban on trawling[152].

---

transport facilities for women fish workers; to give compensation for accident and death; to give compensation for craft damages; to give *pattayam* (property ownership) for fishermen's lands; to conduct democratic elections in village unions; to include fishermen in Scheduled Caste list; to enforce strict licensing of crafts; to give free ration in lean seasons; to ban industrial waste flowing into the sea and polluting rivers; to remove middlemen from exploiting fishermen; and to implement Babu Paul Commission Report.

[151] About the nature of the agitation *The Week* of India reported: «The 53 year old nun (Philomin Mary) refused to relent even after her admission to the intensive care unit of the Trivandrum Medical College Hospital. There were several other priests and nuns on indefinite fasts at different centres including in front of the Secretariat, embarrassing both the church and the government. An open appeal by the Kerala Bishops' Council, the supreme body of ecclesiastical heads in the State, to end the strike went unheeded at all places. The only response that the appeal evoked was a further intensification of the struggle. [...] Sr. Philomin Mary refused to yield even to the persuasions of her own family members including her aged mother. "Fasting is my fundamental right and if you want to help me, give what you can to the poor fishermen", she told the anxious members of the family at the hospital. The nun showed little willingness to heed the advice of either the doctors or bishops, compelling the former to force-feed her and administer glucose intravenously. She threatened to drag the doctors to court and one of her colleagues did it when he filed a writ petition before the High Court seeking her release. The court on June 19 ordered her to be released immediately, since the detention was illegal, because the police had not produced her before a magistrate after the arrest» (*The Week*, July 1-7, 1984, 31). For further details regarding the fishermen's agitation see P. ARAVINDAKKSHAN, «Crusade on the Coast», 10-14; K.G. KUMAR, «The Kerala fishermen's agitation», 112-115; V. MENON, «The Church in Revolt», 14-17; G. ARAVINDAN, «In the Shoes of the Fishermen», 18; P. MARY – *al.*, «Casting the Net on the Right Side», 193-200. [Personal interview with Sr. Philomin Mary on 11-6-1994]. Despite the severe criticisms about the Kerala bishops we have to understand that in the early stages of the agitation Archbishop Joseph Kelanthara, Archbishop of Verapoly and the then head of the Latin Hierarchy of Kerala supported the agitation. See J.J. KALEECKAL, *Oru Samara Katha*, 93-114.

[152] The fishermen agitation continues in different ways even now. In 1994 the Bishop M.S. Pakiam of Trivandrum called the fishermen to fight against the Central Government's policies that threaten the fishing industry of Kerala. As a protest against the Central Government's policies, on 23rd and 24th November 1994 no fishermen in the Trivandrum coast went for fishing. Fr. T. Kochery was on a hunger strike at Porbanthar

5.2.3 The Impact of Fishermen's Agitation in the Diocese

The fishermen agitation had far reaching effects in the Church in Kerala and in India. One of the reasons for the immediate suspension of the agitation was the open appeal of the Bishops of Kerala to stop the agitation[153]. The appeal of the Bishops, although not much welcomed by fishermen leaders, could create a confusion among the faithful. There were mixed reactions from the public, fishermen and priests. After the federation called off the 1984 agitation the bishops came out with a statement forbidding priests and nuns from undertaking fasts and taking part in public demonstrations without permission from their superiors and the local bishops. They also did not favour the manner in which the fishermen agitation was carried out, especially with the involvement of priests and nuns[154].

Since the agitation had taken place *during the time of Liberation Theology*[155] some priests took the occasion to oppose those who were involved in the agitation. The public statements of those priests and nuns who actively took part in the agitation widened the ideological gap. In many coastal parishes the tension continued. The tension increased when the congress party, which had been supported by the fishermen, began to lose its political strength in the coastal villages.

The tension in the Diocese intensified when Fr. D. Gomas S.J., a native of the Diocese of Trivandrum, wrote an editorial in connection with India's 38th Independence Day titled «*Svatantṛiyadina cintakal*» (Independence day reflections) in the diocesan periodical *Jīvanum Velicavum* in the August issue of 1984[156]. In his reflection, Fr. Dominic Gomas said that even after the four decades of independence millions of people are denied the primary needs. In the particular context he referred

---

from 2nd to 8 May 1995. The recent events are sufficient proofs that the ruling governments have never given considerable attention to the cause of fishermen.

[153] See J. MURICKAN, *Struggle for Justice*, 13-14.

[154] The statement of the Bishops was severely criticized point by point in a published reply on 11-11-1984 by Fr. J.J. Kaleeckal, the President of *Kerala Swatantra Matsya Tozhilali Federation* (KSMTF). See J.J. KALEECKAL, *Oru Samara Katha*, 228-247.

[155] See SCDF, *Instruction on Certain Aspect of the «Theology of Liberation»*. See also M. PARINTHIRICKAL, «Roman Document», 454-473. In an interview Sr. Alice, an active member of the fishermen agitation said: «Liberation theology was foisted on the agitation. The agitation began as a purely fishermen's agitation. It was not inspired by what was happening in Latin America. But when it was identified with the agitation we accepted it» (V. MENON, *The Illustrated Weekly*, 16-17).

[156] See D. GOMAS, «*Patrādhipakuruppu*» (Editorial Reflections), 1. 30.

to the pitiable social conditions of the fishermen of Trivandrum. Referring to the fishermen agitation and the response of the bishops, he held the view that there was nothing wrong to fight for the cause of the poor.

The editorial was responded to by Msgr. M. Netto, the then Rector of the diocesan Minor Seminary and the former Administrator of the Diocese. In his «*Patrādhiparkulla Kattu*» (Letter to the Editor) Msgr. M. Netto also raised three accusations against Fr. D. Gomas: it was criticizing the bishops; it was against the canon law no. 287; it was inculcating Marxist ideologies among the faithful. The letter to the editor was published along with a reply of Fr. D. Gomas in the October issue of *Jîvanum Velicavum* in 1984. Fr. D. Gomas, taking into consideration the ideological differences of the priests at that time, wrote a long reply to Msgr. M. Netto quoting from *Justice in the World*, no. 8; *Gaudium et Spes*, nos. 29, 30, 31, and *Populorum Progressio*[157].

The letter to the editor and the reply manifested the ideological tension which existed in the Diocese. The tension took on a new dimension when the Bishop A. B. Jacob decided, out of pressure from a group of priests, to change the diocesan periodical *Jîvanum Velicavum* into a diocesean bulletin in 1985[158]. Together with the ideological differences, the difference of opinion regarding the division of the Diocese caused a total crisis in the Diocese[159]. The tension was such that to envisage a common vision of the Diocese was practically impossible. Even the Priests' Senate was not functioning well, because of the non representation of a section of priests. However, each priest was doing his best for the people of God entrusted to his care, but without a common vision of the Diocese. The people were not ignorant of many of the happenings.

The tensions existing in the Diocese were well articulated by A.Xavier, the first director of the Orientation Centre of the Diocese and Fr. A. Peter, one of the senior priests of the Diocese, in a parish souvenir in 1985. The article «*Kamukinkōdum Miṣanarimārum*» (Kamukincode and Missionaries) by A. Xavier and Fr. A. Peter's article «*Yuvākale Unarū*» (Youngsters Raise up!) though written in the cultural background of the

---

157 See M. NETTO, «*Patrādhiparkulla*» (Letter to the Editor), 26-27. See also D. GOMAS, «*Marupaṭi*» (Reply), 27-32.

158 It was at this time that a group of priests did not even feel the need of priestly fellowship and avoided attending the diocesan gatherings of priests.

159 Already from the time of Bishop P.B. Pereira the division of the Diocese was one of the major concerns of the Diocese. After his death, Bishop A.B. Jacob took charge of the Diocese and he expressed his intention of dividing the Diocese.

Izhava community of Kamukincode, called for an open and sound theological approach towards the existing problems of the Diocese of Trivandrum. Both of them criticized the lack of common vision from the part of authorities. Fr. A. Peter even called for an urgent need of organizing the youth. He suggested the youth, after getting sufficient training from NBCLC, could be the animators of the BECs. In the same article he also urged the need of inculturation, ecumenism and dialogue and the formation of basic human communities.

It was in the above mentioned particular background that Bishop A.B. Jacob convened a meeting of all the priests on 10 March, 1987 to discuss the Golden Jubilee celebration of the Diocese which became a turning point in the life of Trivandrum Diocese leading up to the formation of BECs.

5.3 Jubilee Celebration: The Point of Departure

The year 1987 was the 50th anniversary of the erection of the Diocese of Trivandrum. The Bishop's intention was to have a «modest celebration» of the Jubilee[160]. As scheduled, the meeting was held on 10th March 1987. Only fifty-six priests out of one hundred and nine were present. Everybody felt that the present atmosphere was not fit to celebrate a meaningful Jubilee. The Bishop wrote in his second letter in connection with the Jubilee:

> I invited the opinions of the priests how best to celebrate the Jubilee. The present condition of the diocese was exposed in its various aspects by many priests. The house found that the present atmosphere is not conducive to a meaningful celebration of a jubilee. The *Presbyterium* felt that its internal unity is the vital pre-requisite. To achieve this end it was suggested that the entire clergy live together at least for five days with the Bishop. The living together will help to give vent to each one's internal feelings and foster mutual fellowship and love[161].

5.3.1 The Role of Bishop A.B. Jacob

In order to plan for a fruitful «Living Together» Bishop A.B. Jacob personally appealed to all the priests for another meeting on 7th April

---

160 A.B. JACOB, *Golden Jubilee*, 3-3-1987, ADT.

161 A.B. JACOB, *Golden Jubilee*, 21-3-1987, ADT. The idea of «Living Together» was proposed by Fr. R.P. Lean and supported by some priests. There was no uniformity regarding the decision. But, Bishop A.B. Jacob's final decision was significant and prophetic at that juncture.

1987.[162] The second meeting confirmed the decision of the first meeting and gave valuable suggestions put forward as regards the mode of «Living together». The second meeting elected a central committee giving representation to the ten Vicariates of the Diocese[163]. Two religious priests, two Vicars General and the Chancellor were co-opted in the central committee. The Central Committee also decided to meet the priests personally to get their views and suggestions to work out the programme successfully and eventually to make the living together fruitful. However, the Bishop knew the difficulties inherent in this attempt. So the bishop wrote: «As you know, we need God's help in this work. Therefore, I request your special prayers on this occasion. Also kindly exhort the religious and your parishioners to support us with their special prayers»[164]. Again informing the date of the living together the Bishop exhorted the priests:

> The most convenient time arrived at now for this is [proposed] to be from Sunday the 30th August evening to Saturday the 5th September 1987. Since this is the occasion for the renewal of the entire presbyterium, I desire that all the priests of the diocese join me for this programme from the beginning till the end. This year we would be combining the annual retreat with this living together. I intimate these dates sufficiently early so that you may make yourself available to attend this programme in its entirety [...]. As this is very important event in the life of the diocese, please make a special intention during the Eucharist for the success of the living together. I would also request you to exhort the religious communities and our faithful to pray for the same intention[165].

When some of the priests expressed their pastoral difficulties to leave the parish for «Living Together», the Bishop was ready to arrange religious priests to meet the urgent pastoral needs of the parishes[166]. And again he reminded them not to accept any public engagements during the days of «Living Together»[167]. There were disagreements about the venue being outside the Diocese, but all were happy that Fr. D.S.

---

[162] A.B. JACOB, *Golden Jubilee*, 21-3-1987, ADT.

[163] At the time of Jubilee celebration there were only ten Vicariates.

[164] A.B. JACOB, *Golden Jubilee*, 27-4-1987, ADT.

[165] A.B. JACOB, *Golden Jubilee*, 12-6-1987, ADT.

[166] In the very first meeting some priests expressed their unwillingness for a «Living Together». The pastoral needs of the people were raised in order to avoid such an event.

[167] A. B. JACOB, *Golden Jubilee*, 14-7-1987, ADT.

Amalorpavadass was going to be the facilitator of the «Living Together»[168].

5.3.2 Evolving a New Vision and Mission

The long awaited «Living Together» began on Sunday the 30th August 1987. Eighty five priests in comparison to the fifty six priests on the 10th March, gathered with Bishop A.B. Jacob at the Kottar Animation Centre to participate in the programme. Fr. D.S. Amalorpavadass was the facilitator. The programme began with a Bible Service. Each day the presbyterium spent ten hours in prayer, reflection, discussion and study[169]. In the first four days the following themes were dealt with:
– Basic exigency of renewal
– Self awareness, God awareness and inversely
– Vision and understanding of the Church according to Vatican II
– Theology of the Local Church
– Ministry in general
– Priestly Ministry
– Identity of Priest
– Lay ministries
The last two days were devoted for discussing:
– Pastoral, Social and Educational activities of the Diocese
– Administration of the diocese
It was from prayer, reflection, discussion and study that a new vision and mission evolved in the Diocese of Trivandrum. The major reflection started with the «Vision and understanding of the Church according to Second Vatican Council», in which D.S. Amalorpavadass dealt with: (1) Jesus Christ and Christian identity of the Church; (2) the Church, communion and institution; and (3) the actual contingent reality of the pilgrim Church. The reflection was oriented to the «Theology of the local Church». And then he also dealt with (i) the incarnation and concretization of the mystery of the Church, (ii) the dynamic process and stages of founding a Church, (iii) the constitutive elements of the Church, (iv) some consequences and implementations.

---

168 See A.B. JACOB, *Golden Jubilee*, 14-8-1987, ADT. See also ID., *Golden Jubilee*, 26-8-1987, ADT; ID., *Golden Jubilee*, 6-10-1987, ADT. Since the «Living Together» of priests with the Bishop was held at Kottar, it was also known as *Kottar Sammēlanam* (Kottar Meeting) and *Kottar Synod*.

169 A.B. JACOB, *Golden Jubilee*, 6-10-1987, ADT.

It was against this theological background that D.S. Amalorpavadass challenged the priests for the first workshop of the «Living Together» with a *provoking* question: «Does the Church of God in Trivandrum at Diocesan and parish level function as and project the image of a fraternal community based on sharing?». The discussion following by the input talk by D.S. Amalorpavadass helped the priests to bring home to themselves the *diaconal* aspect of their priestly ministry in the given situation of Trivandrum[170].

In the «Living Together», the idea of beginning the BECs was not dealt with as an important subject, however, the role of laity in the Church, especially in the Indian context was discussed in detail. D.S. Amalorpavadass gave two talks on the laity. The talks were followed by a workshop with the theme «The place and role of lay people in the Church; their participation in the decision-making process; establishing and functioning of pastoral councils»[171].

The «Living Together» was a unique *Pentecostal* experience in the life of the local Church of Trivandrum. It was an earnest attempt to concretize the vision of the *Church in the Modern World*. The theological input by D.S. Amalorpavadass and the reflections that came out from the «Living Together», helped the priests to formulate a common vision on various activities of the ministry in the concrete situation of Trivandrum. The «Vision and Mission» which emerged from the «Living Together» reflects the *contextualized* ecclesiology of the local Church in which the proclamation of the Good News of the Kingdom to the poor was given priority:

> This is a historical moment; the whole *presbyterium* gathered as one community to reflect the mission of the local Church. By the Lord's anointing, we are called to share Jesus' mission which is primarily the

---

170 The main points of discussion were on priestly ministry as humble service of spiritual leadership and fellowship in the ministry; the identity of priests in general, relationship — source of identity and spirituality; the specificity and spirituality of presbyteral ministry, service and sanctification, followed by the worshop with the theme signs and expressions of our presbyteral fellowship: what gathers and unifies us as priests and what divides and fragments us as priests.

171 The talks were on (i) the place and role, vocation and mission of the laity; their leadership in the Church and Society; characteristics of the lay people of India; obstacles and requisites for the emergence of lay leadership; spirituality of the lay people; (ii) co-responsibility of all sections of God's people and ecclesial organs of common participation; pastoral councils/diocesan and parish; requisites, modalities, structure, guidelines and preparation. Already in 1969 parish councils began to be formed in some parishes of the Diocese and by-laws of the parish council were promulgated by the Diocese on 15th June, 1972. See B.L. JOSE, *Parish Council*, 177.

proclamation of the good news of the Kingdom to the poor. Christ gave peace, hope and joy to the people who put their trust in him by building up the Kingdom, realized in healing the sick, setting free the fettered and possessed, comforting the broken hearted, protecting the persecuted, forgiving the sinners, giving hope to the frustrated, sharing bread with the hungry (Lk 4,18-19). This expectation has to be realized in our diocese[172].

The proclamation of the Good News of the Kingdom would in the context mean to work for the integral development of the people and building up of ecclesial communities[173] and the prerequisite for this is the fraternal communion among ministers and the laity[174]. In the life of communion, the servant role of priests and religious was emphasized[175] and team ministry of priests was made the pastoral policy of the Diocese[176]. The lay people on the other hand have a co-responsibility in the building up of ecclesial communities. The formation of the parish pastoral council would be an expression of such co-responsibility[177].

---

[172] See A.B. JACOB, *Golden Jubilee*, 6-10-1987, ADT.

[173] «At present the majority of our people are poor, illiterate, politically unorganized, living in a pluralistic society facing innumerable problems. We are called to work for the integral human development of those people. It is in this life situation we have to realize our vision and mission» (A.B. JACOB, *Golden Jubilee*, 6-10-1987, ADT)

[174] «Since the Church of God in Trivandrum needed a renewal in the light of Vatican II, in order to function effectively and project the image of a fraternal community based on sharing, it was felt that efforts should be made towards building up a fraternal community of the Bishop, priests, religious and laity. This vision of Vat. [Vatican] II has been imitated and shared by the entire *presbyterium* during the six day Living Together at the Animation Centre, Kottar. It was realized that we priests, religious, and laity have to collaborate closely in order to actualize this vision in the life of the diocese» (A.B. JACOB, *Golden Jubilee*, 6-10-1987, ADT).

[175] «Taken from among men to serve the community through our sharing in the leadership-ministry of Christ we made an analysis of our role and mission in the Diocese of Trivandrum. We noticed that our ministry was to a large extent centered around a conventional image of the Church and was mainly ritualistic» (A.B. JACOB, *Golden Jubilee*, 6-10-1987, ADT).

[176] «Team ministry of priests could be integrated into the Diocesan pastoral policy. Besides co-ordinating various charisms, services and ministries this can also foster the fellowship among priests. Orientation programmes are to be organized for priests» (A.B. JACOB, *Golden Jubilee*, 6-10-1987, ADT). It was a major shift in the pastoral approach.

[177] «As priests concerned for the laity, we feel obliged to get the parishioners formed to ensure the all round formation of our people. The laity are to be properly and systematically animated on the Word of God and Vatican II teaching about parish community and co-responsibility. We consider it our duty to make the involvement of the laity active in the whole life of the parish. Formation of the parish pastoral council which is an expression of such involvement must become a pastoral priority. The Parish Council should attend to all the aspects of Parish life such as catechism, liturgy, youth,

5.3.3 Vision and Mission in Practice

The renewal envisaged in the «Living Together» was the spiritual renewal in its holistic sense i.e., a total development. Since the vast majority of the people of the Diocese represent the backward class of the Kerala society it is the responsibility of the Church to take care of its own people. And with a determination to carry out the «vision and mission» of the Diocese, certain important decisions emerged. The top priority was given to the formation of the diocesan pastoral council. This was also designed to assure the participatory role of laity in the Church. To carry out the decisions more effectively a new senate was formed by holding election on the last day of the «Living Together»[178]. The term of the office bearers' was fixed as three years and could be extended to one more term[179]. The *presbyterium* decided that the directorship of various ministries in the Diocese be assigned to people of different charisms and be evenly distributed. Team ministry was envisaged in all the diocesan activities. The term of a parish priest was fixed to five years. As a whole the «Living Together» paved the way for a new administrative structure and as a result, in the course of time, a central working committee was also formed to steer the renewal programme.

The faithful who had been exhorted by the Bishop to pray for the success of the «Living Together» had been eagerly waiting to see the outcome of the «Living Together»[180]. Following the «Living Together» a change has been felt throughout the Diocese. Many priests came forward to give leadership for the ministries and they felt that they have a role to play in the renewal of the Diocese. The renewal also gave an opportunity

---

family, education, maintenance of Church, financec» (A.B. JACOB, *Golden Jubilee*, 6-10-1987, ADT).

[178] In the course of the «Living Together», it was decided that the Senate should be constituted soon. For a long time the Senate of the Diocese was not functioning.

[179] Only the Vicar General and the personal secretary to the Bishop are exempted from the norm.

[180] From 27-4-1987 onwards Bishop A.B. Jacob had been exhorting the faithful to pray for the success of the «Living Together». On 7-8-1987 the Bishop sent a pastoral letter, along with a special prayer which would be recited after Holy Communion in the Mass and to be said during the family prayers. See A.B. JACOB, *Metrānte kattu: Suvarna Jūbili Thiurvananthapuram Rūpata* (Bishop's Letter: Golden Jubilee of Trivandrum Diocese) 7-8- 1987, ADT.

to the lay people to share their charisms for the good of the local Church[181].

5.4 *First Evaluation of the Renewal*

In light of the «Living Together» most of the important activities of the Diocese were brought under six Boards: Board for Sacred Ministries and Board for Lay Apostolate, Board for Mission, Dialogue and Ecumenism, Board for Social Action, Board for Education and Board for Temporalities. In all the Boards there were lay representatives, both men and women. To have an evaluation about the execution of the resolution taken at the «Living Together» and speedy implementation of the resolutions, an animation seminar was held from 5th June 1989 to 9th June 1989 for the members of the senate and the Boards. The facilitator of this seminar was again Fr. D.S. Amalorpavadass.

In the evaluation, the members came to the realization that though some recommendations of the «Living Together» were fully implemented, still many recommendations had yet been implemented. Of these, the non-implementation of the diocesan pastoral council was given serious attention. It was also noted that many parishes had not constituted pastoral councils despite the «Living Together» decisions. In the discussion on the question of establishing diocesan pastoral council it was pointed out that the absence of parish councils in several parishes was not a sufficient reason to justify the non-constitution of the diocesan pastoral council. In the analysis of the formation of parish pastoral councils some said that the parish priests were afraid of being controlled by people on ecclesiastical matters. It was also pointed out that most often in reality, the good people stand apart from the parish activities and hence vested interests creep into the parish administration[182]. In adducing the reasons for the non-implementation of the «Living Together» recommendations, it was agreed that there was a failure on the part of the clergy to possess and maintain the spirit of the «Living Together».

---

[181] It is to be noted that under the auspices of Board of Pastoral Ministry forty people were sent for NBCLC lay leadership course. See X. ALEXANDER, ed., *Report of the Commission*, 7, ADT.

[182] It was also proposed in this regard that a team could go around the Diocese, conscientising the people on the importance and role of parish council and facilitating the formation of it. See R.B. SELVARAJ, *Report of the Animation Seminar*, 3, ADT.

5.4.1 A New Spiritual Dynamism

The first evaluation seminar facilitated the speedy execution of further recommendations of the «Living Together». With an intention of constituting the diocesan pastoral council in 1989 Bishop A.B. Jacob sent a pastoral letter restating the role of laity in the Church. In order to give a correct understanding of the pastoral council, the Bishop arranged different seminars for the lay leaders of the parish[183]. And within two months the members of the pastoral council were elected from all the Vicariates and the diocesan pastoral council was constituted on 1st January 1990.

In the process of renewal, Bishop A.B. Jacob was given a dynamic Co-adjutor bishop in M.S. Pakiam, a native of the Trivandrum Diocese on 2nd December 1989[184]. Bishop M.S. Pakiam had been actively taking part in the renewal programmes at the time of «Living Together». The spiritual dynamism of the new bishop was manifested when he had to address the first Pastoral Council Meeting on 13th January 1990. In the meeting he gave the introductory talk on «Diocesan Pastoral Council: A Theological Approach». In his talk he said that the ultimate aim of the pastoral council is the total development of the Diocese. To achieve this one should know the Church. Referring to *Lumen Gentium* and *Gaudium et Spes* he emphasized the importance of *koinōnia* among the faithful, and said that the Church can become a sign and sacrament of salvation in the particular context only when there is *koinōnia* among the faithful[185].

In the first pastoral council meeting the members raised some of the problems concerning the Diocese. Some of them are: (i) absence of parish councils in parishes, (ii) educational backwardness of the Diocese, (iii) problems in the financial transactions — both in the diocese and in

---

183 In the Pastoral letter the Bishop also recalled the teachings of Vatican II *LG* 37. «The pastors, indeed, should recognize and promote the dignity and responsibility of the laity in the Church. They should willingly use their prudent advice and confidently assign duties to them in the service of the Church, leaving them freedom and scope for acting» (A.B. JACOB, *Rūpata Pastoral Counciline Sambandica Iṭaya Leghanam* (Pastoral Letter on the Pastoral Council), 7-10-1989, ADT). See also *CBCI Evaluation Report*, no. 797.

184 Bishop M.S. PAKIAM, former Professor of Scripture and Liturgy at the St. Joseph's Pontifical Seminary, Alwaye, was then the Rector of the diocesan minor seminary and director of Sacred ministries. He has been participating in the meetings at NBCLC in his capacity as Professor of Liturgy and Bible and also as a representative of the Diocese of Trivandrum. As a priest, having worked both in the coastal, non-coastal and city parishes, he knew well the pastoral situations of the Diocese. Moreover, he had been conducting seminars in connection with the formation of diocesan pastoral council.

185 See E. PEREIRA, *Pastoral Council Report*, 10-3-1990, 1-13, ADT.

the parishes, (iv) competitive attitudes of associations in the parishes, (v) unnecessary expenses for the parish feasts (vi) the growing differences between priests and the laity, (vi) disunity among the priests, (vii) having a «diocesan spirituality» of its own, and (viii) a call for an intensive renewal of the family[186].

During this period two important events speeded up the renewal which facilitated the easy formation of BECs in Trivandrum. The first is the «Christian Life 2000» programme envisaged by the Catholic Bishops' Conference of India and the second is the scientific self evaluation of the diocesan renewal carried out after the «Living Together» with a pastoral out look.

5.4.2 «Christian Life 2000»

Pope John Paul II, in his speeches, has been recalling the need to prepare the faithful for the third millennium which starts with the great Jubilee Year 2000. The response has been varied. On the whole the call was taken very seriously ranging from programmes for «Evangelization of the World 2000» to «Christian Life Renewal 2000». While the Charismatic Movement is more on the line of Evangelization by 2000, the official Church in India through the CBCI Commission for «Christian Life» thought it more fitting to use this occasion to spell out a programme for the renewal of Christian life in India. It envisaged a process of renewal through learning and living the Second Vatican Council more deeply, according to the age and stage of each person[187].

The Diocese of Trivandrum, as it has been engaged in renewal, according to the new programme envisaged by the Indian Church, gave a new impetus to its own renewal and structural planning. On 15th February 1990 Bishop M.S. Pakiam convened a general meeting of priests and the programme of «Christian Life 2000» was explained. It

---

186 See E. PEREIRA, *Pastoral Council Report*, 10-3-1990, 1-13, ADT. The first pastoral council meeting is a testimony that the lay people are really interested in the overall development of the local Church.

187 The All India Convention held at Bangalore from 4th to 8th December 1989 adopted an action plan which was known as the Decennial Programme (1990-99). The main objective of this programme is faith formation. It visualized for: the first three years (1990-92) personification of the faith of every member of every Christian family; the second three years (1993-95) the faith renewal of the parish as an ecclesial community; the third triennium (1996-98) deepening the apostolic aspect of the believer by involving himself in the civic society with the zeal of a missionary to permeate his sphere of influence with Christian values; the final year (1999) to culminate the process with a cosmic vision of creation engendered by a faith formation that is cosmic in dimension.

was welcomed by the priests and on 28th February 1990 the Bishop sent a pastoral letter exhorting the need of the renewal of the Diocese in light of «Christian Life 2000» programme. In order to grow in faith, the Bishop stressed the necessity of reading the Bible. He also emphasized the need to learn the teachings of the Church especially those of the Second Vatican Council and the Encyclicals[188]. As a practical execution of the «Christian Life 2000» programme, some priests had already divided the parishes into small units called *ktumbaunit*[189]. It was during this time some priests and sisters began to speak of BECs, of course, in the context of Christian Life 2000[190].

5.5 *The Second Evaluation of the Renewal: A Major Shift*

The renewal began with the «Living Together» and brought a lot of changes in the Diocese. The «vision and mission» envisaged at the «Living Together» was to render better service for the people of God of Trivandrum. The people had a better knowledge of the «Living Together» as they were sufficiently informed of this great event in the

---

[188] See M.S. PAKIAM, *Kraistava Jîvitam 2000 Āṇṭil*, (Christian Life 2000), 28-2-1990, ADT. The main stress of the pastoral letter was on the faith aspect. See also E. PEREIRA, *The Pastoral Council Report*, 4-7-1990, 17-18, ADT.

[189] R.P. Lean, the director of pastoral ministry, after explaining the «Christian Life 2000» to the members of the Pastoral Council invited the priests and members of the pastoral council to form *basic faith communities* throughout the Diocese. Already by 10-3-1990 in many parishes the initiation programmes have started. Parassala was one among the first parishes to do it. See E. PEREIRA, *The Pastoral Council Report*, 4-7-1990, 17-18, ADT. In many non-coastal parishes because of its geographical vastness, parishes were already divided into small units called wards.

[190] On 21st July 1990 a seminar was conducted for the representatives of lay people, priests and religious of all the Vicariates. Following the seminar the Lay Apostolate planned out an intensive programme for the renewal of the family. In its programme Sr. Marykutty F.M.M., the diocesan co-ordinator for the Lay Apostolate, urged the need of forming *Aṭistāna Kraistava Samūhaṅgal* (BECs). And within the period from 14th July to 15th September 1990, the Lay Apostolate (the Commission for Lay Apostolate) organized 10 seminars covering all the Vicariates. See MARYKUTTY, *Lay Apostolate*, 26-6-1990, ADT. The reports from the Kochuthura Parish show that already in 1990 BECs were formed under the leadership of Fr. V.K. Peter. At Neduvanvila – Parassala, where the present author was the parish priest, thirteen units with a thrust on Christian Life 2000 were started in 1990 and later twenty-six BECs were formed before September 1991. The urgent need of forming family units and BECs for deepening the Christian life was also discussed at the pastoral council meeting on 10-3-1990. See E. PEREIRA, *The Pastoral Council Report* , 4-7-1990, 14-16, ADT. In Trivandrum BECs are known as *Aṭistāna Kraistava Samūhaṅgal, Kuṭumba Units, Kuṭumba Yōgam*.

Diocese and their constant prayers were asked for its success[191]. As there was a positive approach from the part of most of the clergy, the people welcomed the renewal, actively co-operating with programmes carried out in the Diocese. The renewal also gave a new hope among the people. The Liturgy became very active. There was an increase in the number of catechism teachers and students[192]. A special syllabus for catechism-for school-dropouts was prepared, seventy catechism teachers were enrolled for the Bible correspondence course of POC. The renewal also gave an opportunity for the first time to assemble the Dalits.

In the new situation of *enlightenment* the people were given an opportunity to express their observations about the process of renewal and aspirations. The lay people also realized that they have a role to play in the Church. The parish council meetings were an occasion to discuss not only the parochial issues but also the execution of the recommendations made at the «Living Together». The policies regarding education and social action and temporal administration, which had been very sensitive even before the «Living Together» were questioned by some priests and lay people. The various Boards for the ministries also could not rise up to the aspirations of the people who were expecting better results from *above* — priests and the members of Board.

By this time, the term of office, as per the recommendations of «Living Together», for the various Boards, was coming to an end. An evaluation of the functioning of the various Boards was the felt need of the laity and the clergy. There was also an earnest desire on the part of the Bishop, who had been fully aware of the exigencies of the Diocese, to present the image of the Church of Trivandrum in a better way. For that, his first attempt was *to know how the people of God had benefited from the renewal and how far the message of renewal had reached the people in the Diocese after the «Living Together»*. For that, the Bishop appointed four commissions of experts on 10-8-1990[193] to study in detail

---

191 The resolutions taken at the «Living Together» were also printed in vernacular and given to the people.

192 In order to make the Liturgy very active *«Nircālukal»*, a leaflet on the Scripture readings on Sundays with commentary and hymns, was circulated. The number of catechism teachers rose from 2.065 in '89-90 to 2.584 in '90-91. The students increased from 33.274 to 37.110. It is remarkable that in Trivandrum catechism teachers do not receive any remuneration.

193 See M.S. PAKIAM, *Decree*, ADT. The Board of Sacred Ministries and Priestly Formation, Board for Lay Apostolate and Board of Mission, Dialogue and Ecumenism were grouped together under the study of the Commission on Pastoral Ministries. It was remarkable that the Commission members included priests from the Diocese and outside,

and evaluate the present functioning of the different Boards and to give suggestions for improving the functioning of the Diocese. The Bishop also appealed to all priests, men and women religious and laity for cooperation with the commissions[194]. The reports of the Commissions were expected to be submitted before 15th November 1990.

The findings of the Commissions were an eye opener on the situation of the Church of Trivandrum. All the reports invariably gave the impression that most of the renewal programmes were mainly based on the priests[195]. The Commission for social action, for example, noted that several parish priests and a few religious charted out projects and implemented them with foreign aid received through TSSS. Most of these schemes did not have much or any involvement of lay people[196]. Lack of vision, disunity among the members within the Board, and selfish interest that crept in were some of the observations that the Commission made. The commission made an important observation regarding the benefits of the Social Action:

> The relationship between the TSSS and the parish based projects was mainly that of a «post office», i.e., TSSS receives project applications from anybody who would like to send projects; post them to various funding agencies; receive funds from foreign funding agencies and post them to various project holders. While TSSS and the parish based programmes did give services to a handful of people, these programmes were not able to address the two basic situations of our people: namely, fisheries and agriculture which are the two main material bases of our fisher-folk and inland people[197].

---

men and women religious, lay men and women and a Hindu. In the study undertaken, the fact that the Commission members sought even the help of people of different religions and different castes especially in the temporal administrations is itself a proof that the Church of Trivandrum was open to new realities.

[194] Again, in the absence of the Bishop, the Administrator of the Diocese sent another circular letter informing the lay people about the possibility of meeting the commission members. See also J. AMADO, *Thiruvananthapuram Rūpata Atministrētaruṭe Kattu* (Letter of Trivandrum Diocesan Administrator) ADT.

[195] What the Sociologists have been saying about the Kerala Church has proved to be correct. The general tendency of the Church in India is also not different. «For various reasons, historical and otherwise, the Church in India today is perceived to be clerically dominated and it is largely centered on the Bishops and priests» (*CBCI Evaluation Report*, n. 595).

[196] See C. LEON, *Summary Report*, 6, ADT. See also *CBCI Evaluation Report*, ns. 738-750.

[197] C. LEON, *Summary Report*, 10, ADT.

In light of the study, the Commission suggested some major shifts in the social action in the Diocese[198].

Social Service at present	Social action in future
Project oriented	Action Oriented
Priest centered	People centered
Church centered	Village centered
Totally rely on foreign funds	Mainly rely on government resources and resort to foreign funds when it becomes inevitable
Implement programmes mainly initiated by funding agencies	Initiate programmes based on the understanding and analysis of the socio-economic problems of our people

The study carried out by the Commission on the activities of the Education Board found that the educational efforts would not be made complete unless the community reaches the state average in literacy and grows further to total literacy[199]. The report regarding the functioning of the Board of Temporalities bought severe criticism. The commission began with the statement: «The functioning of the Board of Temporalities was far from satisfactory»[200]. In the first paragraph itself the commission

---

[198] C. LEON, *Summary Report*, 11, ADT.

[199] E.J. THOMAS, *Summary of Education Commission's Report*, 1-2, ADT.

[200] The Diocese also gave serious attention to the study report. The Commission held forty-one meetings, visited all the properties under the Board of Temporalities, and Institutions directly under the Diocese, interviewed and obtained suggestions from all the members of the Board and from those who were in one way or other connected with the temporal administration of the Diocese during the last five years. Suggestions were also invited from all the priests of Diocese and lay people. See L. MENDEZ, ed., *Summary of the Report*, 2, ADT.

remarked that the members of the Board spent more time during their meetings fighting for power and authority, instead rather than holding creative discussions for constructive activities.

The Commission on pastoral ministries also made an in-depth study covering its areas[201]. In its study, the Commission analyzed the situations existing in the Diocese before and after the «Living Together». The Commission evaluated the functioning of the Boards on the basis of scope for participation, effectiveness in terms of output, clarity of vision, choice of means and identification of thrusts, coordination provisions, awareness building, training lay leaders, systematic planning procedures which include assessing the existing situation, defining objectives, fixing action programs to arrive at the objectives, scheduling, budgeting, fixing policies and procedures, providing means for communicating and motivating, arranging for viable structures. The availability of key personnel, interest and involvement of members and the over all impact of the renewal on the Diocese was also taken into consideration[202]. In its objective study the Commission remarked:

> In general we are *much impressed* by the work done, given the fact that these three Boards came into being just two years ago, the achievements are remarkable. We also found that the Boards and Committees have created a sense of hope among the people. A good many of them expressed happiness in being able to be participants. Another hopeful trend, during the time of the evaluation is the co-operative attitude of the administration. This augurs well for a more effective functioning[203].

The Commission also pointed out certain weaknesses in the whole process of functioning. They are: lack of specialized training for the personnel involved in the Boards and committees extending even to the directors, non attendance and lack of interest in Board meetings, lack of full-time personnel, non-availability of co-ordination structures, failure to create enough consensus on coordination thrusts among all the Boards,

---

[201] The commission studied: (i) the report submitted by the directors of the three Boards and the committees functioning under these Boards, and (ii) the files and registers kept by some of these structures. In addition, it interviewed the directors and quite a lot of the members of the Board and almost all the persons responsible for the various apostolates in the areas covered by the Boards. Further the Commission had discussions with the co-ordinator of the Boards, the diocesan administrators and a few others. The Commission also made itself available on two days to listen to the grievances the priests or the people had regarding the function of the Boards. The proposals were given in the light of this in-depth study.

[202] See X. ALEXANDER, ed., *Report of the Commission*, 11-12, ADT.

[203] See X. ALEXANDER, ed., *Report of the Commission*, 11-12, ADT.

lack of sufficient efforts at follow-up of seminars, lack of pooling resources, talents and facilities of the various Boards for mutual advantage, lack of proper financial polices for the functioning of the Boards, lack of facilities like communication and transport, lack of enough office space and clerical staff at the centre[204].

In the light of the above key observations the commission called for a structural modification.

5.5.1 Call for Structural Changes

Realizing the importance of the role of pastoral ministries in the local Church of Trivandrum, the main concern of the Commission members was to find out the ways and means to propose a *suitable structure* which promotes the proclamation of the Kingdom of God in the challenging situations of Trivandrum. Considering the vastness of the Diocese in terms of geographical area and the poverty stricken situation of the people, the commission realized the practical difficulties of giving an impact to any kind of renewal worked out in the Diocese felt at the wider level except through Vicariate level structures which will have links in each parish to represent the various renewal programmes. The Commission noted:

> Even a parish is normally a big structure, where the «small men» who are the majority find no role to play and no scope to participate. They feel left out, unimportant, and «nobodies». Unless these people also are somehow involved in the diocesan reflection and planning, our efforts will not reach much beyond a few white collared middle-class men and the usual members of a few pious associations. The vast majority of the «anawim» of the Lord will remain mostly untouched. Until we can get over this situation, any diocesan renewal is bound to be exercised of [by] the few on the top in various levels rather than a peoples' movement[205].

Together with decentralization the Commission also envisaged a vision for better participation in the ecclesial structure[206]. While suggesting the

---

204 See X. ALEXANDER, ed., *Report of the Commission*, 11-12, ADT.

205 X. ALEXANDER, ed., *Report of the Commission*, 14-15, ADT.

206 «Hence we should also aim, beyond parish participation, participation at grassroots community levels. This should mean that the parish level representative at the Vicariate Commission, in turn, is the convenor at the parish level, of basic-community-level animators [...]. This should also mean that there are in each basic community separate "ministries" or animators for concerns like Christian Life, Vocation, Communication Media, Family Apostolate, etc., forming so to say a cabinet at basic community levels. Such a principle of subsidiarity will ensure more action at every level

idea of decentralization of diocesan activities thereby giving more opportunity for increased participation, the Commission was fully aware of the difficulties to execute it in the diocesan context. Still the Commission stated:

> Of course, it looks so good on paper. But when it comes to actualities, it will be a struggle. But, in spite of it all, it is worth to dream the «impossible dream» as a long range strategy and to keep pushing towards it even if, in the beginning [initial] stages, the seats for parish or even vicariate representative, remain vacant in some cases. This effort will gradually ensure a co-responsible and more empowered Church that would respond with better situation flexibility to the challenges of the Kingdom[207].

With this background, the Commission made some *Proposals for Structural Modifications* in which the Board of Pastoral Ministries included: Christian Life Formation (integrating the present Commissions for Bible, Liturgy and Catechetics), Vocation, Communication Media, Family (covering such areas as Pre-Cana Conferences, marriage preparation, responsible parenthood, Marriage Encounter, Family Counseling), Lay Apostolate (consisting of representatives of lay associations), Community building (promoting BCC and Christian Life 2000), Evangelization, Youth, Ecumenism and Dialogue[208].

The Commission also suggested defining the pastoral priorities in the Diocese[209] and strongly recommended that any strategy for pastoral action today should include the formation of BECs and the organization of small-group oriented movements. For, such Communities could help in ensuring a more tangible ecclesial experience besides providing structures for participatory action by people at grassroots. The BECs, the Commission has foreseen, could also offer in the long run a provision for co-ordination from below, in a kind of coordination «as if people mattered», where the people at grassroots will help us to identify priorities for pastoral action[210].

---

with more freedom for those on the top to have a wider vision, better prospective and the wherewith for [possibility of] better guidance» (X. ALEXANDER, ed., *Report of the Commission*, 15, ADT).

[207] X. ALEXANDER, ed., *Report of the Commission*, 15, ADT.

[208] For the other proposals for structural modifications see X. ALEXANDER, ed., *Report of the Commission*, 16-19, ADT.

[209] See X. ALEXANDER, ed., *Report of the Commission*, 20, ADT.

[210] See X. ALEXANDER, ed., *Report of the Commission*, 24-25, ADT. Regarding the financial aspects of the Pastoral Ministry, apart from the diocesan funds, the Commission gave a valuable suggestion: «The diocese should also try to keep pushing [urging] the

5.5.2 Early Christian Communities: A Living Model

The Diocese as a whole and the Bishop in particular has given special attention to the reports of the four Commissions which well expressed the aspirations of the people of God in the Diocese of Trivandrum. This was fully reflected in the Lenten Message of Bishop M.S. Pakiam[211]. In the message, the Bishop exhorted, referring to the Lenten Message of Pope John Paul II, which was translated and circulated along with it, different aspects of Christian life in the light of the findings of the «Commissions». He presented the early Christian community as a model for everyone's reflection, meditation and imitation. He stressed that the early Christian community took part in everything concerning the human life. They were not mere *recipients of projects*[212] from the Church authorities. They were very conscious of their role in the community so much so that they took up responsibilities.

To contextualize the experience of the early Christian community in the Diocese he informed the people about some concrete programmes which were under great consideration. And the most important among them was the formation of BECs consisting of about thirty families each. These communities would be inter-linked within the parishes, Vicariates and in the Diocese so that even the less privileged, the neglected, and the voiceless would experience Christian fellowship and take part in all the ministries. Thus the Bishop communicated his vision about a Church that is decentralized and a Church in which everyone would be participating through their charism[213].

5.5.3 BECs: A Pastoral Option

Following the Lenten Message the Bishop sent a pastoral letter urging the formation of BECs in all the parishes as a time bound programme. He

---

parishes to share a part of the formation expenses. It should be made policy in the diocese to get the parishes to allot a certain percentage in their incomes for formation activities at diocesan and parish levels. If the parish is less a feast celebration crowd, and more a community at the service of the kingdom, the parish budgets also should prove this commitment» (See X. ALEXANDER, ed., *Report of the Commission*, 23, ADT).

[211] See M.S. PAKIAM, *Metrānte Nōymbukāla Sandēśam* (Lenten Message of the Bishop), 13-2-1991, ADT.

[212] As the Church in India is accused of institutionalization the Bishop's statement is prophetic. See *CBCI Evaluation Report*, n. 745.

[213] The pastoral council meeting held on 4-7-1991 also discussed the progress and functioning of BECs in the Diocese. See S. YESUDAS, *Pastoral Council Report*, 26-1-1991, 20-22. The message of the Bishop was fully in tune with the Encyclical of Pope John Paul II, *Redemptoris Missio*, n. 51.

said: «In the light of the renewal process of the Diocese I consider that it is inevitable to form *Aṭistāna Kṛistīya Samūhaṅgal*[214] in all the parishes of our Diocese». He was aware of the difficulties to form the communities in a time bound programme, especially for the laity who were trained in a different way. He added:

> The formation of BECs is not an easy job. The services of people who have good will are extremely needed. It is not necessary to remind you that, for selfless service, people have to come forward and take up responsibilities. Do not belittle the value of such services. Remembering the role of laity in the process of diocesan renewal, act according to it[215].

According to him the spiritual and material benefits of the Diocese should be experienced and enjoyed by every community. The criteria to know the development of the Diocese according to him depends on the true Christian life of the BECs. And he expressed his time bound programme too. «I earnestly desire that the BECs would be formed in all the parishes by the end of May 1991»[216].

From the reports submitted by the Commissions, it became clear that for a total development of the Diocese more decentralization and better participation of the people were necessary. These suggestions of the Commissions fully agreed with the spirit of the Scripture and the vision of the Second Vatican Council. The vitality of the Church is based not on rigid laws and structures but in self giving and *kenosis* which comes from love. This is well expressed in the biblical terminology *koinōnia* or fellowship. A true fellowship can be experienced in small communities of twenty or thirty families.

In the practical aspect, the Bishop envisaged that the communities might gather once in two weeks or at least in a month. In their gatherings they would read the scripture and meditate on it and get a new life from it. Keeping up the family spirit, the people will be able to discuss the problems of life in light of the Gospel. And there should be a common effort to find out the solutions. According to the Bishop no one should have an occasion to feel that he or she is neglected or unheard in the

---

[214] The literal translation of *Aṭistāna Kṛistīa Samūhaṅgal* would mean basic Christian communities. In effect *Aṭistāna Kṛistīya Samūhaṅgal* are basic *ecclesial* communities. So, in the dissertation, we call *Aṭistāna Kṛistīya Samūhaṅgal* as BECs.

[215] M.S. PAKIAM, *Aṭistāna Kṛistīya Samūhaṅgal* (Basic Ecclesial Communities), 10-4-1991, ADT [The translation mine]. See also the Pastoral Council report of 1-6-1991.

[216] M.S. PAKIAM, *Aṭistāna Kṛistīya Samūhaṅgal* (Basic Ecclesial Communities), 10-4-1991, ADT.

BECs. There should be a committed effort to take common decisions and to execute them. The fellowship thus derived should be a *power house* to radiate the Christian life. The people should also be able to fight against the injustices in the society and build up Christian *koinōnia*. Thus, the communities would be a great help to the spiritual and material, cultural and educational welfare of the society[217].

This pastoral letter of the Bishop has become the point of reference for the BECs in Trivandrum and other local Churches in Kerala. The pastoral letter expressed the true desire and commitment of a *pastor* for the spiritual and material development of the voiceless, the marginalized and the less privileged people of Trivandrum. As was mentioned in the pastoral letter, structural changes also had taken place very fast. The power has been decentralized and has become a means of service. As a result, a participatory Church is on the threshold.

5.5.4 New Pastoral Option Calls for New Structures

The formation of BECs brought a change in the whole structure of the administration. The whole diocesan administration is brought under four ministries: Pastoral Ministry, Education Ministry, Social Service Ministry, Finance Ministry. The Pastoral Ministry is divided into seven Commissions: Christian Life (Bible, Liturgy, Catechetics), Family Apostolate, Youth, Evangelization, Vocation, Pious Associations, Ecumenism and Dialogue. The Educational Ministry is divided into three Commissions: Academic, Maintenance & Development, Higher & Technical Education. The Social Ministry is divided into five Commissions: Socio — Economic, Women & Child, Health & Anti-Alcoholism, Labour Justice & Peace, and Backward Class. The Finance Ministry is divided into three Committees: Properties, Constructions, Institutions. The main structure is followed in a parish and in Vicariate levels in the Pastoral, Social and Educational Ministries[218].

---

217 M.S. PAKIAM, *Aṭistāna Kṛistīya Samūhaṅgal* (Basic Ecclesial Communities), 10-4-1991, ADT.

218 For example we see how the diocesan pastoral ministry is inter-related with Vicariate pastoral ministry, parish pastoral ministry and BEC. The elected representatives from BECs will form the parish level commission for pastoral ministry. An executive committee will monitor all the pastoral activities of the parish. The convenor of this commission will become a member of the parish pastoral council. In the Vicariate: seven members elected from the parish pastoral ministry will represent the parish at the Vicariate level commissions of the pastoral ministry. The number of the members of each commission will correspond to the number of the parishes in a Vicariate. In the diocesan

The use of word the «Ministry» is very significant in the structure. Christ came into the world to serve and not to be served (Mk 10,41-45). The Church comes at the service of the people[219]. In the new structure only those who are elected in the BECs can become a member of a parish pastoral council or Vicariate council or diocesan council. One cannot be a member of the parish pastoral council unless one *lives the Church* in the concrete situation. One of the external expressions of this is the participation in the BEC meetings. It is through the participation in the BEC meetings that one can know his or her neighbours better and can be at the service of them. In this major shift, importance is given to fellowship and service. «He has, however, willed to make men holy and save them not as individuals without any bond or link between them, but rather to make them into a people who might acknowledge him and serve him in holiness»[220]. The authority is for service.

With a change in the structure a new *diaconal* culture has been evolving in the Diocese. The scripture becomes the prayer book of the laity too. The liturgy is becoming the *liturgy of the people*. The laity takes up the challenge of being an *evangelizer*. The people begin to read and respond to the signs of the time in light of the Word of God. Women and children give a new vitality to the Church. Women's voices are heard in the BEC fellowships, parish pastoral councils and diocesan pastoral council. A new practical ecumenism and dialogue is taking place beyond the conceptual level. Above all, in the particular diocesan context, a process of *re-peopling the de-peopled*[221] is taking place. In this process priests and religious find more meaning in their personal commitment to serve the people of God.

---

level: as the Diocese has eleven Vicariates each Vicariate commission will elect a representative for the diocesan level commission. Thus there will be eleven members in each of the seven commissions at the centre. Each commission will be animated by a secretary who will work under an executive director. The executive director will be helped by a team of experts called Board to form policies. In education and social service ministries the same method is followed in proportion to the number and necessity of the commissions.

[219] The Church in India has been identified with the institutional model. So the choice of the word «Ministry» is a new paradigm of «servant model». This was a significant shift in the ecclesial life of Trivandrum. This shift has been well reflected in the functioning of BECs. «New ideas will not usher in a new praxis, unless structures are changed. It is anathema today to plead for structural changes in the church, because every institution and structure in the church has theological justification and canonical sanction!» (G. KOONTHANAM, «Option for the Poor», 325).

[220] LG 9/2

[221] The phrase was first used by H.L. Perkins. See H.L. PERKINS, *Roots for Vision.*

6. Conclusion

In the previous pages we discussed the emergence of BECs in the Diocese of Trivandrum. The point of departure of our investigation was from the formation of ecclesial communities in the time of the greatest missionary of India, St. Francis Xavier. From the investigation we came to know that although the Portuguese missionaries were working before Francis Xavier in the Travancore Coast, it was Francis Xavier who gave a sound foundation to the establishment of ecclesial communities.

Francis Xavier arrived in India in 1542 with a missionary zeal to preach the Kingdom of God. His stay for a few months in Goa, where he composed *Doctrina Christiana* in its short form in the Portuguese language[222], gave him an occasion to plan out his future missionary career at the Fishery Coast and Travancore Coast. His arrival in Travancore is very significant. He came prepared to preach the Gospel with a new awareness of the Kingdom of God[223]. From the very moment of his entry into the Travancore Coast, Francis Xavier could attract the poor fisher folk. They loved him, listened to him and received baptism from him. The joy that Francis Xavier had in baptizing ten thousand people from Travancore Coast within one month, thus saving their souls, was beyond description.

The ecclesial vision possessed by the saint has continued in the subsequent years. In the course of time the harmony of ecclesial life was broken partly because of the ecclesial systems and partly because of the clergy. Like the *Pūjaris* of Hindu temples, who were very particular about the rituals, the Catholic priests became *pūjāri* with ecclesiastical power instead of becoming *servants to the people of God*[224]. The clergy together with the *pradhāni* who had an age old tradition of the *arayan*, exploited the people even imposing more taxes. Many solid and imposing churches were constructed taxing the poor who lived in huts[225]. The

---

[222] See *EX*, I, 106-116. The Christian doctrine that he prepared reflects the whole of St. Francis Xavier's spirituality. He was one among the first few who had *Spiritual Exercise* under St. Ignatius of Loyola.

[223] «Quando allegava en los lugares no me dexavan los mochachos ni rezar mi oficio, ni comer, ni dormir, sino que los ensenñase algunas oraciones. Entonces encomencé a conocer quoniam talium est regnum celorum» (*EX*, I, 148).

[224] Pope John Paul II rightly said when he visited Trivandrum that «the Church here, and throughout India, is a servant Church» (JOHN PAUL II, «Address to the Faithful», 387-393.

[225] There have been a minority who raised their voices and protested against the injustices. Many a time their voices were unheard. The ecclesial vision of St. Francis

people contributed money *to save their souls* and took pride in it. The sacraments became mere rituals and Sodalities and Confraternities made every ritual more colourful and Patrons' feasts very expensive. Priests and *pradhāni* had only time to think about celebration of feasts. However, a *well established tradition* had been formed in many of the coastal parishes, even competing with the parishes in the Western countries.

After the Jesuits[226] the Carmelites dominated the scene. The Carmelites had a special mission in the ecclesial history of the Kerala Church. Their important mission in Kerala was in connection with the settlement of disputes which had arisen from the *Coonam Cross Oath* of 3rd January 1653. It took more than one century to concentrate their work in the non-coastal villages of Trivandrum. Their austere life and zeal to convert the people brought satisfactory results. The Carmelites, however, apart from their austere life, could not answer the problems of the non-coastal parishes where the people have a strong kinship relation which goes beyond the institutional religion[227]. So ecumenism and dialogue were not in the *missionary agenda*. They gave importance to primary education[228]. Through pious associations and popular devotions the missionaries deepened the faith of the people.

The native priests who were mainly formed by the Religious priests followed the same pattern of Christian life in the Diocese. However, the people were becoming aware of their own deplorable situations in the society. Inspired by the teachings of the Second Vatican Council and the newly evolving theological vision, the people began to question their own destiny. The socially committed priests, religious and lay leaders took an active role to liberate the people from the clutches of social evils. They fought for the fishermen. The fishermen's agitation had its own repercussions in the Kerala Church. The *Gandhian method of agitation* became a moral question in the Christian circle. Those who were engaged in fishermen's struggle, saw the God's liberative hand. In their struggle for the poor they felt «helplessness as well as strength and mastery»[229]. In

---

Xavier and his immediate successors was practically lost. But the people had kept up a solid faith in the Church. The people were proud of being baptized by St. Francis Xavier though the caste system kept the fishermen away from the main stream of the secular world, even from the neighbours.

[226] By Jesuits, we mean priests under the *Padroado* jurisdiction.

[227] The Protestant missionaries also failed in this respect.

[228] The importance given to primary education is well reflected in the TSSS survey conducted in 1993. See C. LEON, *Sāmūhika Sāmbattika Survey Prāthamika Report* (Socio-Economic Survey Preliminary Report).

[229] T. KOCHERY, «The Cross Now and Here», 245.

their identification with the suffering fishermen they also met *Jesus*.[230] The fishermen's agitation gave an occasion for the Hierarchy of Kerala to think about the fishermen's problem in its depth. The agitation also proved the powerful religious sentiments of a suffering class[231].

The changes that had been taking place caused mixed reaction among the clergy and the laity. In the struggle for the poor, an ideological conflict became evident in the life of the Church of Kerala. Trivandrum became an arena of conflict of ideas and struggle. The cultural differences also played an important role. The *inborn independence*[232] of the people of Travancore was well expressed in the religious matters. Even within the struggle and ideological differences «the people» were the main concern.

At the moment of conflict, the call for celebration of the Golden Jubilee of the Diocese and the «Living Together» which followed was an attempt to find out solutions to the various problems of the Diocese. The «Living Together», like that of the Apostles who gathered to find solution to the complaints of the Hellenists (Acts 6,1-6), was an occasion for the priests to come together and to find out solutions of the various problems of the Diocese. As the Apostles who, realizing their mission, shared the responsibility of *diakonia* to the seven, the «Living Together» gave an opportunity for the priests to realize their role and mission in the Diocese. And this realization assured the involvement of the laity in the ecclesial life of the Diocese. The *conflict* that existed in the Diocese *resulted positively* to find new ways of being the Church. The decisions of the «Living Together» did not remain merely as verbal acceptance of conclusions. The renewal called for constant evaluation of the implementation of the decisions of the «Living Together» in light of the Word of God and the teachings of the Church and in the particular context of Trivandrum. It is through a process of constant self evaluation that BECs became the pastoral option of the Diocese.

The BECs in Trivandrum have their own indigenous nature. The emergence of BECs in Trivandrum traces its origin to the ecclesial communities founded by St. Francis Xavier and the Carmelites missionaries. The Second Vatican Council called the ecclesial

---

[230] See T. KOCHERY, «Where I met Jesus», 185-192. See also P. MARY – *al.*, «Casting the Net », 193-200.

[231] From the *upper-cloth* revolt and the social liberation of Sri Narayana Guru it is clear that religious life is the basis of social change in Kerala.

[232] The people of Travancore have never been under a foreign ruler, even at the time of British regime.

communities for renewal or *aggiornamento*. In the process of renewal, through the moments of painful experiences, prayer, reflection and study, the BECs became the pastoral option of the Diocese. In the new pastoral option the traditional role of the Bishop, priests, religious and the laity changes. In the change, an incarnational spirituality emerges. Since BECs have become a pastoral option, a structural change was inevitable.

The next chapter is an attempt to know how the BECs function in the changing structure. We also will see how *fidelity and creativity* of BECs are actualized in the changing ecclesial administrative structure and changing situations of the society.

CHAPTER IV

The Functioning of Basic Ecclesial Communities in Trivandrum

In the third chapter we discussed how BECs have emerged as the pastoral option in the Diocese. We saw that though the ecclesial life of Christian communities goes back to the time of early missionaries, the BECs are the outcome of the renewal process initiated by the Second Vatican Council and contextualized through the process of «Living Together» and the Golden Jubilee celebration of the Diocese. The historical, theological and sociological factors which influenced the emergence of BECs were also under our investigation in the last chapter. We saw that bishops, theologians and priests have played a significant role in the origin and growth of BECs. Some of the important phases in the formation of BECs in Trivandrum are: (i) the felt need of the people to live like the early Christian community, (ii) the awareness of the clergy about the felt need of the lay people, (iii) the timely response to the felt need of the people by the clergy and the Bishop and (iv) the maturing self-realization of the clergy about their own specific role as servants of the people of God.

In this chapter we investigate the functioning of BECs in the Diocese. This we do in the context of a field study conducted in 1994 in view of this dissertation: it takes into account the findings of a survey conducted through questionnaire method, the results of the personal experience in the BEC meetings and interviews with people in different walks of life. Since the people of the Diocese are mainly of two cultural milieus, two Vicariates from each sector have been selected so as to get an overall vision of the functioning of the BECs in Trivandrum.

In our preliminary inquiry from various animators, priests and lay people who are involved in the BEC formation, we came to know that though the formation of BECs is a diocesan programme all the Vicariates are not functioning equally well. With the background of the preliminary inquiry we first selected two Vicariates which are functioning well — one from the coastal and the other from the non-coastal, and two Vicariates which have to improve — one from the coastal and the other from the non-coastal.

Then within each Vicariate we have selected two parishes one that is functioning well and the other which has to improve. In the third selection, we have taken two BEC units from each parish — one functioning well and the other needing improvement.

The fourth selection was on the respondent. From each unit we have selected two BEC animators, two ordinary members who regularly participate in the BEC gatherings, the co-ordinator of BECs in the particular parish and three irregular or indifferent members. That is to say, from each parish there were selected twelve respondents and altogether ninety-six respondents[1], of which, seventy-two are regular participants and twenty-four irregular. In the questionnaire there were thirty nine objective questions and three open ones.

The results of the questionnaire survey are not to be taken in a sociological sense but are to be considered as elements promoting objectivity to our investigation[2]. The field study gives us a picture of how the BECs are functioning at present, the general trend of the laity, the

---

[1] Age-wise we selected twenty-seven people belonging to the age of less than twenty-five, of which twelve are male and fifteen female, forty-three belonging to the age of twenty-five to forty, of which nineteen are male and twenty-four female, twenty-six belonging to the age of more than forty, of which eighteen male and eight female. From the educational point of view fifty-eight are with SSLC or below SSLC, thirty-five are diploma or graduation certificate holders and three post-graduation. When we analyze the respondents on the basis of job we see that sixteen are coolies, twenty are fishermen or farmers, nineteen are government employees or businessmen and forty-one are house wives.

[2] During the field study I attended as an observer various meetings related to BECs. The important ones are: (i) the reporting session of the theology students' exposure programme on 28-4-1994 at Loyola College Trivandrum; (ii) the BEC unit meetings at Poozhikunnu on 30-4-1994, at Chullimanoor on 7-5-1994, at Kochuveli on 10-5-94, at Kannamthura on 16-5-1994, at Utchakkada on 17-5-1994, at Valiavila on 6-6-1994; (iii) the Neyyattinkara Vicariate animators meeting at Mangalathukonam on 14-5-1994; Kannamthura parish animators meeting on 16-5-1994; Vlathankara parish animators meeting on 17-5-1994; (iv) the diocesan animators' camp at Vellayambalam from 3-6-1994 to 4-6-1994; (v) the two BEC Vicariate conventions — one at Vettucadu on 8-5-1994 and the other at Palayam on 22-5-1994. The interviews both formal and informal include those of with the Bishop, fifty priests and twenty-one women religious of eleven congregations; 112 lay people consisting of literate and illiterate, employees and non-employees. We also collected some information also from children.

involvement of the consecrated ministers and the social commitment of the BECs. The results of the field study will be explored after showing the realization of the pastoral option in the early stages and the efforts made by the Diocese to realize its option.

1. Realization of the Pastoral Option

We have seen that with the Lenten message of Bishop M.S. Pakiam in 1991 and the Pastoral Letter dated 10-4-1991, the formation of BECs was given top priority in the Diocese[3]. As a part of the realization of the Pastoral Option of the Diocese different training programmes were organized in the initial stages.

In the first stage, awareness seminars on community-building were conducted for priests and laity. These were offered by the Commission for Community Building under Pastoral Ministry on parish, Vicariate and diocesan levels[4]. Since there arose the need to elect leaders or animators from each BEC unit, the Commission for the Community Building printed and distributed a booklet explaining the qualities required for Christian leadership[5]. The commission secretary and the director of pastoral ministry visited all the Vicariate centres and held discussions with the forane vicar and forane co-ordinators of pastoral ministry as regards the formation of BEC units in the parishes.

In the second stage, leaders' conventions were held along with the official inauguration of BECs. Within a period of six months about 2.000

---

[3] According to the time bound programme in all the Vicariates study classes were arranged for priests before 20 April 1991. In light of the study classes, the Bishop asked the priests to instruct the people on the importance of the BECs on two consecutive Sundays in the parishes, 21st & 28th April, 1991.

[4] It included a special training programme arranged for priests, sisters and lay people of twenty parishes. The presence of priests, sisters and lay people for the training programmes orients the participants to a new ecclesial culture in the Indian context where the priests and religious have not fully accepted the role of laity in the Church. «[...] all in the Church, whether they belong to the hierarchy or are cared for by it, are called to holiness, according to the apostle's saying: "For this is the will of God, your sanctification" (1 Th 4,3; cf. Eph 1,4)» (*L G* 39).

[5] In the pastoral letter on BECs the Bishop instructed that in the first meeting of BECs itself two leaders — one man and one woman — would be elected. For the description of the qualities required of the leaders see R. GREGORY, ed., *Kuṭumba Unit Netākalkkoru Mārgarēgha* (Guidelines for the Family Unit Leaders). In the booklet guidelines to conduct the BEC gatherings were also given.

BECs were formed and regular meetings began to be conducted[6]. The commission also started to publish a newsletter (bimonthly) called *Navapatham* (New Way). Through the newsletter themes for the meetings, reflections about the image of the Church, news and views of BECs in various parishes were given.

In the third stage the commission started visiting the parishes to give proper guidance to the BEC leaders or animators and to evaluate the activities. In the early period, in order to train more resource personnel, the Diocese made use of the methods of the *Lumko Series*[7], known as the *Lumko Methods* in its training programme. The *Lumko Methods* could easily convey the message of BECs at the grassroots level.

1.1 *New Structure Calls for New Methods*

Inspired by the teachings of the Second Vatican Council, the Lumko Institute in South Africa developed a series of methods known as *Lumko Methods* for training people for community ministries. In Trivandrum the *Lumko Methods* have been in use from the time of the «Living Together» for training the leaders and in the BEC meetings. The methods in the series include materials for models of the Church, Gospel sharing,[8]

---

[6] The number of communities in August 1991 was about 876. See M.S. PAKIAM, *Letter to Bishop Bosco Penha*, ADT. In November the number of BECs increased to around 2.000. See R.P. LEAN, *Briefing of BEC Process*, ADT.

[7] The series consists of nine different kits and fourteen booklets for the use of the average pastoral workers and their co-workers.

[8] The Gospel Sharing Methods include (i) *The 7-step method* which aims at: experiencing the presence of the Risen Lord; helping each member of the group to be touched personally by the word; encouraging mutual deepening in the faith by personal sharing; deepening personal bonds among the members of the group; creating trust within the group; creating a «spiritual climate» for planning the action of the community; (ii) *Group response method* which aims at: seeing daily situation and problems reflected in the biblical text; helping the group to look beyond their immediate personal spiritual needs; making the Gospel a driving force for «self-help» in talking life issues; (iii) *Look-listen-love method* which aims at: starting from the life issue; sharing life experiences in which members of the group are emotionally involved, feeling happy or unhappy about them; listening to God's call regarding these experience or event if no biblical text can be quoted; arriving at a common action; (iv) *Amos programmes* which aim at: beginning with a social, economic or political problem which concerns all; helping a group to analyze a situation and find root-causes for a problem; seeing a social, economic or political problem in the light of the Gospel and Church documents; to help the group follow a detailed problem-solving scheme; (v) *Parish-search method* which aims at: training leaders in preparing «Bible Study» notes for groups; learning how to use a Bible commentary; learning how to prepare guiding questions in order to discuss life-issues in the light of a biblical text and (vi) *Biblical picture programmes* which aim at: helping a

building of small Christian Communities[9], non-dominating leadership[10]. These methods helped in various ways to communicate the Gospel message and the teachings of the Church to the people at the grassroots level and subsequently, the people began to respond to the social situations collectively.

It is beyond doubt that the determination to implement the recommendation of the study report by the Bishop, absorbed and supported by the Diocesan Pastoral Council, was one of the main reasons for the formation of more than 2.000 BECs within a year. We give the Vicariate-wise number of BECs in the Diocese in 1992 and in the year 1994.

BECs in Different Vicariates[11]

	1992	1994
Angengo	120	127
Chullimannor	126	140
Kattakode	237	203
Neyyattinkara	189	222
Palayam	188	225
Pulluvila	222	273
Puthukurichy	189	216
Thothoor	270	283
Undencode	203	202
Valiyathura	253	242
Vlathankara	176	272
	2173	2402

---

group to connect Bible and life by means of photo-posters and Bible pictures; to help a group to «dig deeper» by means of a supplied work-sheet; meditating and reflecting on the main topics of the faith; allowing catechumens to be accompanied by a community on the way to baptism. For a detailed description of each method see O. HIRMER – F.R. BRODERICK, *Gospel Sharing*.

[9] See F. LOBINGER, *Building Small Christian Communities*.

[10] See F. LOBINGER, *Towards Non-dominating Leadership*.

[11] The number of BECs in 1992 is from a report of the Bishop dated 29-6-1992 and the number of BECs in 1994 is from the report of Sr. Jayanthi, the co-ordinator of the animators of the BECs, on 4th June 1994. According to the latest information (24-8-1995) we came to know that there are 2627 communities.

1.2 *Printed Materials*

In the early stage of the functioning of BECs in the Diocese there arose a need of printed materials. Along with the newsletter, *Navapatham* (New Way) and *Kuṭumba Unit Netākalkkoru Mārgarēgha*, (Guidelines for the Family Unit Leaders), the Commission for Community Building published literature on BECs in the native language. The important ones already published are: *Aṭistāna Kraisttava Samūham: Caritra Paścāttalam*, (BEC: A Historical Background); *Aṭistāna Kraisttava Samūham: Bible Velicattil* (BEC: In the Context of Bible); *Kuṭumba Yōga Prabhāṣaṇaṅgal*, (Speeches at the Family Gatherings), *Aṭistāna Kraisttava Samūham: Suviśēṣānubhavam Paṅguvaikkal*, (BEC: Sharing the Gospel Experience); and *Aṭistāna Kraisttava Samūham: Oru Paṭhanam* (BEC: A Study). To extend the message of BECs to the children and to the youth of the Diocese, some of the books were prescribed as texts for Sunday Catechism classes[12].

Despite all the diocesan infrastructure, uncertainties existed in the formation of BECs in the initial stage[13]. This was partly due to the *hasty implementation* of the programme and partly because of *anxiety about the decentralization of power.*

2. BECs: A New Way of Being Church

Ever since the «Living Together», the Diocese has been at the threshold of its renewal of Christian life. The process of renewal gained a momentum when BECs became the pastoral option of the Diocese. This is evident in the participation of the people in the BEC meetings, in the liturgical services and in their social commitments. The parishes have become communities of communities, each consisting of twenty or thirty families. Each BEC is called a *Kuṭumba unit*[14]. Each community gathers

---

[12] From November 1995 the Commission for BECs in Trivandrum began to publish «*Ekatānādam*» (united voice) a news bulletin for the Kerala region.

[13] The invitation of Bishop Bosco Penha, the auxiliarybishop of Bombay, to conduct a seminar on BECs to the priests of the Diocese is to be seen in the context of initial uncertainties in the execution of the programme. See M.S. PAKIAM, *Letter to Bishop Bosco Penha*, ADT. Bishop B. Penha led a seminar for priests on BECs from 17th to 18th December 1991.

[14] 12% of BECs are communities with less than ten families, 21% with families between ten to fifteen and 67% are communities with more than twenty families. Most of the communities in the coastal BECs have more than twenty families. In the survey it became clear that the people who do not participate in the BEC meetings have a general

in its cultural milieu. Within the geographical milieu no one is left out. In the event that one does not frequent the BEC gatherings, other members work as evangelizers to bring that particular member to the BEC gatherings.

2.1 *BECs and Their Gatherings*

The members of a BEC gather once a week, fortnightly or once a month[15] in one of the houses within the BEC geographical unit[16]. The number of participants in a gathering vary from one BEC to the other[17]. Most of the participants are women. This is a common phenomenon in both the coastal and non-coastal BECs[18].

Since women are more numerous in most of the BEC gatherings there is a general complaint that BECs have become *Vanita Samājam* (women's forum). There are various reasons for the high participation of the women in the BECs. One of the main reasons is that in most of the families the male members go for work outside the village and some even outside the State[19]. Other reasons include the inherent religious attitude of

---

idea about what is happening in the BECs. For example 66% irregular respondents have a general idea about the number of families in a BEC.

[15] The response to the question «How often do you gather?» reveals that 70% of the BECs gather once a week, and 24% once a fortnight and 6% once a month. In the coastal areas 91% gather once a week and in the non-coastal areas 49% gather once a week and 42% gather once a fortnight. See Table ns.: Ia – Q3, IIa – Q3, IIIa – Q.3. In the Trivandrum city the people gather once a month.

[16] Gathering in a house is very significant. The Church goes to the people — *Ad Gentes*. The gathering at different houses reminds one of the early Christian house churches.

[17] Generally in 43% of the BEC gatherings, the participants are between fifteen and thirty in number. In 40% of the BEC gatherings, the participants are more than thirty and in 17% the participants are less than fifteen. In the coastal BEC gatherings the participants are comparatively greater in number than in the non-coastal BECs. See Table ns.: I a – Q2, II a – Q2, III a – Q2. The general understanding of the BECs is that at least one adult member of a family be present for a BEC gathering.

[18] The question about the participants «among the participants?»in the questionnaire contained three possible answers (a) 80% ladies, (b) 60% ladies, (c) equal number of ladies and gentlemen. In 74% BECs more than 80% women participate and in 26% of BECs, 60% women participate. See Table ns.: Ia – Q4, IIa – Q4,III a – Q4. Nevertheless in the city both men and women have equal participation.

[19] The fishermen go for fishing far away from the place and quite a good number of them come home only once in two or three months. In the non-coastal BECs a good number of the male members are masons and go to other parts of Kerala. However, according to some priests and lay people, indifference is the main reason for the less participation of male members in the BECs.

women towards the religion[20] and the high *literacy rate* among the
women in Trivandrum[21]. However, a more balanced participation of men
and women would be ideal. As regards the absence of members in the
BEC gatherings 35% of the participants think that the people are not
attending because of their physical absence from the place. About 40%
think that it is because some are not interested in the new system and 25%
hold the view that by attending the gatherings one does not get any
particular experience[22] though 88% of the people prefer the new parish
structure of the local Church which has evolved in Trivandrum[23].

---

[20] In the third chapter we saw that in most of the pious associations women have
better participation than men. In the second chapter we have noted how the Nadar women
fought for their right to wear upper cloth already in the 19th century. We have also seen
the role played by the Mukkuvar women against the Communist Government in 1957 in
Trivandrum. Together with the spontaneous religiosity in addition to the new ecclesial
awareness, the women play a better role in the BECs.

[21] From the point of view of the literacy rate in Kerala State, the literacy of the
Catholic population in Trivandrum is not satisfactory. The literacy rate of the State is
89.79% and in the district of Trivandrum it is 89.22%. See GOVERNMENT OF KERALA,
Kerala at a Glance, 5. 9. In the Diocese of Trivandrum it is 85.30%. See C. LEON,
Sāmūhika Sāmbattika Survey Prādhamika Report (Socio-Economic Report), 9.
According to the report only 2.1% have done professional courses. However, we find an
awakening at present as regards literacy.

[22] To the question «Why one does not participate?», in the BEC gatherings we gave
the possibility of three answers: (a) the person is out of station, (b) the person is not
interested in the new system and (c) the person does not get any religious experience.
Among the respondents, the coastal people are more reluctant to accept the new structure
than in the non-coastal places. See Table ns.: Ia-Q6, IIa-Q6 and IIIa-Q6. Since the new
structure demands active participation in the BEC gatherings, to become a member of the
parish pastoral council or diocesan pastoral council one has to be a regular member in the
BEC gatherings. The response is to be understood in the context of the ecclesial
administrative system explained in the previous chapter. See the interview with Bishop
M.S. PAKIAM by K.C. Francis, «Abhimugham» (Face to Face), 9-13. Neverthless, the
response of 25% persons that some do not attend because they do not get any special
experience by attending the BEC gatherings need special consideration by the BECs.

[23] To know the mind of the people about the new structure of the parish we formed
the question like this: «How do you react to the structural changes brought about in the
parish by the formation of BECs?» We gave three choices for answers: (a) the former
structure was better, (b) the present one is better, and (c) do not have a clear idea. Among
the respondents 9% prefer the old structure and 88% prefer the new structure. See the
CHART n. I and see the Table n.: Ia – Q19. When we analyze the attitude of coastal and
non-coastal people we see that 13% of the coastal people prefer the old structure while
their counterparts in non-coastal areas are only 4%. See Table ns.: IIa – Q19, IIIa – Q19.
To understand the implications of the attitude towards the new structure, see the
ecclesiastical administrative system described in the third chapter.

CHART I

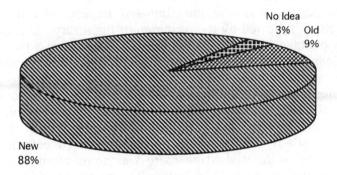

Structure Old or New?

Regarding the economic status of the participants we do not find much disparity between the rich and the poor though in the first years many rich people found it difficult to go to the house of a poor member. In the Diocese we see that almost 43% of the BECs are represented by the poor and in 57% BECs, the percentage of the rich and poor are more or less equal[24].

There are various reasons for a positive approach towards the BECs. Despite the structural aspect such as attendance, reporting and evaluation[25] and constant insistence from the Bishop, priests and

---

[24] From the economical point of view, most of the participating respondents are from the lower strata of the society. See Table ns.: Ia – Q5; IIa – Q5 and IIIa – Q5. Only 20% could be considered above average in the financial standard in the diocesan context.

[25] To know the structural aspect of the gatherings of the BECs we had the following questions and three choices were given as answers. 1. «Is there any particular mode of procedure in your BEC gatherings? (a) yes, (b) no, (c) do not know». 2. «Does anybody write the report of the gatherings and read in the following gathering.? (a) yes, (b) no, (c) do not know». 3. «Do you evaluate the activities of the BEC in your gatherings? (a) yes, (b) no (c) sometimes». According to the respondents 78% of the BEC gatherings have a particular mode of procedure. See Table ns.: Ia – Q10, IIa – Q10 and IIIa – Q10. In 97%

animators[26], the BECs help the participants to live the *Mystagogy*[27]. This Mystagogy is achieved through an organized network of the peoples' gathering in the unit, parish, Vicariate and diocesan levels. To illustrate how BEC functions in a concrete situation we give two instances - one from the coastal and another from the non-coastal.

In one of the BEC gatherings which the author attended[28], a young girl welcomed the participants (in most of the places the head of the family welcomes the participants). She, then, initiated the meeting with a hymn to the Holy Spirit followed by the recitation of the rosary. After praying the rosary a passage from the Gospel was read and after a pause, two more participants read the same passage. Then after a few moments of silence some began to repeat one or other striking verse from the Gospel passage thrice and slowly. It was a Gospel sharing. Afterwards ten women shared how God had inspired them through the Gospel. In the sharing, their life experience was reflected. Then they began to reflect over the responsibility that they had to undertake in the light of the Gospel message. In the discussion there was some clarity about the responsibilities that they were to undertake. The discussion led to decision

---

of the gatherings there is report writing and reading. See Table ns.: Ib – Q14, IIb – Q14 and IIIb – Q14. There is evaluation in 70% of the gatherings. See Ib – Q13, IIb – Q13 and IIIb – Q13.

[26] A few priests and lay people consider that BEC is imposed on them from *above*. A priest who held a very responsible office in the Diocese and had vast experience in the coastal and non coastal parishes said: «In the beginning 75% of the priests were suspicious about the possibility of the formation of BECs. The priests, according to him, did not understand at first, and the Bishop was stern. Then we accepted without understanding the vision of BECs. But now we understand the vision and we need it. The anxiety that people will question the priest is no more. Now importance is given to participation». Some priests see that BECs are the natural outcome of the «Living Together». For most of the lay people BECs are the realization of what they had looked out for with the Second Vatican Council.

[27] Mystagogy is a pedagogy, which leads newcomers into an experience of Christian mysteries, in particular, to the sacraments. In the context of Trivandrum the experience of mystery is manifested in the change of heart and acceptance of the Gospel message in the concrete life. For a treatment on Mystagogy see E. ANCILLI, ed., *Mistagogia e Direzione Spirituale*. The use of the word «Mystagogy» in the context of BECs see D. REGAN, *Experience the Mystery*. F.R. Salvador develops the reciprocal relationship between «mystagogic spirituality» and «pastoral spirituality» in his article «Espiritualidad Mistagogica y Pastoral», 375-393. The use of «Mystagogy» in liturgy is treated by A.M. TRIACCA – A. PISTOIA, eds., *Mystagogie*.

[28] The particular BEC consisted of twenty-five families. The house which hosted the gathering was a hut. So the people gathered in front of the house.

making. For executing the decision who?, when?, and how?, were clarified.

Their discussion first concerned how to extend the Bible to all the twenty-five families[29]. They inquired about the children who were not frequenting the Sunday catechism class in the parish. One of the animators of that BEC gave a report of the Seminar *cum* Convention of BECs held on the previous week at the Vicariate[30]. They had a discussion on issues concerning their lives too. Increase in the price of rice was the major concern of the people. The lack of electricity in ten houses and lack of toilet facilities in five houses were real problems. It was very evident that they were more conscious of the problems of the place. They decided to call the attention of the Trivandrum City Corporation authorities and the government officials. Since they were a minority group in a parish they entrusted the animators to discuss their problems in a general body of the BEC animators in the parish and to send a memorandum to the Government. The women were very keen to discuss the problem of alcoholism among their husbands. After the discussion there were intercessory prayers and a secret collection. It was followed by a concluding song[31].

The general pattern of the functioning of BECs in the non-coastal areas is also the same as that in the coastal areas. A particular BEC consists of thirty two families. At the gathering eighteen families were represented, of which five were male members. Two women religious were also present[32]. The meeting started at 7.15 pm. The people who came after

---

[29] Most of the BEC units in the Diocese take initiative to reach the Bible to every family.

[30] In the Seminar *cum* Convention more than 800 animators were present. The participants were divided into different groups and discussed on various questions concerning the functioning of BECs and the future scope of it in the Vicariate.

[31] The women took active part in the discussion. No male member made any comment during the discussion. After the meeting I inquired about the reason why men did not take part in the discussion. One male member said: «I do not like to discuss when women are present». Another said: «I have taken alcohol and I do not like to speak». A common phenomenon which we see in Kerala is that male members find it difficult to take part in discussions in the presence of more female members. Lack of animation from the consecrated ministers has been also noticed. It has been observed that in the coastal BEC gatherings the participation of priests or religious is less though they live very close to the people.

[32] I came to know that the women religious or a priest, if possible, participate in a BEC meeting, but the lay people themselves conduct it. The people are so happy to see that the women religious visit the house and participate in the BEC gathering. The house

their daily work gathered in a house which could barely accommodate the participants. In the house of this average family there was no electricity. The way the meeting was conducted was similar to that of the previous one. After the reflection there was a discussion. Since it was just before the beginning of the academic year, the main concern of the group was literacy and the distribution of books for the poor children in the unit. The women in the unit participated actively in the discussion. The meeting continued till 9 pm. There was also a registering of attendance, and reading of the report of the previous meeting[33].

The above mentioned concrete instances of the BECs, though not very ideal or lively, shed some light on an ordinary BEC meeting without much animation from a priest or religious.

2.2. *An Organized Network*

One of the remarkable characteristics of the functioning of BECs in Trivandrum is the organized network existing in the Diocese. Each BEC is linked with the parish, the Vicariate and the Diocese. To vitalize the network there are gatherings for parish level animators, Vicariate level animators, as well as those at the diocesan level. These animators gather once a fortnight or once a month not only to evaluate and plan out the programmes but also to live the Mystagogy[34]. It is because of this

---

of the religious and the place of the meeting were not very close as we said in the first case.

[33] In my conversation with the animator I came to know that, that particular unit has taken initiatives in constructing roads and educating the illiterate. Though the male members are normally less in the gatherings they come forward to execute the decisions taken in the BEC gatherings.

[34] In a parish level animators' gathering, which I attended, there were thirty-seven participants. The parish priest was not present, though the parochial house was hardly fifty feet away from the place of the meeting. There were 30% men and 70% women participants. Of the total participants 54% had a personal Bible with them. They conducted their regular animators meeting. There was the reading of the Bible, followed by reflection and personalization of the message of the Gospel in the living context. They evaluated the previous BEC convention held in their Vicariate. From the evaluation it was evident that they responded collectively to the different needs of the people. To the question what drew them to be associated with the BECs, one said that there was an impulse to live according to the Bible. A lady responded: «I got courage to beg pardon». A male participant shared his relation with the BECs like this: «My wife was the leader of *our* BEC for three years and I blamed her always. Now I am an active member of the BECs and I am happy about it». A young man said that he used to conduct the BEC meetings after his office work. The most surprising information was to know about the participation of Hindus in the BEC gatherings in that parish. I came to know that at least in seven units Hindus attended the BECs. One of the main reasons is the spiritual aspect

network that to communicate a message in any part of the Diocese it is enough that eleven co-ordinators of the Vicariates be informed. The impact of such a communication network is such that the Bishop's pastoral letters cannot go unnoticed. The same thing also happens in a parish, and the priests' sermons are not un-discussed. A priest views the present situation like this: «Now a priest cannot hide anything from the people. The people discuss various aspects of the ecclesial life such as the liturgical celebrations, priests' sermons in the Church, financial matters of the parish, Church feasts»[35].

2.3 New Orientation towards the Word of God

In most of the BECs the animators select a Bible passage according to the context of the place. Some BECs follow the passages suggested from the Diocese[36]. One of the remarkable achievements of BECs in the Diocese, even according to the critics of BECs, is the new awareness towards the Word of God[37]. The Bible Pratiṣṭha (exposition of the Bible) in a BEC meeting is a typical symbolism of the importance of the Word of God in the BECs. The Scripture is becoming the prayer book of the people. The people read, reflect upon and personalize the Scripture[38].

---

of the gatherings which is expressed in communion and service. In the non-coastal BECs the presence of people from other faiths is not a rare phenomenon.

[35] According to a priest it is through the BECs that the parish could celebrate a patron's feast without much expense. That particular parish had a tradition of spending even Rs. 72.000 for a Church feast.

[36] As regards the selection of the Bible passage in the gatherings 8% select the Bible passage of the Holy Mass of the following Sunday. 34% follow the Bible passage proposed by the diocesan office. Since the year 1994 was dedicated to the family, the readings proposed were related to the family life. And 58% take the Bible passage as animators plan out. See Table ns.: Ib – Q12, IIb – Q12 and IIIb – Q12.

[37] To the question «Do you think that your participation in the gatherings has helped to read and understand the Bible better?», 92% gave «yes» answer, only 7% gave «no» answer. See Table ns.: Ib – Q15, IIb – Q15, IIIb – Q15. In most of the families Scripture reading is becoming common along with the rosary prayers in the evening.

[38] When Bishop M.S. Pakiam, attended a BEC meeting in a rural village a lady was reading a passage from the Bible and she was giving exegesis. [Interview with the Bishop on 27-5-1994]. «Many "basic Christian communities" focus their gatherings upon the Bible and set themselves a threefold objective: to know the Bible, to create community and to serve the people. Here also exegetes can render useful assistance in avoiding actualizations of the biblical message that are not well grounded in the text. But there is reason to rejoice in seeing the Bible in the hands of people of lowly condition and of the poor; they can bring to its interpretation and to its actualization a light more penetrating, from the spiritual and existential point of view, than that which comes from a learning that relies upon its own resources alone (cf.Matt 11,25)» (PBC, The

This new awareness towards Scripture is seen among the old, the young and the children. It is manifested in the BEC meetings, planning sessions and in the families. It recalls the ancient tradition of *lectio divina* in the Christian tradition[39] and the *shravaṇa* (listening to the Word), *manana* (reflecting on it), *nididhyāsana* (the truth reflected upon is taken down from the mind to the heart in silence), tradition of ancient India[40].

2.4 New Approach to Liturgy

In the third chapter we saw that the people of Trivandrum have been giving great importance to the liturgical practices. Although the liturgy pertains to the whole body of the Church[41], in effect it has been centered on priests. The reforms of Vatican II, as far as the laity is concerned, have not been realized to the extent that they should have been[42]. With the formation of BECs, we witness a change in the liturgical life of the people. They participate in the liturgy expressing their faith and life. The Word of God, which is celebrated in each BEC gathering, leads the people to active participation in the liturgy which in turn leads them to a deeper understanding of the Church[43]. The new approach of the BECs towards the Word of God and the liturgical life is reflected in the growing consciousness of children[44]. We have noticed that the BECs are taking an active role in preparing the liturgy especially on Sundays.

Interpretation of the Bible, 125). Mr. Varghese, an active member of BECs at Parassala, claims that every family in his unit has a Bible. See G. VALIYAPADATH, «Ghaṭnayuṭe Azhicupanikku Śeṣam» (After the Structural Changes), 17.

[39] For a further study on the various aspects of the *lectio divina* in the pastoral context see B. SECONDIN, «Lectio Divina», 63-91.

[40] See V. MATAJI, «Towards an Indian Christian Spirituality», 93-125.

[41] See *SC* 26.

[42] See J.P. PINTO, *Inculturation*, 103-137.

[43] To the question: «Do you think that your participation in the BEC gatherings has helped you to understand the Church better?», 82% gave «yes» answer, 12% gave «no» answer and 6% have no idea about it. As regards the awareness towards the Bible and the Church we do not find much disparity in the thinking of the coastal and non-coastal people. It shows the more or less balanced growth of the BECs both in the coastal and in the non-coastal BECs. We also notice that even those who are not fully aware of the Church are inspired by the Word of God. See Tables ns.: I B-Q15.16.20. See also the CHART n. II.

[44] Once I visited a coastal village and some children came to me. Within a short time I could converse with them. In my conversation I just asked them whether they attended the Sunday Mass. All of them gave a positive response. I asked them what was the Gospel read in the Church that Sunday. All of them immediately recalled the particular

CHART II

Deepening of Faith
Bible — Church — Liturgy

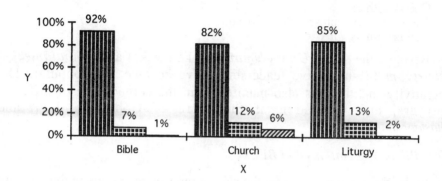

To revitalize the liturgy, the BECs, from time to time, compose hymns[45] in the vernacular which powerfully communicate the new vision of a Church. Through the hymns the people are reminded of God's presence in their daily life as He was present to the Patriarchs and the people of Israel. For instance, a hymn runs like this:
God is with us, Yahweh
God is with us
Immanuel, Immanuel
God is with us
God of our Fathers
God is with us
The God who appeared to Moses and the People
God is with us
The God who shattered the chain of slavery in Egypt
God is with us
The God who gave the promised land to His People

---

passage. This was because they had read the Gospel passage of the coming Sunday in their previous BECs gathering. Normally every BEC unit in diverse ways participates in the Sunday liturgy. Readings during the Mass, prayers of the faithful, community singing, participation in the presentation of gifts are some of the ways by which each BEC unit actively participates. In parishes like Parassala, Kannamthura, the BEC animators arrange special Bible classes for the children of different BEC units together.

[45] Vatican II speaks of the importance of sacred music in *SC* 112-121.

God is with us
The Word became flesh and dwelt among the people
God is with us
The God who sacrificed His life for us On the Cross
God is with us
The God who is present through the Sacraments as the salvific source
God is with us
The God who is present on the Altar
God is with us.

Besides, the songs *Uṇarū uṇarū* (awake awake) and *Pinbalamēkum Netṛtvam* (a supportive leadership) have become very popular. The creativity in liturgy is also manifested in the composition of different prayers, and veneration of the Word of God with *ārati* and *hastapranāmam*[46].

2.5 *Pious Associations and BECs*

In the third chapter we saw the role of pious associations in the Diocese before the «Living Together»[47]. Formerly the pious associations were doing some work for the whole parish. In most of the cases the parish activities were done through different associations. So to do some good work in the parish one had to join one of the associations. Now there is co-ordination of all the pious associations, for all of them come under the pastoral ministry. The peculiarity of the pious associations is that the members do not come from the same neighbourhood, but from the various areas of the parish. The integration of pious associations within the BECs also helps the growth of the functioning of BECs[48].

---

46 *Ārati* is the traditional rite of waving a lighted lamp before an image of a person worthy of honour. It is a form of praise and veneration. *Hastāpranāmam* is the touching of sacred objects and bringing the hands to the forehead.

47 To have a better understanding about a parish only with pious associations and a parish with pious associations and the BECs see F. LOBINGER, *Building Small Christian Communities*, 22-25

48 To the question «How is the relationship between the pious associations and BECs?» 84% of the BEC members say that pious associations promote BECs. 12% think that pious association cannot accept BEC programmes and only 4% think that BECs discourage pious associations. See Table ns.: Ic – Q27, IIc – Q27, IIIc – Q27. Once I visited a Legion of Mary Junior *Presidium* of boys. It consisted of 7 members. I asked their opinion about the relevance of pious association, for example Legion of Mary, in the emergence of BECs. According to them both are two sides of the same coin. The pious association gives more importance to prayer and personal life and the BECs help to go out of oneself to others. BECs have a social aspect. From the conversation with them I realized that they were also active members of the BECs. Some priests wanted to see

2.6 Oneness within the Community

In a coastal parish, according to a priest, the people were divided on the basis of various political parties. Each political party had its own followers. But now, through the BECs the people feel: «we are one». The same priest told me that formerly there were many organizations which would not co-operate with the Church. Now the secular organizations like Trivandrum District Fishermen Federation, PCO, and even Panchayath — the smallest governmental administrative cell — co-operate with the Church. Formerly the Panchayath, for example, wanted to do some programmes for the sake of doing without people's participation. Now the people know that the Panchayath has to work for the people. And the officials also approach the priests with confidence that the programmes will be executed, for there is much participation in the decision making process too.

The oneness within the BEC is well expressed in one's relationship to the other. Formerly, people used to invite one's relatives and friends to the house when there were celebrations connected with baptism, birthday and marriage. There was not so much place for the neighbours unless they were friends and relatives. Now the first persons to be informed and invited are the BEC members[49]. According to Prof. Kitty Lopez, former Principal of Government Women's College, Trivandrum, there is a family spirit in her BEC unit. She says:

> Formerly when we see our neighbours in the Church we used to finish our relationship with a smile. Now there is a family spirit. We know more or less the background of every family in our unit. Now we know how many children are in a family and what they are studying, what is their financial situation and even their family problems. Earlier some rich people were reluctant to participate in the BEC meeting when it was held in a poor house. Now the attitude is changed[50].

BECs only as pious associations or *prārthanayōgaṅgal* (prayer meetings). However, a good number of priests consider that there is no relevance of pious associations. In the Diocese most of the leaders of the pious associations have become the animators of the BECs. Among the respondents 36% are associated with pious association. See Table ns.: Ic – Q26, IIc – Q26 and IIIc – Q26.

[49] See G. VALIYAPADATH, «Ghaṭanayuṭe Azhicupanikku Śeṣam», 16. In a certain BEC when a person is getting married the previous day all the members of the BEC unit go to the house and pray and present a Bible to the bride or bridegroom. According to an animator of *Vanitāvēdi* (Women's forum), *BEC is a family.*

[50] G. VALIYAPADATH, «Ghaṭanayuṭe Azhicupanikku Śeṣam», 16 [Translation mine].

This same fellowship is seen in a good number of BECs. To the question «what effect do the BEC gatherings have on the neighbourhood relationships?» 80% of the respondents believe that BECs have strengthened the neighbourhood relations[51].

2.7 *BECs and Inculturation*

In most of the BEC units, the gatherings begin with the lighting of the *Nilavilakku* (oil lamp) in a traditional Indian way. Usually the head of the family does it. We also find a creative initiative in a non-coastal BEC gathering where a non-Catholic or a non-Christian does this lighting of the lamp. In many places both in the coastal and non-coastal BECs we find *pushpārati* (waving of flowers) before the Bible to show honour and respect[52]. An experienced catechist spoke about the *Attapūvu* competition conducted in connection with the *ōnam*, the State feast of the Keralites, in a non-coastal BEC units in his parish[53]. As the non-coastal Catholics live among the Hindus the *Attapūvu* competition gave an occasion for the Hindus to come closer to the Christians. In the same parish the BECs could arrange *ōnasadyā* (meals on the *ōnam* day) with the participation of Hindus. It created an atmosphere of communion of brothers and sisters of different faiths[54]. Since the Diocese of Trivandrum has a pluriform culture within the Indian culture a cultural integration is also taking place

---

[51] Only 6% think that BECs were detrimental to the neighbourhood relations. See Table ns.: Ib – Q17, IIb – Q17, IIIb – Q17.

[52] As we have said earlier, the participation of people from other religions is not rare in non-coastal BECs. From the field study it became clear that in the coastal BECs also people from other religion participate. One of the reasons could be that they live as neighbours. This is a good initiative especially when people from other religions or denominations participate in the BECs. The lighting of the oil lamp or waving of flowers in itself is not something new. It started with the liturgical renewal movement in India.

[53] *Attapūvu* is a decoration with flowers before the house in preparation of *ōnam*, the State festival of the Keralites. Usually the women decorate the *Attapūvu* in an artistic way. Though *ōnam* is the State feast, it is considered to be a feast of the Hindus. Normally the Christians in the coastal areas are not used to celebrating the feast even at home. The new converts, especially the Nadars, the Ezhavas and the Dalits, used to celebrate *ōnam* at home but not in public. Actually it is a harvest feast having a symbolic meaning of equality and fraternity.

[54] Inculturation in itself is not a new thing in the Diocese. But BECs help its members to reciprocally integrate aspects of the Christian faith with the particular culture. The BECs in Trivandrum generally accept the cultural integration. To the question «How do you react to the statement: The Church has to respect and adapt herself to the cultural traditions of our country?». 87% agree to the statement while 8% do not agree and 5% have no opinion at all. See Table ns. Id – Q39, IId – Q39, IIId – Q39.

through the interaction of the BEC co-ordinators and animators. Such interaction, first of all, helps to respect other's culture and tradition. Pope John Paul II rightly said:

> Through inculturation the Church makes the Gospel incarnate in different cultures and at the same time introduces peoples, together with their cultures, into her own community. She transmits to them her own values, at the same time taking the good elements that already exist in them and renewing them from within. Through inculturation the Church, for her part, becomes a more intelligible sign of what she is, and a more effective instrument of mission[55].

2.8 BECs as Evangelizers

One of the fundamental activities of the Church is to proclaim the Gospel of the Lord Jesus to the world. This is the permanent mission of the Church[56]. This is effectively carried out in small groups. In the context of Trivandrum, at least in 32% of BECs, the presence of brothers and sisters from other faiths is a sign that the BECs work as evangelizers[57] and 60% of the BECs keep up the missionary thrust[58]. Out of the participants from other faiths, 53% are really interested in to joining in the fellowship of the BECs, though 28% participate because they are invited by their friends or neighbours[59]. Among the participants from other faiths 57% participate in the BECs with a good intention of knowing more about Jesus Christ[60].

To illustrate how BECs act as evangelizers, a narration of a few instances will not be out of place. In a small mission station in the

---

[55] JOHN PAUL II, *Redemptoris Missio*, n. 52.

[56] See *AG* 10. See also JOHN PAUL II, *Redemptoris Missio*, n 31; ID., *Christifideles Laici*, n. 35. For further study on the nature and characteristics of evangelization and the dimensions of missionary spirituality see J.E. BIFET, *Spirituality for a Missionary Church*, 11-88.

[57] To the question: «Do the non-Catholic or non-Christians participate in your BEC gatherings?», 32% gave «yes» answer, 67% gave «no» answer and only 1% has no idea about it.

[58] See Table ns.: 1 a – Q7, II a – Q7, III a – Q7. See Table ns.: I c – Q23, II c – Q23, III c – Q23.

[59] According to the opinion of the members of the BECs, 28% of the people from other faiths participate because they are invited while 53% are interested to participate. See Table ns.: I c – Q22, II c – Q22, III c – Q22.

[60] To the question: «Why do the non-Catholics and non-Christians, if any, participate in your gatherings?», 57% say that they come to know more about Christ, 23% say that they come to participate in prayer and 20% say that they come as on-lookers. See Table ns.: I c – Q21, II c – Q21, III c – Q21.

Palayam Vicariate the author went to celebrate Sunday Mass in 1994. There were more than a hundred people present for the Mass. To an inquiry about the functioning of BECs in that parish almost all of them said that after the formation of BECs there has been a growing participation in the Holy Mass and new comers also began to appear in the Church. Some have even publicly confessed that BEC gatherings have been instrumental for them to know Jesus Christ and the Church.

On another occasion a priest told me that the BECs have been instrumental in the conversion of more than twenty-five families. Here the veracity of the cases was personally verified by the author himself. Though there were other influential factors, BECs played an important role in attracting them to the Church. A government employee confessed that it was through BECs that his family received baptism[61].

3. Lay Protagonists in the BECs

In the last chapter we have sufficiently treated the nature of leadership that existed in the Diocese of Trivandrum and in the Church in Kerala. We have also seen that a shift has been taking place in the Diocese with the «Living Together» in sharing the responsibilities with the lay people in a meaningful way. The Bishop's exhortation to the laity on 13-2-1992 reminded them of the early Christian community which took part in everything concerning human life. This had a positive response when BECs became the pastoral option of the Diocese.

---

[61] Some animators of the BECs exaggerate by saying that many non-Catholics have joined the Church. But we cannot deny the fact that BEC deepens the faith of the newcomers. In certain cases we find different denominations in the same family. In such cases BEC gatherings clarify various misunderstandings. «[...] Christians cannot underestimate the burden of *long-standing misgivings* inherited from the past, and of mutual *misunderstandings* and *prejudices*» (JOHN PAUL II, *Ut Unum Sint*, n. 2).

CHART III

Better Lay Participation

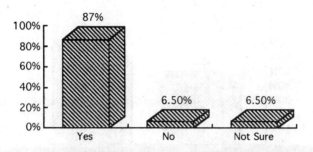

At the very first glance we can see how the lay people have become the protagonists of the BECs[62] and have begun to exercise their priestly, prophetic and kingly roles[63].In an interview, one of the co-ordinators of BECs in a non-coastal parish said: «Formerly, problems were solved by the parish priests and now people accept the leadership of the BEC animators». The very fact that lay people, either the father or the mother of the house where the meeting is held or an animator, presides over the BEC gatherings sheds light on the great change in the nature of leadership[64]. However, a vast majority of BECs prefer the presence of priest or religious in the BEC gatherings[65].

---

[62] See CHART III. See also Table ns.: Ib – Q 18, IIb – Q 18, III b – Q 18. BECs, being the the pastoral programme of the diocese, old people have not stopped coming to the various activities of the Church and new people have a chance to come forward. Formerly priest and *kaikāran* (treasurer) were the important people. In the present system there are at least seven animators involved in different ministries.

[63] See *LG* 31. See also *CCC*, ns. 897-913. For an elaborate theological reflection on the three roles of the lay people, see Y. CONGAR, *Lay People in the Church*, 121-323. See also A.L. PICARDAL, *An Ecclesiological Perspectiv*, 96-258.

[64] From the response to the question «who presides over the BEC gatherings?» we came to know that 70% of the gatherings are presided over by the BEC animators, 27% by the heads of the family hosting the gathering and only 3% by a priest or religious. See Ia – Q8, IIa – Q8, IIIa – Q8. In a good number of the BECs the lighting of the lamp, a traditional Indian custom is done by the father or the mother of the house.

[65] Regarding the presence of priest or religious 39% hold the view that it is necessary and 61% hold the view that the presence of priest is good. The question had a third possible answer «not required» which not even one respondent chose to indicate as his or her position. See Table ns.: Ia – Q9, IIa – Q9, IIIa – Q9. See CHART IV. As regards the preference of priests, a professor told me this: «The Indian tradition has high regard for

CHART IV

Impression about the Presence of Priests and Religious in
the BEC Gatherings

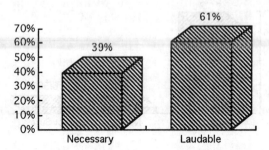

Despite the preference for priests or religious by the lay people in the BECs, most of the respondents agree that BECs paved a way to find new lay leaders[66]. The BECs gave occasion to the laity to exercise their charism for the benefit of the whole community[67] both from an ecclesial

---

the priest. And we consider that his presence is a blessing». He added, «But we expect that the priests respect the role of the laity in the Church». Another person who is very much involved in the BEC programme says: «No one can substitute for the sacramental power of a priest. But the priests must also respect the knowledge of laity in the secular matters». It is very striking to note that among the twenty two irregular respondents, fourteen — seven from the coastal and seven from the non-coastal areas — responded that the priest's presence is necessary. In comparison with the regular participants the irregular participants insist on the presence of priests! In my interview with priests and lay people I came to know that at least in some BECs there is better participation of male members if priests participate.

[66] To the question «Do you think that BECs in your parish have been helpful in finding new leaders and in imparting Christian formation?» 77% gave a positive response. See Table ns. Ic – Q30, IIc – Q30, IIc – Q30. Although most of the respondents agree that a leadership has grown among the lay people no one believes that BECs helped the formation of political leaders. However, 55%, most of whom are poor, answered that it is good to discuss the contemporary politics in the BEC gatherings. See Id – Q37, IId – Q37, IIId – Q37. The poor are the most affected by the contemporary political system. So it is quite natural that the poor seek political leadership from the Church.

[67] For a detailed study on the charism and manifestation of Spirit see J. VADAKKEDOM, «Pros to sympheron». See also A. BITTLINGER, Gifts and Graces; R. VIDALES, «Charisms and Political Action», 68-77; E.J. MALATESTA, «Charism», 140-143; B. SECONDIN, Segni di Profezia, 249-271; M. DE C. AZEVEDO, The Consecrated Life, 100-101; L. BOFF, Church: Charism & Power, 154-164.

and a civil point of view. Since there are animators for pastoral ministry, education ministry and social service ministry a participatory leadership is ensured in every BEC. And it is beyond doubt that the BECs are becoming the nursery of future religious and political leaders[68].

Among the lay animators the role of women, and the youth need a special explanation in the present context of BECs.

3.1 The Women Animators: Vital Force of BECs

A priest in the Diocese of Trivandrum, knowing that I was doing a field study on the BECs in Trivandrum, had only one point to comment about the functioning of BECs in his parish: «The women dominate in the BECs!» A reputed *Prisenti* (president of a confraternity) in a parish told me that BECs are good and there is better participation in the liturgy but women should not be in the parish council!

As we have noticed there is a general tendency to lament that BECs are becoming *Vanita Samājam* (women's forum)[69]. From the survey it is clear that in most of the BECs women participate more actively in the BECs than men do. The women, on their part, are happy that they can actively take part in the BECs[70].

The presence of women in the BECs and especially their leadership role might be seen in the context of the «Living Together» and the various study reports. In the early literature regarding the renewal, the women's role was not in the main agenda, though the role of the laity has been sufficiently treated. The Kerala society, despite its literacy rate and social development, stands behind in sharing of power or in the decision making process of the society. According to George Mathew, Director of

---

[68] See B. SECONDIN, *Segni di Profezia*, 287-291. See also C. DUQUOC, «Charism as the Social Expression», 87-96.

[69] The Bishop sees the better participation of women in the BECs as a positive sign, for, the growth of Christian life depends to a large extent on the women.

[70] During my field study I asked a young lady, a post graduate degree holder from the University of Kerala, in what way BEC helped her. She replied: «Before being involved in the BECs I was not able to look at a man or a priest to say what I wanted. Now I have no fear to speak before anybody». I got similar replies from most of the women whom I interviewed. Even though a few women also complained that male participation is less, the women were happy that they could actively cooperate in the renewal process of the local Church. A woman expressed her impression about the role of women like this: «The women who were *inside* the house came out. Today even if the women religious do not come, the BEC functions».

the New Delhi Institute of Science, religious organizations had an important role in keeping the women away from the power structure[71].

In Trivandrum already in the 19th century Protestant missionaries had shown special interest to educate girls in spite of the cultural prejudices against women[72]. The Latin Catholic women, with an exception of a few like Annie Mascren, who represented the first Parliamentary Constituency of Trivandrum, could not come to the forefront of the society. The main reason was that the women were not given an opportunity. In the BECs the women get an opportunity to be sensitive to the Christian life in a holistic way[73]. There are provision in parish pastoral council by-laws to ensure the participation of women in the life of the local Church of Trivandrum. Even without this provision in the by-laws, women are entering more into the diocesan bodies since active participation in the BECs is a condition for anyone to hold a *office* on the parish, Vicariate and diocesan level.

----

71 Though G. Mathew's argument is in the context of politics, his article in the *Malayala Manorama,* a daily in Kerala, sheds light on the situation of women in Kerala. As he remarks, never in the history of Kerala more than ten women Legislative Members have been in the Kerala Legislative Assembly. Most of the women in Kerala have to be satisfied with office works and the teaching profession. See G. MATHEW, «*Samvaraṇattil Otuṅgunna Vanita Rāṣṭrîyam*» (Women Politics Constrained to Reservations), 6. The same idea had been expressed by a KCYM member of Chullimanoor in 1991. See S. VARGHESE, «*Strîku Niṣedhikkapedunna Svargam*» (The Heaven that is denied to Women) [No page numbering].

72 See M. MAULT, *The Girl's School*, CWMA. At present in the Church of South India (CSI), Trivandrum, there are ordained women in active parish services. According to Bishop Samuel Amirtham, although in the beginning of the ordination of women there were criticisms in the CSI Church, the people accept the service of ordained women in the Church. Most of the missionaries, especially Protestants, held the view that by educating a girl they were saving a family.

73 N. Nayak compares the attitude of women and men at the level of local organizations: «The common feature is that responsibility and opportunity bring out the best in people, and people who have not benefited by any "official" education, have a tremendous capacity for reason, logic and common sense. To move to a level of conceptualization is a slower process but is a possibility. It was my experience that women interacted much more between themselves not shying away from "sensitive" issues that needed to be thrashed out between themselves. Men on the contrary prefer to interact with the functionary of the organization and even if they interact among themselves, it will be mainly on issues more distant from themselves. Men easily avoid "sensitive" issues and in a way one always has to be able to know what is behind "his mind when he speaks". Men seem to take off at a less "enthusiastic rate" than women do. Once women have seen a point, understood it, then there seems no way to keep them from going ahead. They do not seem to see unnecessary barriers that keep them back [...]» (N. NAYAK, *Struggle within the Struggle*, 55).

The present day response of women in the BECs of Trivandrum is be understood also in the context of Pope John Paul II's letter, «Women: Teachers of Peace» in which he emphasizes the significant contribution that women can make towards achieving peace which affects every aspect of human existence. The Pope, invites the women:

> to become teachers of peace with their whole being and in all their actions. May they be witnesses, messengers and teachers of peace in relations between individuals and between generations, in the family, in the cultural, social and political life of nations, and particularly in situations of war[74].

3.2 The Youth: A Dynamic Force in the BECs

In the previous chapter we saw that prior to the «Living Together» the youth movement was active in three Vicariates. The youth became very active with the renewal process of the Diocese[75]. It is laudable that in most of the BECs the youth plays a significant role. In the diocesan campaign against the illicit brewing of alcohol, which created a great impact in Kerala, it was the youth who responded creatively to the Lenten message of the Bishop[76]. In an interview, the Bishop himself confirmed the role of the youth[77]. The youth's ecological concern is also having much effect at the grassroots level[78].

4. Changing Role of the Consecrated Ministers

From the time of «Living Together» we could see a change in the traditional role of priests and religious. The change took on a new dimension when BECs became a pastoral option.

---

[74] JOHN PAUL II, Women: Teachers of Peace, n. 2. See also JOHN PAUL II, Mulieris Dignitatem, n. 30.

[75] In the renewal process the youth movement has adopted a policy of Prārthnan, Paṭhanam, Pravartanam (Prayer, Study and Action).

[76] See M.S. PAKIAM, «Metrānte Kattu», 1-6. To the question about the attitude of the youth towards the BEC programmes 83% have the opinion that the attitude is encouraging but 10% think that the attitude of the youth is discouraging. See Table ns.: Ic – Q28, IIc – Q 28, IIIc – Q28.

[77] «Many youngsters were inspired by the article and took up the fight against illicit brewing» (V. ABRAHAM, «Between brew and blue water», 24).

[78] See E. WILFRED, Kerala Catholic Youth Movement, ADT.

4.1 *Role of the Bishop*

The leadership of the Church is the most decisive factor in the life of the Catholics of Trivandrum. In the previous chapter we saw how the Bishops' decisions have inspired the renewal of the Diocese. In the particular social context of Trivandrum, the Bishop of Trivandrum has a prophetic role. The prophetic role is based on two factors: firstly as the successor of the Apostles and head of the local Church, and secondly as the leader of a backward class, the Latin Catholics of Trivandrum. Bishop M.S. Pakiam's constant effort to combine both these roles is very evident in his talks, pastoral letters and interviews[79]. In combining both roles the Bishop has a message for the people and priests. According to him, the people should not remain a mere *recipient of projects,* but they have to take part in everything concerning human life. He has a specific message to the priests too:

> Priests should not be merely satisfied with the celebration of the Sacraments. They have to enter into the lives of the people. As Jesus stood for changes against the evil structures of the society, the priests have a duty to work for the continuation of the changes. The priests should take initiatives to form loving communities. The priests should become the *offered* as they are the offerers[80].

In a prophetic voice the Bishop can question the policies which are a threat to the human life. His pastoral letters concerning literacy[81], illicit

---

[79] The Bishop's pastoral experience as a diocesan priest in the Diocese helped him to mold his theological thinking and pastoral vision. As a bishop he can speak from his experience. He speaks about his early priestly life like this: «In the early years of my priesthood, my own poverty made me to understand the poverty of the people. During the rain I had to wake up since the roof of the parochial house was leaking. Because of the lack of money I had to starve.[...] The parishioners who knew me well brought food. These experiences helped me to have more contact with the poor» (K.C. FRANCIS, «Abhimugham» , 51 [Translation mine].

[80] K.C. FRANCIS, «Abhimugham», 51 [Translation mine].

[81] Regarding literacy the Bishop wrote two pastoral letters. The first one was in 1990. In it he fully co-operated with the programmes of the State Government in its effort to eradicate illiteracy. He gave the statistics of the illiteracy rate of some of the parishes of the Diocese. See M.S. PAKIAM, «*Metṟānte Kattu* (Bishop's Letter), ADT. In the second pastoral letter on literacy, the Bishop became a critic of the activities of the Government. He says that the literacy programmes carried out in the coastal villages were only *prahasanam* (a mere show). So he called the government and other religious and secular organizations to work sincerely to eradicate the illiteracy. See M.S. PAKIAM, *Sākṣarata Raṇḍām Ghaṭṭam* (Literacy: Second Stage), ADT.

distillation[82], family year, 1995 as non-corruption year are some among them. The effects of the prophetic messages of the Bishop have had their own results.

DR. A. Susaipakiam's [M. Soosa Pakiam] mission of stopping illicit arrack brewing at Pozhiyoor seemed Utopian to most people initially. They wondered how the Latin Catholic bishop of Trivandrum, could achieve what others had tried and failed. None believed that liquor dons would let go of a copious sources of cheap and high-quality arrack. But for the bishop Pozhiyoor was a test case and only the first target in the fight cleansing his diocese of the curse of illicit liquor[83].

Since the pastoral letters were discussed in the BECs it was easy to execute the decisions which the people themselves take. The women, who were the victims of men's alcoholism, became very active in the BECs. The Bishop also participated in many BECs. He knew well how BECs functioned in the city, coastal and non-coastal villages. According to him, the people in the city come prepared to participate in the BECs. A good number of people placed in high positions in the society came down and made much effort to help the poor[84]. In the coastal BEC gatherings, the people do not like discussions. Lack of interest among the priests on the one hand and lack of time for the priests on the other hand affect the functioning of BECs[85]. There is much opportunity for manipulation. People are not fully aware of the renewal process. The absence of male members also affects the BECs in the coastal areas. A better performance is seen in the non-coastal BECs[86].

The Bishop, though a great proponent of BECs in Kerala and in India, far from exaggerating the role of BECs, holds the view that BEC is a

---

[82] See M.S. PAKIAM, «Metṟānte Kattu», 1-6.

[83] Pozhiyoor is a Catholic village consisting of two parish churches with more than 9.000 inhabitants. Until 1992 July 31 more than 95% of the families were involved in the illicit production of alcohol. See V. ABRAHAM, «Between Brew and Blue Water», 24-26. The word «arrack» means country alcohol.

[84] A medical doctor in a city BEC makes himself available for the people of his unit once a week. An engineer, in a city unit, has decided to give technical knowledge freely to his BEC unit. These informations are based on the report read at the BEC convention of Palayam Vicariate on 22-5-1994. The importance of such service is to be understood in the context of the professionals in Kerala who equate time with money.

[85] Compared to the non-coastal areas people in the coastal areas give much importance to religious services. Most of the priests in the coastal areas are busy with religious services and lack of time to animate the BECs. The multiplication of the pious associations and the celebration of different feasts make the priest very busy.

[86] Interview with the Bishop M.S. Pakiam on 27-5-1994.

means to arrive at the Kingdom of God and not an end in itself. But his determination to liberate the people from the backwardness of the society is evident when he says: «When we are convinced of certain things we have to execute it. When we find mistakes we have to correct it. And we have the good will to correct it. As a matter of fact we could integrate lots of things together»[87]. His uncompromising attitude against the *false peace* provokes enough criticism. But in effect his pastoral letters have become a point of reference to the Church in Kerala[88].

4.2 *Role of Priests*

The priests through their ministerial priesthood are called to serve the people of God[89]. In India, particularly in Kerala, because of institutionalization of the Church there exists a gap between priests and the people. In the Diocese, the priests play a prophetic role in visualizing a participatory Church at the grassroots level. In the initial stages of the formation of BECs it was priests who, through sermons, catechesis and seminars, conveyed the new vision of a participatory Church.

The BECs give also an opportunity to understand the problems of the society in a concrete level. The priests in the BEC gatherings become more listeners than speakers. The BECs also help to build up the gap between the clergy and the lay people in Kerala. There is a new approach in the priest — lay relationship. The changes in the attitude can be described like this: formerly priests invited the people to the Church and now people gather and invite the priest to the BEC gatherings.

In unwieldy parishes the BECs are a blessing to the priest, providing better contact with the people. Some priests feel that they lose contact with the people, for their contact is limited to the leaders only. For some others, who had been conducting prayer meetings in the non-coastal parishes, BEC is not a new vision but a new awareness. A few priests

---

[87] Interview with the Bishop M.S. Pakiam on 27-5-1994. One of the major criticisms about the BECs is that it was hastily implemented. To a large extend it was inevitable. For example, regarding the *Vanitā vedi* (women's forum), a woman animator said: «The original aim was conscientization through awareness class. But they had to incorporate issue based programmes such as rape, illicit distillation, homicide».

[88] To give an example, the Bishop's pastoral letter on 3rd January 1995 declaring «1995 as non-corruption year» was re-printed in a popular Catholic weekly of the Syro-Malabar Church *Sathyadeepam* on 26th January 1995. The response of the people from different parts of Kerala is reported in the subsequent issues of *Sathyadeepam,* 8 February, 1995, 3; 1 March, 1995, 1; 22 March, 1995, 3.

[89] See *LG* 24. See also *CCC*, ns. 1551-1553.

think that the lay people consider BEC as a ladder to obtain powers in the parish and diocesan councils. Such priests consider that with the introduction of BECs the priests' power is limited. Nevertheless, every priest acknowledges about the new awareness of the lay people towards the Church and its pastoral activities.

4.3 *Role of Women Religious*

The women religious in India have a great reputation of conducting schools, colleges and hospitals. In Trivandrum, despite the illiteracy and educational backwardness of the Latin Catholics, the schools run by the women religious keep up a high standard competing with any other school in the State. In the parishes, generally, the women religious do a silent service. Nevertheless, there is a general complaint, which the religious themselves admit; they have failed to identify with the people[90].

In Trivandrum some women religious began to identify with the people during the fishermen agitation but lacked a holistic vision of the local Church. Assuming responsibilities to build up Christian communities by the religious is a new phenomenon. It demands prophetic courage to understand the dynamism of their own charism. In a letter dated 2-9-1992 the Bishop invited «sisters with the aptitude of openness, creativity, organizing capacity, ready to put up with hardships, ability to respect popular expressions of faith»[91]to participate in the renewal programme. Some religious congregations have volunteered to take up a new venture of community building in the Diocese. As a matter of fact, in all the Vicariates the animators are the women religious.

The women religious prove that they are competent to deal with pastoral problems and can enter into the lives of the people[92]. Since most of the participants in the BECs are women, the role of women religious

---

[90] «In Indian situation where poverty, misery and oppression are rampant on one side and an inner thirst for *mukthi* or moksha or God - realization persists on the whole, the religious women can give a poignant witness to the masses by their very life» (T. JACOB – PRIMA – R. MONTEIRO – VANDANA, «The Role of Women», 226). Even those congregations that have originated in Kerala have taken more inspiration for their spirituality from the West than from the local culture.

[91] M.S. PAKIAM, *Invitation for full-time Religious Personnel*, ADT.

[92] In some Vicariates it was not easy for women religious to animate the BECs, especially where the priests were not co-operating. But for the religious, the animation of BECs was the exercising of the prophetic role which they derive from the sacrament of baptism and their special consecration. The Synod on the «Consecrated Life» in 1995 also emphasized the prophetic role of religious. See B. SECONDIN, *Per una fedeltà creativa*, 133-134. 349-373. See also B. SECONDIN, «La vita consacrata»,7-17.

has more significance. Realizing the problems that women face in the society, the women religious can fight for the rights of their less privileged sisters. Their active participation in hunger strikes, picketing and demonstrations on various issues of the people are true expressions of their solidarity with the poor and the under privileged. In light of the Gospel and of the teachings of the Church, the women religious understand that their charism is not stagnant, unproductive and unrelated to the people, but it is dynamic, creative and related to the people[93]. Thus, the women religious find more meaning in their consecration[94].

The priests and religious, in so far as they are the leaders of the poor class, the prophetic role demands that they have to be the voice of the voiceless. In being so they cannot forget that all are called to holiness[95]. The priests and religious have to see the link between evangelization and the human advancement — development and liberation[96].

Although the formation of BECs is the Diocesan pastoral option, all the priests and religious have not yet accepted the vision of BECs. However, a good number of priests and religious have realized that they have a special role as *servants* to the People of God[97].

---

[93] «We may have the best theology of Consecrated Life, but it will remain sterile unless this witness is actually borne by our existing institutes and communities of Consecrated Life — unless they are, and are seen to be, *witnesses of the City of God* among men and women» (H. ALPHONSO, *Priestly Vocation*, 80).

[94] To a general question «What would be your reaction if the BEC programmes fail in the diocese,?» 50% of the women religious remarked: «it is our failure». According to the other 50% it is the fault of the animators. The reaction of the religious women shows their growing identification with the local Church.

[95] See *LG* 39. According to Cardinal C.M. Martini, the important thing is to know that no one is in the first row. «Il vero dato è la vocazione di tutti alla santità, come già ricordava il Messaggio conclusivo del sinodo al n. 5. È indispensabile la prima linea, quella linea della santità che è per tutti, è uguale per tutti, è richiesta a tutti. La questione fondamentale non sta nel dire chi è prima, chi è dopo, chi è meglio, chi è più attuale, ma nel dire: tutti» (C.M. MARTINI, «A chi il domani?»,1-3).

[96] See PAUL VI, *Evangelii Nuntiandi*, n. 31. According to Pope Paul VI it is impossible to accept that in evangelization one could or should ignore the importance of the problems so much discussed today, concerning justice, liberation, development and peace in the world. This would be to forget the lesson which comes to us from the Gospel concerning the love of our neighbour who is suffering and in need. See PAUL VI, *Address for the opening of the Third General Assembly*, 562.

[97] It is through the coordinated ministry, that the priests and religious do a meaningful *diakonia* for the people of God. On the part of the religious, in light of the Synod on the Consecrated Life, such a co-ordinated ministry could be called *prophetic diakonia*. For the various aspects of the prophetic role of religious see B. SECONDIN, *Per una fedeltà creativa*, 349-373.

5. BECs in Their Social Commitment

With the emergence of BECs a new vision has evolved in the Christian charity. Formerly people helped each other *without* social awareness.

CHART V

Importance given in the BEC gatherings

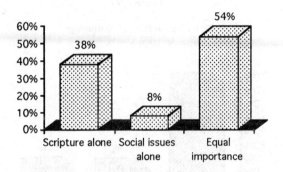

Now people help each other *with* social awareness. Concern for the neighbour has increased. It is true that the Church, as we have seen in the previous chapter, had been doing a lot of charitable works for the people. Now there is a difference in the approach. The Word of God is read in the BECs and the people experience the liberating hands of God in it. «I am Yahweh your God who brought you out of Egypt, where you lived as slaves» (Ex 20,2). Through the Word of God the people realize not only their own sufferings but also realize the causes of their suffering. They receive strength from the Word of God to solve the human-made sufferings. In 54% of the BECs the people give equal importance to both the Scripture and to the social problems[98].The problems of poverty, alcoholism, unemployment, illiteracy, dowry system are some of the important subjects which come under the discussion in the BECs.

To have a deeper insight into the approach of BECs towards the social problems we have formulated three objective questions followed by three possible answers and two direct questions in our questionnaire:

---

[98] See CHART V. See also Table n. Ib – Q11, IIb – Q11, IIIb – Q11.

1. Discussion of the social problems like poverty, alcoholism, unemployment, illiteracy, dowry, evils of caste system, etc., in your gatherings: (a) promotes the growth of the community, (b) leads to conflicts, (c) distracts prayer. 75% hold the view that the discussion promotes the growth of the community, 12% opine that the discussion leads to conflicts and 13% think that the discussion distracts the prayer life[99].

CHART VI

Discussion in the BEC Gatherings

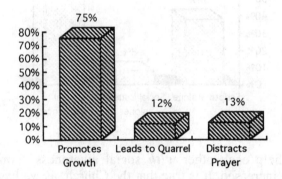

2. Has your BEC ever discussed any of the above mentioned social problems in the BEC gatherings?: (a) yes, (b) no, (c) do not know. 83% of the respondents said that they discussed various issues in the BEC gatherings. But 12% did not have any discussion and 5% have no idea about it[100].
3. If the answer is «yes» could you mention anyone of the problems discussed?.
4. If you had discussion in your gatherings what was the solution of the BEC to that particular problem?

---

99 See Table ns.: Id – Q32, IId – Q32, IIId – Q32. See also CHART n. VI. 25% are distracted or are lead to quarrel or at least they feel so. It is true that in some places proper animation is lacking.

100 See Table ns.: Id – Q33, IId – Q33, IIId – Q33.

5. Was your solution a success or a failure?: (a) successful, (b) partly successful, (c) failure. According to 36%, they could solve the problems successfully, for 48% it was partly successful and for 16% it was a failure[101].

The important aspect of the discussions in the BECs is that it leads the members to make decisions. The decision, thus taken after discussion, will not remain mere in paper and ink but will be executed, despite the possibility of failures in the process of its execution.

5.1 *BECs in Their Fight against the Evils of the Society*

The response to the objective and direct questions sheds light on the concern of the BECs about the social realities. The most discussed social problem, according to the survey and interview, is alcoholism. It is evident that since many families, especially the women, are the victims of alcoholism; both the coastal and non-coastal BECs have given much importance to this issue. Together with the youth wing of the BECs, the TSSS also played a significant role[102]. This was a *test case* also for the BECs in its social commitment.

Though the problems connected with alcohol cannot be fully solved without a serious effort from the State Government, many families and parishes were liberated from alcoholism[103]. The fight against the evils of the society ushered in new ecumenism and dialogue. Since most of the problems are related to the society, irrespective of caste and religions, the initiative of the Diocese brought secular and religious organizations closer[104].

---

[101] See Table ns.: Id – Q36, IId – Q36, IIId – Q36.

[102] See V. RESALAYYAN, *Anti Alcoholism Movement*, PPn. The report, explains the involvement of priests, women religious, people from other denominations and secular organizations in the fight against alcohol in the Vicariate of Undencode.

[103] Some of the popular News Papers and weeklies have given much coverage to the fight against the alcohol. See M. MADHU, «Madya Vimuktamakunna Kaṭaloraṅgal», (Coastal Villages in its path of redemption from Alcohol), 4-5. 18-19. See also *Kerala Kaumidi,* 13 November, 1993, 3; *Mangalam,* 4 November 1993, 3; *Kerala Kaumidi,* 29 October 1993, 3. R. KRISHNAN, «Kerala: A Fall From Grace», 116-117. Even before the pastoral letter of the Bishop an anti-alcohol movement had started in the parishes like Mulluviala, Mambilly.

[104] The Bishop in his pastoral letter has mentioned that the Catholics have to co-operate with the other religious and secular organizations which work for the common good of mankind. The BECs are very sensitive to the urgent need of cooperation with other organizations and associations which work for the betterment of humanity.

5.2 BECs at the Service of the Voiceless

In one of the BECs in the Palayam Vicariate, there are thirty families. The people in the unit are generally poor. The particular BEC came to know about a family where after the death of the mother the father remarried and wanted to send to an orphanage the three children born from the first wife. The members of the particular BEC became aware of it. In their inquiry they came to know that it was because of poverty that the father had decided to send the children to an orphanage. The members of the BEC decided to help the family so that the three children would not lose parental care[105].

In one of the BECs of the Vlathankara Vicariate, the members came to know about a poor cancer patient. The particular BEC unit could not afford to give a financial support to the patient. Through the BEC net work in the parish, each BEC could help the patient by giving Rs. 250/- (i.e. US $ 8.00) every month. The whole parish was involved to protect the life of the person.

Another characteristic feature of the BECs in its social thrust is its approach to the dowry system. In a State where dowry deaths are becoming a common phenomenon with the «business-oriented matrimony»[106], the *samūha vivāham* organized by the social service ministry of the BECs, forms a new attitude towards women and marriage[107].

According to 58% such a creative attitude is good while 39% hold the view that it is necessary. See Table ns.: Id – Q38, IId – Q38, IIId – Q38.

[105] The family was non-Catholic and the BEC members did not have any intention of converting the family to the Catholic faith. However, because of the approach of the members of the BEC, the entire family received the Catholic faith.

[106] «What has particularly worried sociologists and the police is a spurt in the number of dowry deaths and suicides by unmarried girls in the highly literate and socially progressive southern State of Kerala. In this context, Dr. J.V. Jayasinh of the Madras School of Social Works says that education has virtually failed to do away with growing dowry evil. "Dowry deaths have today become so common that they seldom shock the people" [...] Middle-class families, unable on their own to afford the trappings of the upper classes, began offering sons "for sale" in the lucrative matrimonial market. Marriage thus became a stepping stone to wealth and status. In the prevailing social milieu, killing a wife and marrying again was the next step. In Kerala, for instance, dowry was confined largely to the tradition-bound Christian community. Now the economic prosperity which the State acquired through its Gulf connection has brought all its communities under the spell of "business-oriented matrimony"» (R. RAO, «Dowry deaths», 3).

[107] *Samūha vivāham* means conducting the marriage ceremonies of more than one couple. Since marriage celebration is becoming an expensive affair, the Church and other

Since the social problems are increasing in Kerala, the BECs are sensitive to the «culture of death»[108]. It is in this context of *respect for life* that the BECs give serious attention to the problem of abortion. In one of the city BECs, the members discussed matters pertaining family life such as natural family planning, evils of abortion. In the context of Kerala, which has been accustomed to keep silence regarding sex, family planning and abortion, the initiative of BECs in Trivandrum symbolizes the potentiality of BECs for responding to the invitation of Pope John Paul II to «respect, protect, love and serve life»[109].

5.3 *BECs at the Service of the Homeless and the Exploited*

A Government employee in one of the BEC units in the Palayam Vicariate said that the members of his BEC could help a family which did not have a house. The family had a small plot of land but was not in a position to do any manual work. The members of the BEC decided to construct a house for them. One of the members made the plan for the house, another volunteered to do the masonry work and another the carpentry work and still another financial help for he was not a skilled labourer[110].

In the third chapter we have discussed the problem of fishermen in detail. We saw that the exploitation has been continuing. The exploitation has attained new dimensions when the central Government gave permission to the multi-national companies to catch fish from the Indian coast. Since it would affect the traditional fishermen, the Diocese protested such a decision of the Central Government. As a part of the protest, the Bishop supported the All India *fisheries bandh* (not going for

---

secular organizations arrange marriages of more than one couple together. The main purpose is to support the poor who are not able to marry due to lack of money. In Trivandrum, more than three Vicariates have arranged such *samūha vivāham*.

[108] See JOHN PAUL II, *Evangelium Vitae*, n. 21. According to a study conducted in 1995 by Dr. Sheela Shenoy, an assistant professor of gynecology at Trivandrum Medical College, the number of teenage abortions in Kerala have increased by 20% in a period of one year. See C.L. JOSHI, «Teenage Abortions», 98-99.

[109] See JOHN PAUL II, *Evangelium Vitae*, n. 5.

[110] According to the preliminary report of the TSSS survey conducted in 1993, 17% of the families in the Diocese are homeless. Any efforts to help the homeless should be understood in the Diocesan context. According to the TSSS survey 15% families live in huts, 33% live in thatched houses, 34% live in tiled houses and only 12% live in the concrete built houses. See C. LEON, *Thiruvananthapuram Rūpaṭa* (Diocese of Trivandrum), 4. At present every parish of the Diocese is making an effort to build a house for a homeless person in the parish.

fishing in protest) on 4-2-1994[111]. It was a great success in Trivandrum
and could call the attention of the State and Central Governments. It was
organized through the BECs. Compared to the previous agitations it was
also peaceful. Again on November 24 and 25, 1994 the people of
Trivandrum called for a *fisheries bandh*. The «Secretariat March»,
demanding the *reservations* ensured in the constitution for the OBC, on
the 21st of August 1995 by the Latin Catholics was also organized
through the BECs. It shows the growing consciousness of the people
against exploitation. The Bishop's courage to declare 1995 as «Non
corruption Year» is seen in the vitality of the functioning of BECs in
Trivandrum. According to the Bishop, the fight against corruption is part
of combining «faith and life»[112].

5.4 *Breaking the Caste Barriers*

In a planning session of the BEC animators of a Vicariate, I was
present as an observer. When the animators finished their prayer and
planning session, I asked the members to share their life experience in
their involvement in the BEC programme. A government employee said
that he was living among different castes. Formerly he found it difficult
to enter the house of lower castes. Now he has no difficulty to enter the
house of other castes and he is able to share the food that others offer
him[113]. The BEC meetings are held in the houses of former *untouchables*
too. He said that a conversion had taken place in his life.

---

[111] See M.S. PAKIAM, *February 4: Akhilēndia Bandh*, (February 4: All India Bandh),
ADT. No fisherman had gone for fishing on the *bandh* day.

[112] On 3 January 1995 Bishop M.S. PAKIAM, issued a pastoral letter declaring 1995 as
«Non-corruption Year». The significance of the pastoral letter is to be seen in the light of
an article published by Dr. T. Chakiath, the Professor of Sociology at St. Joseph's
Pontifical Seminary, Alwaye on 4-1-1995 in *Sathyadeepam*. The article, based on the
survey conducted throughout Kerala, highlights the moral degradation of the society.
According to the survey thirty-six out of ninety-six priests, thirty out of ninety women
religious, 325 out of 450 laymen and 94 out of 182 lay women had resorted to bribery
for getting various things done. See T. CHAKIATH, «Vardhamānamāya Azhimatiyum
Kraistava Uttaravādittavm» (Increasing Corruption and Christian Responsibility) in
Sathyadeepam, 4 January, 1995, 1.6. The Bishop's pastoral letter was reprinted in
Sathyadeepam, 25 January, 1995, 1.6. See M.S. PAKIAM, *1995 Azhimati Virudha
Varsācaranam* (1995 Anti Corruption Year), ADT. See also M.S. PAKIAM,
Agamanakālam: Viśuāsavum Pravartiyum (Advent: Faith and Life), ADT; KCBC,
Nāmārum Annyaralla (We are not Strangers to each Other).

[113] In some of the BEC meetings the host provides light refreshments.

In a non-coastal BEC a person belonging to a Nadar caste did not like the Dalits drawing water from his well. His participation in the BEC changed his attitude towards the Dalits. A priest working in a non-coastal parish told me that with the introduction of BEC *people from the lower caste gain acceptance in the parish councils*. In a few BECs we find that people from other rites also participate. The participation of people from different rites shows that the ordinary people are able to think beyond the *Rite*. The presence of Hindus in the coastal BECs is really a breaking down of not only caste barriers but also religious barriers.

6. Conclusion

In the previous pages we have attempted to examine how BECs function in the Diocese of Trivandrum. Since it was a contextualized study we tried to give a first-hand knowledge about the functioning. From our study it has become evident that the Christian life of Trivandrum is centered around the BECs though there are disagreements about the structural changes. From the way the BECs function at present it is evident that there is a well organized pastoral planning.

As in other countries where BECs have become the pastoral option, the hierarchy — the Bishop, the priests and the religious — played a significant role in the formation and functioning of BECs[114]. Tremendous efforts came from the hierarchy, especially in the initial stages, in forming 2.402 (at present 2.627) BECs. It was done through the training of the lay people and the priests, getting the cooperation of the religious and laity. Apart from the determined effort there were uncertainties in the initial stage. This was prevalent mainly among the priests. The lay people, in comparison with the priests, are more receptive to BECs. The lay leadership, of 10.000 people, which has emerged through the BECs, is going to play a significant role in the years to come.

With the introduction of BECs we see that there is a new approach to the Word of God and Liturgy. The liturgy is no more a ritual in the Church but an expression of the faith experience of a community in Christ through the Church. The children, youth and elderly people express their faith in the Risen Lord through their participation in the liturgy especially by means of offertory procession, spontaneous prayers and singing. The liturgy becomes truly communitarian. The Bible is

---

[114] According to M. de C. Azevedo the work of the clergy and other pastoral agents was crucial in triggering the process and catalyzing the specific perspective of BECs in Brazil. See M. DE C. AZEVEDO, *Basic Ecclesial Communities*, 35-39.

becoming the prayer book of the people. The people bring the Bible to the BEC gatherings, read, meditate and share their reflections for self-evangelization and for the betterment of the community. There is creativity in the composition of hymns and in the use of symbols. We saw that BECs are becoming Mystagogues — strengthening the faith of the baptized and the new converts leading to religious experience in the paschal mystery of Christ.

In the functioning of BECs we have seen that children, youth and women gather together according to the social background either once a week, once a fortnight or once a month. The women, who were *inside the house, come out and become evangelizers*. They have become the vital force of the BECs. The approach of women can be compared to the Samaritan woman who met Jesus and became an evangelizer of the Good News (Jn 4,39-42). The women who in the past were not represented in the decision making process, now are consulted and they are heard — from the BEC units to the diocesan pastoral council.

However, for an ideal Christian life the presence of men and women is essential. That is why Pope John Paul II exhorts that «the coordinated presence of both men and women is to be pastorally urged so that the participation of the lay faithful in the salvific mission of the Church might be rendered more rich, complete and harmonious»[115]. And the words of the Pope are specially significant in the context of Trivandrum and Kerala where woman is considered as a second class citizen in the Church and in the society[116].

The role of the Bishop in the functioning of BECs is a major factor. The Bishop is fully aware of the fact that he is the head of the one of the weakest sections of Kerala. His prophetic voice is the outcome of his direct contact with the people. He knows how BECs function in different parts of the Diocese. The Bishop's approach towards the laity in sharing the responsibility is very significant in the Indian context.

---

[115] According to the Pope the reason for the coordinated presence of men and women is mainly based on the original plan of God. See JOHN PAUL II, *Christifideles Laici*, n. 52. See also JOHN PAUL II, «Il Vangelo vi rafforzi», 7.

[116] Until recently the Christian personal law of the Syrian Christians did not allow female children equal rights with male children. It is specially noted that J. Kuriedath, in his Sociological Study on *the Changes in the Authority Structure of the Syro-Malabar Church*, has given only a low representation to women because «they were found less knowledgeable about administrative matters of the church». According to him the women religious are not in any way better than any ordinary lay woman in the knowledge of ecclesiastical administration. See J. KURIEDATH, *Authority in the Catholic Community*, 67. See also *CBCI Evaluation Report*, n. 650.

Whatever change takes place in a diocese, the immediate point of reference is the parish priest, for it is he who «actuates the Church's sacramental signs of the presence of the Risen Christ»[117] in a concrete situation of the ecclesial community[118]. So it is quite natural that the priests confront problems in executing programmes of the Diocese especially when there are ideological and cultural differences.

In the Diocese of Trivandrum the implementation of BECs has created some tensions too. The problem arose when BECs were linked with the parish councils, which are formed of the animators or leaders of the BECs. The priest was in the midst of those minority but powerful leaders who refused to go the grassroots level, and those voiceless majority who accepted the new vision of the participatory Church envisaged by the Diocese. In this confrontation we may say that 25% of priests accepted BECs as a vision and work for the building up of the Christian communities[119], 50% of priests participate in the BECs but not very actively[120]. Around 5% reject the basic vision of BECs and 20 % neither fully accept nor fully reject the vision[121]. But a very striking phenomenon among the priests is that most of the senior priests, who were ordained before the Second Vatican Council, accept BEC as a *new way of being the Church*.

---

[117] JOHN PAUL II, *Pastores Dabo Vobis*, n. 16.

[118] «The ecclesial community, while always having a universal dimension, finds its most immediate and visible expression in the *parish*» (JOHN PAUL II, *Christifideles Laici*, n. 26).

[119] «Today in particular, the pressing pastoral task of the new evangelization calls for the involvement of the entire People of God, and requires a new fervour, new methods and a new expression for announcing and witnessing of the Gospel. This task demands priests who are deeply and fully immersed in the mystery of Christ and capable of embodying a new style of pastoral life, marked by a profound communion with the Pope, the Bishops and other priests, and a fruitful cooperation with the lay faithful, always respecting and fostering roles, charisms and ministries present within the ecclesial community» (JOHN PAUL II, *Pastores Dabo Vobis*, n. 18).

[120] Some priests whole heartily accept the vision but they fail to express their conviction. In my interview with priests I realized that a good number of priests expect intellectual output from «above» i.e. the Bishop or pastoral ministry. It is in this context, Pope John Paul II's vision of the *On going formation of priests* is significant. «On going formation helps priests, *within the Church as "communion"*, to deepen their awareness that their ministry is ultimately aimed at gathering together the family of God as a brotherhood inspired by charity and to lead it to the Father through Christ in the Holy Spirit» (JOHN PAUL II, *Pastores Dabo Vobis*, n. 74). For different aspects of the on going formation of priests see ID., *Pastores Dabo Vobis*, ns. 70-81. See also *PO* 6.

[121] We also came to know that the lay people are also very sensitive to the indifferences of priests.

In the functioning of the BECs the role of the religious and priests is also becoming clarified. Since the consecrated ministers are called to be at the service of the people of God, the spirituality of the priests and religious is also to a large extent based on the spirituality of the local Church which is well reflected in the Council statement that «all are called to holiness»[122]. In the BECs the priests and religious find more fulfillment in exercising their priestly, kingly and prophetic roles. They express their solidarity with the less privileged brothers and sisters of the society.

The BECs in Trivandrum give a new thrust to its social commitment. In its social commitment we see a shift from the *recipient Church* to one which makes use of the human resources in the given situation. However, it is evident that the problems like poverty, homelessness, illiteracy, lack of primary facilities cannot be solved easily. Nevertheless, a common thread seen in the functioning of BECs is the meaningful personal and communitarian life as envisaged in the early Christian community.

The BECs in Trivandrum are the contextualization of the early Christian community. Our next task is to discover the spirituality of BECs and to point out its challenges in Trivandrum.

---

[122] See *LG* 39-42.

CHAPTER V

The Spirituality of Basic Ecclesial Communities
and Its Challenges in Trivandrum

In the previous chapter we discussed how BECs function in the Diocese of Trivandrum. From the contextualized study we know that *a new way of being Church through the BECs* is vibrant in the ecclesial life of Trivandrum. We noticed that there is diversity in the functioning of BECs according to the cultural background of each community. This diversity enriches the local Church of Trivandrum. The main concern of the BECs in Trivandrum towards the Word of God, the liturgy, and the ecclesial and social life of the people also formed part of our investigation.

In this chapter our task is to discover the spirituality of BECs and its challenges in Trivandrum. The new ecclesial vision emerged with the «Living Together», and the subsequent self-evaluations had an influence on the People of God in the Diocese of Trivandrum. As a result of this new ecclesial vision, a new ecclesial spirituality specific to the Diocese of Trivandrum is evolving. It is not without challenges. The socio-religious factors are taking new dimensions in the contemporary society. The BECs have a prophetic role not only to understand the old socio-religious factors but also to discern the contemporary problems, to build up «a new culture of human life»[1]. In this context the BECs cannot function simply as an issue based gathering[2]. The danger of institutionalizing the

---

[1] See JOHN PAUL II, *Evangelium Vitae*, ns. 78-101.

[2] The BEC gatherings help to mobilize people especially when there are some special issues. The fishermen *bandh,* campaign against illicit production of alcohol at Pozhiyoor and Pannimala, issues connected with Vizhinjam, the demand for reservation for the backward class of the Latin Catholics are some of the important issues which were strongly supported by the BECs in Trivandrum. Already in the second chapter we

BECs for *better functioning* in the future cannot be ruled out. The challenge to save life is becoming an everyday task especially when new threats to the human life are increasing. In discerning the present and foreseeing the future, the BECs in Trivandrum cannot stand isolated. It has to relate with other local Churches and other communities which work for the Kingdom of God where justice and peace reign (Rom 14,17-18).

1. The Spirituality of BECs in Trivandrum

In the first chapter of our study we saw that there is no uniformity as regards the understanding of spirituality. The pluralistic understanding of spirituality expresses also the difficulty in explaining one's religious experience. Nevertheless, we saw some common traits like «experience», «progressive development», «transformation», «relation», «community», and «cultural milieu» which explain the dynamic nature of spirituality. A common thread in all the definitions and descriptions is the communitarian aspect which originates from the trinitarian communion[3]. The starting point is the God-experience in a community. The Christians have a special experience of God in the person of Jesus Christ. The characteristic feature of the communitarian spirituality is that it is vertical and horizontal: centred on the trinitarian God and centred on the person who is created in the image and likeness of God (Gen 1,26-27).

The spirituality of BECs in Trivandrum would be evaluated from the fact of how the spirit of the trinitarian communion is lived in the socio-religious context of the People of God[4]. The BECs in Trivandrum do not

---

discussed how different backward classes like Nadars, Izhavas, and Dalits fought against the evils of the society.

[3] Though we sometimes attribute the divine manifestations of creation, redemption and sanctification to Father, Son, and Holy Spirit respectively, we cannot relate to one person of the Trinity without simultaneously relating to the other persons. See C. KIESLING, «On Relating to the Persons of the Trinity», 599-616. See also E.R. MARTINEZ, *La vita cristiana*; I.A. KAIGAMA, *The Trinitarian Implications*.

[4] Giving importance to the existing context of the people is a new phenomenon in the recent literature on spirituality. H. Alphonso writes: «Christian spirituality does not arise or grow in a vacuum: the Christian's habitual religious attitudes at their deepest and fundamental level are necessarily conditioned by the situation, the age and the world in which he / she lives. [...] Present-day Christian spirituality, then, can only be described in terms of the present-day situation» (H. ALPHONSO, *Placed with Christ the Son*, 153). According to M. de C. Azevedo spirituality emerges from concrete expressions of life, while it inspires and guides the people who are experiencing that reality. This is why we can talk about several spiritualities, and we can even identify streams and schools of

function in a vacuum. They have a cultural background with existential realities which sometimes turn into existential anxieties caused by pseudo developments[5]. The history of the people, the geographical factors, the presence of different religions, and the caste differences are important factors for understanding the background of the BECs. Problems such as poverty, illiteracy, unemployment, «scientifically and systematically programmed threats»[6] to life, negative influence of media, are some of the existential factors.

Ever since the beginning of ecclesial communities in the 16th century, the people of Trivandrum were trying to live the message of the Gospel despite their sufferings caused by the civil and religious authorities[7]. With the introduction of BECs, the people of God in the Diocese began to have a new awareness of the Christian life. This awareness created a new way of being the Church. More than a change in the institutional model, a new model, BEC model, has emerged[8].

The Word of God began to be the light and life of the people. The ordinary people began to show extraordinary interest in the Word of God[9]. They began to interiorize the Word of God through *lectio divina*.

---

spirituality within the wider unified context of a basic Christian spirituality. See M. DE C. AZEVEDO, *The Consecrated Life*, 109-118.

[5] Regarding the pseudo developments, S. Rayan, who bears the ethos of Trivandrum, poses certain thought provoking questions. Criticizing the aggressive penetration of multinationals in the developing countries like India he remarks: «Most of the time their advent is unnecessary and absurd. Do we indeed need Coca Cola and Pepsi Cola to come to India so we can find something to drink when we are thirsty?» (S. RAYAN, «The Search for an Asian Spirituality», 15). «The "Growth-Model Development" pursued in our country since independence, has also involved the use of high and dangerous technology, mega-projects which benefit an elite and destroy the lives of vast numbers of the population. This development-model with its ally, consumerism, is seen by the sensitive as a subtle destructive force striking at the root of ecological balance and adversely affecting the survival of many people and the quality of our culture» (STATEMENT OF THE INDIAN THEOLOGICAL ASSOCIATION, «Towards an Indian Christian Spirituality», 79-88). See also F. WILFRED, «No Salvation Outside Globalization?», 80-92.

[6] JOHN PAUL II, *Evangelium Vitae*, n.17.

[7] We have explained in the second and third chapters about the attitude of the civil and religious authorities towards the people of Travancore in the early stages of their Christian life.

[8] In the BEC model we find a convergence of the positive aspects of *institutional model, communion model, sacramental model, kerygmatic model*, and *servant model*.

[9] «Reflection on biblical hermeneutic tells us that it is the community which, out of its own current experience and life situation, reads the Bible in such a way as to draw from it the nourishment it needs at the moment. The community is not an inert spectator during Bible reading; it is an active participant bringing its own experience and questions to the

Since the Word of God is alive and active in the people (Heb 4,12-13), they began to discover their own self or to recover the lost self from the false self[10]. They also discover the compassionate Self of God who liberates the mankind from all sorts of evils of the society.

The study of the socio-religious background helped us to understand and assess that the BECs in Trivandrum is in a pilgrimage (*cammino*) towards the Kingdom of God. In praxis this pilgrimage is following Jesus Christ. In order to arrive at the Kingdom of God the BECs have taken the life of the early Christian community as a model. As a result, despite the cultural and ideological differences, there is a new awareness in the ecclesial life. This new awareness is expressed in the BEC gatherings, pastoral council meetings, celebration of sacraments. The sacraments do not remain a mere *pūja* in which the priest does everything and the people remain as onlookers. The gatherings become events of grace and mutual up-building. The gatherings impart grace to take up the challenges, individually and collectively, to express concern and commitment to one's neighbour. An integral development of the people is the outcome.

As in the first Christian community there is an effort to share the common goods (Acts 2,42-47; 4,32-35). The compassion of Jesus Christ is manifested visibly (Mk 6,34). There is an attempt at sharing of money[11], and sparing time for the poor and needy. There is concern for each individual and commitment from everyone. The neighbour gains acceptance like that of a friend and a relative. There is an opening of doors to the members of the neighbourhood families as a sign of the opening of one's heart to God. This opening extends not only to the Catholics but also to the people belonging to other Christian denominations and other religions.

In a cultural situation where caste tends to dominates over religion, people of different castes get equal acceptance in the community. The

---

Word of God» (D. REGAN, *Experience the Mystery*, 81). It deserves special attention to note the general attitude of the people in Brazil and in Trivandrum towards the Word of God. Such an attitude towards the Word of God is to be understood in the context of the Catholic tradition which always expected the priest even to select a passage from the Bible. See J. FUELLENBACH, *The Kingdom of God*, 17.

[10] See D.S. AMALORPAVADASS, «A Theology of Mission», 323-346.

[11] «Solutions must be sought on worldwide scale by establishing a true economy of communion and participation in goods on both international and national levels» (JOHN PAUL II, *Address to the Fourth General Conference*, n. 15). See also ID., *Evangelium Vitae*, n. 91. The theme *economy of communion* is further developed by Chiara Lubich, the founder of Focolari Movement, after her visit to Latin America in 1992.

human dignity of the guest and host is respected. The different cultures are recognized and appreciated. This is an important factor in the spirituality of BECs especially when the host is of a different caste and class[12].

There is an effort to protect life which includes a fight against the evils of the society. The people realize that BEC gatherings are the best occasion to speak about the values of human life. The common problems of the society are discussed with an open mind. There is an effort to analyze the problems and an effort to solve them as in the early Christian community (Acts 6,1-7). In the process of analyzing a particular problem each member in the BEC gets an occasion to express his or her views. The voiceless in the early ecclesial communities can raise their voice and their opinions are heard and respected[13]. The members of the BECs, as a part of their commitment to follow Jesus Christ, try to respond to the problems actively[14]. There is a constant effort to combine life and faith[15]. Those who fight against injustice come together and pray together[16]. Actually it is the prayer experience in the BECs that inspires the people to take up any task in the community.

---

[12] In Acts we see how St. Peter himself was awaiting the revelation of God to enter the house of the centurion Cornelius (Acts 10,1ff.). See I. DE LA POTTERIE, «The Christian's Relationship», 175-182. We have noticed in the previous chapter how caste and class distinctions dominate the society and how BEC gatherings try to break the caste barriers. The opening of doors to other is not a new thing in the contemporary situation. «In a charismatic household, the doors of a nuclear family are opened to non-relatives, who then live as intimate members of the household as if living within their own immediate family» (W. AU, By Way of the Heart, 52-53). But the difference in the BECs is that they open the doors to all the neighbours despite the caste and class distinction.

[13] In the ecclesial communities of earlier times there existed domination of rich and powerful in the society and they decided everything.

[14] «We cannot but think of today's tendency for people to refuse to accept responsibility for their brothers and sisters. Symptoms of this trend include the lack of solidarity towards society's weakest members — such as the elderly, the infirm, immigrants, children — and the indifference frequently found in relations between the world's peoples even when basic values such as survival, freedom and peace are involved» (JOHN PAUL II, Evangelium Vitae, n. 8).

[15] The need to combine faith and life is emphasized by Pope John Paul II. The Pope says: «We need to begin with the renewal of a culture of life within Christian communities themselves. Too often it happens that believers, even those who take an active part in the life of the Church, end up by separating their Christian faith from its ethical requirements concerning life, and thus fall into moral subjectivism and certain objectionable ways of acting» (JOHN PAUL II, Evangelium Vitae, n. 95).

[16] Coming together and praying together are very important especially as the Christians are divided on the basis of liturgical rites which multiply churches and

It is in the above mentioned existential situations that we describe the spirituality of BECs in Trivandrum. Since the Christian life through BECs in Trivandrum is a new way of being the Church in the contemporary time we are not able to give a definition of the spirituality of BECs in Trivandrum. Therefore, more than a definition we may describe the spirituality of BECs in Trivandrum as the maturing of personal and communitarian commitment to follow Jesus Christ and to love one's neighbour in the living cultural situation.

1.1 *Personal and Communitarian Commitment*

The spirituality of BECs is personal and communitarian. God calls everyone personally[17].

> Look, I am standing at the door, knocking. If one of you hears me calling and opens the door, I will come in to share a meal at that person's side. Anyone who proves victorious I will allow to share my throne, just as I have myself overcome and have taken my seat with my Father on his throne (Rev 3,20-21).

The response to the personal call implies the building up of a community. The first words in the Bible to the human person, «Where are you?»(Gen 3,9), implies that we have been created as *response-able*, interpersonal, cognitive-affective subjects whose perfection consists in the authentic communicating of divine and human fellowship[18]. The dynamic relation between «person» and «community» in human life is relevant also in the case of Christian life[19].

The dynamic and intimate relation between «person» and the «community» is well expressed in the exhortation of St. Paul to the

---

institutions in an unchristian way. The differences in Kerala have gone in such a way that not even the «Our Father» can be prayed uniformly. As it is commonly said pluralism is not a reason nor a justification for the divisions in the Church caused in the past or sustained at present by motives that are alien to the nature and mission of the Church. «[...] *fellowship in prayer leads people to look at the Church and Christianity in a new way*» (JOHN PAUL II, *Ut Unum Sint*, n. 23). «There is no important or significant event which does not benefit from Christians coming together and praying» (ID., n. 25).

[17] See H. ALPHONSO, *Placed with Christ the Son*, 159 See also ID., *The Personal Vocation*.

[18] See J. NAVONE, *Self-giving and Sharing*, 24

[19] A «person» arrives at one's total personality only within community, and a «community» is a genuine community only if it is made up of living responsible persons who, each of them, make the community goals and tasks as their own. See H. ALPHONSO, *Placed with Christ the Son*, 159-161.

Corinthian community. According to him the particular manifestation of the Spirit granted to each one is to be used for the benefit of others:

> There are many different gifts, but it is always the same Spirit; there are many different ways of serving, but it is always the same Lord. There are many different forms of activity, but in everybody it is the same God who is at work in them all. The particular manifestation of the Spirit granted to each one is to be used for the general good. To one is given from the Spirit the gift of utterance expressing wisdom; to another the gift of utterance expressing knowledge, in accordance with the same Spirit; to another, faith, from the same Spirit; and to another, the gifts of healing, through this one Spirit; to another, the working of miracles; to another, prophecy; to another, the power of distinguishing spirits; to one, the gift of different tongues and to another, the interpretation of tongues. But at work in all these is one and the same Spirit, distributing them at will to each individual (1 Cor 12,4-11)[20].

The spirituality of BECs in Trivandrum is personal (not individualistic) and communitarian. This aspect is well expressed in the pastoral letters of the Bishop, in the meetings of the diocesan pastoral council, the parish pastoral council, etc. The spirituality of BECs derives from the biblical understanding of *koinōnia* (communion) which we explained in the first chapter. The communion of BECs is two dimensional: vertical and horizontal. These two dimensions are inseparable[21]. This is well explained when Jesus Christ replies to the question about the greatest commandment of the Law.

> You must love the Lord your God with all your heart, with all your soul, and with all your mind. This is the greatest and the first commandment. The second resembles it: You must love your neighbour as yourself. On these two commandments hang the whole Law, and the Prophets too (Mt 22,37-40).

Recalling the experience of the early Church, the Acts of the Apostles make it clear that community life is foundational to Christian living. Right at the very beginning of Christianity, the followers of Jesus Christ:

> remained faithful to the teaching of the apostles, to the brotherhood, to the breaking of bread and to the prayers [...]. And all who shared the faith owned everything in common and sold their goods and possessions and

---

[20] For a theological and exegetical study of the passage see J. VADAKKEDOM, «*Pros To Sympheron*», 144-157. 172-241. See also PBC, *Unity and Diversity in the Church*, 14-36.

[21] Although the concept of communion is elaborated in the Second Vatican Council, in the Diocese of Trivandrum the idea of communion remained mainly in the theoretical realm as in most of the local Churches in India.

distributed the proceeds among themselves according to what each one needed. Each day, with one heart, they regularly went to the Temple but met in their houses for breaking of bread; they shared their food gladly and generously; they praised God and were looked up to by everyone. Day by day the Lord added to their community those destined to be saved (Acts 2,42-47).

The NT theme of togetherness is an excellent criterion of what the reality of a Christian community is intended to be[22]. The communitarian aspect of Christian life was also a major theme in the writings of the Apostolic Fathers. For example, St. Ignatius of Antioch exhorts the people of Ephesus to gather often[23]. The spirit behind the foundation of the religious orders is also to be seen from the perspective of common witnessing Jesus Christ in an individualistic society.

In Trivandrum, most of the people come from the Hindu background which, despite its philosophical richness, is individualistic. Adding to the Hindu philosophical background, Western individualism which was symbolized in the principle of *saving one's soul*, influenced the Christians of the place[24]. Consequently, the people were satisfied with the practices of going to the Church receiving the sacraments and thus *saving their souls*. Through the BECs, however, the people realize that they have to respond to God's call personally which implies a communitarian commitment[25]. The personal and communitarian response becomes meaningful when it helps one to follow Jesus Christ. And the following of Jesus Christ is the *sine qua non* factor of the spirituality of BECs in Trivandrum.

---

[22] For elaborate Bible references to the communitarian aspect of Christian life see S.P. KEALY, *Spirituality for Today*, 17-33.

[23] «Be Zealous, therefore, to assemble more frequently to render thanks and praise to God. For, when you meet together frequently, the powers of Satan are destroyed and danger from him is dissolved in the harmony of your faith» (ST. IGNATIUS OF ANTIOCH, «Letter to the Ephesians», n. 13).

[24] In the third chapter of our study we have discussed sufficiently how most of the missionaries were only preoccupied with the *salvation of souls*. And many a time the missionaries did not think about the integral development of the persons who lived there. As a result, the Catholics stood behind other backward communities.

[25] «God's covenant-creating and covenant-sustaining initiative in Jesus Christ awaits our appropriate response in authentic fellowship (*Koinōnia*)» (J. NAVONE, *Self-giving and Sharing*, 22).

1.2 *To Follow Jesus Christ*

One of the important expressions of the spirituality of BECs is the determination of its members to follow Jesus Christ[26]. Since the BECs in Trivandrum have taken the first Christian community as a model, the major tenets of the spirituality of the first Christian community is reflected. We note that the early Christian spirituality was Christological by nature[27]. The early community realized that Jesus Christ is the one Saviour of all, the only one able to reveal God and able to lead them to God[28]. They experienced the presence of the risen Lord in their midst. For them there was no opposition between belief and fact, because their belief is built on fact[29]. The Christians were aware that through baptism

---

[26] To follow Jesus Christ in the biblical point of view signifies a response to the call of Jesus Christ. For example, Jesus Christ calls his disciples to follow Him (Mk 1,16-20). The initiative comes from Jesus Christ. The characteristic feature of «following» both in the OT and in the NT comes from a divine initiative. The response of Abraham, Moses, the prophets, the Apostles and the disciples testify to this divine initiative. So, following Jesus Christ means responding to the call of Jesus Christ with the assistance of His Spirit. «when the Spirit of truth comes he will lead you to the complete truth, since he will not be speaking of his own accord, but will say only what he has been told; and he will reveal to you the things to come. He will glorify me, since all he reveals to you will be taken from what is mine» (Jn 16,13-14). According to St. Paul all the blessings which unite the Christians in fellowship are gratuitous, and he never thinks of them apart from Jesus Christ, the embodiment of all that grace signifies. And in our description of «to follow Jesus Christ», we mean that the divine initiative to follow Jesus Christ comes from the Spirit of Jesus Christ.

[27] «It is quite certain that the soul of Christian spirituality lies in the absolutely unique influence of Jesus' words and of his personality, exercised first on his immediate disciples» (L. BOUYER, *A History of Christian Spirituality*, I, 35). See also J. AUMANN, *Christian Spirituality*, 19-34. The Christological nature of early Christian spirituality is well explained by the Apostolic Fathers too. For example, St. Clement of Rome writes: «Through Him let us strain our eyes toward the heights of heaven; through Him we see mirrored His spotless and glorious countenance. Through Him the eyes of our heart have been opened; through Him our foolish and darkened understanding shoots up into the light; through Him the Lord willed that we should taste immortal knowledge, [...]» (ST. CLEMENT OF ROME, «Letter to the Corinthians», 38). Like St. Clement of Rome, St. Ignatius of Antioch emphasized the uniqueness of Christ in the life of Christians. He admonished his readers to be «imitators of Christ, as He is of His Father» (ST. IGNATIUS OF ANTIOCH, «Letter to the Philadelphians», n. 7).

[28] See JOHN PAUL II, *Redemptoris Missio*, ns. 4-11. Even in the early Christian community there was doubt regarding the divinity of Jesus Christ. That is why St. Ignatius of Antioch exhorts the Trallians to be deaf if anybody speaks apart from Jesus Christ. See ST. IGNATIUS OF ANTIOCH, «To the Trallians», n.9. See also G. RAVASI, «Linee Bibliche», 56-123.

[29] See L. CERFAUX, *Christ in the Theology of St. Paul*, 69-70. «The power which raised Christ from the dead does not confine itself to one resurrection, but brings about

they were living a new life. They believed that through baptism they were participating in the life of Jesus Christ in a real sense. St. Paul explains:

> So by our baptism into his death we were buried with him, so that as Christ was raised from the dead by the Father's glorious power, we too should begin a new life. If we have been joined to him by dying a death like his, so we shall be by a resurrection like his [...] (Rom 6,4-11)

Following Jesus Christ is the visible expression of Christians' response to God's call[30]. Jesus Christ is at the centre of Christian faith. In Him, God's age-long self-manifestation through human history has come to a climax[31]. The studies on the various schools of spirituality also highlight the fact that the Christological focus was one of the main characteristics of Christian spirituality throughout the history of the Church. For example there is an explicit focus in French spirituality on the person of Jesus Christ. Names like Bernard of Clairvaux, Cardinal Bérulle, Marguerite-Marie Alocoque and Pierre Teilhard de Chardin hold a privileged place in the annals of christological piety of the Catholic Church[32]. According to John Paul II, the Church's fundamental function in every age, and particularly in ours, is to direct the human person's gaze, to point the awareness and experience of the whole of humanity towards the mystery of Jesus Christ[33].

1.2.1 New Experience in Following Jesus Christ

In the BECs in Trivandrum the people see the invisible presence of God in the Paschal mystery of Jesus Christ. Since the people are belonging to the backward class of the society they experience also the liberative hand of God in Jesus Christ. They experience a personal God

---

in Christians a life which is of the same nature as that of the risen Christ. It is as if the new and divine life poured over from Christ into all Christians, so as to create them anew. Thus the risen Christ is once more the centre or source from which there flows out a life which is a continuation of his own» (ID., *Christ in the Theology of St. Paul*, 323-324).

[30] See G. GUTIERREZ, *We Drink*, 39-53.

[31] See *FAPA*, 341-342.

[32] See D. DIDOMIZIO, «French Spirituality», 161-165. One of the classical spiritual books of the modern period which called for the interior conversion is titled *Imitation of Christ*. See also L. BORRIELLO, «Spirituality in Modern Times», 47-59.

[33] See JOHN PAUL II, *Redemptor Hominis*, n. 13.

in Jesus Christ who not only speaks to them but also seeks them out[34]. The close relation the following of Jesus Christ might not be the immediate result of the formation of BECs, for, already from the beginning of ecclesial communities, the people began to hear Jesus Christ and His Church, and began to worship the God of Jesus Christ in the Church.

The difference which we notice in the present life of the ecclesial communities is the new awareness of the nature of God manifested in Jesus Christ. More than the ecclesial communities of the early times of Christianity in the South Travancore, the BECs try to realize the personal and communitarian commitment in following Jesus Christ. Behind this commitment we see the concern and compassion of each individual for the other. The people are now in a process of re-discovering the spirituality of Jesus Christ's message. It is in a way a re-discovery of the basic principles of Christian spirituality. The awareness of the ecclesial life of the people of Trivandrum can be compared to the biblical episode of the Samaritan woman and the people. «Now we believe no longer because of what you told us; we have heard him ourselves and we know that he is indeed the Saviour of the world» (Jn 4,1)[35]. Their faith goes beyond the theoretical explanations[36]. In the context of BECs the people might say that their faith depends not on the

---

[34] «In *Jesus Christ* God not only speaks to man but also *seeks him out.* The Incarnation of the Son of God attests that God goes in search of man. Jesus speaks of this search as the finding of a lost sheep (cf Lk 15,1-7). It is a search which *begins in the heart of God* and culminates in the Incarnation of the Word. If God goes in search of man, created in his own image and likeness, he does so because he loves him eternally in the Word, and wishes to raise him in Christ to the dignity of an adoptive son. God therefore goes in search of man who *is his special possession* in a way unlike any other creature. Man is God's possession by virtue of a choice made in love: God seeks man out, moved by his fatherly heart» (JOHN PAUL II, *Tertio Millennio Adveniente*, n. 7).

[35] In the episode of the Samaritan woman we find the divine initiative from Jesus Christ and a personal response from the woman. The individual response of the woman had a tremendous impact on the community. It is through her that the community comes to know Jesus Christ. When the community heard Him directly and personally they also began to give a powerful testimony. In the BECs also the initiative came from the ministers of the Church. But now the lay people as individuals and as communities try to give testimony through their words and deeds.

[36] See M. VIDALE – R.D.O. SIERRA, «The Spirituality of the Brazilian Base Communities», 39-49. The religious experience that one gets in the ecclesial community is very significant. The starting point of the emerging Indian theology focuses this aspect of religious experience too. See M. AMALADOSS, «An Emerging Indian Theology», 473-484. ID., «An Emerging Indian Theology», 559-572. See also G. GUTIERREZ, *We Drink*, 33-53.

faith of the priests, whose *diaconal* role is never denounced, but God has revealed Himself in Jesus Christ to them in and through the Church[37].

1.2.2 A New Experience from the Suffering of Jesus Christ

The people discover God's preferential love for them through Jesus Christ in the Church. They realize their closeness to the cross of Jesus Christ in their sufferings[38]. They are becoming aware that they can be sharers in the Paschal Mystery of Jesus Christ through their social backwardness and gain hope from the victory of Jesus Christ. The resurrection of Jesus Christ gives them hope. The death and resurrection invites the people to the life of Jesus Christ and his prophetic message.

The people, who had accepted the Christian faith in the context of social humiliation and backwardness, find in the Nazareth proclamation of Jesus Christ — «The spirit of the Lord is upon me, for he has anointed me to bring the good news to the afflicted. He has sent me to proclaim liberty to captives, sight to the blind, to let the oppressed go free, to proclaim a year of favour from the Lord» (Lk 4,18-19) — a spiritual experience of the children of God, a consolation and a liberation.

Like the Churches in the developing countries, the people for a long time used to have a low self-esteem. The discovery that they are really children of God, made in his image, is productive of a rich spirituality which inspires them to struggle to rediscover the image in which they were created[39]. This phenomenon of the religious experience of God in

---

[37] This new experience has influenced more women than men. As we have noted in the previous chapter the women who were *inside* the house *came out* and began to be evangelizers.

[38] See JOHN PAUL II, *Salvifici Doloris*, ns. 19-24. «Christian spirituality is a *spirituality of Kenosis* — of powerlessness, of continual purification from self-centeredness, of growing more and more in openness to our partners in dialogue. *Kenosis* implies death and resurrection, that dying to self which brings fullness of life (Phil 2,6-11). Hence, it is communitarian; it is centered on the eucharist, where together we experience death and resurrection in Christ» (*FAPA*, 331). Although, theologically, the resurrection of Jesus Christ is the important feast in a liturgical year, in Trivandrum the well attended celebration is Good Friday. «One could take several ways of expressing the core of the gospel. It is quite intriguing to note that in the Hindu thinking on the Cross in Indian setting, it is God's identification with human suffering rather than Paul's emphasis on the atonement of human sin that has been crucial» (M.M. THOMAS, «Mission of the Church», 84). See also M. AMALADOSS, «The Pluralism of Religions», 100.

[39] D. REGAN, *Experience the Mystery*, 65-66.

Jesus Christ was one of the main reason for the Nadar women to fight for the right to wear upper cloth in the 19th century[40]. The Latin Catholics of Trivandrum, with the emergence of BECs, not only began to realize their social backwardness but also began to fight for their rights in accordance with the teachings of the Church[41].

1.2.3 The Word of God and the Eucharist

In the BEC gatherings, recalling the presence of Jesus Christ in their midst, the people enthrone the Bible in their midst and gather around it[42]. Although, Jesus Christ is the centre of their life, they do not look upon Him as an idol to be worshipped. Rather, they find in Him a person to be followed and a message to be lived[43]. In reading the Word of God the people gain access to the Father, through Christ, the Word made flesh, in the Holy Spirit and thus become sharers in the divine nature (cf. Eph 2,18; 2 Pet 1,4)[44]. Thus the BECs try to realize the salvific plan of God for them[45]. Unlike the early ecclesial communities in Trivandrum which gave more importance to the rituals, the Word of God is read in the communities, meditated upon and understood in their own living

---

[40] In the second chapter we have sufficiently discussed the upper cloth struggle. We have also seen that the upper class in Kerala did not like the lower class joining Christianity in the 19th century. The Gospel message has also influenced the Hindus belonging to the poor class to fight for their human rights.

[41] It is true that the fishermen's agitation took place before the formation of BECs. But a collective approach to the social issues on the part of the local Church of Trivandrum is seen after the formation of BECs.

[42] According to W. Kasper the Church stands under the word of God. See W. KASPER, Transcending All Understanding, 105-124. See also B. SECONDIN, ed., Parola di Dio e Spiritualità, 13-31.

[43] The importance given to the Word of God is an important phenomenon we see in every BEC in the Church whether in Latin America or in Africa or in Asia. With the Second Vatican Council we find that a great importance is given to the Word of God. «É questo un grande principio che si riallaccia all'antica visione della vita spirituale come capacità di leggere le Scritture e di comprenderne il messaggio profetico di vita che essa propongono» (B. SECONDIN, «La Spiritualità contemporanea», 214-215). See also «Puebla Final Document», n. 629 [J. EAGLESON – P. SCHARPER, eds., Puebla and Beyond, 211].

[44] See DV 2. See also B. CALATI, «Parola di Dio», 1134-1151; C.A. BERNARD, Theologia Spirituale, 362-370.

[45] According to J.M. Tillard the Christian experience is to be understood in the context of the Covenant, which God made with Abraham. Then only we can grasp God's fidelity to his Words. See J.M.R. TILLARD, «I Cammini dello Spirito», 330-403. Reading the Word of God implies remembering the past and discerning the present. See B. SECONDIN, Nuovi Cammini dello Spirito, 205-231.

context[46]. The Word of God, which is living and active (Heb 4,12) in the BECs, leads the faithful to the eucharistic sacrifice which is the «source and summit of Christian life» (*LG* 11)[47]. The gathering for the eucharistic celebration is significant:

> Christians come together in one place for the Eucharistic assembly. At its head is Christ himself, the principal agent of the Eucharist. He is high priest of the New Covenant; it is he himself who presides invisibly over every Eucharistic celebration. It is in representing him that the bishop or priest acting *in the person of Christ the head* (*in persona Christi capitis*) presides over the assembly, speaks after the readings, receives the offerings, and says the Eucharistic Prayer. All have their own active parts to play in the celebration, each in his own way: readers, those who bring up the offerings, those who give communion, and the whole people whose «Amen» manifests their participation[48].

Since there is sufficient preparation for the Eucharist in the BECs, the eucharistic celebrations, more than a cultic act, become expressions of their faith in Jesus Christ[49]. What D. Regan speaks of in Brazil is also relevant in Trivandrum. He says: «The liturgy of basic communities frequently recalls the salvific interventions of God in history; not in the past history of his people, but in history here and now»[50]. The liturgical celebrations constantly call them to combine the faith they proclaim in the sacraments and the life they live in the world.

1.2.4 Aiming at the Kingdom

Following Jesus Christ means living the message which he preached. The sum and substance of the teachings of Jesus Christ is the Kingdom of

---

[46] «Contemporary hermeneutics insists that every reading of a text is a rereading. Every time a person reads a text he or she brings to it a new awareness, fruit of accumulated experience, and this new viewpoint prompts the reader to ask new questions of the text, questions which it had not occurred to him or her to ask before» (D. REGAN, *Experience the Mystery*, 65).

[47] See *CCC*, ns. 1324-1327.

[48] *CCC*, n. 1348.

[49] Most of the BECs take much initiative to prepare the liturgical celebrations in the Church in a meaningful manner. This new liturgical experience prevents the people from spending huge amounts of money for feast celebrations.

[50] D. Regan shows the relation between BECs and liturgy. See D. REGAN, *Experience the Mystery*, 74. See also *CCC*, ns. 1356-1372.

God. The people realize the universal application of the message[51]. The elements of the teachings of Jesus Christ on the Kingdom of God cannot be separated from the person who taught it. John Paul II writes:

> The Kingdom of God is not a concept, a doctrine, or a programme subject to free interpretation, but is before all else a person with the face and name of Jesus of Nazareth, the image of the invisible God. If the Kingdom is separated from Jesus, it is no longer the Kingdom of God which he revealed[52].

The Kingdom message of Jesus Christ is to be lived in the concrete situations by doing service to others. This is what John Paul II wished for the people of Trivandrum during his visit to Trivandrum in 1986. The Pope exhorted:

> The signs of the presence of God's Kingdom are the preaching of the Good News to the poor, the proclaiming of the sight by [to] the blind, the setting free of those who are oppressed, the proclamation of the acceptable year of the Lord. All these mean that the Church's service to the Kingdom of God is accomplished in her service to the poor and to the suffering[53].

1.3 *To Love One's Neighbour*

The commitment to follow Jesus Christ leads the members of BECs to express their concern and commitment to their neighbours. The members are challenged to love not an imaginary neighbour[54] but the neighbour who lives close to one, the neighbour whose children are to be sent to school, who is not able to build a house for his family, who has no means to meet the hospital expenses, who does not have a vision about his family[55]. Loving one's neighbour is loving God himself. «Anyone who

---

[51] The universal application of the message of the Kingdom of God is one of the contemporary concern of the Asian theologians. See *FAPA*, 341. See also F. WILFRED, *From the Dusty Soil*, 161-175; J. DUPUIS, «FABC Focus», 132-156.

[52] JOHN PAUL II, *Redemptoris Missio*, n. 18.

[53] JOHN PAUL II, «Address to the Faithful of Kerala», 390-391.

[54] The phenomenon of *imaginary neighbour* we see in the cities both in the developed and developing countries. Many a time the people who live in the cities may not even know the names of their neighbours but show much zeal in helping the people of other countries and continents. Jesus Christ's command, on the other hand, has two dimensions: one is to love those who are close to one (Jn 13,1) and the other is to love those who are beyond one's inner circle of caste, colour and creed (Lk 10,29-37).

[55] In the Diocese we observe that most of the people because of the financial constraint — not because of lack of intelligence — do not have proper plan of their own family. Many parents do not have even an idea about the future of their children and their children fail to plan for their studies or their future. In addition to the financial

says "I love God" and hates his brother is a liar, since whoever does not love the brother whom he can see cannot love God whom he has not seen» (1 Jn 4,20). In the concrete situation of the BEC gatherings, the members encounter the poor and needy[56]. They are called to love one another. Their love is a challenging one, for, to love the «neighbour' in another village, country or continent is easier than to love the one who lives close to the house. In a way the BECs call for a solidarity with the poor and the needy.

1.3.1 Solidarity with the Poor

Solidarity with the poor is closely connected with the spirituality of BECs. A follower of Jesus Christ cannot but be in solidarity with the poor. «True solidarity with one's neighbour is rooted in the conviction that Christ has united himself with each and every person by means of his redemptive incarnation»[57]. Jesus Christ openly declared that he came to bring good news to the poor (Lk 4,18-19), exhibited a special concern for those who marked by deprivation (Mt 11,4-5) and exhorted his followers to identify with the poor who suffer from hunger, thirst, sickness, homelessness, imprisonment (Mt 25,31-46)[58]. As a response to the divine command of identification with the poor the Council says: «the joy and hope, the grief and anguish of the men of our time, especially of those who are poor or afflicted in any way, are the joy and hope, the grief and anguish of the followers of Jesus Christ as well» (*GS* 1). Contextualizing *Populorum Progressio* of Paul VI, the present Pope John Paul II says:

> Solidarity helps us to see the «other» — whether a person, people or nation-not just as some kind of instrument, with a work capacity and physical

---

constraints, the Hindu concept of «fate» impedes the people from taking up responsibilities. Realizing this aspect we find a lot of conscientiousation programmes going on in the Diocese through BECs.

[56] In many BECs only the poor and needy will be present. Not that the rich do not come but there may not be any rich in the BEC. The sociological survey conducted by the TSSS in 1993 sheds light on the economic situation of the people. According to the survey 26% of the families do not have their own property.

[57] JOHN PAUL II, «La grande primavera del cristianesimo», 4. See also *GS* 22.

[58] «When Christians practise the virtue of charity in the specific form of solidarity with the "least of the brethren", who bear the indestructible image of Christ (cf. Mt 25,46), the gratuity of that love calls forth God's abundant blessings upon the local Church» (JOHN PAUL II, «La grande primavera del cristianesimo»,4). «Il tempio di Dio, da sempre, è il fratello povero, il bisognoso, lo straniero, l'orfano, l'eunuco» (B. SECONDIN, «La vita consacrata e il dialogo», 17).

strength to be exploited at low cost and then discarded when no longer useful, but as our «neighbour», a «helper» (cf. Gen 2,18-20), to be made a sharer, on a par with ourselves, in the banquet of life to which all are equally invited by God[59].

The Pope calls solidarity a Christian virtue[60] and confirms the urgent need to join with other Christian communities to take «a stand in the name of Christ on important problems concerning man's calling and on freedom, justice, peace, and the future of the world»[61]. Solidarity with the poor which is a Christian virtue has to take concrete form. It has to be realized at the grass roots level[62]. The Council strongly affirms that the Church is able, indeed it is obliged, if times and circumstances require it, to initiate action for the benefit of all, especially of those in need, such as works of mercy and similar undertakings[63].

1.3.2 Charism: Inner Spirit of BECs

In the BECs one expresses solidarity with the poor and works for the well being of the community according to the charism, he or she receives from God (1 Cor 7,7. 17; 12,7). Charism is a free gift of God to a person for the community[64]. The Council says:

> It is not only through the sacraments and the ministrations of the Church that the Holy Spirit makes holy the People, leads them and enriches them with his virtues. Allotting his gifts according as he wills (cf. Cor 12,11), he also distributes special graces among the faithful of every rank. By these gifts he makes them fit and ready to undertake various tasks and offices for

---

[59] JOHN PAUL II, *Sollicitudo Rei Socialis*, n. 39. See also SCDF, *Instruction on Christian Freedom*, n. 89.

[60] JOHN PAUL II, *Sollicitudo Rei Socialis*, n. 40. See also B. SECONDIN, *Nuovi Cammini dello Spirito*, 49-60.

[61] JOHN PAUL II, *Ut Unum Sint*, n. 43. «There is a new consciousness on the part of the marginalized that the situation is not an inevitable fate but something to be struggled against. Coupled with this is a new consciousness of solidarity — people are not isolated in the struggles against injustice» (*FAPA*, 277).

[62] «To proclaim the universal salvific will of God is in Christ means not just to talk about it, but to make it happen» (M. AMALADOSS, «The Pluralism of Religions», 100. See also J. PADIPURA, *Development and Culture*, 50-64; F. WILFRED, «Human Rights», 62-78.

[63] *GS* 42. See also JOHN PAUL II, *Christifideles Laici*, n. 41; J. SCHASCHING, «From the Class War», 466-481; L. LADARIA, «Humanity in the Light of Christ», 386-401.

[64] For a study on Charism see E.J. MALATESTA, «Charism», 140-143. See also C. MOLARI, «Mezzi per lo sviluppo spirituale», 466-524; L. BOFF, *Church: Charism & Power*, 154-164.

the renewal and building up of the Church, as it is written, «the manifestation of the Spirit is given to every one for profit» 1 Cor 12,7 (*LG* 12).

According to St. Paul the variety of gifts are not something extraordinary or unexpected but for the good of the community (1 Cor 12,4-11). The gifts of God are beyond comparison (Rom 5,15-21). It is functional, so much so everyone enjoys equal dignity[65]. Paul reminds:

> And through the grace that I have been given, I say this to every one of you: never pride yourself on being better than you really are, but think of yourself dispassionately, recognizing that God has given to each one his measure of faith. Just as each of us has various parts in one body, and the parts do not all have the same function: in the same way, all of us, though there are so many of us, make up one body in Christ, and as different parts we are all joined to one another [...] (Rom 12,3-13).

In his description of charism, Paul had the Christian communities in mind. So charism, for Paul, is meant to build up the community.

> Whether they be exceptional and great or simple and ordinary, the charisms are graces of the Holy Spirit that have, directly or indirectly, a usefulness for the ecclesial community, ordered as they are to the building up of the Church, to the well-being of humanity and to the needs of the world[66].

The discerning principle of charisms is love (1 Cor 13,1-13). Love is to be expressed in service. «Welcome each other into your houses without grumbling. Each one of you has received a special grace, so, like good stewards responsible for all these varied graces of God, put it at the service of others» (1 Pet 4,10). In effect, each BEC tries to be at the service of the others. The talents are not hidden (Mt 25,14-30). God's gifts are used for the common good in their diversity[67]. Each BEC creates a more ample space for communion in a dynamic way, beginning

---

[65] «The dignity of the person constitutes *the foundation of the equality of all people among themselves*. As a result all forms of discrimination are totally unacceptable, especially those forms which unfortunately continue to divide and degrade the human family, from those based on race or economics to those social and cultural, from political to geographic, etc. [...] Just as personal dignity is the foundation of equality of all people among themselves, so it is also the *foundation of participation and solidarity of all people among themselves: dialogue and communion are rooted ultimately in what people "are", first and foremost, rather than on what people "have"*» (JOHN PAUL II, *Christifideles Laici*, n. 37).

[66] JOHN PAUL II, *Christifideles Laici*, n. 24

[67] «The great cannot exist without the small, nor the small without the great; there is a certain organization, and it is of benefit to all» (ST. CLEMENT OF ROME, «Letter to the Corinthians», 39). See also E. DUSSEL, «The Differentiation of Charisms», 38-55.

from the smallest and the simplest, towards the definitive up-building of the Kingdom. It is remarkable that St. Paul also instructs the community to regulate the use of the gifts of the Spirit (1 Cor 14,26-32)[68]. Thus, various charisms in BECs will be better discerned and utilized.

1.4 *Living in the Cultural Situation*

The spirituality of BECs is closely linked with the living cultural situation of the people[69]. We saw, in the second chapter, that the important cultural factors are based on the castes. The castes, the Mukkuvar, the Nadar, the Izhavas, and the Dalits with all its derivations, have their own caste identity which may go beyond the norms of established religion. At the same time, these communities try to make a cultural identity. We call it as the *Latin Catholic cultural identity*[70]. This cultural identity is complex. The spirituality of BECs evolves around this cultural complexity[71].

The complexity is deepened by the external factors which are related to the daily life of the people and the internal factors which are fully integrated into the personality of people. The external factors are poverty, illiteracy, homelessness, unemployment, diseases, injustices at work and in society, the privation of fundamental rights, and discrimination because of race, religion and sex[72]. The internal factors

---

[68] See K. KUNNUMPURAM, «Towards A Theology of Ministries», 9-34.

[69] Appreciating the relation between the spirituality and the living cultural situation is one of the concerns of the present day theologians. See M. AMALADOSS, «The Spirituality of Dialogue», 58-69. See also B. UGEUX, «Inculturation», 134-141. Appreciating the spirituality of people in the living situation is not lacking in the history of spirituality also. For example according to Francis de Sales (1567-1622) it is an error, or rather a heresy, to banish the devout life from the regiment of soldiers, the mechanic's shop, the court of princes, or the home of married people. See F. DE SALES, *Introduction to the Devout Life*, 44.

[70] By Latin Catholic cultural identity we mean two things: a Latin liturgical identity and social backwardness.

[71] It is a common phenomenon we see among the people that the same story will be understood differently by the people of differing living situations. For example the story of Joseph in the OT would be understood differently by the people of two cultural situations. The European missionaries see Joseph as a man who *remained faithful to God*. The people of Africa would see Joseph as a man who, no matter how he travelled, *never forgot his family*. For a detailed study of various cultural aspects of practical life see C.H. KRAFT, *Christianity in Culture*. See also P.C. PHAN, «Cultural Diversity», 195-211; F. WILFRED, «Images of Jesus», 51-62.

[72] See JOHN PAUL II, «Address to the Faithful of Kerala», 390. To get a holistic picture of the social situation of the people of Trivandrum see C. LEON, *Sāmūhika*

are those of cultural values inherited from caste consciousness[73], the unity of family and moral principles[74], popular beliefs[75]and religious consciousness inherited from the Indian spiritual tradition which is wrongly understood or interpreted as Hindu tradition[76]. The living cultural situation also includes the new developments that are taking place in the socio-political and religious realms[77].

It is in the above said complex living situation that the people come together as BECs and express their commitment to follow Jesus Christ and love their neighbour. It is in these situations that the people try to combine their faith and life.

2. The Laity in the Threefold Mission of Jesus Christ

Until the Second Vatican Council the place of the laity in the Church was not sufficiently recognized though there is no distinction between 'lay people' and 'clerics' in the vocabulary of the New Testament[78]. As John Paul II observed, there even existed a negative approach towards the laity[79]. It is after the Second Vatican Council that the role of the laity in the Church, their vocation, charism, are being fully recognized. The

---

Sāmbattika Survey Prādhamika Report (Socio-Economic Survey Preliminary Report), 1993.

[73] We have noticed that caste consciousness is becoming an important factor both in politics and in religion.

[74] The unity of family and moral principles are closely interrelated. See JOHN PAUL II, *Letter to Families*, ns. 6-15.

[75] By popular beliefs we mean those beliefs which are inherited from the age long tradition. For example, most of the people look at a inauspicious hour of the day known as *rāhu-kala* for blessing of a house, for marriage ceremony, laying the foundation stone of a building. The popular beliefs come from the popular culture. Nowadays scholars used to speak of the influence of powerful «popular tradition» or «the little tradition» in India against the minority «dominant» or «great tradition» (P. PUTHANANGADY, «Which Culture for Inculturation?», 295-309).

[76] For example the *Gayatri Mantra*, a hymn sung in the Hindu Temples or the *Santi Mantra*, a prayer, recited in the Āsram is part of Indian tradition. See D.S. AMALORPAVADASS, «A Theology of Mission in India», 323-346.

[77] We have noticed that caste consciousness is becoming an important factor both in politics and in religion.

[78] Y. CONGAR, *Lay People in the Church*, 27.

[79] See JOHN PAUL II, *Christifideles Laici*, n. 9.

laity, through the sacrament of baptism, is incorporated into Jesus Christ, and share the priestly, prophetic and kingly office of Jesus Christ[80].

> The participation of the lay faithful in the threefold mission of Christ as Priest, Prophet and King finds its source in the anointing of Baptism, its further development in Confirmation and its realization and dynamic sustenance in the Holy Eucharist. It is a participation given to each member of the lay faithful *individually*, in as much as each is one of the *many* who form the *one Body* of the Lord: in fact, Jesus showers his gifts upon the Church which is his Body and his Spouse. In such a way individuals are sharers in the threefold mission of Christ in virtue of their being members of the Church, as St. Peter clearly teaches, when he defines the baptized as «a chosen race, a royal priesthood, a holy nation, God's own people» (1 Pet 2,9). Precisely because it derives *from* Church *communion*, the sharing of the lay faithful in the threefold mission of Christ requires that it be live and realized in *communion* and *for the increase of communion itself*[81].

Being partakers of the threefold mission of Jesus Christ, the laity obtain the common dignity or the baptismal dignity which gives them autonomy in the Church.

2.1 *Autonomy of the Laity*

Derived from the baptismal dignity, the lay faithful obtain the filial grace and the identical vocation to perfection. They share a responsibility, together with the ordained ministers and men and women religious, for the Church's mission[82]. The Council exhorts:

> The laity, however, are given special vocation: to make the Church present and fruitful in those places and circumstances where it is only through them that she can become the salt of the earth. Thus, every lay person, through those gifts given to him, is at once the witness and the living instrument of the mission of the Church itself «according to the measure of Christ's bestowal» Eph 4,7 (*LG* 33).

The special vocation of the lay faithful implies a secular character which is properly and particularly theirs. It is deeply rooted in the mystery of the Word Incarnate, and which is realized in different forms

---

[80] See *LG* 30-38. For an extensive treatment on lay faithful see *CCC*, ns. 897-913; Y. CONGAR, *Lay People in the Church*, 121-323. T. GOFFI, «Tracce di vita», 404-465; A. BARRUFFO, «Laico», 810-828; B. SECONDIN, *I Nuovi Protagonisti*, 207-230.

[81] JOHN PAUL II, *Christifideles Laici*, n. 14.

[82] JOHN PAUL II, *Christifideles Laici*, n. 15.

through her members[83]. It is exercised as individuals and as groups[84]. The Council says:

> The faithful are called as individuals to exercise an apostolate in the various conditions of their life. They must, however, remember that man is social by nature and that it has been God's pleasure to assemble those who believe in Christ and make of them the People of God (cf. 1 Pet 2,5-10), a single body (cf. 1 Cor 12,12) (*AA* 18).

The Council, reading the signs of the time further exhorts: «In present circumstances it is supremely necessary that wherever the laity are at work the apostolate under its collective and organized form should be strengthened» (*AA* 18). The Council also recognizes the right of the laity, with necessary link with the ecclesiastical authority, to establish and direct associations and to join in the existing ones[85].

2.2 *Autonomy of BECs*

The autonomy of the laity necessarily follows the autonomy of the BECs. In the BECs the lay people share their baptismal dignity to exercise their priestly, kingly and prophetic mission of Jesus Christ in a concrete situation[86]. The autonomy which a BEC experiences in the concrete situation inspires its members to be creative ministers of the Church in the modern world. Each BEC has to enjoy its autonomy not only in electing its members to parish pastoral council but also in conducting each BEC gathering, in celebrating the liturgy of the Word in the BEC gatherings, in composing hymns, in adapting new symbols.

Since the BECs share a secular character, each BEC becomes a prophetic sign. Because of its secular character the BECs not only animate the world with the spirit of Christianity, but also witness Jesus Christ in all the circumstances of humankind[87]. In this context what the Council says of the laity is also applicable to the BECs. The Council says:

> It is to the laity, though not exclusively to them, that secular duties and activity properly belong. When therefore, as citizens of the world, they are engaged in any activity either individually or collectively, they will not be

---

[83] See JOHN PAUL II, *Christifideles Laici*, n. 15.

[84] See *A A* 17-19. See also JOHN PAUL II, *Christifideles Laici*, n. 29

[85] See *AA* 19. See also *CIC*, n, 215. Many a time the teachings of the Church are not given any attention because of clericalism. See B. SECONDIN, *I Nuovi Protagonisti*, 207-218. See also J. NEUNER, «Paths of Mission», 259-267.

[86] See A.L. PICARDAL, *An Ecclesiological Perspective*, 124-258.

[87] See *GS* 43.

satisfied with meeting the minimum legal requirements but will strive to become truly proficient in that sphere. They will gladly cooperate with others working towards the same objectives. Let them be aware of what their faith demands of them in these matters and derive strength from it; let them not hesitate to take the initiative at the opportune moment and put their findings into effect. It is their task to cultivate a properly informed conscience and to impress the divine law on the affairs of the earthly city (*GS* 43).

Another important factor we see in the BECs is the autonomy within the members — adults, youth and children. In its autonomy, each group whether adults or youth or children has its own specific role. Pope John Paul II observes: «Within them, the individual Christian experiences community and therefore senses that he or she is playing an active role and is encouraged to share in the common task»[88].

3. Challenges of BECs

Although BECs in Trivandrum are the out-come of the renewal programme initiated in 1987, they became a diocesan pastoral option only in 1991. Since they are of recent development in the local Church of Trivandrum (a contemporary phenomenon) we still need time to assess how far BECs have become part of the ecclesial culture of the people. Some priests have not yet accepted the BEC model as the best means to proclaim the Gospel in the Diocese. However, looking forward to the third millennium, the BEC model gives hope for the future mission of the Church in India and in that respect the BECs have an important role to play at present. Therefore, the BECs have to be sensitive to the challenges of the time.

The challenges of BECs are posed in this way. How far can BECs be «light» and «salt» in the local Church of Trivandrum and in the other local Churches? How far can BECs in Trivandrum, by reading the signs of the time, function with the spirit of *aggiornamento* on the one hand and *ad gentes* thrust on the other hand?

3.1 *Challenges of BECs Within in the Diocese*

One of the greatest challenges of BECs is to live the Christian faith in the day to day life. «One of the gravest errors of our time is the dichotomy between the faith which many profess and the practice of their

---

[88] JOHN PAUL II, *Redemptoris Missio*, n. 51.

daily lives» (*GS* 43). An issue based coming together cannot create a lasting ecclesial community. It cannot witnesses Jesus Christ and proclaim the message of the Kingdom. If the BECs gather only based on issues, whatever be their nature, it deviates from the true spirit of the Church of Jesus Christ. We have also observed in the fourth chapter that not all the priests have accepted the vision of the BECs.

Too much institutionalization of BECs may produce counter results. The people will find no difference between the well established hierarchical model and the new BEC model of the Church. The new model can be promising in any context only when it takes Jesus Christ's compassion as the guiding principle, and a *diaconal* approach in its leadership.

3.1.1 To Live the Christian Faith

It is true that the BECs are growing up in the midst of various socio-political issues. The fight against illicit distillation of alcohol, the efforts to irradicate illiteracy, the fight for justice when Christians are persecuted, and the struggle for minority rights[89] give a new vitality to the members of the BECs. The most important factor is that BECs are the protagonists in all these issues and the BECs in Trivandrum showed their ability to respond to the different needs of the society. To a large extent the response of the BECs was also a success[90]. But the coming together of Christians as BECs has a still deeper meaning[91]. It is not a

---

[89] On 21st August the Latin Catholics of Trivandrum from all the castes conducted a «Secretariat March» against the denial of reservations ensured in the Indian Constitution. The «Secretariat March» was organized through the BECs.

[90] It is a common phenomenon that when something affects the whole community or a society, the people unite together and react to it. In Trivandrum the upper cloth struggle, temple entry struggle and fishermen agitation are typical examples of this sort.

[91] The very fact that the BECs could attract people of other faith is because of the deeper spiritual experience which the people get from the Word of God and the Christian fellowship. C. Boff rightly observes in the context of Brazil like this: «I remember when I was in a small diocese in the interior of Brazil which held a synod for pastoral workers. The books provided for them had two special chapters on spiritual renewal. We had prepared a programme for base communities, with the usual treatment of the bible, the formation of community, participation, social questions, etc. But the members of the base communities asked why they should not be concerned also about spirituality. They wanted this. This whole question of the hunger for spirituality needs to be studied, because people want it» (C. BOFF, «The Church in Latin America», 131-132).

social grouping alone[92]. First of all they come together because they are called. They come as *ekklēsia*[93]. They are called by the triune God. They are called to have communion with the triune God and communion with the people of God. This communion, without doubt, is realized in the sacraments and especially in the Eucharist. And it is from the Eucharist, which can be even celebrated in the BEC gatherings, that all the activities of the Church are directed[94]. The BECs in its *pilgrimage* of a new way of being the Church celebrates the Word of God and takes its nourishment from the Eucharist, the culmination of all the sacraments. In this regard what the Puebla Conference said about the authentic ecclesial community is worth mentioning:

> As a community, the CEB [BEC] brings together families, adults and young people, in an intimate interpersonal relationship grounded in the faith. As an ecclesial reality, it is a community of faith, hope and charity. It celebrates the Word of God and takes its nourishment from the Eucharist, the culmination of all the sacraments. It fleshes out the Word of God in life through solidarity and commitment to the new commandment of the Lord; and through the service of approved coordinators, it makes present and operative the mission of the Church and its visible communion with the legitimate pastors. It is a base-level community because it is composed of relatively few members as a permanent body, like a cell of the larger community[95].

3.1.2 Approach to Social Issues

The BECs are not just pious associations. If they are mere pious associations it is enough to gather in the churches. At the same time the BECs have to «embody the Church's preferential love for the common people»[96] and have to take up issues which affect the human life in all its dimensions in the light of the teachings of the Church[97]. Here the BECs

---

[92] See JOHN PAUL II, *Evangelii Nuntiandi*, n. 58. See also ID., *Ecclesia in Africa*, n. 89; B. SECONDIN, *I Nuovi Protagonisti*, 142-147.

[93] See our discussion on «Church» in the first chapter.

[94] See *SC* 10. «no Christian community is built up which does not grow from and hinge on the celebration of the most holy Eucharist. From this all education for community spirit must begin» (*PO* 6). See also E. RUFFINI, «Eucaristia», 601-622.

[95] «Puebla Final Document» n. 641 [J. EAGLESON – P. SCHARPER, *Puebla and Beyond*, 212].

[96] «Puebla Final Document» n. 643 [J. EAGLESON – P. SCHARPER, *Puebla and Beyond*, 213].

[97] It is the prime duty of any government to look into the social welfare of its citizens. But in effect even the democratically elected governments effectively move towards a

differ also from the nature of pious associations or even those movements which close the eyes to the social needs of the people. John Paul II holds the strong view that every community has a responsibility to respond to the needs of the people in the concrete situations:

> The Church well knows that *no temporal achievement* is to be identified with the Kingdom of God, but that all such achievements simply *reflect* and in a sense *anticipate* the glory of the Kingdom, the Kingdom which we await at the end of history, when the Lord will come again. But that expectation can never be an excuse for lack of concern for the people in their concrete personal situations and in their social, national and international life, since the former is conditioned by the latter, especially today[98].

In taking up social issues the BECs cannot be narrow minded. If the BECs take up issues only related to the Latin Catholics of Trivandrum they cannot claim to be the «light of the nations». It might also fail to be the «joy and hope» of the modern world. Instead, joining with other religious and secular organizations the BECs have to work for the common good of the «People of God».

3.1.3 Institutionalization?

Another challenge of BECs in the Diocese is from its very structure. Though the idea of the participatory Church was the long cherished desire of the lay people, the form and structure of BECs came from above[99]. The structure is organized in such a way that no one in the Diocese is excluded from the BECs. In other words, everyone becomes automatically a *member* of BEC. The automatic membership has both positive and negative effects. Positively we can say that all are included in any one of the BECs and negatively a member need not be a participant in the BEC which in turn demands personal commitment.

Since the formation of BECs is the pastoral option of the Diocese, we find a great effort on the part of priests, religious and lay animators to bring everyone to the BEC gatherings. In this process a tendency to

---

form of totalitarianism. See JOHN PAUL II, *Evangelium Vitae*, n. 20. Bishop M.S. Pakiam, in his pastoral letter on 3rd January 1995, reminded the people about the importance of being familiar with the social teachings of the Church.

[98] JOHN PAUL II, *Sollicitudo Rei Socialis*, n. 48. See also ID., *Ecclesia in Africa*, n. 109.

[99] This is the phenomenon we see in Latin American, in Africa and in Asia. The greater initiative comes from the bishops or priests or religious who have been committed to the people's cause.

institutionalize the whole programme is seen, forgetting the spirit of the
BECs[100]. The question is how far a *member* can remain, without
participating in the BEC gatherings. What is the reaction of the
participants towards the non-participants?[101] Are the BECs tempted to
say that there is salvation only through BECs?

3.1.4 BECs and the Parish Structure

Though BECs are the new way of being the Church the foundations of
Christian faith are provided not in the BECs but in the parishes.

> The *parish* carries out a function that is, in a way, an integral ecclesial
> function because it accompanies persons and families throughout their lives,
> fostering their education and growth in the faith. It is a centre of
> coordination and guidance for communities, groups, and movements. In it
> the horizons of communion and participation are opened up even more. The
> celebration of the Eucharist and other sacraments makes the global reality of
> the Church present in a clearer way[102].

In Trivandrum, the diocesan structures are set up on the basis of the
BECs. As a result, one cannot become a member of the pastoral council
unless one does frequent the BEC gatherings. The problem comes when
BECs begin to dictate norms about those who do not participate in the
gatherings. Tension may arise if BECs insist that one should pass through

---

100 *Institution* is needed if it does not lose the original vision of a programme. For the
positive and negative aspects of the Church seen as Institution see A. DULLES, *Models of
the Church*, 34-46. «Every inspired idea goes through a similar evolution, whether it is
in society or in the Church. It happened to the religious orders, to theological schools,
pious and devotional movements, and to lay religious organizations. A prophetic
movement that is incapable of becoming a stable institution will die or disappear. It may
leave behind memories, stamp its mark upon history, and build an occasional monument
to its passage through time, but it will disappear nonetheless» (J. COMBLIN «Brazil: Base
Communities», 201-202).

101 In the BEC conventions conducted in 1994 in all the Vicariates the question about
the non-participants was discussed. The question was «how to bring together the people
who are not participating in the BECs?» This question was discussed in the seminars
conducted on the days of BEC Vicariate conventions. Though the aspect of compassion
was reflected in the discussions towards the non-participants, some of them thought that
BECs should be institutionalized. See W. LOURDAYYAN, *Report on the BEC Convention*,
ADT. In some of the BEC meetings which I attended, the same question was discussed
informally. The spontaneous reaction of at least some of the members was to make the
structure of BECs very rigid.

102 «Puebla Final Document» n. 644 [J. EAGLESON and P. SCHARPER, *Puebla and
Beyond*, 213]. For the practical problems related to the structure of BECs see
J. COMBLIN, «Brazil: Base Communities», 201-225.

the BECs for parish services like baptism, confirmation and marriage[103]. Sometimes priests also will insist that participation in the BECs is essential to receive the sacraments. Such administrative or bureaucratic attitudes defeat the spirit of the BECs and ultimately the spirit of the Church[104].

3.1.5 Compassion

Another important challenge of the BECs is to show Jesus Christ's concern and compassion to everyone. If the greatest value of spirituality is love, it must express itself in terms of compassion[105]. It is through compassion that BECs can present a correct image of God. The compassion of God is such that «*not even the murderer loses his personal dignity*, and God himself pledges to guarantee this»[106]. And John Paul II sees in the compassion of God «*the paradoxical mystery of the merciful justice of God*»[107].

---

[103] In the context of Trivandrum, at least in some parishes the parish councils impose certain *regulations* which do not correspond with the spirit of the Church. One such case is when a person from other denomination or religion wishes to accept the Catholic faith, the parish councils impose certain *rules*. To impose certain pastoral regulations is easier than to show Jesus Christ's concern and compassion. In the case of mixed marriages also the local Churches in Kerala cling to pastoral reasons which in no way express the mind of the Church. To compare the situation in Brazil see J. COMBLIN, «Brazil: Base Communities», 206-208. According to C. Boff, the Sects know how to receive newcomers, how to welcome them and make them feel at home. They know how to put the believer in direct contact with Jesus Christ, with the Holy Spirit and with the Father without any institutionalized intermediary. They can give believers a real ecclesial feelings, with the conviction of being part of the Church, in touch with God, responsible for mission, battling with the devil. They are in immediate touch with God, whereas Catholics have to go through a whole series of mediators. See C. BOFF, «The Church in Latin America», 139-140.

[104] «In a servant Church, the structures of the Church herself are at the service of the Gospel and of the people. Church structures were developed to support the mission of the Church. Thus structures are for the Church, not the Church for structures. The Gospel, not canon law, is the guide and guard of the Church. The Church is a community. As such, her laws and social structures should not stand in the way of her faith communication» (*FAPA*, 340).

[105] It is «to suffer with, to go where it hurts, to be with people in their suffering before we do anything for them. Ultimately, it means achieving solidarity with them in the same way Jesus showed solidarity with them. As we cannot understand the poor without Jesus, neither can we understand compassion independently of Jesus» (J. FUELLENBACH, *Hermeneutics*, 148).

[106] JOHN PAUL II, *Evangelium Vitae*, n. 9.

[107] JOHN PAUL II, *Evangelium Vitae*, n. 9

In sending Moses to liberate the people of Israel God says to Moses: «I have indeed seen the misery of my people in Egypt. I have heard them crying for help on account of their task-masters. Yes, I am well aware of their sufferings» (Ex 3,7). Here we see the God who is directly involved in the misery of humankind[108]. Jesus Christ further describes the nature of God when he says: «Be compassionate just as your Father is compassionate» (Lk 6,36)[109]. The compassion takes the form of courage and it breaks the human imposed barriers. Jesus Christ's compassion leads to courage so as to break the barrier between Jews and Samaritans (Jn 4,1-42). It is from the compassion that a new diaconal leadership emerges.

3.1.6 *Diaconal* Leadership

From our previous study it is clear that the BECs try to actualize the ecclesiological vision of *diakonia* which has been rediscovered with Vatican II[110]. The assurance of people's participation in the administrative structures of the parish and the Diocese is the realization of the *diaconal* vision evolved in the local Church of Trivandrum.

In the Church, «lay members of the Christian faithful can cooperate in the exercise of this power [of governance] in accordance with the norm of law». And so the Church provides for their presence at particular councils, diocesan synods, pastoral councils; the exercise in solidum of the pastoral care of a parish, collaboration in finance committees, and participation in ecclesiastical tribunals, etc.[111]

---

[108] The aspect of compassion is well developed in Liberation Theologies beginning from 1970.

[109] The word «compassion» comprises the whole message of Jesus Christ. The compassion of Jesus Christ is not giving some *help* to a person but to make him aware of his or her human dignity. In the Gospel the most loyal followers were people who had been given a sense of dignity and hope. Magdalen, Levi and Peter are some among them. In the final analysis only the attitude of compassion can sustain a Christian community. The starting point of liberation theology is also the compassion of God to the poor and the needy. See PBC, *The Interpretation of the Bible*, 63-66. See also SCDF, *Instruction on certain aspects of the «Theology of Liberation»*; G. GUTIÉRREZ, *A Theology of Liberation*.

[110] «The Church is not motivated by an earthly ambition but is interested in one thing only — to carry on the work of Christ under the guidance of the Holy Spirit, for he came into the world to bear witness to the truth, to save and not to judge, to serve and not to be served» (*GS* 3). For a detailed study on the ecclesiological vision of service see A. DULLES, *Models of the Church*, 89-102. See also M.M. THOMAS, *A Diaconal Approach*.

[111] See *CCC*, n. 911. See also *CIC*, Can. 129§ 2.

To put into practice this vision the *diaconal* leadership is a challenge to the consecrated ministers especially in the Indian Church which has been known for its clericalism.

Another aspect of *diaconal* leadership is the ability to work with others and share the responsibility of the Church and society. The enormous increase of lay leadership in the local Church of Trivandrum has to be considered as a blessing rather than a threat to the ministerial service of a priest. «They should unite their efforts with those of lay faithful and conduct themselves among them after the example of the Master, who came amongst men "not to be served but to serve, and to give his life as a ransom for many" (Mt 20,28)» (*PO* 9).

In the Diocese of Trivandrum some priests feel that they cannot cope with the new system especially with regard to the administration of the parish. Although a good number of lay leaders feel that the BECs will function in the Diocese even if the priests do not cooperate, the risk of non-effectiveness cannot be denied. For example, in a parish where more than fifty BECs functioned, the parish priest was able to remove the coordinator of BECs from the parish without any prior information and without any request from the animators of the BECs from the parish[112]. The effect of such reaction is evident in those parishes where BECs are supported and encouraged by the priests and those parishes which are not guided by the priests. Neverthless, the future priests, permanent deacons which we foresee in the near future, religious men and women, catechists will be born from these communities, bearing a new Christian culture of service.

The role of the lay ministers of BECs is so important that it is they who work for the communion of each BECs within the parish, within the Diocese and within the universal Church. So much so, the lay leaders have to transmit not their own thinking or doctrine, but that which they learn and receive from the Church. In any case, each leader or animator of the BECs is much more than a teacher, he or she is a witness, and the

---

[112] The person who was removed from the responsibility still does not know the reason why he was removed. Though it may be a rare incident the distorted understanding of the *power* of parish priests is a major factor. In this context what C. Boff says is worth mentioning: «The structures for participation are there in place, but all of them can be reversed at a stroke, changed overnight, with the arrival of a new bishop or a change of a parish priest. Even the most thriving community of participation can be reduced to nought. We have so many sad experiences of this kind. The problem is that none of these very successful experiences have any structural, juridical guarantee to enable them to continue. The new developments have not been institutionalized, recognized in law» (C. Boff, «The Church in Latin America», 137).

community has the right to receive from him or her a persuasive example of Christian life, of a dynamic and radiating faith, of disinterested love[113].

As we have observed in the previous chapter the lay people give respect to the priests but the lay people also do expect that the consecrated ministers are real followers of Jesus Christ who gave a deeper meaning to service by washing the feet of his disciples (Jn 13,1-13)[114]. The *diaconal* commitment demands more openness and accountability to the people not only in the parishes but also in the institutions whether they belong to religious or to diocese[115].

From the *diaconal* commitment of both the consecrated ministers and lay ministers a new collegial style of leadership can emerge. Such a leadership will be ready to do *the washing of the feet* of the other. The consecrated ministers will realize that they are not called to dominate over others but to serve the people of God, respecting the common priesthood that derives from baptism[116]. And in such an emptying of oneself the message of the Gospel will be proclaimed.

---

[113] See JOHN PAUL II, «Mensagem deixada às comunidades eclesiais de base», 257-261.

[114] It is laudable that auxiliary bishop Vincent Concessao, New Delhi, before the consecration, as a symbol of service to humanity, instead of honour, washed the feet of six people representing various sections of the society. See I.P. SARTO, «Delhi Auxiliary Consecrated», 1-2.

[115] The Church in India is well known for its instituionalism and clericalism. In most of the cases the religious congregations and the leaders of the Church fail to be open to the people they serve. «The financial management of the church suffers very much in the absence of talents and skills. We refuse to open our account books to lay people except to income tax Officers. This unnecessary shroud of secrecy creates heavy loss, suspicion and hostility!» (K.T. SEBASTIAN – S. ZACHARIA, «The Role of the Laity», 218). As regards the religious too the lay authors are critical. They say: «today what image of major religious congregations in the mind of an ordinary lay man? He feels that these congregations are like multinational companies! They have no accountability to the local church — neither to the bishop nor to the laity» (*Ibid.*, 218). See also *CBCI Evaluation Report*, n. 749.

[116] See JOHN PAUL II, *Letter to Priests*, 1995, n. 7. See also ID., *Letter to Women*, 1995, n. 11. «We dream of a servant Church: servant of God, servant of Christ, servant of his plan of salvation; servant also of the Asian peoples, of their deep hopes, longings and aspirations; servant of the followers of other religions, of all women and men, simply and totally for others» (*FAPA*, 340).

3.1.7 BECs: Nurseries of Political Leaders

One of the important achievements of BECs in general is the emergence of various lay leaders in the Church[117]. According to John Paul II Christians who occupy positions of responsibility are to be carefully prepared for political, economic and social tasks by means of a solid formation in the Church's social doctrine, so that in their places of work they will be faithful witnesses to the Gospel[118]. Formation of good political leaders has become a vital subject in Asia too.

> The involvement of the lay person in political activity confirms his/her rootedness in Christ, who called his community of disciples to be a leaven in the world and thus to labor for the common good. A Christian is a member of a God-peopled and of the wider community, the good of which he/she is called to promote, protect and serve. To shut oneself totally away from the demands of the political transformation of Asia is, surely, in a sense, a denial of Christianity[119].

In the Diocese of Trivandrum, BECs are also becoming the nurseries of future political leaders. It is a fact that a great number of the BECs, despite their social commitment, are not in favour of discussing political matters in the BEC gatherings. Nevertheless, we have noticed that the poor wish to discuss political matters in the BECs.

In the particular context of Kerala, where high political polarization takes place on the basis of caste and religion, the BECs have to take up a prophetic challenge to form good political leaders[120].

3.2 BECs and Their Missionary Thrust

The Church by its very nature is missionary and every Christian by his/her baptism is consecrated to the mission of Christ. One of the important concerns of the Church, especially as it prepares for the great Jubilee, is to illustrate and explain the truth that Jesus Christ is the one Mediator between God and humanity and the sole Redeemer of the

---

117 See B. SECONDIN, Segni di Profezia, 287-291.

118 See JOHN PAUL II, Ecclesia in Africa, n. 90. See also ID., Evangelium Vitae, n. 93. See also GS 74. See also KCBC, Nāmārum Annyaralla (We are not Strangers to each Other), 5-6.

119 FAPA, 180.

120 «The need of the hour in Asia is for competent and principled lay people to enter into the realm of party politics and, from within, influence the philosophies, programs and activities of political parties and personalities for the common good in the light of the Gospel» (FAPA, 180).

world, to be clearly distinguished from the founders of other great religions[121]. In India, after Vatican II, we see that there has been a lack of clarity as regards the missionary vision of the Church. As the CBCI Evaluation Committee observes, for many Christians, the Church is a body that is meant for the welfare of the Catholic community only, instead of being a community that has been entrusted with a mission[122]. The message of Jesus Christ cannot be presented to the modern man and woman with simple theoretical explanations or only with apologetical arguments[123]. The method to achieve this mission depends on each local Church.

In Trivandrum, because of the particular cultural situation, we find better chances for evangelization. We have noticed that in many of the BECs people from other religions participate. The participation of people from other faiths in the prayer meetings prior to the BECs was not a rare phenomenon. Nevertheless, a growing interest is seen among the Catholics to invite brothers and sisters of other faiths to their BEC gatherings. Another feature of the present missionary thrust in the BECs is that unlike the previous times the lay people show much interest in preaching the Word of God. As Pope Paul VI envisaged, the BECs are privileged to receive the Gospel and are becoming the proclaimers of the Gospel[124]. The increase in the number of priestly vocations and vocation to religious life from Trivandrum is to be seen in light of this missionary thrust.

3.3 Relation to Other Local Churches

The local Church of Trivandrum, is the first Diocese in Kerala which has taken BEC as its pastoral option in its full sense[125]. The Diocese

---

[121] See JOHN PAUL II, *Tertio Millennio Adveniente*, n. 38. «The Years leading up to the Jubilee should become a time of hope for the Church in India!" (ID., «Il Vangelo vi rafforzi», 7).

[122] *CBCI Evaluation Report*, n. 794. «We welcome the decision of the Council to recognize the equal status of Oriental rites in the Church and so to resist its total Latinization. Still it is deplorable that at a time when all energy and resources of the Church should be used to face the immense problems of the country and the growth of a truly Indian Church in this vast nation much work is lost in rivalry and competition» (J. NEUNER, «Paths of Mission», 262).

[123] See J.E. BIFET, *Spirituality for a Missionary Church*, 45-88.

[124] See PAUL VI, *Evangelii Nuntiandi*, n. 58

[125] By the term «full sense» we mean all the parish and diocesan activities are based on the BECs.

functions as a communion of BECs. This communion of BECs takes up a new initiative of communion with other BECs in other local Churches in Kerala and outside Kerala. The «Inter-diocesan Seminar» organized for the BEC leaders of the dioceses of Trivandrum, Quilon and Kottar (Tamil Nadu) on 25th January 1995[126], and the All Kerala Seminar on «Community Building» from 1st to 5th May 1995[127] deserve special attention. It has been observed that in both seminars the lived experience of the BECs in Trivandrum was highly appreciated[128]. The seminar gave also an occasion to recognize the common problems of different local Churches in the same region. And the possibility of witnessing Jesus Christ despite the Rite differences was realized in the community building seminar[129].

At present most of the local Churches in India are moving in the direction of BECs[130]. There are some dioceses still having anxiety about accepting BEC as the pastoral option in their dioceses, though the renewal is taking place through the Bible sharing groups following the *7 steps method* introduced by the Lumko Institute. Already in 1978 the Diocese of Kottar moved in this direction and at present there are 1698 BECs functioning[131]. There are 10.000 lay animators associated with

---

[126] There were fifty-two participants including priests, religious and lay animators who took part in this seminar. It is worth mentioning that nearly 5.000 BECs function in these dioceses. The most important factor is that all these dioceses have people belonging to different castes and cultural backgrounds. The initial problems connected with the formation of BECs were also the same. See R.B. GREGORY, *Inter-diocesan BCC Seminar Report*, ADT.

[127] See ANTONIETTA, *Report of the All Kerala Workshop*, 1-3, ADT.

[128] In the second seminar there were sixty representatives from fourteen dioceses. The presence of Bishop B. Penha, the Chairman of the CBCI Commission for Laity; Bishop M.S. Pakiam, member of the CBCI Commission for Laity; Frs. V. Thomas the out going Secretary of the CBCI Commission for Laity; A. Fernandez, the new Secretary of the CBCI Commission for Laity; Sr. Antonietta the Animator of the CBCI Commission for Laity shows the concern and commitment of the National Team in executing the vision of the Church in India towards the formation of BECs in each local Church.

[129] We notice that in the seminar there were participants from Oriental Churches too. See ANTONIETTA, *Report of the All Kerala Workshop*, 2, ADT

[130] See R. TIGGA, «Churches Moving», 3. «A new trend which seems to have gained a fair amount of popularity in a certain parts of the country is the formation and growth of Basic Christian Communities. There are strong appeals from respondents that these communities should be formed all over the country» (*CBCI Evaluation Report*, n. 632).

[131] According to the official report there are 1698 BECs in 183 villages in the four Vicariates. See DIOCESE OF KOTTAR, *Newsletter*, 99.

BECs in the Archdiocese of Bombay[132]. The diocese of Quilon has BECs as its pastoral option since 1992, and there 1.500 BECs are functioning at present[133]. Msgr. L. Coutinho writes about the BECs in Goa like this:

in this Archdiocese of Goa our prime pastoral concern is focused on the formation of Small Christian Communities, which when established on a solid basis, will hopefully contribute to turn each parish from administrative and bureaucratic unit into a real «family of God», a big community made up of small communities». He adds, «It is not a question of simply adding new structures to the existing ones, but rather of creating by all means a new spirit[134].

The relation of BECs with other BECs in the same region and other regions opens the way for a new communion of communities in India[135]. Such a communion broadens the ecclesial life of the Church in India at large which has been wounded by divisions of various kinds especially on the basis of Rites[136]. This also makes a break-through in the *introvert* approach of each BEC or local Church to an *ecclesiastical exchange* with a *horizontal dimension*[137] of the communion (*koinōnia*) taking up a new initiative for the missionary Church of India. It is a fact that a renewal of

---

[132] Personal interview with Bishop B. Penha on 21-6-1994. In the Archdiocese of Bombay the BEC programme was initiated with the Bombay Synodal decision in 1980. The decision began to be realized from 1984. See B. PENHA, «Revitalization of the Church», 55-62. The contribution of Bishop B. Penha deserves special mentioning in spreading the vision of BECs in many parts of India. He writes: «On the regional level we have tried to conscientize other dioceses of the Western Region [...]. We have also tried to reach out to other dioceses in India. I have personally visited several dioceses on this mission — Ahmedabad, Bangalore (the Redemptorists) Baroda, Belgaum, Calcutta, Goa, Khandwa, Kottar, Mangalore, Mysore, Nashik, Port Blaair, Pune, Rajkot and Trivandrum» (B. PENHA, «Small Christian Communities», 1-2). See also ID., «Small Christian Communities Must Be Missionary», 1-2.

[133] See R. ANTONY, *Report of the Committee for the Formation of BCCs*, PPn. On 25th May Bishop J.G. Fernandez of Quilon has written a pastoral letter exhorting the urgent need of the formation of BECs. See J.G. FERNANDEZ, *A ṭistāna Kraistava Samūhaṇgal* (Pastoral Letter on BECs).

[134] L. COUTINHO, «More Brothers than Fathers», 1-2.

[135] B. PENHA, «Small Christian Communities Must Be Missionary», 1-2.

[136] The seriousness of the division on the basis of Rites is reflected even among the theologians of India who have to be the prophets of the Indian Church. See S. ARULSAMY, «Some Comments», 67-71.

[137] See W. BÜHLMANN, «The Mission of the Church», 313-322. During the process of the CBCI Evaluation there was a widespread realization that there should be an effective link from grassroots to the national level and vice versa. See *CBCI Evaluation Report*, n. 779.

missionary spirit in the present context of India is possible only through the local Churches and especially through the BECs.

This is a new initiative because already in 1977 the Bishops of Asia did think about the formation of BECs in every diocese in Asia as the best means of evangelization and incarnating the Church in the living culture[138]. The «Church in India Today» seminar held in the light of Vatican II shows the dream of the Church in India to incarnate the ecclesial life in the cultural situations of India. Unfortunately, instead of incarnating the Church in the cultural situation we witnessed the institutional growth of the Church in India. It is in this context of such a institutionalization that we see the emergence of BECs in many local Churches in India. In this regard the observation of J. Neuner is important. He says:

> In keeping with the ecclesiology of the Council the life of the Church must be understood not merely as activity of hierarchy and clergy but as the unfolding of the Christian community in the frame of the social and cultural conditions of each nation. The emphasis on the responsibility of the laity is of special significance in the strongly clerical Indian Church. Through the laity the message of Jesus Christ is present and must become effective in the many secular spheres of Indian society. Lay people, however, must find their legitimate place also in the Church itself, in planning, decision-making and apostolic involvement. Much of it is realized in basic communities which are being formed in many regions[139].

4. Promise of A New Vision: Church as Communion of Communities

Our research so far led us to the belief that BECs are a «cause for great hope for the life of the Church»[140] especially in the local Church of Trivandrum. The BECs function in the local Church of Trivandrum in communion with the universal Church. It is in this communion we find the unity and catholicity of the BECs. St. Paul says: «If one part is hurt, all the parts share its pain. And if one part is honoured, all the parts share its joy. Now Christ's body is yourselves, each of you with a part to play in the whole»(1Cor 12,26-27). Pope John Paul II has rightly said: «It has always been necessary for local Churches to assist and support one another, especially to assist those who are near and those with the

---

[138] See *FAPA*, 67-92.148-152.

[139] See J. NEUNER, «Paths of Mission in India», 264-265.

[140] JOHN PAUL II, *Redemptoris Missio*, n. 51.

greatest needs. Such actions foster communion among these Churches and show *the fruitful nature of the catholicity* of the Church»[141].

The BECs try to live the spirit of the early Christian communities despite some failures. In living the spirit of the early Christian communities the BECs give a great witness to the people who live around them. The Holy Spirit which guided the first Christian community to accept «Cornelius» and «Saul» challenges the BECs in Trivandrum to have a communion with God's people in the local situations for the realization of the Kingdom of God.

The BECs in Trivandrum, despite its vitality, functions in the «Third World» context. They carry the ethos of the BECs of Latin America, Africa and other Asian countries. More similarities than differences have been noticed in the functioning of BECs in most of these countries. So the BECs in Trivandrum can function in solidarity with other BECs of the developing countries[142]. Such an expression of solidarity may inspire those countries which are estranged from «Christian roots»[143].

Since there is a change in the relation between third world countries and first world countries on economic bases, is it not possible to have a meaningful sharing of pastoral experiences between the Churches of the first worlds and the third world? According to M.de C. Azevedo just as Europe launched out to share with others around the world from the abundance of its culture and religiosity, the entire first world must now open itself to receive from those who are seemingly inferior and poor. In fact, the poor can give first world Christians the vital capacity to be intuitive and to relate to others[144].

---

[141] JOHN PAUL II, L'Omelia durante la concelebrazione Eucaristica», 1543. See also *LG* 13.

[142] Recent development in the Archdiocese of Adelaide in Australia shows that the BEC model is effective also in the developed countries. According to Archbishop Leonard Faulkner the emergence of BECs is the work of the Holy Spirit in our time. See M. HEBBLETHWAITE, «Earthing the Church», 11.

[143] «The *more the West is becoming estranged from its Christian roots, the more it is becoming missionary territory,* taking the form of many different "areopagi"»(JOHN PAUL II, *Tertio Millennio Adveniente,* n. 57). See also ID., *Redemptoris Missio,* n. 37.

[144] See M. DE C. AZEVEDO, *The Consecrated Life,* 98-106. «India with its 14 million Catholics as the biggest catholic Church in Asia (except the Philippines) has a special responsibility towards the European Churches: It has to push them, not by words, but by deeds, to implement more courageously the impetus of the Council» (W. BÜHLMANN, «The Mission of the Church», 315).

4.1 *Towards Basic Human Communities*

To concretize the communion of God's people first of all there should be real communion within the local Church. Such communion gives way to pluralism respecting the various cultures. It also keeps in dialogue with other cultures, for which, BECs are proving to be a good pastoral method. The spirituality of the BECs is such that it can easily keep in touch with the people of other denominations and religions. The BECs can respond to the exhortation of Pope John Paul II in this regard. The Pope exhorts:

> Indeed all the faithful are asked by the Spirit of God to do everything possible to strengthen the bonds of communion between all Christians and to increase cooperation between Christ's followers: «Concern for restoring unity pertains to the whole Church, faithful and clergy alike. It extends to everyone according to the potential of each»[145].

And the Church cannot ignore the vast majority of the people who are not baptized[146]. They are God's people who «possess an impressive patrimony of deeply religious texts»[147]. To them, as Pope Paul VI says, the dialogue of salvation has been already opened by God[148]. And the Church has to continue the same dialogue initiated by God. For that, the BECs can initiate the process of forming basic human communities which can break through all the human made barriers[149]. The Christian

---

[145] JOHN PAUL II, *Ut Unum Sint*, n. 101. See also *UR* 5.

[146] At least some of them, although are not baptized, adore the God of Jesus Christ. For some, baptism causes another caste and cultural identity which they do not want to accept. «The person of Jesus is admired and loved today by millions of Asians who are 'non-Christians'. And there are others who, while committed to Jesus Christ, for serious social reasons are not able to be members of the visible church» (F. WILFRED, «Images of Jesus Christ», 55). See also H. STAFFNER, *Jesus Christ and the Hindu Community*; R. PANIKKAR, *The Unknown Christ*; J. DUPUIS, *Jesus Christ;* E. SCHILLEBEECKX, «The Church and Mankind», 34-50.

[147] PAUL VI, *Evangelii Nuntiandi*, n. 53.

[148] PAUL VI, *Ecclesiam Suam*, ns. 58-118.

[149] See PONTIFICAL COUNCIL FOR PROMOTING CHRISTIAN UNITY, *Directory*. For further theological discussion and practical application of ecumenism and dialogue. See S.WOOD, «Ecclesial *Koinōnia* in Ecumenical Dialogues», 124-145. S. Wood treats the aspect of ecumenism from a theological point supported by various documents of the Churches and ecclesial communities. In the Asian and Indian context see J. DUPUIS, «Dialogue and Proclamation». See also M. AMALADOSS, «Interreligious Dialogue», 2-5; ID., «Being a Christian community», 23-33; J.H. WONG, «Anonymous Christians», 609-637; F. WILFRED, «Ecumenism as a Movement», 573-583. For a concrete experience with a theological reflection on dialogue see A.L. GAJIWALA, «The Spirit of

communities in India should not be closed, exclusive communities. They must be open communities where all people in each place, irrespective of religion, caste, creed and ideology, are brought together and basic human communities are formed[150]. Since the co-existence of people of various faiths are seen in the same family the formation of basic human communities become easier in the local context of Trivandrum[151].

4.2 Basic Human Communities: Towards the Kingdom of God

The spiritual dynamism of BECs — a maturing of personal and communitarian commitment to follow Jesus Christ and to love one's neighbour in the living cultural situation — may make it possible to broaden the vision of BECs to the basic human communities with fidelity to Christian faith and more creative openness embracing everyone to God's Kingdom.

> The Kingdom of God encompasses relationships between God and humankind. It symbolizes the presence of the powerful yet compassionate God who brings salvation to the universe. It is a sphere in which humankind accepts God's sovereignty in personal and social life consisting in «Justice, peace and joy» (Rom 14,17)[152].

The inner dynamism of BECs is that it helps one to *put off the mantle* like that of the Bartimaeus to follow Jesus Christ (Mk 10,46-52)[153]. In the basic human communities, the Christians can take a prophetic role to be the *light of the world*[154] helping the people to see from partial vision to the global vision (Mk 8,22-26)[155]. Since the basic human communities

---

Dialogue», 485-495. The relevance of ecumenism and dialogue can no more be considered a problem of the East it has become a necessity of the West too.

[150] See K. PATHIL, «Basic Christian Communities», 336.

[151] To understand the inner dynamism of neighbourhood communities see V. ABRAHAM, «Neighbours in Love», 14-17. See also J.P. PINTO, *Inculturation*, 182-233.

[152] *FAPA*, 314.

[153] See B. SECONDIN, *Per una fedeltà creativa*, 411-413.

[154] See *LG* 1. J. Fuellenbach speaks of the role of Church in the changing world comparing to a ship that is equipped with enormous lights moving through the centuries indicating to other ships on the ocean which way they should move in order to reach the shores of salvation. According to him the Church's mission is perceived not as taking people from their ship into the «bark of St. Peter» but rather to indicate to them which way to steer their boats. See J. FUELLENBACH, *The Kingdom of God*, 276. See also M. AMALADOSS, «The Pluralism of Religions», 85-103; A. DE FELIPE, «Año 2.000 ¡Viva la diferencia!», 48.

[155] See B. SECONDIN, *Per una fedeltà creativa*, 403-406.

are in dialogue with the world, they can give sympathetic response to the new forms of poverty in an unjust and impoverished world.

> It is the Father's will that we should recognize Christ our brother in the persons of all men and love them with an effective love, in word and in deed, thus bearing witness to the truth; and it is his will that we should share with others the mystery of his heavenly love. In this way men all over the world will awaken to a lively hope (the gift of the Holy Spirit) that they will one day be admitted to the heaven of surpassing peace and happiness in their homeland radiant with the glory of the Lord (*GS* 93).

In the basic human communities, the Kingdom message can also incarnate into the socio-religious milieu.

> Christians are called to prepare for the Great Jubilee of the beginning of the Third Millennium by renewing their hope in the definitive coming of the Kingdom, preparing for it daily in their hearts, in the Christian community to which they belong, in their particular social context, and in world history itself [156].

5. Conclusion

In the present chapter of our study we tried to discover the spirituality of BECs and its challenges in Trivandrum. In the light of the functioning of BECs in Trivandrum we tried to describe the spirituality of BECs in Trivandrum. We saw that it is a maturing of personal and communitarian commitment to follow Jesus Christ and to love one's neighbour in the living cultural situation.

As the BECs are a challenge in the present situation of the Church which had been institutionalized, the spirituality evolving from the BECs is also challenging. The challenges are multidimensional. The inner dynamism of this spirituality challenges each BEC to evaluate and discern the social issues undertaken after the formation of BECs. At the same time, the BECs have a prophetic role not only to take up issues pertaining to the Catholics of Trivandrum but also to be involved in all matters pertaining to humankind. The BECs have to express their solidarity with the poor and the marginalized. We saw that the institutionalization of BECs, though inevitable to a certain extent, may deviate from the spirit of the *diaconal* vision which has emerged in the Diocese unless they retain the spirit of the compassion of Jesus Christ.

---

[156] JOHN PAUL II, *Tertio Millennio Adveniente*, n. 46.

The BECs in Trivandrum cannot be considered as an isolated phenomenon. They share the ethos of most of the local Churches in India. The BECs also share the ethos of other developing countries. The reciprocal relations existing among the local Churches through the communion of BECs are giving a new direction to the mission of Church in India which has been marked for its contradictions and high institutionalization. The similarities seen in the BECs of the developing countries give further scope of expressing a new solidarity within the Churches of the developing countries. Such a solidarity can be a preparation of a broader communion which may be realized through the basic human communities.

GENERAL CONCLUSION

One of the important contributions of the Second Vatican Council is the rediscovery of the understanding of the Church as the «People of God». The incarnate effect of such an understanding is reflected in the emergence of BECs. The BEC is described as a *new way of being the Church*. In the new way of being the Church, the People of God experience new spiritual depths and give new meaning to spirituality.

In the foregoing pages we, through a moderate elaboration, have been exploring the spirituality of BECs in the socio–religious context of Trivandrum/Kerala, India. We have discovered that the BECs have a theological basis, and that the spirituality of BECs in Trivandrum is something related to the ethos of the people, and that the spirituality of BECs in Trivandrum is in the process of maturing and that it calls for the personal and communitarian commitment to follow Jesus Christ and to love one's neighbour in the living cultural situation.

Our findings could be summarized as: (1) the BECs have a theological basis; (2) the BECs in Trivandrum trace their roots back in the ecclesial communities founded by St. Francis Xavier and the Carmelite missionaries; (3) the formation of BECs in Trivandrum is a saga of the creative fidelity of a local Church; (4) there is an emergence of Latin Catholic identity in the particular socio–religious context of Trivandrum; (5) the Christian life, at present, in Trivandrum revolves around the BECs; (6) the Spirituality becomes the lived experience of the people as it is (i) a maturing of personal and communitarian commitment to follow Jesus Christ and (ii) a maturing of personal and communitarian commitment to love one's neighbour in the living cultural situation; (7) it provides an occasion for everyone to realize and to exercise his or her charism; (8) there evolves a diaconaland participatory leadership; (9) BECs are becoming the nursery of religious and political leaders; (10) the Gospel is becoming the liberative force for women; (11) the BECs are occupying pride of place in the proclamation of the Gospel in Trivandrum and in other local Churches in India; (12) the BECs in

Trivandrum give scope for further theological and missiological reflection and action.

(1) *The BECs have a theological basis.*

The theological basis of BECs is the new understanding and awareness of the local Church. In the NT the word «Church» is used 114 times. Nevertheless, from Jesus Christ's mouth we hear the word Church only one time (Mt 16,18-19). This does not mean that the «Church» does not have any significance in the mind of Jesus Christ. Actually the message of Jesus which we call the Kingdom message, or the vision of Jesus, has grown up in the communities called Churches.

The word «Church», which comes from the Greek word *ekklēsia,* has a great religious significance in the biblical context. It is used in the place of *qāhāl.* It indicates God's assembly, characterized by having answered Yahweh's call. St. Paul uses the word *ekklēsia* intending *ekklēsia tou theou* as in Acts 20,28 (Church of God). He uses the word in the singular (Rom 16,23; 1 Cor 14,23) and in the plural (2 Cor 11,8; 12,13; Phil 4,14). The number of persons is not an essential factor to becoming a Church. Even a small fellowship as a house Church could be called an *ekklēsia* (1 Cor 16,19) and each local community is Church in its fullness. For the Church Fathers like Ignatius of Antioch, Justin and Ireneus, Church is primarily a local Church, a Church incarnated in the particular place and context.

The importance given to the local Church by St. Paul or the Fathers in no way belittles the importance of the universal Church. Vatican II shows the relation between the universal Church and the local Church by saying that the Church of Christ is really present in all legitimately organized local groups of the faithful, in so far as they are united to their pastors. Although these groups may be often small and poor, or existing in diaspora, Christ is present through whose power, or influence the One, Holy Catholic and Apostolic Church is constituted[1].

Despite the Council's broader vision of the Church, the present Code of Canon Law restricts the understanding of local Church to a diocese[2]. A parish is a local Church in so far as it is related to that diocese. But in the existential situation the accomplishment of the Church's task cannot be left to the *parish alone.* The development of BECs is a response to the realization of Vatican II's vision of the Church as the «People of God» in

---

[1] See *LG* 26.

[2] See *CIC,* n. 369.

the concrete life situation. In other words, it is the realization of the Church in a given locality. They are the smallest cells of the Church in terms of community. The BECs, like the first Christian communities, take up the mission of Jesus Christ and bear the responsibility of carrying it under the guidance of the bishops in communion with the universal Church.

The theological foundation of BECs is further articulated in the word *communion*[3]. It is the dynamic expression of Christian life. Communion does not originate in a person but in God. In Christ, the communion becomes a reality, because he is God and human. Incarnation is the first moment of God's communion with humanity. Christ has created a new openness among men and women introducing the concept of communion as an open reality. And the primitive Christians lived in that communion (Acts 2,42). According to St. Paul the communion should be the guiding principle of Christian life (1 Cor 12,12-30).

The communion is concretely experienced in a community. It is manifested when two or three people are gathered in Christ's name. It is vitalized when the «Word of God» is read, listened to and lived in a community. It is expressed when the «Eucharist» is celebrated. It is manifested when one shares the joy and sufferings of one's neighbours. And such a communion takes place better in «small groups» and more meaningfully in BECs because such gatherings give a new religious experience. BEC gatherings integrate all the aspects of human life. Each BEC gathering leads one to have communion with the triune God who is incarnated in their midst and to have a communion among themselves. They commit themselves to Jesus Christ and express their commitment in loving others in their cultural situation.

This new understanding of ecclesial communion experienced in the BECs inspires each local Church to discover its own spirituality in the particular context.

(2) *The BECs in Trivandrum trace their roots back to the ecclesial communities founded by St. Francis Xavier and the Carmelite missionaries.*

The formation of BECs in Trivandrum traces its origin to the ecclesial communities founded by St. Francis Xavier and the Carmelite missionaries. Though there were missionaries before the coming of Francis Xavier, the people of Trivandrum still consider him as a person

---

[3] See JOHN PAUL II, *Christifideles Laici*, n. 26.

who imparted the Christian faith. He mainly concentrated his missionary work among the Mukkuvar in the coastal villages. The people witnessed his holy life and experienced the presence of a personal God in his message.

Although the primary goal of his missionary work was salvation of souls, as uderstood at that time, his instruction to the priests shows that he was very much concerned about the welfare of the people. He was convinced that without the help of lay people an ecclesial community could not be fostered. So he appointed *kanakapula* (like a catechist) to foster Christian faith in the ecclesial communities which he founded. The main concern of the Carmelite missionaries was also salvation of souls. They offered instruction in the Christian faith and formed Christian communities mainly in the non-coastal villages. They converted the Nadars, the Izhavas and the Dalits. Since the people had a Hindu religious background the conversion work and the formation of ecclesial communities were not easy as was evidenced in the coastal villages. The Carmelite missionaries appointed *upadēsi* (catechist) in the non-coastal villages as animators of Christian life.

Both in the coastal and non-coastal villages the ecclesial communities were vitalized through confraternities (*combria sabha*), popular devotions, pious associations and prayer meetings. The ecclesial communities were strengthened, especially in the coastal villages, by an administrative system taking into account the ecclesial norms adapting to the cultural situation of the people. Thus *ūrukottam* (parish assembly) played a significant role in the parish structure and the *pradhāni* (important person) became the influential people in the parish. Since the coastal parishes were under the Portuguese missionaries, the *Padroado* system of administration influenced the people. Although the people were protected from the native higher castes of Travancore the missionaries did not work for the *integral development* of the people. Those who participated in the administrative structure of the parishes, like *pradhāni* and *kanakapula* could not present the real problems pertaining to the community to the missionaries. The Christian life became more cultic and the people were trained to spend more income on the celebration of feasts than to sustain their families. However, the people sustained a deep Christian faith even in the midst of their miseries.

In the non-coastal villages, the missionaries saw that the caste system played an important role. The Protestant missionaries worked for the social development of the people together with the spiritual development. The Catholic missionaries converted many people to the faith and looked after the spiritual matters of the people. The result was that the people in the non-coastal villages also remained socially backward.

The ecclesial communities which trace their roots back to the time of St. Francis Xavier and the Carmelite missionaries were structured ones. This did not help the integral development of the people. Even in the formation of ecclesial communities how far the missionaries succeeded in to incarnating the Church in the given place is doubtful. The ecclesial communities remained largely a replica of the Western Church. The 1659 message of the *Propaganda Fide* regarding the integration of faith and culture had little impact on the missionaries[4].

(3) *The formation of BECs in Trivandrum is a saga of the creative fidelity of a local Church.*

The impact of Vatican II had great importance in the local Church of Trivandrum. The spirit of the renewal has been reflected in many corners of the Diocese. The people's participation in the Church was the felt need of the time. The formation of parish councils could not make much impact in the Diocese because of the strong centralized administrative structure that existed in the Diocese.

The social awareness was well reflected in the organizations like the *Kerala Catholic Youth Movement* (KCYM) and the *All India Catholic University Federation* (AICUF). They did not remain as pious associations. The members in these organizations began to involve themselves in the life of the people. Together with the other secular organizations the KCYM and AICUF began to understand the situations of the people and tried to find out the causes for the deteriorated situations. They made efforts to change the living situations of the people. They opposed all those factors which caused the misery of the poor. In their opposition, the fishermen's agitation caused unrest both in the secular and religious circles. The priests and religious who were inspired by the teachings of Vatican II supported the move.

---

4 The Propaganda Fide gave a clear message to the missionaries in 1659 stating: «What is more absurd than to transport France, Spain, Italy or some other part of Europe to the Chinese? Do not introduce among them our countries but faith, this faith which does not reject nor hurt the rites or customs of any people [...]. So there is no more powerful motive for alienation and hate than to introduce these changes in the customs peculiar to a nation, principally those which have been practised as long as the elders can remember» (*Collectana S. Congregationis de Propaganda Fide*, 1, 42 quoted by J.P. PINTO, *Inculturation*, 60).

In the non-coastal villages the priests and people felt that they did not have any say in the administration of the Diocese. Combined with the ideological differences, the difference of opinion regarding the division of the Diocese caused a total crisis in the Diocese. It was in the context of such a crisis that Bishop A.B. Jacob convened a priests' meeting to discuss the mode of celebrating the Golden Jubilee of the Diocese in 1987. The *Presbyterium* found that the existing atmosphere was not conducive to a meaningful celebration of the jubilee. The *presbyterium* felt that its internal unity was a vital pre-requisite. To achieve this end, it was suggested that the entire clergy live together at least for five days with the Bishop.

In order to have an internal unity within the Diocese, the priests along with the Bishop spent five days in prayer, study and discussion at Kottar. It is known as «Living Together» or «*Kottar Sammēlanam*». The «Living Together», like that of the Apostles who gathered to find solutions to the complaints of the Hellenists (Acts 6,1-6), was an occasion for the priests to come together and to find solutions to the various problems of the Diocese. A «vision and mission» emerged from the «Living Together» which reflected the *contextualized* ecclesiology of the local Church.

Since the vast majority of the people of the Diocese represent the backward class of the Kerala society it was made clear in the «Living Together» that a holistic development of the people was to be envisaged. Following the «Living Together» a change in the administrative structure has taken place. All the activities of the Diocese were brought under six Boards and in each Board lay participation was assured. Various programmes emerged in different parishes within the renewal programme. «Christian Life 2000» was one of the major renewal programmes which helped the people *to live* the Church. It was an occasion to form BECs in informal way in various parishes. After three years of the renewal programme, Bishop M.S. Pakiam in 1990 appointed four commissions, consisting of lay people, to study how the People of God had benefited from the renewal and how far the message of renewal had reached the people in the Diocese after «Living Together». The findings were an eye-opener to assess the situation of the local Church of Trivandrum. All the reports invariably gave the impression that most of the programmes were mainly based on the priests. To realize any kind of renewal among the people, the commission proposed that the formation of BECs would be an effective method.

The conflict existing in the Diocese resulted positively in finding new ways of being the Church in light of the Word of God, and the teachings of the Church applied to the particular cultural situation of the people.

(4) *There is an emergence of Latin Catholic identity in the particular socio-religious context of Trivandrum.*

The people of the Diocese of Trivandrum live in a pluriform cultural background. The dominant castes in the region, though not numerically, are the Brahmins and the Nairs. The important religions are Hinduism, Islam and Christianity. The social situation of the Diocese is complex, mainly because of the caste factors. The Mukkuvar, the Nadar, the Izhava and the Dalits are the major castes. Though in the caste hierarchy all these castes have lower status on economical ground they had a prestigious past. They even now keep caste identity. They do not wish to live on *borrowed identities*. The caste consciousness among them gives a caste cultural identity on the one hand, and on the other hand a Latin Catholic identity. Whatever be the caste or religious identity the people are listed among the backward communities (OBC) in Kerala.

The complexity is deepened by factors which are related to the daily lives of the people. Some of these factors are poverty, illiteracy, homelessness, unemployment, diseases, injustices at work and in society, and discrimination because of race and sex. With the English education, Kerala has witnessed a social awakening. In the social awakening religion played a significant role especially for the emancipation of the poor. The liberation from slavery, the right of women to wear upper cloth, the right to walk on the public roads, the right to enter the temple, etc., are closely related to religion. According to J.W. Gladstone, there was hardly any social movement without a religious aspect nor any religious movement without the social aspect during the 19th century[5]. In the socio-religious inter relation the Protestant Nadars, the Hindu Izhavas, and the Hindu Dalits had a better chance to rise socially. The Catholics, because of the over emphasis of the *other world* remained in the lower strata of the society. The people retained their faith despite suffering and starvation. The lay people were conscious of their deplorable social situations but since the parish administrative system was mainly based on the priests the people could not raise their voices. Since the Latin Catholics have a complex caste culture in Trivandrum and in Kerala, they also failed to create a social identity. The Kerala Latin Catholic Hierarchy also did not take much effort to understand the problems of the Latin Catholics of Trivandrum.

The Diocese has also a peculiar religious background. In the Diocese the Mukkuvar are fully identified with the Catholic Church, even though

---

[5] J.W. GLADSTONE, *Protestant Christianity*, 416.

most of them were Hindus before the coming of the Portuguese missionaries. The Nadars, the Izhavas and the Dalits, because of a strong kinship relation, have a close contact with the Hindus and Christians of various denominations. As a result, we find people of different faiths in the same family. All these castes are very much influenced by the Hindu popular culture.

The renewal initiated by Bishop A.B. Jacob and continued by Bishop M.S. Pakiam helped the people to have their own Latin Catholic identity. Since the renewal envisaged was an integral one, the people welcomed and adopted it; and the people experience a *new way of being the Church* through BECs.

(5) *The Christian life, at present, in Trivandrum revolves around the BECs.*

Although BECs were functioning in the Diocese in various parishes with the renewal initiated in 1987 it became the pastoral option of the Diocese in 1991. At present there are 2.627 BECs. They are functioning in the capital city, coastal and in the non-coastal villages. Like the first Christian communities the people gather in houses, a reminiscent of the house churches in the early Church. The people gather once a week, fortnightly or once a month. In the gatherings the people read the Bible, meditate on it, and share their reflections for the growth of the community. One feels that he or she *is* the Church against the feeling that he or she is *in* the Church. They take up responsibilities in light of the Gospel message.

There is an organized net work from the BECs to the Diocese. The lay people, religious and priests are involved in the animation of BECs on the parish, Vicariate and diocesan levels. Compared to the early ecclesial communities of Trivandrum, the BECs assure better participation of the lay people. The people experience that they are the Church. A new approach to the Word of God is visible. The liturgy is no more a ritual in the Church but an expression of the faith experience of the community in Christ. The children, youth and elderly people express their faith in the Risen Lord through their participation in the liturgy by means of presentation of gifts, spontaneous prayers and singing.

However, there are also parishes and Vicariates where the message of BECs has not reached. Some priests cannot yet digest the idea that BECs are a *new way of being the Church.* Although better participation of women in the BECs is welcomed overall in the Diocese, less participation of male members in good number of BECs also poses lot of unanswered questions in a male dominated society like Kerala.

(6) *The Spirituality becomes the lived experience of the people* as it is (i) a maturing of *personal and communitarian commitment to follow Jesus Christ* and (ii) *a maturing of personal and communitarian commitment to love one's neighbour in the living cultural situation.*

In the functioning of BECs in Trivandrum one can easily notice that apart from the organized network which comes mainly from above, there is something that compels the people to come together, pray together and share their Christian experiences. They read the Word of God and interiorize it through *lectio divina*. Since the Word of God is alive and active in them (Heb 4,12-13) they discover their own *self* or recover the «lost self» from the «false self». They also discover the compassionate Self of God who liberates them from all sorts of evils in the society.

There is a constant effort from the people to combine faith and life. The change that is taking place in the social life of the people testifies that the religious life of the people is related to the social life. Accordingly many people stopped the habit of drinking alchol. Some villages are liberated from illicit distillation and the sale of alcohol. There is a process of *re-peopling the de-peopled*. People began to build up good relations with their neighbours. The neighbours gain a new acceptance even if they belong to different castes. There is sharing of money and material goods. The gatherings become the events of grace and mutual up- building. The gatherings impart the grace to take up the challenges, individually and collectively, to express concern and commitment to one's neighbour. And an integral development of the people is the outcome.

In each BEC there is personal and communitarian commitment to follow Jesus Christ. They experience the tangible presence of Jesus Christ in the Word of God and in the sacraments. The sacraments do not remain a mere *pūja* in which the priest does everything and the people remain as onlookers. They believe that Jesus Christ is the Saviour of all, the only one able to reveal God and able to lead them to God. So they follow Him and they are led by Him. The tangible presence of Jesus Christ challenges them to have communion with their neighbours both personally and collectively. Each member of the BECs has not an imaginary neighbour but a neighbour who lives close to one's door. The neighbour gains acceptance like that of a friend and a relative. There is an opening of doors to the members of the neighborhood families as a sign of the opening of one's heart. The opening extends not only to the Catholics but also to the people belonging to other Christian denominations and to other religions. In a cultural situation where caste dominates over religion BECs have helped people of different castes to give and receive equal acceptance in the community. The human dignity of the guest and the host is respected.

However, there are variations in the functioning of BECs in the Diocese. Lack of vitality in the functioning of BECs is evident if priests do not show much interest in the BECs. The changing of animators may affect its functioning. Despite the organized network we find that quite a number of people, both men and women, do not participate in the BEC gatherings. The variations in the functioning of BECs demonstrate that BECs are still in the process of maturing.

(7) *The BECs provide an occasion for every one to realize and to exercise his or her charism.*

One of the important effects of the Spirituality of BECs in Trivandrum is that it helps the laity to realize his or her own particular charism and to exercise it for the benefit of the community. Charism is a free gift of God to a person for the community. The gifts are different (1 Cor 12,4-11) and the discerning principle is love (1 Cor 13,13). The charism enables one to realize his or her personal vocation in the world and in the Church. It is an event that takes place in a specific historical setting and goes on enriching, readjusting to the needs of the time and actualizing itself with the contributions of new researches.

As human persons are created in the image and likeness of God (Gen 1,27), everyone has a fundamental human dignity. This is enriched by the reception of the sacrament of baptism, through which one becomes the child in the Son sharing His priestly, prophetic and kingly office. The baptismal dignity challenges one to share the salvific mission of the Church. In this mission there is no difference between slave or free person; male or female; Mukkuvar or Nadar; traditional Catholic or new convert; Latin Catholic or Syrian Catholic; politicians or non-politicians; literate or illiterate (Gal 3,28). Every individual is respected as a person and not as «a thing» or an «object» to be used. Each one is a responsible «subject», endowed with conscience and freedom, called to live responsibly in society and history, oriented towards spiritual and religious values[6].

As in the early Church, the BECs take up the responsibility to recognize, to regulate and to coordinate the charisms (1 Cor 14,26-40). This coordination encourages new leadership within the community and enables the members to meet the various needs of the ecclesial community

---

[6] JOHN PAUL II, *Christifideles Laici* , n. 5.

and the society, both spiritual and temporal (Acts 6,1-6). Thus, the sick and needy in a community will not be so unnoticed; the homeless will not be un-cared for; the violation of human rights will not be ignored; threats to life will not remain unchecked.

Each BEC becomes innovative in conducting its gathering, in celebrating the Word of God, in formulating prayers, in composing hymns and in creating symbols. The people try to understand the Word of God in the light of the living context and try to evaluate their life in the light of the Word of God. And each one develops his or her charism for the benefit of the community.

(8) *There evolves a diaconal and participatory leadership.*

The Church in India, as John Paul II said at Trivandrum on 8th February 1986, is a *servant Church.* Actually it was a reminder to the Church in India which has conveniently neglected the aspect of service due to its over-institutionalization. Although the post Vatican period showed some signs of hope of a *servant Church* with «Church in India Today» seminar in 1969, most of the local Churches have been preoccupied with the multiplication of various structures and institutions especially in Kerala. In the process of institutionalization, the people, a vast majority of them poor, had to undergo double discrimination: one from the State and the other from the *privileged Christians.* This discrimination continues in different shapes and forms in the Church in India even now[7].

Since the institutions are in the hands of the clergy and various Religious Congregations of both men and women, the role of the laity in the life of the Church has been *cleverly avoided* and *conveniently ignored.* Looking at the *un-Christian side of the Indian Church* the lay faithful are led to a strong feeling that they are meant *to pray, pay, and obey* and nothing more[8]. Hence, to a vast majority of the people in India the Church remains nothing but another social institution of influence and power[9].

Neverthless, the Church in India has a mission to proclaim the Kingdom of God. This is possible when each local Church realizes the potentiality of the lay faithful in the given locality. It is their right to hold

---

[7] The injustices within the Church include discriminations on the basis of caste, region, language, etc. See *CBCI Evaluation Report,* n. 791.

[8] See *CBCI Evaluation Report,* n. 641.

[9] See *CBCI Evaluation Report,* ns. 785. 794.

positions of leadership and responsibility because they are more in touch with the day-to-day realities of life. The economic backwardness or caste barriers should not be a hindrance in extending leadership and responsibility to the local people. All the more as the CBCI Evaluation Report observes: «among the *lay people, those who are poor and those who are really committed to the cause of the poor are closer to the realities of life.* Hence the need to promote an active role for them in the mission of building up the Kingdom»[10]. The report further states:

> The 21st century will face difficult problems that cannot be solved without lay participation and lay leadership. That is, lay participation and lay leadership is the answer to all that the Church is visualizing for the future. Hence it is the pastoral duty of the common National Body to find ways and means to ensure that the existing state of affairs as regards lay participation and lay leadership is corrected as quickly as possible and that lay persons get their legitimate share of responsibility in the management of the Church affairs and in the life of the Christian community[11].

Such an approach to realize the potentiality of the lay faithful favours the formation of BECs. In the early ecclesial communities of Trivandrum the leadership was limited to the priests and *kanakapula or pradhāni*. With the BECs a participatory leadership has been evolving. Thus in Trivandrum more than 10.000 lay leaders or animators have emerged. These leaders are called to be at the service of the People of God in their respective communities. A collegiality (co-responsibility) takes place at the grass roots level. Through a pastoral coordination a collegiality is also taking in a wider level especially among the clergy and the lay people. The new leadership is more open to realities of the Church and to the world. They can give the Church a new relevance, a new vitality, a new modernity, and a new sense of mission. The leaders of BECs, like Vaikunda Swami, Sri Narayana Guru and Chattambi Swamikal, can combine spirituality and social life.

(9) *The BECs are becoming the nurseries of religious and political leaders.*

The BECs, in its new way of being the Church, have to take responsibility to form Christian leaders. The structure of BECs is such that all the members of the Diocese belong to one or the other BEC. So, from an existential point of view, the future leaders have to emerge from

---

[10] *CBCI Evaluation Report*, n. 645 [emphasis in italics mine].

[11] *CBCI Evaluation Report*, n. 647.

these communities. It is from these BECs that the young boys and girls will respond to God's call. It is from these communities that the future political leaders emerge. Each BEC becomes a *sign of prophecy* in the Indian Church.

It is true that a great number of the BECs, despite its social commitment, are not in favour of discussing political matters in the BEC gatherings. Nevertheless, the BECs have a prophetic role in the society to take a stand on political matters. Since BECs are also becoming the nursery of permanent deacons, priests and religious, we hope that the ecclesial leaders take up the task of being servants of the «People of God».

The new leadership evolving through BECs has to be in solidarity with the poor. *True solidarity with one's neighbour is rooted in the conviction that Christ has united himself with each and every person by means of his redemptive incarnation.* Walking with those who are poor is closely connected with the spirituality of BECs. Jesus Christ openly declared that he came to bring good news to the poor (Lk 4,18-19). He exhibited a special concern for those who were marked by deprivations of hunger, thirst, sickness, and imprisonment (Mt 25,31-46). A follower of Jesus Christ cannot but be in solidarity with the poor.

(10) *The Gospel is becoming the liberative force for women.*

According to Indian thought wherever women are honoured, there the gods bestow their blessings; where they are dishonoured, there all sacrifices are rendered fruitless[12]. However, in practice, women are the most discriminated section in the society. The killing of «girl babies» by *amnio-centesis* is the best example of such a discrimination towards women[13]. The Hindu society has imposed various customs which prohibit women from entering temples. Their taking part in the administration of the temple became *unthinkable*. The role of women in the Church also had been highly negligible. In many parts of India the discrimination of women still continues[14]. In the so called *glorious* pre-Portuguese period of the Syrian Christians, lay participation meant only male members from the *noble* families. The women from the backward classes were not allowed to wear upper cloth in the presence of the *higher castes*. In the

---

[12] See M.D. CHATURVEDI, *Hinduism*, 197.

[13] See H.S. D'SOUZA, «Vogliamo rassicurarvi», 4 See also JOHN PAUL II, «La grande primavera del cristianesimo», 4.

[14] See *CBCI Evaluation Report*, n. 785.

Diocese of Trivandrum too, any discussion on the role of women in its «Living Together» was left in oblivion.

However, we find the Word of God as a liberative force for women. It was the Word of God that gave strength to the Nadar women to fight for their right to wear upper cloths in 1859. The Word of God had been the inspiration for the struggle of the Kerala fisher folk, in the 80's. In the BECs the women experience not only an inner freedom through the Word of God but also a new ecclesial awareness. The women, who were *inside* the house, *come out* and become evangelizers. The increased participation of women in the BECs may be the *silent beginning of a new ecclesial culture in Kerala*[15]. Their active participation in the BECs and the new biblical and ecclesial awareness can challenge many administrative structure that is not led by the spirit of the Gospel.

The women religious, who were not considered different from the ordinary lay women as regards the administrative matters of the Church, play a prophetic role in the BECs. In light of the Gospel and of the teachings of the Church the women religious understand that their charism is not stagnant, unproductive and unrelated to the people, but it is *dynamic, creative* and *relational*. The women religious, who were concerned about *enriching* their *congregations* and their founders' *charism of the past*, began to realize that charism is a gift of God for the People of God of the present and not for the building up of an institute[16]. This awareness led many of the congregations to endure any hardships for the sake of building up the local Church of Trivandrum.

Their active participation in the fight against the evils of the society should be considered as a new attempt to give *new meaning to religious life*. The women religious are all the more convinced of the fact that they cannot be the *bystanders in the struggle of the people*. It has been significantly noted that in every Vicariate the animator is a woman religious. They prove that they are competent enough to deal with pastoral problems and can enter into the lives of the people. Being

---

[15] «I renew the appeal I made last September, for the whole Church to be willing to foster feminine participation in every way in her internal life, with the exception of those tasks which belong properly to the priest, by making use of the ample room for a lay and feminine presence recognized by Church law [...]. By promoting respect for women's true dignity, you will contribute to freeing reserves of wisdom and sensitivity which the Church and society greatly need» (JOHN PAUL II, «Il Vangelo vi rafforzi nel legame di unità», 7).

[16] See B. SECONDIN, *Per una fedeltà creativa*, 134.

animators of the BECs, they are expressing a solidarity with the humanity especially taking up the role of *universal sisterhood.*

(11) *The BECs are occupying pride of place in the proclamation of the Gospel in Trivandrum and in other local Churches in India.*

One of the major findings of our study is that BEC is the best means to proclaim the Gospel in the pluralistic culture of Trivandrum. The Gospel incarnates itself in the local culture of the people. The BECs help the people to come together in their social situations. Each BEC gives an occasion for people to know each other and to share the joys and sorrows of one another. The breaking of caste barriers signals that each person is important in the BECs. Therefore, no one is denied the chance of sharing one's thoughts. The lay faithful can exercise their priestly and prophetic and kingly roles in the Church in a concrete way. The people try to resolve the problems of a socio-cultural nature in light of the Word of God. The spirituality of BECs is such that it helps one to follow Christ personally and to love one's neighbour in the living cultural situation.

In recent years the focal point of the bishops' conferences in Asia is termed as dialogue. The bishops maintain that dialogue frees the Church from becoming a self-centered community. In the BECs a meaningful dialogue takes place. This is evidenced concretely in the way people welcome *the brothers and sisters of other faiths* in an informal way. The BECs respect other religious faiths and customs. *Ōnam* becomes a common feast of Christians and Hindus. *Gayatri Mantra*, a hymn sung everyday in the Hindu Temples, becomes a part of the Indian Christian heritage. The fellowship achieved through the dialogue in the BECs will help to probe the common problems of the society. Since the BECs are concerned about the problems of the society, they have communion with other organizations and human communities to work for the betterment of the society. The present day threats to the human life force us to have a new solidarity with all those who love human life.

Although the BECs in Trivandrum have their own particular context, to a large extent the people in other local Churches share the same experience. The functioning of BECs in Quilon, Kanjirappally (Kerala), Kottar (Tamil Nadu), Nalgonda (Andhra Predesh), Mangalore (Karnataka), Goa and Bombay (Maha Rastra), show that the people share a common ecclesial life despite the cultural and the linguistic differences. It may also be because of the common cultural heritage of the people of India and Asia who have inherited a tradition of combining culture and spirituality. The BECs could function like the ancient village community which preserved certain perennial elements of Indian culture and civilization amidst political turmoil and a succession of invasions[17]. In the new «areopagus»[18] the BECs can function like *the ark of Noah* (Gen 6,13-8-22).

The impact of BECs in the new mission of the Church in Asia is also well reflected in the orientations of the Asian Bishop's Conferences.[19] Throughout our study we have noted the vital role of BECs in the different parts of the world. BECs is considered to be the work of the Holy Spirit in our time. It is generally accepted that BECs are to be given priority in adopting the means to proclaim the Gospel.

(12) *The BECs in Trivandrum give scope for further theological and missiological reflection and action.*

(i) A BEC is described as *a new way of being the Church*. Each BEC is not a part of the whole Church but it is a whole in a miniature form. How far BECs could be called a Church without the Eucharist celebration? Since Eucharist is the fountain from which all the activities of the Church are directed BECs open a new scope of celebrating the Eucharist in the BECs *i.e.,* in the houses.

(ii) In the BEC gatherings we notice that brothers and sisters of other faiths also participate. They do believe in Christ. The social situations do not permit them to receive baptism as it causes another cultural identity. In such situation can the BECs lead them to the Lord's supper?

(ii) Can the BECs in Kerala form a *Kerala liturgy* which would be the cultural expression of the people of Kerala? Or the Latin or Syrian liturgy in Malayalam would be continued? As the Church in Kerala is divided on the basis of foreign liturgical traditions, will a *Kerala Liturgy*, as the cultural expression of the people of Kerala, be the ideal?

(iv) In Trivandrum all the faithful are geographically included in any one of the BECs. The members of the pastoral councils are elected from the BEC gatherings. How far can the New Code of Canon Law interpret the BECs?

---

[17] F. WILFRED, *From the Dusty Soil*, 87.

[18] «After preaching in a number of places, Saint Paul arrived in Athens, where he went to the Areopagus and proclaimed the Gospel in language appropriate to and understandable in those surroundings (cf. *Acts 17: 22-31*). At that time the Areopagus represented the cultural centre of the learned people of Athens, and today it can be taken as a symbol of the new sectors in which the Gospel must be proclaimed» (JOHN PAUL II, *Redemptoris Missio*, n. 37). See also JOHN PAUL II, *Tertio Millennio Adveniente*, n. 57.

[19] See *FAPA*, xxix

Some of the above mentioned challenges need further theological and missiological studies. Until the message of the Kingdom reaches the hearts of every human person in the Diocese, the BECs have to expect further challenges. Neverthless, as the spiritual dynamism of BECs provide a methodology to face the challenges of various types; it is our hope that the BECs in Trivandrum will also be able to face different challenges in the years to come.

In facing different challenges each BEC will be *creative* by reading the signs of the time and *faithful* by listening the voice of the Spirit. The Apostles read the signs of the time when the Hellenists complained and when they listened the voice of the Spirit a new *diakonia* emerged (Acts 6,1-6). This is our hope that the BECs in Trivandrum would be also *creative* and *faithful* in the years to come.

APPENDIX[1]

A.

1. Name:

2. Age:
   1. Between 15 and 25
   2. Between 25 and 40
   3. Above 40

3. Sex:
   Female —— Male ——

4. Education:
   1. Std. 10 and below
   2 B.A. and below
   3 Post Graduate

5. Profession:
   1. Coolie
   2. Farmer/ Fisher
   3. Govt. Employee/ Business
   4. Other

6. Designation in the BECs:
   1. Leader (Male)
   2. Leader (Female)
   3. Secretary
   4. Treasurer

B. Instructions:

1. *Kindly select only one answer and tick exactly in the bracket given against the chosen answer*
2. *Be brief while answering questions 34, 35 and 41*

C

1. How many families are there in your BEC?

   a) less than 10   ( )
   b) between 10-20   ( )
   c) more than 20   ( )

---

[1] A Questionnaire survey on the Spirituality of Basic Ecclesial Communities in the Socio-Religious context of Trivandrum/ Kerala, India, conducted within the period of 5-5-1994 to 5-6-1994 in view of Doctoral Dissertation in the Institute of Spirituality, Pontifical Gregorian University, Rome, by Ponnumuthan Selvister.

2. The number of participants in your BEC meeting:

a) less than 15   (   )
b) between 15 and 30   (   )
c) more than 30   (   )

3. How often do you gather?

a) once a week   (   )
b) once a fortnight   (   )
c) once a month   (   )

4. The participants are:

a) 80% are ladies   (   )
b) 60% are ladies   (   )
c) both ladies and gents in equal number   (   )

5. The economic status of the participants are mainly:

a) rich   (   )
b) poor   (   )
c) rich and poor alike   (   )

6. One does not participate because one:

a) is out of station   (   )
b) is not interested in the new system   (   )
c) does not get any particular experience   (   )

7. Do the non-Catholics or non-Christians participate in your BEC gatherings

a) yes   (   )
b) no   (   )
c) do not know   (   )

8. Who presides over the BEC gatherings?

a) the head of the family where the gathering is held   (   )
b) priest / religious/ catechist   (   )
c) one of the office-bearers of BEC   (   )

9. The presence of priests and the religious is:

a) necessary   (   )
b) good   (   )
c) not required   (   )

10. Is there any particular mode of procedure in your BEC gatherings?

a) yes   (   )
b) no   (   )
c) do not know   (   )

11. In your gathering importance is given to:

    a) reading and reflection of the Scripture   ( )
    b) discussion of social issues   ( )
    c) both   ( )

12. The Bible passage read in your gatherings is:

    a) the reading of the Holy Mass of the following Sunday   ( )
    b) the one proposed by the diocesan office   ( )
    c) the one selected by the animator of the gatherings   ( )

13. Do you evaluate the activities of your BEC in your gatherings

    a) yes   ( )
    b) no   ( )
    c) sometimes   ( )

14. Do you have the practice of someone writing the report of the
    gathering and reading it in the following meeting?

    a) yes   ( )
    b) no   ( )
    c) do not know   ( )

15. Do you think that your participation in the gatherings has helped
    you to read and understand the Bible better?

    a) yes   ( )
    b) no   ( )
    c) do not know   ( )

16. Do you think that your participation in the BEC gatherings has
    helped you to understand the Church better?

    a) yes   ( )
    b) no   ( )
    c) do not know   ( )

17. What effect do the BEC gatherings have on the neighbourhood
relationships?

    a) strengthening   ( )
    b) detrimental   ( )
    c) do not know   ( )

18. Do you think that through the formation of BECs lay people have
    access to get better participation in the parish functioning?

    a) yes   ( )
    b) no   ( )
    c) not sure   ( )

19. How do you react to the structural changes brought about in the
    parish by the formation of BECs?

   a) the former structure was better   ( )
   b) the present one is better   ( )
   c) do not have a clear idea   ( )

20. Has your participation in BEC gatherings prompted you to parti-
    cipate better in the liturgical services and in other church activities

   a) yes   ( )
   b) no   ( )
   c) not sure   ( )

21. Why do the non-Catholics and non-Christians, if any, participate in
    your gatherings?

   a) to know more about Christ   ( )
   c) to participate in prayer   ( )
   d) only as on-lookers   ( )

22. They participate because:

   a) they are invited   ( )
   b) they are interested   ( )
   c) do not know   ( )

23. You invite the non-Catholics and non-Christians to your gatherings:

   a) to attract them to the Church   ( )
   b) because they are neighbours   ( )
   c) since they show interest to attend   ( )

24. Out of your experience how do you evaluate the BEC programme
    in your diocesan context?

   a) the only way to witness Christ   ( )
   b) the best way to witness Christ   ( )
   c) one of the many ways to witness Christ   ( )

25. The different BEC groups in the same parish:

   a) help the common growth of the parish   ( )
   b) create enmity between the groups   ( )
   c) engender unhealthy competition   ( )

26. Are you a member of any pious association like Legion of Mary,
    Marian Sodality or Christian life communities, Charismatic groups, etc.?

   a) yes   ( )
   b) no   ( )

27. How is the relationship between the pious associations and BECs?

    a) pious associations promote BEC   ( )
    b) pious association can not accept BEC programmes ( )
    c) BECs discourage pious associations   ( )

28. What is the attitude of the youth towards BEC programmes

    a) encouraging   ( )
    b) discouraging   ( )
    c) do not know   ( )

29. How does the lack of interest from the part of the parish priest affect BECs?

    a) negatively   ( )
    b) partly   ( )
    c) does not affect   ( )

30. Do you think that BECs in your parish have been helpful in finding new leaders and in imparting Christian formation?

    a) yes   ( )
    b) no   ( )
    c) do not know   ( )

31. If your answer is "yes" what kind of leadership has emerged from such groups

    a) lay leadership   ( )
    b) political leadership   ( )
    c) participatory leadership   ( )

32. Discussion on the social problems like poverty, alcoholism, unemployment, illiteracy, dowry, evils of caste system, etc., in your gatherings:

    a) promotes the growth of the community   ( )
    b) leads to conflicts   ( )
    c) distracts prayer   ( )

33. Has your BEC ever discussed any of the above mentioned social problems in the gathering

    a) yes   ( )
    b) no   ( )
    c) do not know   ( )

34. If "yes" could you mention anyone of the problems discussed

35. If you had discussion, what was the solution of the BEC to the particular problem?

36. Was your solution a success or a failure?

    a) successful   ( )
    b) partly successful   ( )
    c) failure   ( )

37. Discussion of the contemporary politics in BEC gatherings is

    a) good   ( )
    b) necessary   ( )
    c) not needed   ( )

38. What is your opinion about BECs having cooperated with other organi-zations like *Mahilā Samājam* (Organization for women) co-operative societies to work for the betterment of the humanity

    a) good   ( )
    b) necessary   ( )
    c) not needed   ( )

39. How do you react to the statement: "The Church has to respect and adapt herself to the cultural traditions of our country?"

    a) agree   ( )
    b) do not agree   ( )
    c) no pinion   ( )

40. In light of your experience in the BEC do you hope to create a community where the members share everything and help one another like the early Christian communities?

    a) I hope   ( )
    b) It is very difficult   ( )
    c) It is impossible   ( )

41. What is your overall opinion about BECs?

The Tables[2]

Table I a: Total Response

	Q1	Q2	Q3	Q4	Q5	Q6	Q7	Q8	Q9	Q10
A	10	15	62	69	00	30	25	24	37	73
B	18	38	21	24	40	34	50	03	58	15
C	57	35	06	00	53	21	01	63	00	02
N	11	08	07	03	03	11	20	06	01	06
Total	96	96	96	96	96	96	96	96	96	96

Table I b: Total Response

	Q11	Q12	Q13	Q14	Q15	Q16	Q17	Q18	Q19	Q20
A	34	07	61	82	78	70	74	79	08	74
B	07	29	11	06	06	10	06	06	83	11
C	48	49	15	01	01	05	13	06	03	02
N	07	11	09	07	11	11	03	05	02	09
Total	96	96	96	96	96	96	96	96	96	96

[2] The tables summarize the questionnaire survey report of the coastal and non coastal BECs. The first set of four tables i.e., Ia, Ib, Ic, and Id, shows the results of the total response i.e. of 96 respondents.

The second set of tables, namely II a, II b, II c, II d, presents the total response from the coastal BECs.

The third set of tables, namely III a, III b, III c, III d, places before the total response from the non-coastal BECs.

In all the three sets of Tables questions 34, 35, 41 are left out because their answers are descriptive in nature.

In the tables:

Q = Question

A = the first of the given answer options

B = the second of the given answer options

C = the third of the given answer options

N = unanswered

Table I c: Total Response

	Q21	Q22	Q23	Q24	Q25	Q26	Q27	Q28	Q29	Q30
A	28	13	25	14	79	31	57	77	40	69
B	11	25	07	41	07	53	08	09	24	09
C	10	09	10	31	06	00	03	07	26	12
N	47	49	54	10	04	12	28	03	06	06
Total	96	96	96	96	96	96	96	96	96	96

Table I d: Total Response

	Q31	Q32	Q33	Q36	Q37	Q38	Q39	Q40
A	18	69	72	25	27	54	82	74
B	00	11	11	33	24	36	07	16
C	53	12	04	11	41	02	05	02
N	25	04	09	27	04	04	02	04
Total	96	96	96	96	96	96	96	96

Table II a: Response from the Coastal BECs

	Q1	Q2	Q3	Q4	Q5	Q6	Q7	Q8	Q9	Q10
A	00	04	40	37	00	11	06	09	19	33
B	12	20	02	09	13	22	26	01	28	11
C	33	19	02	00	33	11	01	35	00	01
N	03	05	04	02	02	04	15	03	01	03
Total	48	48	48	48	48	48	48	48	48	48

Table II b: Response from the Coastal BECs

	Q11	Q12	Q13	Q14	Q15	Q16	Q17	Q18	Q19	Q20
A	14	02	25	38	38	33	34	38	06	36
B	03	12	07	06	04	06	06	04	40	07
C	27	30	12	01	00	03	06	04	02	01
N	04	04	04	03	06	06	02	02	00	04
Total	48	48	48	48	48	48	48	48	48	48

Table II c: Response from the Coastal BECs

	Q21	Q22	Q23	Q24	Q25	Q26	Q27	Q28	Q29	Q30
A	15	02	11	07	38	16	26	33	16	35
B	04	09	01	22	06	27	07	09	14	06
C	01	07	04	16	04	00	02	05	16	05
N	28	30	32	03	00	05	13	01	02	02
Total	48	48	48	48	48	48	48	48	48	48

Table II d: Response from the Coastal BECs

	Q31	Q32	Q33	Q36	Q37	Q38	Q39	Q40
A	06	30	38	10	11	26	41	36
B	00	11	06	17	13	21	02	10
C	31	06	02	10	23	01	04	02
N	11	01	02	11	01	00	01	00
Total	48	48	48	48	48	48	48	48

Table III a: Response from the non-coastal BECs

	Q1	Q2	Q3	Q4	Q5	Q6	Q7	Q8	Q9	Q10
A	10	11	22	32	00	19	19	15	18	40
B	06	18	19	15	27	12	24	02	30	04
C	24	16	04	00	20	10	00	28	00	01
N	08	03	03	01	01	07	05	03	00	03
Total	48	48	48	48	48	48	48	48	48	48

Table III b: Response from the non-coastal BECs

	Q11	Q12	Q13	Q14	Q15	Q16	Q17	Q18	Q19	Q20
A	20	05	36	44	40	37	40	41	02	38
B	04	17	04	00	02	04	00	02	43	04
C	21	19	03	00	01	02	07	02	01	01
N	03	07	05	04	05	05	0 1	03	02	05
Total	48	48	48	48	48	48	48	48	48	48

Table III c: Response from the non-coastal BECs

	Q21	Q22	Q23	Q24	Q25	Q26	Q27	Q28	Q29	Q30
A	13	11	14	07	41	15	31	44	24	34
B	07	16	06	19	01	26	01	00	10	03
C	09	02	06	15	02	00	01	02	10	07
N	19	19	22	07	04	07	15	02	04	04
Total	48	48	48	48	48	48	48	48	48	48

Table III d: Response from the non-coastal BECs

	Q31	Q32	Q33	Q36	Q37	Q38	Q39	Q40
A	12	39	34	15	16	28	41	38
B	00	00	05	16	11	15	05	06
C	22	06	02	01	18	01	01	00
N	14	03	07	16	03	04	01	04
Total	48	48	48	48	48	48	48	48

ABBREVIATIONS

AA	*Apostolicam Actuositatem*, Vatican II, Decree on the Apostolate of Lay People, 18 November 1965 (All the documents of the Vatican II are cited from FLANNERY, A., ed. [Study Edition], New York 1987)
al.	*alii* [others]
AAS	*Acta Apostolicae Sedis* (official gazette of record for Papal and Vatican curial statements)
AC	Archives of Cochin
ACP	M. J. TYLOR, ed., *A Companion to Paul*, New York 1975
AD	*Anno Domini*
ADT	Archives of the Diocese of Trivandrum
AfER	*African Ecclesial Review*
AFJ	S. SUGIRTHARAJAH, ed., *Asian Faces of Jesus*, London 1993
AG	*Ad Gentes* (Vatican II, Decree on the Missionary Activity of the Church, 7 December 1965)
AGOCD	*Archivium Generale Ordinis Carmelitarum Discalceatorum*
AICUF	All India Catholic University Federation
AMECEA	Association of Member Episcopal Conferences of Eastern Africa
AncBD	D.N. FREEDMAN, *The Anchor Bible Dictionary*, I-VI, New York 1992
B.C	Before Christ
BB	*Bible Bhashyam*
BCC/ BCCs	Basic Christian Communities
BEC/ BECs	Basic Ecclesial Communities
BI	*Business India*
BIMA	Bishop's Institute for Missionary Apostolate
BPCDIR	*Bulletin Pontificium Concilium pro Dialogo inter Religions*
BZ	*Biblische Zeitschrift*
CBCI	Catholic Bishops' Conference of India

CBCK	Catholic Bishops' Conference of Korea
CC	*Celebrating Community*
CCC	*Catechism of the Catholic Church*
CCEO	*Codex Canonum Ecclesiarum Orientalium*
CD	*Christus Dominus* (Vatican II, Decree on the Pastoral Office of Bishop's in the Church, 28 October 1965)
CDe	*Current Dialogue*
CELAM	Consejo Episcopal Latino Americano
CHK	*Christian Heritage of Kerala*, Fs. L.M. Pylee, Cochin 1981
CIC	*Codex Iuris Canonici*
CleM	*Clergy Monthly*
CM (F)	*Le Christ au monde*
CMAA	A. D'SILVA, ed., *Creative Ministries and Affirmative Action in Todays's India*, Pune 1984
col.	Column
Conc (E)	*Concilium* (English)
Conc (I)	*Concilium* (Italian)
CS	T. GOFFI – B. SECONDIN, eds., *Corso di Spiritualità*, Brescia 1989
CWMA	Council for World Mission Archives, School of Oriental and African Studies, London
DBT	X. LÉON-DUFOUR, ed., *Dictionary of Biblical Theology*, London 1988[2]
DCEVS	S. GAROFALO – T. FEDERICI, eds., *Dizionario del Concilio Ecumenico Vaticano Secondo*, Roma 1969
DCS	G.S. WAKEFIELD, ed., *A Dictionary of Christian Spirituality*, London 1983
DES	E. ANCILLI, ed., *Dizionario enciclopedico di spiritualità*, I-III, Roma 1990
DI	J. WICKI, ed., *Documenta Indica*, I-XVII, 1948-1984
DL	*Doctrine and Life*
Dr.	Doctor
DSp	*Dictionnaire de Spiritualité*, I-XIV, Paris 1936
dt	Dated
DV	*Dei Verbum* (Vatican II, Dogmatic Constition on Divine Revelation, 18 November 1965)
EAPR	*East Asian Pastoral Review*
ed. / eds.	Editor/ Editors
Epist.	Epistula
ES	*Esperienza e Spiritualità*, Fs. C.A. Bernard, Roma 1995
ESQ.	Esquire

EX	G. SCHURHAMMER – J. WICKI, eds., *Epistolae S. Francisci Xaverii*, I, Roma 1944-45
F	Folder
FABC	Federation of the Asian Bishops' Conferences
FAPA	G. ROSALES – C.G. ARÉVALO, ed., *For All the Peoples of Asia: Federation of Asian Bishop's Conferences Documents from 1970 to 1991*, Quezon City 1992
FC	H. DRESSLER, ed., *The Fathers of the Church*, I, Washington, D.C. 1947
FCM	S. KAROTEMPRAL, ed., *Following Christ in Mission*, Bombay 1995
Fs.	Festschrift/Studies in Honour of
FX	*Francis Xavier* (G. SCHURHAMMER, *Francis Xavier*, II, Roma 1977)
Greg	*Gregorianum*
GS	*Gaudium et Spes* (Vatican II, Pastoral Constitution on the Church in the Modern World, 7 december 1965)
Her.	*Herderkorrespondenz*
IBMR	*International Bulletin of Missionary Research*
i.e.	*id est* [that is]
IMR	*Indian Missiology Review*
Irén.	*Irénikon*
IT	*India Today*
ITS	*Indian Theological Studies*
IW	*Illustrated Weekly*
J	Jacket
JDh	*Journal of Dharma*
JeDh	*Jeevadhara*
JV	*Jîvanum Velicavum*
KCBC	Kerala Catholic Bishops' Conference
KCYM	Kerala Youth Movement
LCK	M. ARATTUKULAM, ed., *The Latin Catholics of Kerala*, Kottayam 1993
LG	*Lumen Gentium* (Vatican II, Dogmatic Constituion on the Church, 21 November 1964)
LMC	*Les Missions Catholique*
LMS	London Missionary Society
LouvSt	*Louvain Studies*
LV	*Lumen Vitae*
Mal	Malayalam
MEB	*Movimento de Educacção de Base*
MilSt	*Milltown Studies*

MIT	K. PATHIL, ed., *Mission in India Today: The Task of St. Thomas Christians*, Bangalore 1988
Mons. / Msgr	Monsignore
Ms	Manuscript
MX	A. VALIGNANO, ed., *Monumenta Xaveriana*, I-II, Matriti 1899-1912
n. / ns.	number / numbers
NA	*Nostra Aetate* (Vatican II, Declaration on the Relation of the Church to non-Christian Religions, 28 October 1965)
NBCLC	National Biblical Catechetical & Liturgical Centre
NDCS	M. DOWNEY, ed., *The New Dictionary of Catholic Spirituality*, Minnesota 1993
NDS	S. DE FIORES – T. GOFFI, eds. *Nuovo dizionario di spiritualità,* Roma 1979[5]
NIDNTT	C. BROWN, ed., *The New International Dictionary of the New Testament Theology*, I-IV, Grand Rapids 1975
NJBC	R.E. BROWN – J.A. FITZMYER – R.E. MURPHY, eds., *The New Jerome Biblical Commentary*, London 1992
OBC	Other Backward Communities
OR	*L'Osservatore Romano* (Daily Italian edition)
OR (E)	*L'Osservatore Romano* (English Weekly edition)
OT	*Optatam Totius*, (Vatican II, Decree on the Training of Priests, 28 October 1965)
PAC	Parish Archives of Chullimanoor
PAK	Parish Archives of Kochuthura
PAP	Parish Archives of Parassala
PBC	Pontifical Biblical Commission
PCO	Programme for Community Organization
PL	*Patrologia Latina*
PMV	*Pro Mundi Vita*
PO	*Presbyterorum Ordinis* (Vatican II, Decree on the Ministry and Life of Priests, 7 December 1965)
POC	Pastoral Orientation Centre
PPn	Personal Possession
PUU	Pontificia Universitas Urbaniana
Ref. n.	Reference Number
Rs	Rupees
SC	*Sacrosanctum Concilium* (Vatican II, The Constitution on the Sacred Liturgy, 4 December 1963)
SCDF	Sacred Congregation for the Doctrine of the Faith
SEDOS	*Servizio di documentazione e studi*
SFSp	*Studies in Formative Spirituality*

SIRD	*Studies in Inter-religious Dialogue*
SM (E)	*Sacramentum Mundi* (New York)
SpTo	*Spirituality Today*
Sr.	Sister
SSLC	Secondary School Leaving Certificate
St.	Saint
STCEI	G. MENACHERY, ed., *The St. Thomas Christian Encyclopedia of India*, I-II, Trichur 1973
StMiss	*Studia missionalia*
StS	*Studies in Spirituality*
STW	K.C. ABRAHAM – MBUY-BEYA, eds., *Spirituality of the Third World*, New York 1994
SU	Studia Urbaniana
TDC	Trivandrum District Council
TDNT	G. KITTEL – G. FRIEDRICH, eds., *Theological Dictionary of the New Testament*, I-X, Michigan 1990
ThStud	*Theological Studies*
Th.Inv.	*Theological Investifgations*
TR– IL	Travancore – Incoming Letters
TR– R	Travancore – Report
tr.	Translated
TSA	Trivandrum Seminary Archives
TSSS	Trivandrum Social Service Society
TVM	Trivandrum (Thiruvananthapuram)
UBSP	Urban Basic Services for the Poor
UR	*Unitatis Redintegratio* (Vatican II, Decree on Ecumenism, 21 November 1964)
VAP	R. LATOURELLE, ed., *Vatican II: Assessment and Perspectives*, II-III, New York 1989
VFTW	*Voices from the Third World*
VJTR	*Vidyajyoti Journal of Theological Reflection*
VN	*Vida Nueva*
VSVD	*Verbum SVD* (*Verbum Societatis Verbi Divini*)
WoWo	Word & Worship
ZThK	*Zeitschrift für Theologie und Kirche*

BIBLIOGRAPHY

1. Sources

ALEXANDER, X., ed., *Report of the Commission on Pastoral Ministries*, Trivandrum (1990) in ADT.

ALLEN, *To R. W. Thompson*, Letter, 9 January, 1894, India Odds, Box 16, F 1, J B in CWMA.

ALPHONSE, A. M., *La Religion dans les Missions des Carmes Déchaussés au Malabar – Diocèse de Quilon: Tableau comparatif des Pagodes, Mosquées Temples Protestants & Églises Catholiques*, Aprilis (1903) A, Plut 452 in *AGOCD*.

AMADO, J., *Thiruvananthapuram Rūpata Aṭministrētaruṭe Kattu*, [Letter of Trivandrum Diocesan Administrator] n. 337/90/18b (8d-Com) in ADT.

ANTONIETTA, *Report of the All Kerala Workshop on Community Building at Trivandrum from 1 to 5 May*, (1995) in ADT.

ANTONY, K., – al., *Petition for the Approval of the Rules of Confraternity of Mother of Sorrows to His Lordship the Bishop of Cochin*, n. 322, 25 February, 1936 in AC.

ANTONY, R., *Report of the Committee for the Formation of Basic Christian Communities*, 12 February, 1992 in PPn.

———, *Basic Christian Communities: A short Report*, Quilon, (1994) PPn.

ANTONY, R., *Letter*, 16 November, 1994 in PPn.

Authorization by Ringeltaube to Vedamanikam [A true copy of the certificate to the late Maha Rasan Vethamanikam, the oldest catechist of Mylaudy], India Odds, Box 15, F 1 in CWMA.

BENZIGER, A.M, *To Rev. Fr. Brocard: Parassala & Manivila*, n. 2540, Letter, Quilon, 23 March, 1917 in PAP.

———, *Division du Diocèse de Quilon en trois*, Quilon, 24 Mai, 1929, A, Plut 452 in *AGOCD*.

———, *To the Carmelite General*, Letter, Trivandrum, 16 July, 1932, A, Plut – 452 in *AGOCD*.

BENZIGER, A.M, *Copie d'une lettre de son Exc. Mgr. Alois-Marie Benziger, Arch. Tit. d'Antinoe (ci-devant Evêque de Quilon) au Très Rév. P. Guillaume de S. Albert, Général de's Carees Déchausés, au sujet de l'érection du Siège archiépiscopal de son Exc. Mar Ivanios à Trivandrum, capitale du Travancore*, Trivandrum, 24 Août, 1932, A, Plut 453 in *AGOCD*.

BERNARDIN, *To Rev. Fr. Damascene: Tettiode – Trithuvapuram: Baptism & Conversion*, n. 300, Letter, Quilon, 7 February, 1930 in PAP.

———, *Accounts & Church Contribution, Parassala*, Letter, n. 6207, Quilon, 22 April, 1932 in PAP.

———, *To Rev. Fr. Damascene: Parassala House in Church Property*, Letter, n. 10949, Letter, Quilon, 18 October, 1934 in PAP.

———, *To Rev. Fr. Damascene: Parassala: Church Money & Feast*, n. 12418, Quilon, 4 July, 1935 in PAP.

———, *To Rev. & Dear Fr. J. Damascene» Airy–Manivila New centre of conversions & Catechists*, n. 11918, Letter, Quilon, 30 March, 1935 in PAP.

———, *To Fr. Herman*, Letter, Quilon, 19 July, 1932, A, Plut 453 in *AGOCD*.

———, *To Mons. Leone P. Kierkels, Delegate Apostolico delle Indie, Bangalore* (Copy) no. 9765, Letter, A, Plut 452 in *AGOCD*.

———, *Muthukolam, Conversion of Jacobites*: Ref. n. 3474/34, 25 March 1934, A, Plut 452 in *AGOCD*.

———, *Number of conversions in the Mission of Quilon, India, from July 1933 to June 1934*, Quilon, July, 1934, A, Plut 452 in *AGOCD*.

BROWN, *As a Missionary Opportunity*, Trivandrum, (1859) India Odds, Box 16, F 1856-1859 in CWMA.

CLARKE, W.S., – al., *Slavery in Travancore: From the Friend of India*, (copy) 10 February, 1853, India Odds, Box 16, F 1852-55 in CWMA.

«"Comprimssio"[sic] *of the Confraternity of O. L. Mother of Doloures established in Mullavalappu Chapel*», n. 321 (1936) in AC.

«Correspondence Regarding Mr. Mead's Marriage to a Native Woman», TR–IL, Box 4, F 2, J C in CWMA.

COX, J., *The Assault Case: Trivandrum*, (1850) India Odds, Box 16, F 1846-51 in CWMA.

———, *Movement among Ezhavars at Vakkum*, Trivandrum, (1852) India Odds, Box 16, F 1852-55 in CWMA.

———, *Report of Trevandrum and Quilon for the year 1859*, (1859) TR – IL, Box 5, F 4, J A in CWMA.

Cox, J., *Replies of Missionaries to Dr. Tidman's Enquiries on the Upper Cloth Controversy*, Nagercoil, September 12(1859) India Odds, Box 16, F 1856-59 in CWMA.

——, *To R.W. Thompson*, Letter, 8 May, 1893, India Odds, Box 15, F 1, J B in CWMA.

Dereere, V.V., *The «Status Missionis» of the Latin Diocese of Trivandrum for the year 1 July 1938 to 30 June 1939 to His Eminence Peter Cardinal Fumasoni-Biondi, Prefect S. Congr. Prop. of the Faith*, Trivandrum, 26 September, 1939, A, Plut 452 in *AGOCD*.

——, *Circular Letter: Consecration of the Diocese to the S. Heart*, n. 1757, Trivandrum, 30 December, 1941 in ADT.

——, *To Reverend Fathers Parish Priests*, n. 7711, Letter, Trivandrum, 24 May, 1950 in ADT.

——, *Advent & the Erection of the Catholic Action Society*, n. 7036, Pastoral Letter, Trivandrum, 21 November, 1950 in ADT.

Devadas, *Report on the Dalit Christians*, TSSS Trivandrum (1994) PPn.

Duncan Esq. D., *Acting Director of Public Instruction, to the Chief Secretary to Government*, Madras, 5 October, 1893, TR – IL, Box 15, F 3, J B in CWMA.

First National Council of India, *Synodal Letter*, 19 February, 1950 in ADT.

Gregory, R.B., *Inter-diocesan BCC Seminar Report*, Trivandrum, 25 January, 1995, in ADT.

Gudgeon, B., *Mar Ivanios and the Jacobites*, A, Plut 453 in *AGOCD*.

Hacker, «Marriage with Heathen», in *Printed Report*, Neyoor (1885) India Odds, Box 17, F 1884-99 in CWMA.

——, «Printed Report, 1886», Neyoor, (1886) India Odds, Box 17, F 1884-99 in CWMA.

Hacker, «Palmyra Climbing and Sunday Observance», in *Printed Report*, Neyoor, (1888) India Odds, Box 17, F 1884-99 in CWMA.

Ildaphonse, *Summarium Relationum Annualium Districtus Trevandrum – Neyyattinkara a I Julii 1931 ad Junii 1932*, 10 Julii, 1932, A, Plut 454 in *AGOCD*.

——, *Letter to Msgr. Bernardine*, 11 April, 1934, A, Plut 452 in *AGOCD*.

——, *Legion of Mary*, 19 January 1934 in A, Plut - 454 in *AGOCD*.

Ivanios, M., *To the Jacobite Patriarch of Antioch, Ignatius Elias*, Letter, (copy) Tiruvalla, 19 January, 1931, A, Plut 453 in *AGOCD*.

——, *To the Fides Service in Roma*, Letter, Quilon, 20 November, 1931, A, Plut 453 in *AGOCD*.

IVANIOS, M., *Christmas Message*, Translation from Malayalam (1930) A, Plut 453 in *AGOCD*.

JACOB, A.B., *Golden Jubilee of Our Diocese: Meeting,* n. 75/87/18b, 3 March, 1987, Trivandrum (1987) in ADT.

———, *Golden Jubilee of Our Diocese: Meeting* (II) n. 92/87/18b, 21 March, 1987, Trivandrum (1987) in ADT.

———, *Golden Jubilee of Our Diocese: Meeting* (III) n. 117/87/18b 27 April, 1987, Trivandrum (1987) in ADT.

———, *Golden Jubilee of Our Diocese: Living Together* (IV) n. 18b/87, 12 June, 1987, Trivandrum (1987) in ADT.

———, *Golden Jubilee of Our Diocese: Living Together* (V) n. 18b/87 14 July, 1987, Trivandrum (1987) in ADT.

———, *Metrānte Kattu: Suvarnajūbili – Thiruvananthapuram Rūpata* [Bishop's Pastoral Letter: Golden Jubilee–Diocese of Trivandrum], n. 18b/87, 7 August, 1987, Trivandrum (1987) in ADT.

———, *Golden Jubilee of Our Diocese: Living Together* (VI) n. 18b/87, 14 September, 1987, Trivandrum (1987) in ADT.

———, *Priests of our Diocese and to those priests who would render their services during our absence, Golden Jubilee of Our Diocese: Living Together* (VII) n. 18b/87, 14 August, 1987, Trivandrum (1987) in ADT.

———, *Golden Jubilee of Our Diocese: Living Together* (VIII) n. 18b/87, 26 August, 1987, Trivandrum (1987) in ADT.

———, *Priests and Religious, Golden Jubilee of Our Diocese: Living Together* (IX) n. 18b/87, 6 October, 1987, Trivandrum (1987) in ADT.

———, *Rūpata Pastoral Counciline Sambandicca Iṭaya leghanam* [Pastoral Letter on the Pastoral Council], n. 310/89/8b, 7 October, 1989, Trivandrum (1987) in ADT.

JAMESTOWN, *1856: A General Description,* India Odds, Box 16 F. 1856-59 in CWMA.

JESSINA, *A Study of Chullimanoor Forane,* (1994) in PAC.

JONES, E., «Work among Fishermen», in *Printed Report,* Neyoor, (1888) India Odds, Box 17, F 1884-1899 in CWMA.

KUMAR, S. – RAJADAS, *The Report of the Pastoral Exposure Programme Submitted to Fr. George Paul on 1May 1994,* Trivandrum (1994) in TSA.

LEAN, R.P., *Briefing of BEC process in Trivandrum given to Bishop Bosco Penha of Bombay,* Pastoral Ministry, Trivandrum, 15 November, 1991 in ADT.

LEON, C., ed., *Summary Report of the Commission on Social Action Board*, Trivandrum, (1990) in ADT.

LOURDAYYAN, W., *Aṭistāna Kṛstîya Samūham* [Basic Ecclesial Communities], Palayam Forane Covention Report, Thiru-vananthapuram, (1994) in ADT.

LUCAS, *Au Venerable Définitoire General O.C.D.*, Trivandrum, 13 fevrier, 1947, A, Plut 452 in *AGOCD*.

MARY, A., *To Fr. Bernardine*, Letter, Ernakulam, 12 July, 1932, A, Plut 453 in *AGOCD*.

MARYKUTTY, *Lay Apostolate*, FA/1/90, 26 June, 1990, Trivandrum (1990) in ADT.

MATEER, S., «Position in Trivandrum», in *Printed Report*, Neyoor, (1864) India Odds, Box 17, F 1863-64 in CWMA.

————, *To Duhie*, Letter, (copy) Trevandrum, 20 August, 1867, TR – IL, Box 7, F 2, J B in CWMA.

————, *Parachaley Report: Position in Trivandrum*, (1864) Box 17, F 1863-64 in CWMA.

MATTHIAS, *Review of the History of the College*, 20 December, 1906, India Odds, Box 17 in CWMA.

MAULT, M., *The Girl's School and Slavery: Nagercoil*, (1830), India Odds, Box 16, F 1829-1835 in CWMA.

MAULT, C., *To Mead C.*, Letter, (copy) 9 July, 1850, Box 4, F. 2 in CWMA.

————, *To the Directors of LMS*, Letter, 25 September, 1851, Box 4, F 2, J C, in CWMA.

MEAD, C., *To Burder*, Letter, Quilon, 4 April, 1818, TR – IL, Box 1, F 1 in CWMA.

————, *To Burder*, Letter, Nagercoil, 10 August, 1819, TR – IL, Box 1, F 1 in CWMA.

————, *To Rev. Clayton*, Letter, Neyoor, 12 January, 1833, India Odds, Box 16 in CWMA.

MEAD, C., *Replies to Questions Drawn Up by G.H. Baber on the Condition of Slaves in Travancore and Cochin*, 18 April, 1843, TR – IL, Box 3, F 2, J E in CWMA.

————, *Written report*, March 6 (1846) India Odds, Box 16, F, 1836-1845 in CWMA.

MENDEZ, L., ed., *Summary of the Report of the Commission for Temporalities*, Trivandrum, (1990) in ADT.

MERCATI, A., ed., *Monumenta Vaticana*, Roma MCMXXII.

«Minutes of the Travancore District Committee» (LMS), 12 November, 1894, India Odds, Box 16, F2, J C in CWMA.

NICHOLAS, M., Letter, Trivandrum, 2 June, 1995 in PPn.

PAKIAM, S.M., Kraistava Jîvitam 2000 Āṇṭil [Christian Life – 2000], n. 18b/90, 28 February, 1990, Trivandrum (1990) in ADT.

———, Metrānte Kattu: Sākṣarata [Bishop's Letter: Literacy], n. 18b/90, 25 July, 1990, Trivandrum, (1990) in ADT.

———, Decree, n. 306/90/18b, Trivandrum, (1990) in ADT.

———, Metrānte Nōymbukāla Sandēśam [Lenten Message of the Bishop], n. 18B/91, 13 February, 1991, Trivandrum (1991) in ADT.

———, Aṭistāna Kraistava Samūhaṅgal, Pastoral Letter [Basic Ecclesial Communities], n. 18 B/91, 10 April, 1991, Trivandrum, (1991) in ADT.

———, Letter to Bishop Bosco Penha, Trivandrum, 4 September, 1991 in ADT.

———, Sākṣarata Raṇḍām Ghaṭṭam [Literacy: Second Stage], n. 18 B/92, 1 August, 1992, Trivandrum (1992) in ADT.

———, Invitation for Full-time Religious Personnel, Letter, 2-9-1992, Trivandrum (1992) in ADT.

———, Metrānte Kattu: Tapasukāla Sandēśam [Bishop's Lenten Message], n. 2/92, 4-2-1992, Trivandrum, February, 1992 in ADT.

———, February 4: Akhilēndia Bandh [February 4: All India Bandh], 29 January, 1994, Trivandrum, (1994) in ADT.

———, 1995: Azhimati Virudha Varṣācaranam (1995: Anti-corruption Year), n. 18b/95, 31 January, 1995 in ADT

———, Thiruvananthapuram Latîn Kattōlikka Rūpata Bodhipikkunna Apēkṣa [Memorandum submitted by the Latin Catholics of Trivandrum], n. 126/95/9g, Trivandrum, 13 March 1995 in ADT.

———, Āgamanakālam: Viśuāsavum Pravarttium [Advent: Faith and Life], Pastoral Letter, 27 November, 1995, Trivandrum (1995) in ADT.

PEREIRA, E., Pastoral Council Report, Trivandrum, 10 March , 1990, in ADT.

PEREIRA, E., The Pastoral Council Report, 4 July, 1990 in ADT.

PLATINHO, C. A., Diocese of Cochin, no 49 [The order to erect the Confraternity of Our Lady Mother of Douloures in the Mullavalappu Chapel attached to the Parish of St. Antony's Church, Amarabady, by the Vicar General], n. 324 (1936) in AC.

Premier Anniversaire de la Conversion des deux Eveques Jacobites: Discours Emouvants des Deux Prelats, (1931) A, Plut 453 in AGOCD.

Relatio «Extraordinaria» Diocesis Quilonensis – Anno 1927, (1927) A, Plut 452 in *AGOCD*.

Report of the Nagercoil Station, January – June (1829) India Odds, Box 16 in CWMA.

«*Report of the Nagercoil Station For The Year 1844*», India Odds, Box 16 in CWMA.

RESALAYYAN, V., *Report: Anti-alcoholism Movement in the Foranate of Undencode*, 13 June, 1994 in PPn.

RINGELTAUBE, *Letter*, Mylaudy, 4 January, 1813 in South India General, Box 2, F 1, J A in CWMA.

———, *Journal from January 7, 1813 to January 20, 1816*, India Odds, Box 15, F 1 in CWMA.

RUSSEL – LEWIS – WHITEHOUSE, *To C. Mead*, Letter, (copy) 9 July, 1850, TR – IL Box 3, F 2, J C in CWMA.

RUSSEL, *The Shanars and Pariars: A General Description*, 24 January, 1856, India Odds, Box 18, F 1856-1859 in CWMA.

SANTHA, *Kṭumbayōga Report*, Kochuthura, Trivandrum, October 22 (1990) in *PAK*.

SINCLAIR, R.S., *Report of the Parachaley Mission District for the Year 1914*, Letter to Foster, Box, 9, TR – R in CWMA.

SELVARAJ, R.B., *Report of the Animation Seminar at Vettuthura* – 5th June to 9th June 1989, Trivandrum (1989) in ADT.

THALIATH, J., *To I. C. Chaco*, Letter, Trivandrum, 10 March, 1934, A, Plut 453 in *AGOCD*.

THE CLERGY AND THE LAITY OF THE TRIVANDRUM PROVINCE, *Letter to His Excellency the Most Rev.Dr.Aloysius M. Benziger, D.C., Archbishop of Antinopolis*, 12 March, 1933 in *AGOCD*.

THOMAS, E.J., ed., *Summary of Education Commission's Report*, Trivandrum (1990) in ADT.

THOMAS, S., *Letter*, Trivandrum, 22 August, 1994 in PPn.

«*Translation of a Proclamation by Her Highness The Ranî (Ranee) of Travancore*», 3 February, 1829, TR – IL, Box 3, F2, J E in CWMA.

TSSS, *Reports on each Vicariate conducted in 1992-93*, (1993) in ADT.

VALIGNANO, A., *Monumenta Xaveriana*, Matriti 1899-1990.

WHITEHOUSE, «To Tidman, Seminary Report», 30 August, 1852, India Odds, Box 16 in CWMA

WICKI, J., ed., *Documenta Indica*, I-XVII, Roma 1948-1984.

WILFRED, E., *Kerala Catholic Youth Movement*, KCYM 90/C – 10, Trivandrum, 3 October, 1990 in ADT.

WILLS, H,T., *Trivandrum City–1914*, (1914) Box 9, TR – R, in CWMA.

———, *To Rev. F. Lenwood*, Letter, Trivandrum, 21 November, 1914, Box 25, F 2, TR – IL, in CWMA.

YESUDAS, S., *Pastoral Council Report*, 26 January, 1991 in ADT.

2. Church Documents

BENEDICT XV, *Maximum Illud*, Apostolic Letter, Roma 1919.

Catechism of the Catholic Church, Roma 1992, [English Edition, 1994].

CBCI, *Church in India Today* [All India Seminar], New Delhi 1969.

———, *Report of the of the General Meeting of the CBCI: Ernakulam, January 7- 16, 1970*, New Delhi 1970.

———, *Report on the General Meeting, Calcutta 1974*, Delhi 1974.

———, *Report of the Standing Committee Meeting, Bombay, March 21 – 22 & Kottayam April 12 – 13 & 22, 1988*, New Delhi 1988.

———, *Report of the General Committee Meetings: Kottayam, April 1988*, New Delhi 1988.

CBCI EVALUATION COMMITTEE, *CBCI Evaluation Report, The Catholic Bishops' Conference of India: Retrospect and Prospects*, New Delhi 1995.

Codex Iuris Canonici, Roma 1983.

Instrumentum Laboris: The Consecrated Life and its Role in the Church and in the World, Roma 1994.

JOHN PAUL II, *Redemptor Hominis*, Encyclical Letter, Roma 1979.

———, *Catechesi Tradendae*, Apostolic Exhortation, Roma 1979.

———, «Mensagem deixada às comunidades eclesiais de base, no Brasil», 10-7-1980, in *Todos os pronunciamentos do Papa no Brasil*, São Paulo (1980) 257-261.

———, «Address to the Bishops of India», Delhi, 1 February, 1986, *AAS* 78 (1986) 745-753.

———, «Address to the Faithful of Kerala and Tamilnadu at Trivandrum», 8 February, 1986, in *Insegnamenti di Giovanni Paolo II*, IX, 1, Roma 1986, 387-393.

———, «L'Omelia durante la concelebrazione Eucaristica nel "Domain Park" di Auckland», 22 November, 1986, in *Insegnamenti di Giovanni Paolo II*, IX, 2 Roma 1986, 1538-1545.

JOHN PAUL II, *Sollicitudo Rei Socialis,* Encyclical Letter, Roma 1987.

——, *Christifideles Laici,* Apostolic Exhortation, Roma 1988.

——, *Mulieris Dignitatem,* Apostolic Letter, Roma 1988.

——, *Redemptoris Missio,* Encyclical Letter, Roma 1990.

——, *Pastores Dabo Vobis,* Apostolic Exhortation, Roma 1992.

——, «Address to the Fourth General Conference of Latin American Bishop's in Santo Domingo», in *Santo Domingo and Beyond,* ed. A. T. Hennelly, New York 1993.

——, *Letter to Families,* Roma 1994.

——, *Tertio Millennio Adveniente,* Apostolic Letter, Roma 1994.

——, «Homily for Closing Mass of the Ninth Synod», *OR*(E) 2 November, 1994.

——, *Women: Teachers of Peace,* Apostolic Message, Roma 1995.

——, «Homily in Sri Lanka on 21 January 1995», *OR*(E) 1 February 1995, 6-7.

——, «New Evangelization Needs Sound Spirituality of Communion», *OR*(E) 22 February, 1995, 1.

——, *Ecclesia in Africa,* Apostolic Exhortation, Roma 1995.

——, *Evangelium Vitae,* Encyclical Letter, Roma 1995.

——, *Letter to Priests,* Roma 1995.

——, *Letter to Women,* Roma 1995.

——, *Ut Unum Sint,* Encyclical Letter, Roma 1995.

——, «La grande primavera del cristianesimo, importante tema dell'Assemblea Speciale per l'Asia del Sinodo dei Vescovi, ora in preparazione» [Address to the Bishops of the Provinces of Bhopal, Calcutta, Delhi and Ranchi at the «ad limina»], *OR* 28-29 agosto, 1995, 4.

——, «Il Vangelo vi rafforzi nel legame di unità e di carità, affinché tutti insieme i Vescovi dell'India formino una sola mente e un solo cuore» [Address to the Bishops of the Provinces Bombay, Goa, Hyderabad, Nagpur and Verapoly], *OR* 14 dicembre, 1995, 7.

KCBC, *Namārum Annyaralla* [We Are Not Strangers to Each Other], 15 August, 1993.

——, *Report of the Kerala Catholic Bishops' Conference, Commission for Family,* Cochin 1983.

——, *The Report of All Kerala Family Apostolate Consultation,* Alwaye 1983.

KCBC, *Report of the General Body Meeting of the KCBC Commission for the POC held on 26th May*, Kochi 1992.

PAUL VI, *Ecclesiam Suam*, Encyclical Letter, Roma 1964.

————, *Populorum Progressio*, Encyclical Letter, Roma 1967.

————, «Address to the Bishops of Asia», *ASS* 63 (1971) 21-27.

————, L'Eucaristia centro di unità comunitaria e gerarchica della chiesa», in *Insegnamenti di Paolo VI*, X (1972) 909-913.

————, «Address to the College of Cardinals», 22 June, 1973, *AAS* 65 (1973) 381-391.

————, «Address for the opening of the Third General Assembly of the Synod of Bishops», 27 September, 1974, *AAS* 66 (1974) 557-564.

————, *Evangelii Nuntiandi*, Apostolic Exhortation, Roma 1975.

————, «Homily for the Closing of the Holy Year», 25 December, 1975, *AAS* 68 (1976) 143-145.

PBC, *The Interpretation of the Bible in the Church*, Roma 1993.

————, *Unity and Diversity in the Church*, Roma 1991.

PIUS XI, *Rerum Ecclesiae,* Encyclical Letter, Roma 1926.

PIUS XI, *«In Ora Malabarica»*, *AAS* 30 (1938) 90-92.

PONTIFICAL COUNCIL FOR PROMOTING CHRISTIAN UNITY, *Directory for the Application of the Principles and Norms of Ecumenism*, Roma 1993.

PONTIFICIUM CONSILIUM PRO LAICIS, *Spirituality of the Laity: Forms and Movements Today*, Roma 1981 [Documentation Service, n. 7].

————, *Lay Voices at the Synod*, Roma 1988 [Documentation Service, n. 19].

SCDF, *Instruction on Certain Aspects of the «Theology of Liberation»*, Roma 1984.

————, *Instruction on Christian Freedom and Liberation*, Roma 1986.

————, *Some Aspects of the Church Understood as Communion*, Roma 1992.

3. General Works

AA. VV., «Planning for the Church in Eastern Africa in the 1980's», *AfER*, 1 & 2 (1974).

AA. VV., *AMECEA Plenary 1976: Building Christian Communities*, *AfER*, 5 (1976).

AA. VV., *Le Organizzazioni Revoluzionarie nelle Chiesa Europee*, Roma 1973.

AA. VV., *The Cultural Heritage of India*, I, Calcutta 1953-58.

AA. VV., *The Documents of Vatican II*, New York 1966.

AA. VV., *The World's Great Religions*, New York 1957.

ABRAHAM, K.C., – MBUY-BEYA, B., eds., *Spirituality of the Third World*, New York 1994.

ABRAHAM, V., «Between Brew and Blue Water», *The Week* 14 February, 1993 24-26.

————, «Neighbours in Love: Experiment in Ideal Society in a Kerala Village», *The Week* 30 January, 1994, 14-17.

ACHARUPARAMBIL, D., *Induismo: vita e pensiero,* Roma 1976.

————, «The Problem of Presenting Christianity to Hinduism», in *Evangelization e Culture*, Roma 1976, 162-182.

————, *Spiritualità e mistica indù,* Roma 1982.

————, «Hinduism» in *FCM*, 256-265.

ACHUTHAMENON, C., *The Cochin State Manual*, Ernakulam 1911.

AGUILAR, M.I., «An African Theology of Praxis through Small Christian Communiites», *AfER* 37 (1995) 142-155.

AGUR, C.M., *Church History of Travancore*, New Delhi 1903.

AIYA, V.N., *Travancore State Manual*, I-III, New Delhi 1906.

ALBARIS, J., *The Trivandrum Latin Diocese and Social Service Society 1937-1985*, Madura 1986. A Master Degree dissertation, Madhura Kamaraj University, Tamil Nadu.

ALEXANDER, J., «What Do Recent Writers Mean by Spirituality?», *SpTo* 3 (1980) 247-256.

ALPHONSO, H., *The Personal Vocation: Transformation in Depth through the Spiritual Exercises*, Roma 1992

————, *Building up the Church: An Exegetico-Theological Inquiry into the New Testament Teaching on «Edification»,* Roma 1992.

————, *Placed with Christ the Son*, Anand 1993.

————, *Priestly Vocation and Consecrated Life,* Anand 1993.

ALPHONSO, H., ed., *Esperienza e Spiritualità*, Fs. C. A. Bernard, Roma 1995.

AMALADOSS, M. – JOHN, T.K. – SAUCH, G.G., eds., *Theologizing in India*, Bangalore 1981.

AMALADOSS, M., *Becoming Indian: The Process of Inculturation,* Roma 1992.

————, «The Pluralism of Religions and the Significance of Christ», in *AFJ*, 85-103.

————, «The Spirituality of Dialogue», *SIRD* 3 (1993) 58-69.

AMALADOSS, M., «An Emerging Indian Theology: Some Exploratory Reflections», *VJTR* 58 (1994) 473-484. 59(1994) 559-572.

————, «Being a Christian Community among Other Believing Communities», *CDe* June, 1994, 23-33.

————, «Inter-religious Dialogue: A View from Asia», *IBMR* 19 (1995) 2-5.

AMALORPAVADASS, D.S., ed., *Post - Vatican Liturgical Renewal in India at All Levels*, Bangalore 1972.

————, *Gospel and Culture*, Bangalore 1978.

————, ed., *Indian Christian Spirituality*, Bangalore 1982.

————, «Meaning and Role of the Charismatic Renewal in India Today – Its Challenges», *WoWo* 10 (1977) 92-93.

————, «A Theology of Mission in India Today», in *MIT*, 323-346.

AMATO, A., ed., *La Chiesa locale*, Roma 1976.

AMBEDKAR, D.R., *Slavery and Untouchability*, New Delhi 1989.

————, *Christianising the Untouchables*, Madras 1994.

ANCILLI, E., ed., *Mistagogia e direzione spirituale*, Roma 1985.

ANTON, A., «Iglesia universal, Iglesias particulares», *EE* 47 (1972) 409-435.

ANTONY, E.P., «Origin and Growth of the Latin Catholics», in *LCK* 9-100.

————, «Hierarchy and the Community» in *LCK,,* 329-456.

APREM, M., «The Nestorian Church in India from 5th to 16th Ventury», in *CHK,,* 37-47.

ARATTUKULAM, M., ed., *Latin Catholics of Kerala,* Kottayam 1993.

ARAVINDAKKSHAN, P., «Crusade on the Coast», *The Week* 17-23 June, 1984, 10-14.

ARAVINDAN, G., «In the Shoes of the Fishermen», *IW* 29 July, 1984, 18.

ARULSAMY, S., «Some Comments on a Recent "Final Statement on the Indian Theological Association"», *ITS,* 31 (1994) 67-71.

AU, W., *By Way of the Heart: Toward a Holistic Christian Spirituality*, New York 1989.

AUMANN, J., *Christian Spirituality in the Catholic Tradition*, London 1989.

————, tr., *Compendium of Spirituality*, New York 1992.

AYYAR, L.K.A., *Anthropology of the Syrian Christians*, Ernakulam 1926.

AZARIAH, M., *The Un-Christian Side of the Indian Church*, Bangalore 1989.

AZEVEDO, M. DE C., *Basic Ecclesial Communities in Brazil: The Challenge of a New Way of Being Church*, Washington 1987.

AZEVEDO, M. DE C., *The Consecrated Life: Crossroads & Directions*, New York 1995.

BALASUNDARAM, F.J., «The Prophetic Voices of Asia: Part II», *Logos* 1-2 (1994) 1-7.

BALASURIYA, T., «Contestation in the Church in Asia», *Con* (E) 8/7 (1971) 60-65.

BALI, G., «The Basic Features of Life in an Ashram», *OR* (E) 19 October, 1994, 8

BALTZEL, E.D., *The Search for Community in Modern America*, New York 1968.

BARBÉ, D., *Grace and Power: Basic Communities and Nonviolence in Brazil*, New York 1987.

BARRUFFO, A., «Laico», in *NDS*, 810-828.

BARTOLOMEO, P.S., *India Orientalis Christiana*, Roma 1794.

———, *Viaggio alle Indie Orientali*, Roma 1796.

BASELIOS, C.M., «The Reunion Movement: Its Contribution to Christian Heritage», in *CHK*, 308-315.

BASHAM, A.L., *The Wonder that Was India*, New York 1954.

———, «Jainism and Buddhism», in *Sources of Indian Tradition*, New Delhi 1963, 37-202.

BECKER, K.J., «The Teaching of Vatican II on Baptism: A Stimulus for Theology», in *VAP*, II, 47-99.

BENZIGER, M., *Archbishop Benziger: A Carmelite in India*, California 1977.

BERNARD, C.A., *Teologia Spirituale*, Roma 1989.

BERNARD, C.A., ed., *La Spiritualià come Teologia*, Milano 1993.

BESNARD, A.M. «Tendencies of Contemporary Spirituality», *Conc*(E) 9/1(1965) 14-24.

BIFET, J.E., *Spirituality for A Missionary Church*, Roma 1994.

BITTLINGER, A., *Gifts and Graces*, London 1967.

«Bishops 1995 Pastoral Letters Focus on Family Values and Small Christian Communities», in *CBCK News Letter* 4 (1994) 3.

BLÖCHLINGER, A., *The Modern Parish Community*, London 1965.

BOFF, C., «The Nature of Basic Christian Communities», *Conc*(E)144/4 (1981) 53-58.

———, «The Church in Latin America: between Perplexity and Creativity», *SEDOS Bulletin* 15 May, 1995, 131-141.

BOFF, L., *Ecclesiogenesis: The Base Communities Reinvent the Church*, New York 1986.

BOFF, L., *Church: Charism & Power*, New York 1992.

BORRIELLO, L., «Spirituality in Modern Times», in *Compendium of Spirituality*, tr. J. Aumann, New York 1992, 47-59.

BOUYER, L., *L' Eglise de Dieu*, Paris 1970.

BOUYER, L. – VANDENBROUCKE, F., *A History of Christian Spirituality*, I-II, Kent 1968.

BROWN, C., ed., *The New International Dictionary of the New Testament Theology*, I, Grand Rapids 1975.

BROWN, L.W., *The Indian Christians of St. Thomas: An Account of the Ancient Syrian Church of Malabar*, Cambridge 1956.

BROWN, R.E. – OSIEK, C. – PERKINS, P., «Early Church», in *NJBC*, 1338-1353.

BÜHLMANN, W., «The Mission of the Church in India in the 21st Century» in *MIT*, 313-322.

BUNNIK, R.J., «Common-purpose Groups in Western Europe», *Conc*(E) 8/7 (1971) 22-31.

BUSA, R., ed., *Index Thomisticus: Sancti Thomae Aquinatis operum omnium indices et Conciliumordantiae,* Sectio II: *Conciliumordantiae operum thomisticorum: Conciliumordantia prima,* XXI, Stuttgart, 1975.

CALATI, B., «Parola di Dio», in *NDS*, 1134-1151.

CALDWELL, R., *The Tinnevelly Shanars*, London 1850.

CAPRILE, G., ed., *Il Sinodo dei Vescovi 1974,* Roma 1975.

——, *Il sinodo dei Vescovi 1977,* Roma 1978.

CARAMURU, R.B., *Comunidade ecclesial de base: uma opção pastoral decisiva,* Petrópolis 1967.

CAVALCA, M., «La méthode des groupes missionnaires au Japon», *CM*(F) *Le Christ au monde,* 4 (1959) 496-500.

CERFAUX, L., *La Théologie de l'Église suivant S. Paul*, Paris 1965.

——, *Christ in the Theology of St. Paul*, New York 1959.

——, «L'Église», in *Populus Dei*, II: *Ecclesia,* Roma 1969, 865-917

CHACKO, P.T., «Towards a Theology of Politics», *JeDh* 1 (1971) 12-28.

CHAKIATH, T., «Vardhamānamāya Azhimatiyum Kraisttava Uttaravādittavm» [Increasing Corruption and Christian Responsibility], *Sathyadeepam* 4 January, 1995, 1. 6.

CHATURVEDI, M.D., *Hinduism: The Eternal Religion, Its Fundamentals, Beliefs and Traditions*, Bombay 1992.

CLARK, D., *Basic Communities: Towards An Alternative Society,* London 1977.

CLAVER, F., «Forms of Christian Community Living in Asia», *EAPR* 20 (1983) 65-75.

CLEMENT OF ROME, ST., «The Letter to the Corinthians», in *FC*, 9-58.

CODINA, V., «The Wisdom of Latin America's Base Communities», *Conc*(E) 4 (1994) 71-80.

COENEN, L., «Church», in *NIDNTT*, I, 291-307

COMBLIN, J., «Brazil: Base Communities in the Northeast», in *New Face of the Church in Latin America*, ed. G. Cook, New York 1994, 202-225.

COUTINHO, L., «More Brothers than Fathers», *CC*, April, 1994, 1-2.

GOVERNMENT OF INDIA, *Complete Works of Mahatma Gandhi*, LXIV, , 1976.

CONGAR, Y., «The Church: The People of God», *Conc*(E) 1/1 (1965) 7-19

————, *Lay People in the Church*, London 1985.

————, «The Need of Pluralism in the Church, *DL* 7 (1974) 343-353.

COOK, G. ed., *New Face of the Church in Latin America,* New York 1994.

COSTA, C.J., «A Missiological Conflict between Padroado and Propaganda Fide in India», in *ITS* 32/1-2 (1995) 131-160.

COSTELLOE, M.J., tr. *The Letters and Instructions of Francis Xavier*, Anand 1993.

COUTINHO, L., «More Brothers than Fathers», *CC* June, 1993, 16-30.

CULLMANN, O., *The Early Church*, London 1956.

DA SILVA, G.U., *Ecclesial Basic Communities and the New Evangelization at the Light of the Redemptoris Missio with Reference to the Diocese of Larantuka Indonesia,* Roma 1995.

DAY, F., *The Land of the Perumals,* Madras 1863.

D'COSTA, G.A., «Inculturation, India and Other Religions: Some Methodological Reflection», *StMiss* 44 (1995) 121-147.

DE FELIPE, «Año 2.000 ¡Viva la diferencia!», *VN* 8 Julio, 1995, 48

DE FIORES, S. – GOFFI, T., eds., *Nuovo Dizionario di Spiritualità,* Milano 1985.

DE GUZMAN, E.S., «Communautés chrétiennes de base et participation des laïcs», *Convergence* 1 (1987) 33-37.

DE LA POTTERIE, I, «The Christian's Relationship to the World», in *ACP*, 175-182.

DE LETTER, P., «The Local Church», *Sevartham* (1976) 3-29.

DE LIMA, G., *Local Church and Basic Christian Communities in the Service of the Kingdom of God*, Roma 1992.

DE LUBAC, H., *Les églises particulières dans l' Église universelle, suivi de La maternité de l'église, et d'une interview recueillie par G. Jarczyk*, Paris 1971.

————, *Les Eglises Particulières dans L'Eglise*, Paris 1971.

————, *The Splendour of the Church*, London 1986.

DEPARTMENT OF ECONOMICS & STATISTICS TRIVANDRUM, *Statistics for Planning 1988*, Government of Kerala 1988.

DEPARTMENT OF ECONOMICS & STATISTICS THIRUVANANTHAPURAM, *Kerala at a Glance*, Government of Kerala 1993.

DE SALES, F., *Introduction to the Devout Life*, New York 1989.

DE SÉVÉRAC, J.C., *Mirabilia Descripta*, Paris 1925.

DE STE-MARIE, F.A., «Vers la fin d'un long Schisme», *LMC* 1 October, 1931, 509-514.

DEVADAS, P., *K ālpāṭukal* [Footsteps (Social & Church History)] Thiruvananthapuram 1992.

DE WIT, C., «Viewpoint: Which way for the laity?», *The Tablet* 12 September, 1987, 962.

DHAVAMONY, M., *Classical Hinduism*, Roma 1982.

————, «Christian Theology of Inculturation», *StMiss* 44(1995) 1-43.

DIOCESE OF KOTTAR, *News Letter*, March (1995).

DIDOMIZIO, D., «French Spirituality», in *DCS*, 161-165.

DRESSLER, H. eds., *The Fathers of the Church: The Apostolic Fathers*, Washington D.C. 1981.

D'SA, M., *History of the Catholic Church in India*, I-II, Bombay 1910.

D'SILVA, A., ed., *Creative Ministries and Affirmative Action in Today's India*, Pune 1984.

D'SOUZA, H.S., «Vogliamo rassicurarvi del nostro costante sforzo in difesa della vita», *OR* 28-29 agosto, 1995, 4.

DUFF, F., *The Spirit of the Legion of Mary*, Glasgow 1956.

DULLES, A. ,«The Church: Introduction», in *The Documents of Vatican II*, ed. W.M. Abbott, New York 1966, 9-13.

————, *Models of the Church*, New York 1987 [Expanded Edition].

————, *The Catholicity of the Church*, Oxford 1987.

DUPUIS, J.,«Nagpur International Theological Conference», *CleM* 35 (1971) 458-471.

――― , «Lay People in Church and World: The Contribution of Recent Literature to a Synodal Theme», *Greg* 68/ 1-2 (1987) 347-390.

――― , *Jesus Christ at the Encounter of World Religions*, New York 1991.

――― , «Dialogue and Proclamation in Two Recent Documents», *BPCDIR*, XXVII/2, 80 (1992) 165-172.

――― , «FABC Focus on the Church's Evangelical Mission in Asia Today», in *Dialogical Dynamics of Religions*, ed. A. Thottakara, Roma 1993, 132-156.

――― , «The Church, the Reign of God, and the "Others"», *BPCDIR, Theological Colloquium, Pune, India, August 1993* (1994) 85-86.

DUQUOC, C., «Charism as the Social Expression of the Unpredictable Nature of Grace», *Conc*(E) 109 (1977) 87-96.

DUSSEL, E., «The Differentiation of Charisms», *Conc* (E) 109 (1977) 38-55.

DUTT, N.K., *Origin and Growth of Caste in India*, 1, London 1968.

EAGLESON, J., – SCHARPER, P., *Puebla and Beyond*, New York 1979.

ERINGELY, J.T., *Coalition Game Politics in Kerala after Independence,* New Delhi 1985.

ESTEBAS, R., «Evangelization, Culture and Spirituality», *The Way* 4 (1994) 273-282.

FALEYE, M., «A Layman in a Small Christian Community», *AfER* 6 (1982) 343-346.

FALLICO, A., *Chiesa – mondo: un movimento per le comunità ecclesiali di base*, Roma 1982.

FAVALE, A., ed., *Movimenti ecclesiali contemporanei: Dimensioni storiche, teologico-spirituali ed apostoliche*, Roma 1982.

FERNANDEZ, D., «Spanish Carmelite Missionaries in Kerala», in *CHK*, 175-197.

FERNANDEZ, D.A., «Search and Fidelity», *JeDh* 123 (1991) 222-231.

FERNANDEZ, J.G, *Atistāna Kraistava Samūhaṅgal* [Pastoral Letter on BECs], 25 May, 1992 Quilon (1992).

FERNANDEZ, J., «The Diocese of Quilon», in *CHK*, 382-391.

FERNANDEZ, J.V., *A Quarter Century of Progress in the Diocese of Quilon 1900-1925: Souvenir of the Episcopal Silver Jubilee of The Rt. Rev. Aloysius Maria Benziger — Bishop of Quilon*, Trichinopoly 1925.

FERROLI, D., *The Jesuits in Malabar*, I-II, Bangalore 1939-1951.

«Final Consulation on CBCI Evaluation», *Indian Currents* 22 April, 1995, 2.

FITZMYER, J.A., *Paul and His Theology: A Brief Sketch*, New Jersey 1989.

FRANCIS, K.C., «Abhimugham» [Face to Face (Interview)], *JV* December, 1993, 51.

FREEDMAN, D.N., ed. *The Anchor Bible Dictionary,* I-VI, New York 1992.

FREEMAN, L., «A Hindu Saint: A Sign to Indian Christians», *The Tablet* 11 February, 1995, 173-175.

FUELLENBACH, J., *Hermeneutics, Marxism and Liberation Theology,* Manila 1989.

————, *The Kingdom of God: The Central Message of Jesus' Teachings in the Lght of the Modern World,* Manila 1993.

GAJIWALA, A. L., «The Spirit of Dialogue», *VJTR* 58 (1994) 485-495.

GALILEA, S., «The Spirituality of Liberation», *The Way* 25 (1985) 186-194.

GAZO, G., *Pour une Sainteté Ecclesiale Aujourd'hui à la lumière des Communautés Ecclésiales de Base: Une analyse de l'expérience du Diocèse de Man en Côte d'Ivoire,* Roma 1995.

GEDDES, M., *The History of the Church of Malabar from the Time of its Being First Discovered in the Year 1501,* London 1694.

GEORGE, V.C., «The Seven Churches», in *STCEI,* I, 179-181.

GHIRLANDA, G. «Universal Church, Particular Church, and Local Church at the Second Vatican Council and in the New Code of Canon Law», in *VAP,* II, 233-271.

GIBLET, J. – GIRAD, R., «Covenant», in *DBT,* 93-98.

GLADSTONE, J.W., *Protestant Christianity and People's Movements in Kerala 1850-1936,* Trivandrum 1984.

GOFFI, T., «Tracce di vita», in *CS,* 404-465.

GOMAS, D., «Pūnthurayil Oru Mahāyannam» [A great effort in Poonthura], in *AICUF All Kerala Annual,* Cochin 1978, 95-100.

————, «Patrādhipakuruppu: Svatantriyadina Cinthakal», *JV* August, (1984) 1. 30.

————, «*Marupaṭi*» (Reply), *JV* October (1984) 1. 30

GOVERNMENT OF KERALA, *Economic Review,* State Planning Board 1977.

GOVERNMENT OF KERALA, *Kerala at a Glance — 1992,* Thiruvananthapuram 1993.

GRÉA, A., *L'Eglise et sa divine constitution,* Paris 1884.

GREGORY, R., ed., *Kuṭumba Unit Nētākalkoru Mārgarēgha* [Guidelines for the Family Unit Leaders], Thiruvananthapuram 1991.

GUBUAN, W.C., *The Basic Christian Communities in the Church in the Philippines: A Historico-Theological Reflection on the Ecclesial Identity of Basic Christian Communities*, Roma 1992.

GUTIÉRREZ, G., *We Drink from Our Own Wells: The Spiritual Journey of a People*, London 1987.

————, *A Theology of Liberation*, London 1988.

HAMBYE, E. R., «Image of the Church Through Centuries», *JeDh* 22 (1974) 293-310.

HARDAWIRYANA, R. – *al.*, *Building the Church in Pluricultural Asia*, Roma 1986.

HARDGRAVE, JR. R.L., *The Nadars of Tamilnad: The Political Culture of a Community in Change*, Bombay 1969.

HÄRING, B., «Profeti», in *NDS*, 1271-1282.

HARPER, S.B., «Ironies of Indigenization: Some Cultural Repercussions of Mission in South India», *IBMR* 19 (1995) 13-20.

HAUCK, F., «*Koinos*», *TDNT*, III, 789-809.

HEALEY, J.G., «BCCs in the 1987 Synod of Bishop's Documents», *AfER* 2 (1988) 74-86.

HEBBLETHWAITE, M., «Earthing the Church», in *The Tablet* 6 January, 1996, 11-12.

HENNELLY, A.T., ed., *Santo Domingo and Beyond*, New York 1993.

HEUT, E.V., «Religious and AMECEA Key Pastoral Priority: Some Reflections after the AMECEA Study Conference 1979», *AfER* 5(1982) 265-268.

HIRMER, O., – BRODERICK, F.R., *Gospel Sharing*, Secunderabad 1990.

HOUTART, F. – NAYAK, N., *Kerala Fishermen – Culture and Social Organization*, Trivandrum 1988.

HOUTART, F. – LEMERCINIER, G., *Church and Development in Kerala*, Bangalore 1979.

IGNATIUS OF ANTIOCH, ST., «To the Ephesians», in *FC*, 87-95.

————, «To the Magnesians», in *FC*, 96-101.

————, «To the Trillians», in *FC*, 102-106.

————, «To the Romans», in *FC*, 107-112.

————, «To the Philadelphians», in *FC*, 113-117.

IGNATIUS OF ANTIOCH, ST., «To the Smyrnaeans», in *FC*, 118-123.

INDIAN THEOLOGICAL ASSOCIATION, «Towards an Indian Christian Spirituality in a Pluralistic Context» [Statement] Fourteenth Annual Meeting, December 28-31, 1990, Pune, *JeDh* 121 (1991) 79-88.

IYER, V.R.K., *Justice in Words and Injustice in Deeds for the Depressed Classes*, New Delhi 1984.

JACOB, T. – PRIMA – MONTEIRO, R. – VANDANA, «The Role of Women in the Mission of the Church in India», in *MIT*, 219-248.

«Jacobite Conversions in Malabar», *The Examiner* 13 September, 1930, 442-443.

JAMES, T., «Adeodatusacan Oranusmaranam», [Fr. Adeodatus. A Reminiscence], in *Platinum Jubili Smaranika: St. Albert's Church 1917-1992* [Platinum Jubilee Souvenir: St. Albert's Church 1917-1992], ed. D. Selvaraj, Muthiyavaila 1992 [No page numbering].

JANSSEN, H., «Ein Spannungsreicher Aufbruch: Kirchliche Basisgemeinschaften auf den Philippinen», *Her.* 39/11 (1985) 532-536.

JEFFREY, R., *The Decline of Nayar Dominance*, New Delhi 1976.

JOHN, K.J., «Emergence of Latin Christians», in *CHK* 347-354.

JOHN, T.W., *Malsyatozhilali Samarangalum, kristîyānikalum* [Fishermen's Agitation and Christians], Trivandrum, 1990. A Bachelor's Degree dissertation, Serampur University, India.

JOSE, B.L., *The Parish Council: An Investigation into the Parish Council System of Today with Special Reference to Kerala, India,* Roma 1976. A doctoral dissertation, Pontifical Urbanian University.

JOSE, N.K., *Cānar Lahala* [Upper Cloth Revolt], Cochin 1979.

JOSHI, C.L., «Teenage Abortions: The Perils of a Permissive Age», *IT* 15 April 1995, 98-99.

KAIGAMA, I.A., *The Trinitarian Implications of the Pauline Spirituality of Communion*, Roma 1991.

KALATHIL, M., «Caste Discrimination», *JeDh* 63(1981) 196-202.

KALEECKAL, J.J. – al., *Oru Samara Katha* [History of a Struggle], Thiruvananthapuram 1988.

KAIMLETT, J., *An Evaluation of the Protective Legisalation for the Sceduled Castes in India in the light of Religious Freedom,* Roma 1980-81. A doctoral dissertation, Pontifical Urbanian University.

KALLUNKALPURAYIDAM, A., «The Involvement of the Kerala Church in Politics», *JeDh* 1 (1971) 61-71.

KAMUGISHA, D., «The AMECEA Pastoral Priority and Its Implementation», *AfER,*3 (1982)138-141.

KANANAIKAL, J., «Caste Discrimination: A Challenge to the Christian Conscience in India», *VJTR,* 11 (1982) 522-529.

———, *Scheduled Castes in Search of Justice:* Part I& II, New Delhi 1986.

KANJIRATHINKAL, M., «Christian Participation in Politics: A Case Study of the Kerala Church's Political Involvement», *JeDh* 31 (1976) 125-147.

KANTROWITZ, B., «The Search for the Sacred», *News Week* 28 November, 1994, 38-41.

KAPPAN, S., «Christian and the Call to Revolution», *JeDh* 1 (1971) 29-45.

KARIYIL, J., *Rajata Jubili Aghōṣikunna P.O.C.* 1968-1993, [POC Celebrates its Silver Jubilee], Kochi 1993.

KAROTEMPREL, S., ed., *Following Christ in Mission*, Bombay 1995.

KARUNAN, V., «Expert Committee Demanded to Examine Traditions of St. Thomas Christians», *The Herald* 11-17 November, 1994, 7.

KASPER, W., *Transcending All Understanding: The Meaning of Christian Faith Today*, San Francisco 1989.

KAVUMKAL, J., «Christian Ashram: a Study of the Ashram in the Context of Basic Communities», *VSVD* 20 (1979) 68-78.

KEALY, S.P., *Spirituality for Today*, Dublin 1994.

KERALA REGIONAL CHRISTIAN LIFE COMMUNITY, *Yearly Programme – 1992*, Trichur 1992.

KERKHOFS, J., «Basic Communities in Europe», *PMV* 62 (1976) 23-26.

――――, «Basic Christian Communities in Europe», *PMV* 81 (1980) 30-36.

KEYES, R., *We the Lonely People: America's Search for Community*, New York 1970.

KIESLING, C., «On Relating to the Persons of the Trinity», *TS* 47 (1986) 599-616.

KILIYAMPURACKAL, F., *Aloysius Maria Benziger: A Missionary and A Pastor, 1864-1942*, Roma 1992.

KIRISWA, B., «Small Christian Communities in a Keniyan Parish», *AfER* 2 (1982) 90-93.

KOCHERY, T., «The Cross Now and Here», *JeDh* 39 (1977) 240-246.

――――, «Where I met Jesus», *JeDh* 123 (1991) 185-192.

KODA, J.V., *Small Christian Communities: A Vital Force for New Evangelization with Reference to the Diocese of Same* (Tanzania), Roma 1995.

KOILPARAMBIL, G., *Caste in the Catholic Community in Kerala*, Cochin 1982.

KOLLAPARAMBIL, J., *The Archdeacon of All-India*, Roma 1972.

KOLLAPARAMBIL, J., *The St.Thomas Christians' Revolution in 1653*, Kottayam 1981.

KOMONCHAK, J.A, «The Church Universal as the Communion of Local Churches», *Conc*(E) 146/6 (1981) 30-35.

KOMONCHAK, J. A., – al., eds., *The New Dictionary of Theology*, Dublin 1987.

KONINGS, N., «Christian Communities in Nangina Parish, Kenya», *AfER* 4 (1981) 247-254.

KOONTHANAM, G., «Option for the Poor and its Challenges to the Present: Ecclesial Structures and Praxis», *JeDh* 136 (1993) 319-329.

KOSHY, N., *Caste in the Kerala Churches*, Bangalore 1968.

KRAFT, C.II., *Christianity in Culture: A Study in Dynamic Biblical Theologizing in Cross-Cultural Perspective*, New York 1982.

KRISHNAN, R., «Kerala: A Fall From Grace», *IT* 15 November, 1994, 116-117.

KUMAR, K.G., «The Kerala fishermen's agitation», *BI* 16-29 July, 1984, 112-115.

KUNNEL, S., *Family-centered Catechesis: Towards a New Family-centered Catechesis Adapted to the Religious Traditions of the St. Thomas Christians*, Roma 1995. A doctoral dissertation, Pontifical Salesian University.

KUNNUMPURAM, K., «Towards A Theology of Ministries», in *CMAA*, 9-34.

KURIAN, J., *Fishermen's Cooperatives in Kerala: A Critique*, Madras 1980.

KURIEDATH, J., *Authority in the Catholic Community in Kerala*, Bangalore 1989.

KWAME, G.K., «Basic Ecclesial Communities as Communion», *AfER* 37 (1995) 160-179.

LABAYEN, J.X., «Basic Christian Communities», *AfER* 3 (1988) 135-144.

«La Conversione dei Giacobiti in India», *OR* 6 Novembre, 1930, 1.

LADARIA, L., «Humanity in the Light of Christ in the Second Vatican Council», in *VAP* II, 386-401.

LANNE, D.E., «L'Église locale et l'Église universelle», *Irén.* 43 (1970) 481-511.

LANNE, E., La Chiesa locale è diritto divino», in *DCEVS*, Roma 1969, 797-804.

LEE, B.J., – COWAN, M.A., *Dangerous Memories: House Churches and Our American Story*, Sheed & Ward 1986.

LEEUWEN, G.V., «Spirituality of II Vatican Council», in *Indian Christian Spirituality*, ed. D.S. Amalorpavadass, Bangalore 1982, 88-90.

LEGRAND, H.M., «Inverser Babel, Mission de l'Église», *Spiritus* 43 (1970) 323-346.

LEGRAND, H.M., «La realizzazione della Chiesa in un luogo», in *Iniziazione pratica della teologia*, 3, *Dogmatica II*, Brescia 1986.

LELL, J. – MENNE, F.W., eds., *Religiöse Gruppen*, Düsseldorf 1976.

LEMBAGUSALA, P.C., «Approfondissement de la foi dans une communauté de base», *LV* 36 (1981) 450-456.

LEON, C., *Sāmūhika Sāmbattika Survey Prādhamika Report* [Socio-Economic Survey Preliminary Report], Trivandrum 1993.

LOBINGER, F., *Building Small Christian Communities*, Secunderabad 1990.

————, *Towards Non-dominating Leadership: Aims and Methods of the Lumko Series*, n. 1, Secunderabad 1990.

LOGAN, W., *Malabar Manual*, I, Madras 1887.

LOMBARD, F., «Confraternities and Arch-confraternities», in *New Catholic Encyclopedia*, IV, New York 1967, 154.

LOPEZ, A., *Translated Extracts of Letters from the Ancient Province of Malabar*, 1907 [No Place of Publication].

LOPEZ, C., «Latîn Kattolikkarude Sāmuhika Munnēttam?» [Social Revival of Latin Cathoilic Community?], *JV* December (1993) 41-48; January (1994) 8-9, 14; February (1994) 14-16.

————, *Latîn Janata Sāmūhika Navōthanattileku* [Latin Catholic Community in its Social Renaissance],Thiruvananthapuram 1995.

LÓPEZ-GAY, J., «La missione come aiuto scambievole fra le Chiese», in *Chiesa locale e inculturazione nella missione*, Roma 1987, 9-32.

LOPEZ, L., *A Social History of Modern Kerala*, Trivandrum 1988.

LOYOLA EXTENSION SERVICES, *Report on the Benchmark Survey of Slums under UBSP Programme in Thiruvananthapuram Corporation, May-October, 1993*, Sreekaryam 1993.

MACKENZIE, G.T., «History of Christianity in Travancore», in *Travancore State Manual*, II, ed. V.N. Aiya, New Delhi 1906, 135-223.

MADHU, M., «Madya Vimuktamakunna Kaṭalorangal» (Coastal Villages in its path of redemption from Alcohol) *Vanita*, 15-30 June, 1994, 4-5. 18-19.

MALANCHARUVIL, C., *The Syro-Malankara Church*, Alwaye 1974.

MALATESTA, E., «Sacred Scripture: Pure and Perennial Source of Spiritual Life», *Tripod* 24 (1984) 64-78.

MALATESTA, E.J., «Charism», in *NDCS*, 140-143.

MALIEKAL, J., *Caste in India Today*, Bangalore 1991.

Manorama Year Book – 1986, Kottayam 1986.

MARINS, J., «Comunità ecclesiali di base in America Latina», *Conc*(I) 11/4 (1975) 43-54.

————, «What Are Basic Christian Communities?», *Priests & People* 7 (1993) 142-144.

————, ed., *Basic Ecclesial Community: Church from the Roots*, Bangalore 1981.

MARTINEZ, E.R., *La vita cristiana e la spiritualità secondo San Paolo*, Roma 1992.

――――, «"In Christ Jesus": Spiritual Experience in St. Paul», in *ES*, 45-62.

MARTINI, C.M., «A chi il domani?», *Testimoni* 15 dicembre, 1994, 1-3.

MARY, P. – *al.*, «Casting the Net on the Right Side», *JeDh* 123 (1991) 193-200.

MASCARENHAS, L., «Basic Christian Communities in an Islamic Setting in Pakistan», *PMV Bulletin*, 81 (1980) 26-30.

MATAJI, V., «Towards an Indian Christian Spirituality», in *The Church in India: Institution or Movement*, ed. P. Puthanangady, Bangalore 1991, 93-125.

MATANIC, A., «Spirituality», in *DES* III, 2383-2385.

MATEER, S., *Land of Charity: A Descriptive Account of Travancore and its People*, London 1870.

――――, *Native Life in Travancore*, London 1883.

MATHEW, G., «Samvaranattil otuṅgunna Vanita Rāṣṭrīyam» [Women Politics Constrained to Reservations], *Malayala Manorama*, 16 March, 1995, 6.

MAURICE, – MAGEE, M. «Which way for the laity?», *The Tablet* 19 September, 1987, 999.

MBINDA, J.M., «AMECEA Bishops' Consultations», *AfER* 1&2 (1986) 17-21.

MC CARTHY, D. J., *Treaty and Covenant*, Roma 1981.

MC LOUGHLIN, B., «Christian Life Communities», *MilSt* 30 (1992) 87-90.

MC DERMOTT, M., «The Biblical Doctrine of *KOINONIA*», *BZ* 19 (1975) 64-77 & 219-233.

MEJIA, R., *The Church in the Neighbourhood*, Nairobi 1990.

MENDENHALL, G.E. – HERION, G.A., «Covenant», in *AncBD*, I, 1179-1202

MENON, A.S., *Social and Cultural History of Kerala*, New Delhi 1979.

――――, *A Survey of Kerala History*, Kottayam 1970.

MENON, D.M., «Prospects in Kerala», *Seminar*, May (1994) 40-41.

MENON, K.P.P., *History of Kerala*, III, Ernakulam 1929.

MENON, P.S., *History of Travancore from the Earliest Times*, New Delhi 1878.

MENON, V., «The Church in Revolt», *The Illustrated Weekly of India*, 3 March 1985, 14-17.

MILLER, R.E., «Trialogue: The Context of Hindu-Christian Dialogue in Kerala», in *Hindu Christian Dialogue: Perspectives and Encounters*, ed. H. Coward, New York 1989, 47-63.

MOLARI, C., «Mezzi per lo sviluppo spirituale», in *CS*, 466-524.

MORAES, G.M., *A History of Christianity in India*, Bombay 1964.

MULAKARA, G.J., *History of the Diocese of Cochin*, I, Roma 1986.

――――, «Portuguese missionaries in Cochin till 1558», *STVDIA Lisboa* 49 (1989) 69-94.

MÜLLER, A., – GREINACHER, N., «Comunità di base come tema di teologia pratica», *Conc*(I) 11/4 (1975) 17-23.

MUNDADAN, A.M. , *History of Christianity in India*, I, Bangalore 1984.

MUNDADAN, A.M., ed., *Cardinal Parecattil: The Man, His Vision, and His Contribution*, Alwaye 1988.

MURICKAN, J., *Struggle for Justice*, New Delhi 1987.

MURICKAN, J., *Religion and Power Structure in Rural India: A Study of Two Fishing Villages in Kerala, Poovar – Saktikulangara*, New Delhi 1991.

NAMBIARPARAMBIL, A., «From the "SARANAM" of Sabarimala Pilgrimage to the "SARANAM" of the Dialogue-Pilgrimage», in *Popular Devotions*, ed. P. Puthanangady, Bangalore 1986.

NAVONE, J., *Self-giving and Sharing: The Trinity and Human Fulfillment*, Collegeville 1989.

NAYAK, N., *A Struggle within the Struggle*, Trivandrum 1992.

NEDUNGATT, G., «The Spirituality of the Syro-Malabar Church», *Thanima* June, 1994, 4-39.

NESTI, A., ed., *L'altra Chiesa in Italia*, Milano 1970.

NETTO, M., «The Diocese of Trivandrum», in *CHK*, 374-381.

――――, «Patradhiparkulla kattu» [Letter to the Editor], *JV* October, 1984, 26-27.

――――, «Kamukinkode Idavaka Caritram» [History of the Kamukinkode Parish], in *Smaranika 1985: St Antony's Church, Kamukincode*, ed. J. Pereira, Kamukincode 1985 [no page numbering].

NEUNER, J., «Paths of Mission in India Today: National Consultation on Mission, Pune, 4-9 January, 1994», *VSVD* 35 (1994) 259-267.

NEUNHEUSER, B., «Chiesa Universale e Chiesa locale», in *La Chiesa del Vaticano II*, Firenze 1966, 616-642.

NEWBEGIN, L., «What Is a Local Church Truly United?», *ER* 29 (1977) 115-128.

NINAN, K., *Caste in the Kerala Churches*, Bangalore 1968.

OCHAGAVIA, J., *The CLC World Community*, Roma 1983.

OKEYO, V., «Small Christian Communities in KISII», *AfER* 4 (1983) 226-229.

O'NEILL, M., *God Hears the Cry of the Poor: The Emerging Spirituality in the Christian Communities in Peru (1965-1986)*, Roma 1990.

OSTO, A.D., «La Chiesa guarda all'Asia: nuovo modo di essere Chiesa», *Testimoni* 15 Febbraio, 1995, 19- 21.

PADIPURA, J., *Development and Culture: A Moral Theological Analysis of the Theological Approach in India since the Second Vatican Council*, Roma 1993.

PANACKAL, A.J., «The Archdiocese of Verapoly», in *CHK*, 361-373.

PANIKKAR, R., *The Unknown Christ of Hinduism*, London 1964.

PANIKULAM, G., *Koinōnia in the New Testament: A Dynamic Expression of Christian Life*, Roma 1979.

PARAMKUZHI, J., ed., *Smaranika:–1976-1991: KCYM Thiruvananthapuram Rūpata*, [Souvenir-1976-1991: KCYM Diocese of Trivandrum], Trivandrum 1991.

PARECATTIL, J., «Adaptation and Future of Christianity in India», in *STCEI* II, 186-191.

PARINTHIRICKAL, M., «Roman Document on the Theology of Liberation – a Pastoral Assessment», *JeDh* 90 (1985) 454-473.

PASCAL, V.A., *The Latin and Syrian Hierarchies of Malabar*, Ernakulam 1937.

POC, *First Three Years 1968-1971: A Report*, Kochin 1972.

PATHIL, K., «Basic Christian Communities: A New Ecclesial Model», *JeDh* 88(1985) 326-336.

————, ed., *Mission in India Today: The Task of St. Thomas Christians*, Bangalore 1988.

PENHA, B., «Revitalization of the Church through Small Christian Communities», in *The Church in India: Institution or Movement*, ed. P. Puthenangady, Bangalore 1991, 55-62.

————, «Small Christian Communities Must Be "Ecclesial"», *CC* September (1993) 1-2.

————, «Small Christian Communities Must Be Missionary», *CC* July (1992) 1-2.

PEREIRA, A. , ed., *The Sodalist*, II, Trivandrum 1936.

PERKINS, H.L., *Roots for Vision: Reflections on the Gospel and the Churches' Task in Re-peopling the De-peopled*, Singapore 1985.

PERUMAL, V., *Glimpses of Tamil Culture*, Chidambaram 1982.

PETER, A., «Yuvākale Unarū» [Youth Wake Up!], in *Smaranika 1985: St. Antony's Church, Kamukinkode*, ed. J. Pereira, Kamukinkode 1985 [No page numbering].

PHAN, P.C., «Cultural Diversity: A Blessing or a Curse for Theology and Spirituality?», *LouvSt* 19 (1994) 195-211.

PICADAL, A.L., *An Ecclesiological Perspective of the Basic Ecclesial Communities in the Philippines*, Roma 1995.

PICKETT, J.W., *Christian Mass Movements in India*, New York 1933.

PIEPER, K., *Paulus und die Kirche*, Paderborn 1932.

PILLAI, E.K., *Studies in Kerala History*, Kottayam 1970.

PIMENTA, S., «La nostra Chiesa è un "piccolo gregge" al servizio di 18 milioni di fedeli», *OR*, 14 dicembre 1995, 7.

PINTO, J.P., *Inculturation Through Basic Communities: An Indian Perspective*, Bangalore 1985.

PODIPARA, P.J., *The Hierarchy of the Syro-Malabar Church*, Alleppey 1976

————, *The Latin Rite Christianity of Malabar*, Kottayam 1986.

————, *The Thomas Christians*, Bombay 1970.

PONNU, R., «Vaikunda Swami: A Case Study of the Socio-Religious Awakening in South India», *JDh* 10 (1985) 186-199.

PUU, *Evangelizzazione e Culture*, III, Roma 1976.

POOVATHUMKUDY, K., *Missionary Task as Building Christian Communities with Special Reference to Redemptoris Missio*, Roma 1993.

PRINCIPE, W., «Toward Defining Spirituality», *Studies in Religion/Sciences Religieuses* 2 (1983) 127-141.

————, «Christian Spirituality – Terminology», in *NDCS*, 931-938.

PCO, *Annual Report*, Trivandrum, 1985.

PUTHANANGADY, P., «Which Culture for Inculturation: The Dominant or the Popular?», *EAPR* 3/4 (1993) 295-309.

————, ed., *Popular Devotions*, Bangalore 1986.

————, *The Church in India: Institution or Movement*, Bangalore 1991.

PUTHENKALAM, J., *Marriage and the Family in Kerala with Special Reference to Matrilineal Castes*, New Delhi 1977.

PUTHENVEETTIL, T., «The Diocese of Cochin», in *CHK*, 404-412.

PYLEE, L.M., *St. Thomas Christians and the Archdiocese of Verapoly*, Ernakulam 1977.

RADHAKRISHNAN, M.G., «Kerala: Lessons to Learn», *IT* December 31 (1994) 98-99.

————, «Sabarimala Temple: What in God's Name?», *IT* January 15 (1995) 117.

RADHAKRISHNAN, S., *East and West : Some Reflections*, New York 1956.

RAE, G.M., *The Syrian Church in India*, London 1892.

RAHNER, K., «Church and World», in *SM*(E), I, London 1968, 346-357.

————, «Towards a Fundamental Theological Interpretation of Vatican II», *TS* 40 (1979) 716-727.

————, «Structural Change in the Church of the Future» in *Th.Inv.* XX, London 1981, 115 132.

————, «The Future of Christian Communities», in *Th.Inv.* XXII, London 1991, 120-133.

————, «South American Base Communities in A European Church», in *Th.Inv.* XXII, London 1991, 148-154.

RAJ, C.A., «Creative Ministries in a Parish Set-up», in *CMAA*, 47-56.

————, «Book of God – Book of Human Beings», in *Th.Inv.* XXII, London 1991, 214-224.

R A M, K., *Mukkuvar Women: Gender, Hegemony and Capitalist Transformation in a South Indian Fishing Community*, London – New Jersey 1991.

RAO, R., «Dowry deaths: Growing Social Evil», *Indian Communicator* April 3 (1995) 3.

RAVASI, G., «Linee bibliche dell'esperienza spirituale», in *CS*, 56-123.

R A Y AN, S., «The Search for an Asian Spirituality of Liberation», in *Asian Christian Spirituality*, eds. V. Fabella – P. K. H. Lee – D. K. Suh, New York 1992, 11-30.

REGAN, D., *Experience the Mystery: Pastoral Possibilities for Christian Mystagogy*, London 1994.

RICHARD, L., «Theology in Need of Spirituality», *SFSp* 2 (1992) 161-172.

RING, N.C., «Fuga Mundi», in *DCS*, 167-168.

PCO, *Ripples and Repercussions*, Trivandrum 1984.

ROCHE, L., «Diocese of Trivandrum», in *Post – Vatican Liturgical Renewal in India at All Levels*, ed. D. S. Amalorpavadass, Bangalore 1972, 81-83.

————, «The Latin Catholics of Kerala in the Pre-Portuguese Period», in *Journal of Kerala Studies*, VI, University of Kerala, (1979) 599-606.

ROEST-CROLLIUS, A., – NKÉRAMIHIGO, T., *What Is So New about Inculturation*, Roma 1991.

ROEST-CROLLIUS, A., *Theologia dell'Inculturazione*, Roma 1994.

ROSARIO, A.J., ed., *Kollam Kṛistiyānikal* [Christians of Quilon], Kottayam 1995.

ROSSI, A. , «Uma Experiência de Catequese Popular», *REB* 17(1957) 731-737.

«Row over Sabarimala Priest's Church Visit», *The Hindu* March 3, 1995, 16 [International Edition].

RUFFINI, E., «Eucaristia», in *NDS*, 601-622.

SALVADOR, F.R., «Espiritualidad Mistagogica y Pastoral», in *ES*, 375-393.

SAMUEL, V.T., *One Caste, One Religion, One God: A Study of Sree Narayana Guru*, New Delhi 1977.

SANMIGUEL, V., *Parish Welfare Orientations*, Alwaye, 1963.

————, *Carmelite Seminaries in Kerala (1682-1685 – 1776-1975)*, Vemsur 1987.

————, *Three Century Kerala Carmelite Mission: 1656-1975*, Vemsur 1986.

SARTO, I.P., «Delhi Auxiliary Consecrated», *The Herald* 21-27 April (1995) 1-2.

SCHASCHING, J., «From the Class War to the Culture of Solidarity: A Fundamental Theme of the Church's Social Teaching», in *VAP*, 466-481.

SCHILLEBEECKX, E., «The Church and Mankind», *Conc*(E) 9/1 (1965) 34-50.

SCHMAUS, M., *Dogma* 4: *The Church its Origin and Structure*, London 1989.

SCHMIDT, L.K., «Ekklesia», in *TDNT*, III, 501-536.

SCHNACKENBURG, R., «The Pauline Theology», in *ACP*, 213-223.

SCHNEIDERS, S.M., «Theology and Spirituality: Strangers, Rivals, or Partners», *Horizons* 13 (1986) 253-274.

SCHRAGE, W., «"Ekklesia" und Synagoge: Zum Ursprung des urchristlichen Kirchenbegriffs», *ZThK* 60 (1963) 178-202.

SCHREUDER, O., ed., *Gemeindereform – Prozeß an der Basis*, Freiburg 1970.

SCHURHAMMER, G., *Francis Xavier: His Life and His Time*, II, Roma 1977.

SCHURHAMMER, G. – WICKI, J., eds., *Epistolae S. Francisci Xaverii* I-II, Roma 1944-45.

SCIUBBA, R. – PACE, R.S., *Le Comunità di base in Italia*, I-II, Roma 1976.

SEBASTIAN, K.T. – ZACHARIA, S., «The Role of the Laity in the Mission of Church», in *MIT*, 208-218.

SEBASTIAN, M., *Kānikāruṭe Lōkam* [The World of Kanikar], Nedumangad 1990.

SECONDIN, B., ed., *Parola di Dio e spiritualità*, Roma 1984.

SECONDIN, B., *Segni di Profezia nella Chiesa: comunità gruppi movimenti*, Milano 1987.

————, *Nuovi cammini dello Spirito. La spiritualità alle soglie del terzo millennio*, Milano 1990.

SECONDIN, B., *I Nuovi Protagonisti:* Movimenti, associazioni, gruppi nella Chiesa, Milano 1991.

――――, *Lecture Notes: Temi, problemi e prospettive della spiritualità oggi,* Pontificia Università Gregoriana, Roma 1993-94.

――――, *Per una fedeltà creativa: La vita consacrata dopo il Sinodo,* Milano 1995.

――――, «Alla prova della nuova cultura», in *CS,* 080-152.

――――, «Lectio divina: natura e prasi», in *ES,* 63-91.

――――, «La spiritualità contemporanea e la sfida delle nuove culture», in *ES,* 209-240.

――――, «La vita consacrata e il dialogo fra le culture: Sfida per una nuova profezia...», *Consacrazione & Servizio* 44 (1995) 7-17.

SELVARAJ, D., ed. *Platinum Jūbili Smaranika: St. Albert's Church 1917-1992* [Platinum Jubilee Souvenir: St. Albert's Church 1917-1992], Muthiyavaila, 1992.

SESBOÜÉ, D. – GUILLET, J., «Covenant», in *DBT,* 85-87.

SIVARAMAN, K., ed., *Hindu Spirituality: Vedas through Vedanta,* London1989.

SMART, N., *The World's Religions,* Cambridge 1992.

SMITH, D., «What Spirituality Can Resource the Democratic Culture», *The Way* 3 (1994) 183-191.

SOBHANAN, B., «Glimpses into the Disputes between the Carmelites and the Jesuits during the Dutch Period», in *CHK,* 223-244.

SOLIGNAC, A., «Spiritualité», in *DS,* XV, 1142-1160.

SPINSANTI, S., «Ecologia», in *NDS,* 440-460.

SRINIVAS, M.N., *Caste in Modern India and Other Essays,* Bombay 1962.

STAFFNER, H., *Jesus Christ and the Hindu Community: Is a Synthesis of Hinduism and Christianity Possible?,* Anand 1987.

STATEMENT OF THE INDIAN THEOLOGICAL ASSOCIATION, «Towards an Indian Christian Spirituality in a Pluralistic Context» (Fourteenth Annual Meeting, December 28-31, 1990), *JeDh* 121 (1991) 79-88.

STEPHEN, S.H.M., «Basic Community», in *CMAA,* 57-69.

SUDA, J.P., *Religions in India: A Study of their Essential Unity,* New Delhi 1978.

SUGIRTHARAJAH, R.S., ed., *Asian Faces of Jesus,* London 1993.

SULLIVAN, F.A., «The Significance of the Vatican II Declaration That the Church of Christ "Subsists in" the Roman Catholic Church», in *VAP,* II, 272-287.

SWAMI, D.T., *History of Hindu Imperialism*, Madras 1992.

SECOND GENERAL CONFERENCE OF LATIN AMERICAN BISHOPS: *The Church in the Present-day Transformation of Latin America in the Light of the Council,* Washington, D.C. 1979.

THALIATH, J., «The Thought of the Seminar», in *Church in India Today* [All India Seminar], ed. CBCI, New Delhi 1969, 511-542.

TAYLOR, M.J., ed., *A Companion to Paul*, New York 1975.

TERNANT, P., «Church», in *DBT*, 72-78.

THE CAPUCHIN MISSION UNIT, *India and Its Missions*, The Macmillan Company 1923.

THEKKEDATH, J., *The Troubled Days of Francis Garcia, Archbishop of Cranganore, 1641-59*, Roma 1972.

THOMAS, E.J., «Caste and the Syrian Rite in Keralam», *JeDh* 135 (1993) 227-233.

THOMAS, M., *The Catholic Youth Movement and the Emerging Youth of Kerala,* Roma 1983.

THOMAS, M.A., *An Outline History of Christian Churches & Denominations in Kerala,* Trivandrum 1977.

THOMAS, M.M., *The Acknowledged Christ of the Indian Renaissance*, London 1969.

————, *A Diaconal Approach to Indian Ecclesiology*, Roma 1995.

————, «Mission of the Church in the Pluralistic Context of India», *Bible Bhashyam*, 21 (1995) 81-88.

THOMAS, M.M – CONE, J.H., «Spirituality, Culture and Justice», *VFTW* 2 (1993) 176-181

THOTTAKARA, A., «Sankara», in *Le grandi figure dell'Induismo*, ed. N. Giostra, Assisi 1991, 35-68.

————, ed., *Dialogical Dynamics of Religions*, Roma 1993.

————, ed., *Eco-Spirituality: Perspectives from World Religions*, Roma 1995.

THURSTON, E. – RANGACHARI, K., eds., *Castes and Tribes of South India*, V-VII, New Delhi 1909.

TIGGA, R., «Churches Moving towards Grassroots», *The Herald* November 19-25 (1993) 3.

TILLARD, J.M.R., «I Cammini dello Spirito», in *CS*, 330-403.

TOMBÉR, J., *Led by God's Hand*, Trivandrum 1990.

TRIACCA, A.M., – PISTOIA, A., eds., *Mystagogie: Pensée liturgique d'aujourd'hui et liturgie ancienne*, Roma 1993.

Travancore Census Report, 1891.

TRIVANDRUM DISTRICT FISHERMEN'S UNION, *Facts and Reflections on the Recent Struggle of the Fishermen in Kerala*, Trivandrum 1981.

UGEUX, B., «Inculturation Through Small Christian Communiites», *AfER* 37 (1995) 134-141.

VADAKKEDOM, J., «*Pros To Sympheron*» – *The Nature and Function of the Manifestation of the Spirit according to 1 Cor 12,7*, Roma 1995. A doctoral dissertation, Pontifical Greogorian University.

VALIYAPADATH, G., «Ghaṭhanayuṭe Azhicupanikku Śeṣam» [After the Structural Changes], *Assisi*, July (1994) 5-20.

VAN LEEUWEN, J.A.G.G., *Fully Indian – Authentically Christian*, Bangalore 1990.

VANDENBROUCKE, F., «Spirituality and Spiritualities», *Conc*(E) 9/1 (1965) 25-33.

VARGHESE, S., «*Strîku Niṣedhikkapedunna Svargam*» [The Heaven that is denied to Women], in *Smaranika:–1976-1991: KCYM Thiruvananthapuram Rūpata* [Souvenir–1976-1991: KCYM Diocese of Trivandrum], ed. J. Paramkuzhi, Trivandrum 1991[No page numbering].

VARKEY, C., ed., *St. Francis Xavier,* Thevara 1952.

VELLANICKAL, M., «Image of the Church in the NT», *JeDh* 22 (1974) 333-346.

VIDALE, M. – SIERRA, R.D.O., «The Spirituality of the Brazialian Communities» in *STW*, 39-49.

VIDALES, R., «Charisms and Political Action», *Conc*(E) 109 (1977) 68-77.

VIJAYAKUMAR, K.G., «Kerala Samskārattinu Oru Anubandhanam» [An Appendix to the Kerala Culture], in *Smaranika 1985: St. Antony's Church, Kamukinkode*, ed. J. Pereira, Kamukinkode 1985 [No page numbering].

VIJAYANUNNI, M., *District Census Handbook: Trivandrum District*, Kerala 1983.

VODOPIVEC, G., «La teologia e la Chiesa locali in diverse aree culturali», *Lateranum* 50 (1984) 38-76.

VODOPIVEC, J., «La Chiesa Locale e La Missione», in *Chiesa e Missione*, Roma 1990, 97-139.

VON ALLMEN, J.J., «L' Église locale parmi les autres Églises locales», *Irén.* 43 (1970) 512-537.

VON BALTHASAR, H.U., «The Gospel as Norm and Test of all Spirituality», *Conc*(E) 9/1 (1965) 5-13.

WAAIJMAN, K., «Toward a Phenomenological Definition of Spirituality», *StS* 3 (1993) 4-57.

WILFRED, F., «In Service and Fellowship: The Diocese of Kottar in Contemporary Times (1962-1980)», in *Called to Serve: A Profile of the Diocese of Kottar*, ed. J.R. Narchison – *al.*, Nagercoil 1983, 125-230.

——, Faith without "Faith"? Popular Religion», in *Popular Devotion*, ed. P. Puthanangady, Bangalore 1986, 594-613.

——, «Human Rights and the Mandal Movement», *JeDh* 121 (1991) 62-78.

——, «Images of Jesus Christ in the Asian Pastoral Context», *Conc*(E) 2(1993) 51-62.

——, «Ecumenism as a Movement of Justice: Focus on Asia», *VJTR*, 58 (1994) 573-583.

——, «No Salvation Outside Globalization?: Some Theological Reflections on Modern Economic Dogma», *JeDh* 145 (1995) 80-92.

——, *From the Dusty Soil*, Madras 1995.

WILKENHAUSER, A., *Die Kirche als der mystische Leib Christi nach dem Apostel Paulus,* Münster 1940.

WONG, J.H., «Anonymous Christians: Karl Rahner's Pneuma-Christocentrism and an East – West Dialogue», *TS* 55 (1994) 609-637.

WOOD, S., «Ecclesial *Koinonia* in Ecumenical Dialogues», *One in Christ* 2 (1994) 124-145.

WOODCOCK, G., *Kerala: A Portrait of the Malabar Coast*, London 1967.

XAVIER, A., «Kamukinkōdum Miṣanarimārum» [Kamukinkode and Missionaries] in *Smaranika 1985: St. Antony's Church, Kamukinkode*, ed. J. Pereira, Kamukinkode 1985 [No page numbering].

YESUDAS, R.N., *People's Revolt in Travancore*, Trivandrum 1975.

YESUDASAN, J., *Maha Rasan Vedamanickam* [Biography of Maha Rasan], Thiruvananthapuram 1993.

ZAGO, M., «John Paul II's Redemptoris Missio: A Cry for Mission», *OmTer* 215 (1991) 59-66.

ZALESKI, L.M., *The Martyrs of India*, Mangalore 1913.

INDEX OF AUTHORS

Ambedkar: 82
Ancilli: 202

TABLE OF CONTENTS

TESI GREGORIANA

Since 1995, the series «Tesi Gregoriana» has made available to the general public some of the best doctoral theses done at the Pontifical Gregorian University. The typesetting is done by the authors themselves following norms established and controlled by the University.

Published Volumes

1. D'DOUZA, Rudolf V., *The Bhagavadgītā and St. John of the Cross*. A Comparative Study of the Dynamism of Spiritual Growth in the Process of God-Realisation, 1996, pp. 484.

2. PONNUMUTHAN, Selvister, *The Spirituality of Basic Ecclesial Communities in the Socio-Religious Context of Trivandrum/Kerala, India*, 1996, pp. 360.

Riproduzione anastatica: 27 settembre 1996
Tipografia Poliglotta della Pontificia Università Gregoriana
Piazza della Pilotta, 4 – 00187 Roma